THE TRIUMPH
OF CHRISTIANITY

ALSO BY RODNEY STARK

God's Battalions: The Case for the Crusades

Discovering God: The Origins of the Great Religions and the Evolution of Belief

Cities of God: The Real Story of How Christianity Became an Urban Movement and Conquered Rome

The Victory of Reason: How Christianity led to Freedom, Capitalism, and Western Success

For the Glory of God: How Monotheism Led to Reformations, Science, Witch Hunts, and the End of Slavery

One True God: Historical Consequences of Monotheism

The Rise of Christianity: How the Obscure, Marginal Jesus Movement Became the Dominant Religious Force

THE TRIUMPH

OF

CHRISTIANITY

HOW THE JESUS MOVEMENT BECAME THE WORLD'S LARGEST RELIGION

RODNEY STARK

HarperOne

An Imprint of HarperCollins*Publishers*

HarperOne

Map 9.1 by Lynne Roberts
Map 13.1 by Topaz Maps

FIRST HARPERCOLLINS PAPERBACK EDITION PUBLISHED IN 2012

Library of Congress Cataloging-in-Publication Data
  Stark, Rodney.
    The triumph of Christianity : how the Jesus movement became the
      world's largest religion / by Rodney Stark.
      p. cm.
    ISBN 978–0–06–200769–8
      1. Church history. I. Title.
    BR145.3.S73   2011
    270—dc23   2011031294

21 22 23 LSC(H) 10 9 8

CONTENTS

INTRODUCTION

HE WAS A TEACHER AND miracle worker who spent nearly all of his brief ministry in the tiny and obscure province of Galilee, often preaching to outdoor gatherings. A few listeners took up his invitation to follow him, and a dozen or so became his devoted disciples, but when he was executed by the Romans his followers probably numbered no more than several hundred. How was it possible for this obscure Jewish sect to become the largest religion in the world? That is the question that brings us here.

Of course, that question has inspired thousands of other books. Why another? In 1996 I partly addressed that issue in *The Rise of Christianity*, as I applied some new social scientific principles, considered several overlooked possibilities, and used simple arithmetic to help explain the early success of Christianity—how it conquered Rome. The response to that book by many distinguished reviewers went far beyond my most optimistic imaginings. Even so, in recent years I have become increasingly eager to make a far more extensive visit to Christian history: to start with the religious and social situation prior to Christmas Eve and, instead of stopping with the conversion of Constantine early in the fourth century, to continue on to the present.

I began *The Rise of Christianity* in about the year 40 CE in order to avoid dealing with questions concerning the "historical" Jesus and the authenticity of the Gospels—matters on which I did not then feel sufficiently informed. I ended with Constantine for the same reason—I was not prepared to deal with the whole panorama of Christian history. Since then I have written other books that gave me the opportunity to greatly expand my knowledge and historical competence, so now I am ready to write a far longer book on Christianity that hopefully will seem nearly as fresh and original as the earlier one was said to be.

Although the present book begins with events just prior to the birth of Jesus and ends in the present, it is *not* another general history of Christianity. Many eras, topics, and prominent persons are skipped. For example, I devote one sentence to the Puritans and none to the Quakers. I barely mention the Orthodox Churches, Henry VIII, John Calvin, or Ignatius Loyola. Little attention is given to theological councils and controversies; I completely ignore the bloody battles over Trinitarianism that erupted in the fifth century. I have, rather, selected important episodes and aspects of the Christian story through the centuries and assessed them from new perspectives.

What do I mean by new perspectives? I mean new answers to old questions and new interpretations of well-known events. Some of these answers and interpretations are based mainly on the work of other scholars whose landmark studies have received far too little attention, but most of the new perspectives are mine or at least partly mine. Although I often dispute the traditional views of what went on and why, I am deeply respectful of the many great scholars who have, through the centuries, contributed to our knowledge of Christian history. I have depended on hundreds of them, as I make plain in the endnotes.

Let me be clear that my concerns are historical and sociological, not theological. While I am not unfamiliar with Paul's theology, for example, my primary concern in this book is not with what Paul believed, but who he was; not with what Paul said, but to whom he said it. Similarly, I will not assess the validity of Luther's disagreement with Rome; my interest is in how he got away with it.

Finally, I have continued to write for the general reader, based on my belief that if I can't say it in plain English, it must be because I don't understand what I am writing about.

Plan of the Book

THE BOOK IS DIVIDED into six parts.

Part 1: Christmas Eve surveys the religious situation within which Christianity began: the nature of pagan temple societies, the religious makeup of the Roman Empire, and the conflicts going on among the many forms of Judaism that prevailed in Israel.

Part 2: Christianizing the Empire begins with a sketch of what is known about Jesus during his life on earth and then examines the formative days of the movement he inspired. Next is an assessment of the mission to the Jews (which was far more successful than has been recognized) and the mission to the Gentiles (oddly, some of the most basic elements of this mission have been ignored). The next chapter dispels the traditional belief that the early church was recruited from the lowest social strata. To the contrary, as with most new religious movements, early Christianity appealed particularly to people of privilege. Then comes a portrait of the misery of daily life, even for the rich, in Greco-Roman cities. The chapter describes how the commitment of early Christianity to mercy was so effective in mitigating suffering that Christians even lived longer than their pagan neighbors. In addition, most early Christians were women. When the circumstances of pagan and Christian women are compared, the wonder is that *all* of the women in the Roman Empire didn't flock into the church. Then comes the great irony that Roman persecution made the church much stronger. Finally, a model of Christian growth within the Roman Empire from the year 40 to 350 shows that the most likely rate of Christian growth is very similar to the growth rates achieved by several modern movements.

Part 3: Consolidating Christian Europe starts with the implications of Constantine's conversion, suggesting it was at best a mixed blessing that, while ending persecutions, encouraged intolerance toward dissent within the church and greatly reduced the piety and dedication of the clergy. Then comes the demise of paganism. Contrary to tradition, it was not stamped out by Christian persecution, but disappeared very slowly. In fact, paganism may never have entirely died out, and even the presumed conversion of the Northern societies did not occur until nearly a millennium after Christianity became the favored faith of Constantine. By the seventh century, Christianity probably was far stronger and more sophisticated in North Africa and Asia than in Europe. Then came the Islamic onslaught, and eventually Christianity disappeared in many parts of Asia and all but vanished in North Africa and the Middle East. But after more than four hundred years of defensive efforts, in the eleventh century Christian Europe struck back. First, Muslims were driven from Sicily and Southern Italy. Then, the Crusades were launched to liberate the Holy Land. Recent claims that the crusaders really marched east in pursuit of loot and colonies are exposed as malicious nonsense.

Part 4: Medieval Currents first examines the received wisdom that the rise of Christianity ushered in many centuries of ignorance subsequent to the fall of Rome. The work of recent historians shows that not only did Christianity not cause the "Dark Ages"; nothing did. They never existed, and this era was instead a period of rapid and remarkable progress. Next, the image of deeply pious medieval Europeans is exposed as a total fiction—hardly anyone even went to church. Finally, silly claims that Western science managed to arise despite the impediments placed in its way by the church are exposed— the truth is that science arose only in the West because Christianity was essential to its birth.

Part 5: Christianity Divided begins with the rise of two very distinctive and opposed Roman Catholic "Churches" and contrasts their impact on the outbreak of heretical movements in the twelfth century as well as their brutal repression. Chapter 18 notes that the new religious movements that arose in Europe prior to the fifteenth century are identified as heresies because they failed. Luther's "heresy" is called the Reformation because it survived. Many prevailing explanations for the origin and success of Luther's Reformation are assessed and some are dispelled. The final chapter in this section reveals that the prevailing image of the Spanish Inquisition as a monstrously bloody and brutal institution is a fiction mainly reflecting Protestant (especially British) hostility toward Catholicism in general, and toward Catholic Spain more specifically. Extraordinary new research based on access to the complete, highly detailed archives of the Spanish Inquisition reveals that the Inquisition caused very few deaths and was mainly a force in support of moderation and restraint. The Inquisition played a major role in ending the witch hunts that swept over other parts of Europe.

Part 6: New Worlds and Christian Growth begins by showing how the development of religious pluralism in the United States, with the consequence that churches must successfully compete for support or disappear, resulted in the exceedingly high levels of religiousness that currently prevail. The chapter examines what features separate the successful churches from the unsuccessful ones, given the vigorous competition that takes place among American religious "firms." Finally, the chapter explores the development of remarkable levels of civility among American religions. The next chapter demonstrates how the widespread assumption among Western intellectuals that religion must disappear in response to modernization (the secularization thesis) is refuted by the continuing vigor of faith everywhere—except in parts of Europe. It then traces Europe's exceptionalism to repressive and lazy state churches. The last chapter shifts to the rebirth of global missions—to Africa, to Latin America, to Asia, and recently even to Europe. The remarkable success of these missions explains why, even though it has become the world's largest religion, the rise of Christianity continues.

The conclusion reflects on the three most crucial events, aside from the Christ story, influencing the course of the two thousand years of Christian history.

PART I

Christmas Eve

CHAPTER ONE

The Religious Context

ON CHRISTMAS EVE, ALMOST EVERYWHERE on earth the gods were thought to be many and undependable. Aside from having some magical powers, and perhaps the gift of immortality, the gods had normal human concerns and shortcomings. They ate, drank, loved, envied, fornicated, cheated, lied, and otherwise set morally "unedifying examples."[1] They took offense if humans failed to properly propitiate them, but otherwise took little interest in human affairs. The Jews in the West and the Zoroastrians in the East rejected these ideas about the gods, opting instead for a morally demanding monotheism. But aside from these two marginal faiths, it was a pagan world.

However, this pagan world was far from static. Travel and trade applied not only to people and commerce, but to the gods as well. As a result, Rome acquired an extremely complex religious makeup that brought about considerable competition and often inspired bitter conflicts and repression.

Pagan Temple Societies

DESPITE WORSHIPPING MANY GODS, aside from Rome, most societies were not religiously diverse. Even when gods had their own individual temples, they were part of a unified system, fully funded and often closely regulated by the state. Consequently, the primary mission of pagan temples was to ensure that the gods favored the state and its ruling elite—often to such an extent that only the privileged few could gain admission to the temples. Some temples did provide an area accessible to the public, but it usually was located so that it was not possible to catch even a glimpse of the temple's image of god—the idol.

In most societies, pagan temples were served by an *exclusive priesthood*—either based on an hereditary religious caste or recruited from the elite—and they served a *clientele* rather than a membership. Clients came to the temples for various festivals and sometimes in pursuit of personal spiritual or material benefits, but most often the temples served as eating clubs. From time to time, someone would donate an animal to be sacrificed, after which the donor and the donor's friends would have a feast on the meat (temples employed skilled chefs). For many of those involved in the temples, these banquets were the sum of their participation.

Of course, such tepid temple activities were relatively incidental to the lives and activities of those involved: people only *went* to temples, they did not *belong* to them. Those who favored a particular god did not identify themselves in those terms—no one claimed to be a Zeusian or a Jovian. In fact, most people patronized several temples and various gods, depending on their tastes and needs. There was no congregational life, because there were no congregations, in the sense of regular gatherings of groups having a common religious focus and a sense of belonging. Nor did the pagan priests need (or want) the support of congregations. They charged substantial fees for all their services and were, in any event, usually well funded by the state.

And what of the gods? For all their faults they were very appealing because they were so human! Compared with the distant, mysterious, awesome, demanding, and difficult to comprehend God presented by monotheists,[2] people often seemed more comfortable with gods that were less awe-inspiring and more human, less demanding and more permissive—gods who were easily propitiated with sacrifices. These preferences help explain the very frequent "backsliding" from monotheism and into "idolatry" that took place repeatedly in both ancient Israel and Persia. There is something reassuring and attractive about nearby, tangible, very "human" gods.

Zoroastrians and the Magi

WHETHER THE JEWS OR the Zoroastrians were the first major group of monotheists cannot be determined, but it is clear that they influenced one another, especially during the captivity of the Jewish elite in Babylon at the time when Zoroastrianism was in its early and most energetic days.[3] Most historians now accept that Zoroaster grew up in what is today eastern Iran during the sixth century BCE.[4] He was initiated into the local pagan priesthood when he was about fifteen and five years later took up a wandering life devoted to intense spiritual reflection and searching. Then, when he was about thirty, he had a revelation that Ahura Mazdā was the One True God.

All monotheisms face the need to account for the existence of evil. If God is responsible for everything, including the existence of evil, he would appear to be an utterly incomprehensible and terrible being. To avoid that conclusion, monotheisms either posit a God so remote and inactive as to be, in effect, responsible for nothing, or they pose the existence of an inferior evil creature, a sort of godling, whom God allows to cause evil for a variety of reasons, many of them involving "free will." Judaism, and subsequently Christianity, postulates the existence of Satan. Zoroaster revealed that Ahura Mazdā is engaged in a battle with the inferior Angra Mianyu, the "Fiendish Spirit." He also taught that each human is required to choose between good and evil, and the outcome of the battle "rests on mankind: the support which each man lends to the side he has chosen will add permanent strength to it; in the long run, therefore, the acts of man will weight the scales in favor of one side or the other."[5] No more powerful doctrine of "free will" and its implications has ever been stated. In keeping with his explanation of evil, Zoroaster taught that the souls of the virtuous will ascend to an attractive heaven, while evildoers will plummet into hell.

Zoroastrianism spread rapidly and soon became the official religion of the kingdom of Chorasmia (in modern Uzbekistan). In the sixth century BCE, when Cyrus the Great submerged Chorasmia into his newly established Persian Empire, Zoroastrianism initially lost its official standing. But Cyrus's son Darius became a convert, and when he gained the throne, Zoroastrianism regained power.[6] As the years passed and new Persian emperors followed one another to the throne, and especially as new societies committed to the old religions were made part of the empire, the influence of Zoroastrianism began to wane. Long before Christmas Eve, Persia was once again a pagan temple society—except for the Magi.

The Magi were a guild of professional Persian priests who served any and all pagan religions in the Persian Empire. They also were famous astrologers who taught that practice to the Greeks (who referred to them as the Chaldeans). At some point they began to serve as priests of Zoroastrianism too, and eventually they converted.[7] Through the centuries the Magi served as the primary proponents of Zoroastrianism and preservers of its scriptures. They also were widely acknowledged throughout the classical world, even by such famous authors as Plato and Pliny,[8] as able to decipher omens and forecast the future, as related in the account of their arrival in Bethlehem.

Religions in Rome

THE ROMANS WERE FAR more religious than the Greeks, Persians, Egyptians, or other pagans of their era. "Every public act began with a religious ceremony, just as the agenda of every meeting of the senate was headed by religious business."[9] Nothing of any significance was done in Rome without the performance of the proper rituals. The senate did not meet, armies did not march, and decisions, both major and minor, were postponed if the signs and portents were not favorable. Such importance was placed on divination that, for example, if lightning were observed during the meeting of some public body, "the assembly would be dismissed, and even after the vote had been taken the college of augurs might declare it void."[10]

The ubiquity of very public rituals and the constant rescheduling of public life, including festivals and holidays, in response to the "temper of the gods," made religion an unusually prominent part of the everyday life, not only of the Roman elite, but of the general public.[11] In contrast to other pagan societies, the temples were not closed to ordinary Romans, nor were the idols hidden from public view. Everyone was welcome and their patronage was solicited. Consequently, even many poor people and slaves contributed funds to the construction of temples—as is attested by temple inscriptions listing donors.[12]

By Christmas Eve, Rome was ruled by a tyrant emperor, but religiously Rome sustained the first relatively free marketplace. Granted that there was an official Roman paganism, but it was mainly supported by voluntary contributions, as were an extraordinary array of other faiths, not only across the empire, but within the city of Rome itself. Many of these were "Oriental" faiths that had come to Rome from Egypt and the Middle East. There also was a large Jewish enclave in Rome and in many major Roman cities.

A remarkable aspect of the absence of a subsidized state religion in Rome is found in the priesthood. Even the traditional Roman temples were not served by professional, full-time priests. Of course, priests showed up to conduct festivals or supervise a major sacrifice, but most of the time the Roman temples seem to have been served only by a few caretakers who lacked any religious duties or authority. In addition, except for a very small number of priests who were advisors to the senate and those who undertook divination, nearly all other priests were prominent citizens who served in the priestly role only part-time. Presumably these amateur Roman priests received some training for their duties, but it could only have been minor compared with the full-time, professional priests found in Greece, Egypt, or Persia.[13] It does not follow, however, that Roman priests were less sincere than were the full-time priests in other pagan societies. To the contrary, it is a closed, hereditary priestly elite that is most susceptible to cynicism and unbelief.[14] In addition, because Roman priests were amateurs for whom being a priest was not their primary role, "Roman temples were not independent centres of power, influence, or riches . . . they did not . . . have priestly personnel attached to them and they did not therefore provide a power base for the priests."[15] Hence, Roman Temples were rather inexpensive to operate since support of a professional priesthood was the major cost involved in sustaining temples elsewhere.

If Roman paganism differed by needing to be financially self-reliant, it did not differ in the number, character, and specializations of its gods. Nor could it have done so given that nearly all of Rome's gods were of Greek origins, they in turn having come from Egypt, whose gods originated in Sumer! As the gods migrated, only their names were changed.[16]

Seven major gods were established prior to the founding of the Roman Republic, headed by Jupiter (also called Jove) who was regarded as the supreme father of the gods and eventually equated with Zeus. Once the Republic was established, the gods proliferated rapidly. But even when official paganism possessed an abundance of temples, both in Rome and in all the other cities of the empire, somehow they didn't seem able to provide enough religion. New faiths continued to arrive from the East and Egypt—the so-called Oriental faiths.

Oriental Faiths

THE ORIENTAL FAITHS INSPIRED remarkable levels of public enthusiasm. All were "pagan" faiths, but with some very significant differences. For one thing, they didn't simply promote another temple to another god—each was intensely focused on one god, albeit they accepted the existence of other gods. This intense focus resulted in something else new to paganism: congregations.

One of these new faiths came from Greece where it had developed as a movement devoted to Dionysus, whom the Romans knew as Bacchus. The Bacchanalians were intense, proselytizing mystery religionists who aroused vicious persecution by the Roman Senate on what probably were spurious grounds that they engaged in drunken immorality.

Another of the Oriental faiths was devoted to the goddess Cybele, known to the Romans as Magna Mater (the Great Mother), and to an unusually handsome Phrygian shepherd named Attis (who, in some accounts, is of supernatural origins) with whom Cybele fell in love. Unfortunately, the young man became sexually involved with a nymph and Cybele found out. In a fit of extreme anger Cybele caused Attis to become insane, and in his mad frenzy he castrated himself, lay down under a pine tree and bled to death. Cybele sorrowed and caused Attis to be reborn, and he became her companion ever after. Attis never became a major figure, remaining only a member of his lover's supporting cast. However, his self-castration became a major feature of Cybelene worship. For one thing, the most solemn ritual of Cybelene worship was the *taurobolium*, wherein a bull was slaughtered on a wooden platform under which lay new initiates who were then drenched in the bull's blood—all in commemoration of Attis's mutilation. It was believed that the blood washed away each initiate's past, giving each a new life. But perhaps the most remarkable aspect linking the Attis story to Cybelene worship is that all "priests of Cybele were eunuchs; self-castration in ecstasy was part of the process of [their] initiation."[17] This Cybelene mythology and the self-castration of her priests must have developed in Greece, because both were fully developed by the time that Magna Mater reached Rome.

The next Oriental faith to reach Rome brought the goddess Isis, who eventually became the focus of a serious pagan attempt to approximate monotheism. Isis began as an Egyptian nature goddess who was responsible for the annual flooding of the Nile and gained substantial followings throughout the Grecian world after Ptolemy I, a comrade of Alexander the Great and the first Greek ruler of Egypt, had her promoted to the savior goddess, "or more explicitly 'saviour of the human race.'"[18] Isis also inspired *congregations*. Her followers set themselves apart and gathered regularly; they did not disparage the other gods and temples, but neither did they attend to them. The first temple of Isis in the West was built in Pompeii in about 100 BCE. Soon after that came her first temple in Rome, and many more were to follow.

Mithraism can be considered an additional Oriental religion even though, contrary to long tradition, it was not related to the Persian religion involving the god Mitra, but was of Roman origin—evidence of its existence suddenly appears in the historical record dating from about 90 CE. Some of the confusion over Mithra's origins was caused by the fact that Mithraism represented itself as based on the wisdom of Zoroaster and of Persian origin. But this seems to have been a bogus attempt to gain credibility and prestige,[19] very similar to claims by many modern cults to be descended from various ancient groups such as the Druids.

In any event, Mithraism mainly recruited Roman soldiers, including even a few senior officers. It was a mystery cult that promised an attractive life after death and inspired deep commitment among its male-only members. They were so observant of their oaths of secrecy that very little is known today about Mithraic doctrines, their mysteries, or what went on at their secret meetings. What is known is they met in small caverns constructed for that purpose and the congregations were small since there were only seats for about fifty members. Several hundred of these caverns have been found and a map[20] of the sites shows them to have been located along the frontiers of the empire close by the ruins of old legionary camps and fortresses. No Mithraic caverns have been found in Rome.

Table 1.1 reports the number of known temples in the city of Rome exclusively devoted to each major God in about the year

100 CE Isis had by far the most (eleven) and Cybele (six) was a strong second. Then came Venus and Jupiter with four each, Fortuna with three, and Apollo and Sol Invictus each had two. Nine other gods had a single temple in Rome. Of course, many other gods had a niche in the Pantheon, and small shrines to various gods were abundant throughout the city. A number of temples also were devoted to "divine" emperors.

Table 1.1: Number of Known Temples Devoted Exclusively to a Major God in the City of Rome (ca. 100 CE)

God	Number of Temples
Isis	11
Cybele	6
Jupiter	4
Venus	4
Fortuna	3
Apollo	2
Sol Invictus	2
Aesculapius	1
Ceres	1
Diana	1
Janus	1
Juno	1
Liber	1
Mars	1
Neptune	1
Quirinus	1

Source: Beard, North, and Price, Religions of Rome *(1998), 1: maps 1 and 2.*

The essential question is, why were the Oriental faiths so popular? A very insightful analysis of why these new religions achieved great popular success in Rome was written a century ago by Franz Cumont (1868–1947), the great Belgian historian.[21] Cumont argued that the Oriental religions succeeded because they "gave greater satisfaction." He believed they did so in three ways, to which I will add a fourth and fifth.

First, according to Cumont, "they appealed more strongly to the senses," having a far higher content of *emotionalism*, especially in their worship activities. In Rome, the traditional religions mainly involved tepid, civic ceremonies and periodic feasts. They sought to enlist the traditional gods to provide protection and prosperity both for the individual and the community. Mostly this involved public rites conducted by priests and little more than some chanting and a sacrifice. In this way, traditional Roman paganism had relegated religious emotionalism "to the periphery of religious life."[22]

In contrast, the new faiths stressed celebration, joy, ecstasy, and passion. Music played a leading role in their services—not only flutes and horns, but an abundance of group singing and dancing. As for ecstasy, the behavior of participants in the worship of some of these groups sounds very like modern Pentecostalism—people going into trancelike states and speaking in unknown tongues. As Cumont summed up, the Oriental "religions touched every chord of sensibility and satisfied the thirst for religious emotion that the austere Roman creed had been unable to quench."[23]

Although Cumont made no mention of it, the chief emotional ingredient lacking in the traditional Roman faiths was *love*. Romans thought the gods might come to their aid, but they did not believe that the gods loved them—indeed Jupiter was depicted as quite unfriendly to human concerns. Consequently, pagan Romans often feared the gods, admired some of them, and envied them all, but they did not love them.

The second advantage of the Oriental faiths was, according to Cumont, their stress on *individualism and virtue*. The traditional gods of Rome were "primarily gods of the state," not the individual.[24] As did the temple religions of Egypt and Persia, the traditional Roman religions pursued "salvation," not for the individual, but for the city or state. Moreover, aside from requiring humans to venerate them properly, the Roman gods seemed to care little about human behavior, moral or immoral—"moral offences were not treated as offences against the gods."[25] Worse, as noted, these gods set bad examples of individual morality.

In contrast, the Oriental religions were not devoted to sanctifying civic affairs, but were instead directed toward the individual's spiritual life and stressed individual morality, offering various means of atonement—it was not primarily *cities* that were punished or saved; *individuals* could "wash away the impurities of the soul . . . [and] restore lost purity."[26] Some paths to atonement were built into the initiation rites of many of these new religions, which stressed purification and the washing away of guilt; various forms of baptism were common. In addition, formal acts of confession were practiced by followers of both Isis and Cybele, but no such practices existed in the traditional temple faiths.[27] Nor was atonement achieved through rites alone; many of the new faiths required acts of self-denial and privation, sometimes even physical suffering—actions that gave credibility to doctrines of individual forgiveness.

Thirdly, Cumont noted that, for a society abundant in historians and written philosophies, it is remarkable that the traditional Roman religions had no *scriptures*. "They had no written works which established their tenets and doctrines, or provided explanation of their rituals or moral prescription for their adherents."[28] In contrast, the Oriental faiths were religions of the book: Bacchanalian, Cybelene, Isiaic, and Mithraic religions offered written scriptures that "captivated the cultured mind."[29] Moreover, the new faiths presented a far more rational portrait of the gods—even many worshippers of Cybele, Isis, Bacchus, and Mithras "recognized no other deity but their god,"[30] and if they did not claim theirs was the *only* God, they did regard theirs as a supreme God.

As Cumont summarized, the new "religions acted upon the senses, the intellect and the conscience at the same time, and therefore gained a hold on the entire man. Compared with the ancient creeds, they appear to have offered greater beauty of ritual, greater truth of doctrine and a far superior morality. . . . The worship of the Roman gods was a civic duty, the worship of the foreign gods the expression of personal belief."[31]

But Cumont failed to recognize two additional factors that were at least as important as the three he noted, and probably even more important: *gender* and *organization*. Although women were permitted to attend "most [pagan] religious occasions . . . they had little opportunity to take any active religious role"[32] in the traditional Roman religions. There were some priestesses in various traditional temples, but only in those dedicated to a goddess. Worse yet, priestesses were subject to severe regulations quite unlike anything imposed on priests: Vestal Virgins were buried alive for transgressions! In contrast, many of the Oriental religions offered women substantial religious opportunities as well as far greater security and status within the family.

But it wasn't only a matter of having scriptures and moral concerns, of singing and speaking in tongues, or even a more equitable view of sex roles that gave the new religions such an advantage. Above all else was their capacity to mobilize a lay following by involving people in *congregations*, in *active communities of believers*.

Roman paganism offered very little in the way of community. Most Romans were very irregular and infrequent visitors to the temples. But the Oriental religions expected their followers to worship daily on their own and then to gather for services weekly or even more often. Sheer frequency, let alone the intensity of these gatherings, made these religious groups central to the lives of their adherents. This was something that had not previously existed: "at least until the middle of the Republic, there is no sign in Rome of any specifically religious groups: groups, that is, of men or women who had decided to join together principally on grounds of religious choice. . . . [T]here were no autonomous religious groups."[33] Put another way, the Roman gods had only clients and festivals, not members and regular services. In contrast the Oriental religions "offered a new sense of community . . . a much stronger type of membership."[34] As John North expressed it, "the degree of commitment asked of the new member when he joins is patently far higher . . . [and involves an] intensified awareness to direct personal experience of contact with the divine. The new structure corresponds to the intensification of religious life and to the new place which religious experience will occupy in the life of the initiate."[35]

Thus, followers of the new religions had a singular religious identity. "They could and did identify themselves by their religion as well as by their city or their family, in a way that earlier centuries would not have understood at all. . . . It is hard to exaggerate the importance of this change."[36] Although not so exclusive as Judaism, initiates into Bacchanalianism, Mithra, Isiacism, and Cybelene worship were expected to cease temple-hopping and devote themselves fully to their respective deity. To support this commitment they adopted a clear religious identity that required and sustained a closely knit and very active religious community—a congregation, not a clientele. Like the Jews, the followers of the Oriental faiths made their religious group the focus of their social life. In doing so, not only did they strengthen their commitment, but they gained far greater rewards from being committed, as other members rewarded them for it. It is by being set apart and offering opportunities for intense interaction and the formation of close social ties that religious groups generate the highest levels of member commitment and loyalty.[37] But this was also the basis for bitter conflicts with the rulers of Rome.

Fear of Congregations

MOST ROMAN EMPERORS SUSPECTED that nearly everyone was plotting against them. And rightfully so. Of the seventy-six emperors who took the throne from the reign of Augustus to the ascension of Constantine, only nineteen died natural deaths. Seven were killed in battle, forty-two were murdered, two others probably were murdered, and six were forced to commit suicide. Consequently, emperors feared all formal organizations as providing an opportunity for political conspiracies. Thus, late in the first century BCE, edicts were issued regulating the formation of all private gatherings. Under Augustus a "more extensive Law on Associations was passed which required that all associations be authorized by the senate or emperor,"[38] and such permission was seldom granted.[39] Consider that during the first decade of the second century CE, Pliny the Younger wrote to the emperor Trajan asking permission to establish a company of volunteer firefighters in Nicomedia, following a serious blaze in that city. The emperor wrote back, denying his request on grounds that "it is societies like these which have been responsible for political disturbances. . . . If people assemble for a common purpose, whatever name we give them and for whatever reason, they soon turn into a political club."[40]

As noted, what most dramatically set the Oriental faiths apart from Roman paganism was their capacity to generate congregations. While people only went to temples, they *belonged* to an Oriental faith. Given the imperial opposition even to volunteer fire departments, religious groups that met once a week or even more often, that swore members to secrecy and did not admit outsiders to their sacred services, could hardly have been ignored. And although it has not generally been noted by religious historians, the Oriental faiths often were viciously persecuted. Not Mithra, of course, since not even the most foolhardy emperors risked offending the army—and still many emperors were murdered by the Praetorians charged with protecting them. But the Bacchanalians, the followers of Isis, and (to a lesser degree) the Cybelenes fell victim to imperial repression, all because of the "sin" of congregationalism.

Suppressing the Bacchanalians

TODAY THE TERM *Bacchanalian* refers to people committed to drunken orgies, because that's what the Roman Senate claimed about the group when they "ferociously suppressed"[41] the cult of Bacchus in 186 BCE—although the charges probably were false.[42] Unfortunately, there are only two quite unsatisfactory sources. The first is Livy, whose report seems more like fiction than history: it is a story of how a good boy is led by his evil mother into this dreadful group.[43] The second source is the actual senatorial decree, which condemned the group and laid down regulations by which it must abide. Based on Livy's account it has been assumed by far too many historians that this group engaged in all manner of vile deeds: human sacrifice, rape, unrestricted sex, drunkenness, and the like. According to Livy, at least seven thousand people were involved, including "certain nobles, both men and women." Subsequently the male leaders of the group were rounded up and executed; others committed suicide, and the "women were handed over to their relatives for punishment."[44] But if these sentences were actually imposed, and if the charges brought against the group were true, then the restrictions laid down in the Senate decree were absurdly mild.

The Senate decree[45] began by prohibiting Bacchic shrines (allowing ten days from the receipt of the decree for them to be dismantled). However, the group itself was not outlawed, but was only limited as to the size and functions of its gatherings. The Senate commanded that they no longer meet in groups larger than five (no more than two of the five being male), that they hold no funds in common, and that they not swear oaths of mutual obligations. In addition, they were forbidden to celebrate rites in secret, and men were not permitted to be priests. And that was it! Nothing was said about refraining from rape, drunkenness, group sex, or human sacrifice, which makes it obvious that these claims were "fantasies" knowingly invoked by at least some senators "to provide legitimation for . . . [their] very controversial decision."[46]

Equally spurious is the frequent assumption that this was a group that had appeared suddenly and was of Roman origin. The Bacchanalians had been in operation for a considerable time before the Senate took action, long enough to have built up a substantial following all across Italy.[47] Moreover, the cult of Bacchus did not originate in Rome; it was an Oriental import from Greece—even Livy blamed an anonymous Greek priest and missionary for bringing the cult to Rome.[48] Consequently, we need not try to read between the lines of Livy's account or of the Senate's edict to discover the group's origins, what it actually taught and practiced, why it was so attractive, and what it was that the Senate really feared. All that is required is that we to turn to the many studies of the group by historians of religion in Greece. Here one finds an extensive literature on the Bacchic or Dionysiac mysteries, including recent reports of many important new discoveries.[49]

Drawing on this literature allows insight into two fundamental questions. What was the movement really like? Why did it provoke such a violent, yet limited, response from the Senate?

Specifically, the cult of Bacchus (or Dionysius) promised the initiated that they would be welcomed into a blissful life after death, enjoying the company of their fellow initiates. A recently discovered gold plate shaped in the form of an ivy leaf instructed the dead to "Tell Persephone that Bacchus himself has set you free."[50] The ordinary person need only become an initiated and committed Bacchanalian in order to escape the dreary afterlife envisioned by the traditional religions of Rome and to gain everlasting joy: "Now you have died, and now you have been born, thrice blest, on this day."[51] This was a remarkable innovation and gave everyone, rich or poor, a substantial reason to join.

Had the promise of an attractive afterlife been the only unusual feature of Bacchanalians, it seems certain that the Roman Senate would have ignored them—as indeed it did for several generations. But of perhaps even greater importance in gaining converts, the cult of Bacchus surrounded its members with a very intense group life.

Originally in Greece it had been a group restricted to women, and subsequently there were separate male and female groups. Transplanted to Italy, the congregations became mixed. Moreover, rather than meeting several times a year, as they had in Greece and as was typical of groups devoted to other traditional pagan gods, the Bacchanalians now met at least weekly. In order to do so without disrupting their affairs, they held their meetings at night in temples and shrines built for that purpose. To become a member required initiation into the group's mysteries and the swearing of solemn oaths of devotion and loyalty.[52]

What these facts tell us is that the Bacchanalians were not casual participants in periodic sacrificial feasts; they were closely united into intense, very self-conscious congregations. And it was this that aroused the senators against them. No doubt senatorial fears also were inflamed by stories about lurid activities (similar claims were routinely leveled at many other "unpopular" religious groups, including Christians and Jews), but what the Roman Senate actually suppressed were the *congregational features* of the group—its regular meetings, its formal organizational structure, the strong ties among members, the prominent role of women in a group including both sexes, and, most of all, the high level of member commitment. These things, not noisy revelry, were what the Senate perceived as a threat and "wished above all to destroy."[53]

Against Isis

ISIS ALSO INSPIRED CONGREGATIONS. Her followers set themselves apart and gathered regularly; they did not disparage the other gods and temples, but neither did they attend to them. This singularity did not escape official attention. In 58 BCE the Senate outlawed Isis and ordered her altars and statues torn down.[54] They repeated their ban ten years later, and Roman consuls around the empire responded by destroying Isiac altars as "disgusting and pointless superstitions."[55]

Next, Isiacism was "vigorously repressed by Augustus"[56] and Tiberius had the Isiac temple in Rome destroyed, the statue of the goddess thrown into the Tiber River, and its priests crucified.[57] Indeed, it was the emperor Caligula, hardly a paragon of tolerance, but who had a taste for the exotic, who first allowed a temple dedicated to Isis to be built on the Campus Martius, and it was not until the reign of Caracella early in the third century that an Isiac temple was allowed on the Capitol.[58] Even so, as noted, there were more temples to Isis built in Rome than to any other god or goddess.

Despite these frequent attempts by the Roman authorities to suppress Isiacism, almost no details about these matters have survived. There are indications that attacks on Isis worship were said to be precipitated by sexual immorality associated with the temples.[59] But this was a standard charge also leveled against every religious group that engendered opposition, and there is no reason to believe it. In this case, too, what upset the Romans was congregationalism. Cumont put it plainly: "Its secret societies . . . might easily become clubs of agitators and haunts of spies."[60] Moreover, there was nothing secret about the Isiac "commandoes" enlisted by Publius Clodius Pulcher (92–52 BCE), who took to the streets in 58 BCE when the Senate had demolished the temple. "The relentless pressure and obstinacy of the Isiasts gave the [Senate] . . . no respite. They [the followers of Isis] restored their places of worship [whenever they were destroyed]. . . . Like the Christian faith later, Isiac perseverance was forged and strengthened in persecutions."[61]

Isolating Cybele

JUST AS CHRISTIANITY GAINED immense influence by being credited with bringing Constantine victory at the Battle of Milvian Bridge, Cybele (also known to the Romans as Magna Mater or Great Mother) was brought to Rome by order of the Senate in 204 BCE (personified by a hunk of meteorite) because of a prophecy inferred from the Sibylline

Books and confirmed by the oracle at Delphi that she would deliver victory for Rome over Hannibal. Within months after her arrival in Rome, the prophecy was fulfilled. Soon after, a temple was erected to Cybele on the summit of the Palatine, the meteorite was set as the face in a silver statue of the goddess, and she was officially recognized as one of the gods of Rome and was worshipped there for more than five hundred years. Every March 27, the silver statue of Cybele was borne by a procession of her priests to a nearby tributary of the Tiber River and bathed, then carried back to the temple.

The Romans soon learned that having Cybele on their side was a very mixed blessing. Cybelene worship was a wild, disruptive affair. "The enthusiastic transports and somber fanaticism of [Cybelene worship] contrasted violently with the calm dignity and respectable reserve of the official religions."[62] Her priests, known as the *galli*, excelled at ecstatic frenzies. Not only did they castrate themselves during their initiation; subsequently they cross-dressed, wore makeup, frizzed their hair, drenched themselves in perfume, and acted like women. Although Romans were not offended by homosexuality, they were absolutely appalled by effeminacy. Yet, they could not doubt the power of the goddess—she had ended the Carthaginian threat. Hence came the decision to isolate the religion before it could infect the populace, but to permit the "barbaric" rites to continue on her behalf. Once a year Cybele was honored by all Romans, and her "priests marched the streets in procession, dressed in motley costumes, loaded with heavy jewelry, and beating tambourines."[63] During the rest of the year the priests were "segregated and inaccessible to the Romans, their cultic activities were confined to the temple."[64] Moreover, Roman citizens were prohibited by law from becoming Cybelene priests.

Persecution of the Jews

ANTI-SEMITISM WAS VIRULENT AND widespread in the classical world. The great Roman philosopher and statesman Lucius Annaeus

Seneca (4 BCE–65 CE) denounced Jews as an "accursed race"[65] and condemned their influence. The esteemed Roman historian Cornelius Tacitus (56–117 CE) railed against the Jews because they "despise the gods," and called their religious practices "sinister and revolting." Not only that, according to Tacitus the Jews had "entrenched themselves by their very wickedness," and they sought "increasing wealth" through "their stubborn loyalty" to one another. "But the rest of the world they confront with hatred reserved for enemies."[66] And, as with the other Oriental religions, the Romans often justified repression of the Jews on spurious grounds of immorality: Ovid claimed that "the Jewish synagogue was an assembly place for prostitutes."[67]

In any event, the Jews were expelled from Rome in 139 BCE by an edict that charged them with attempting "to introduce their own rites" to the Romans and thereby "to infect Roman morals."[68] Then, in 19 CE the emperor Tiberius ordered the Jews and the followers of Isis to leave Rome. The Jews were required to burn all their religious vestments, and all Jewish males of military age were ordered to serve in Sardinia to suppress brigandage, where, according to Tacitus, "if they succumbed to the pestilential climate, it was a cheap loss."[69] In addition, all other Jews were banished not only from the city, but from Italy "on pain of slavery for life if they did not obey," as told by Paulinus Suetonius.[70] In 70 CE the emperor Vespasian imposed a special tax on all Jews in the empire, thereby impounding the contributions that had been made annually to the temple in Jerusalem. And in 95 CE the emperor Domitian executed his cousin Flavius Clemens and "many others" for having "drifted into Jewish ways," as Cassius Dio put it.[71]

Of special interest is that, as reported by Suetonius, in about 49 CE, Emperor Claudius expelled the Jews from Rome for rioting at the instigation of "Chrestus." Since *Christus* was often spelled with an *e* instead of an *i*, this report is taken to mean riots concerning Christ, as is acknowledged in Acts 18:2 where Paul is reported to have met two Christians in Corinth who had been forced to leave Rome. However, historians think that if the entire Jewish population of Rome, by then numbering many tens of thousands, had been banished, many other writers of that time would have at least mentioned it—and they did not. What seems more likely is that everyone involved in the riots, which probably involved Christians attempting to teach in the local synagogues (as Paul so often did elsewhere), was ordered out of Rome, but this probably only involved a few hundred people.[72]

No doubt many Romans did resent that Jews dismissed the gods as illusions and their temples as blasphemous, but it seems likely that the most compelling objection on the part of the state was the standard complaint—that the major sin of the Jews was to be a strong, well-organized, separated community, in addition to which the Jews sought converts, as did all of the Oriental faiths. This likely created hard feelings in the pagan temples because converts to Judaism or to the other Oriental faiths ceased patronizing the temples. This might have been ignored in a society wherein the temples enjoyed lavish state support. But in Rome, even the temples of Jupiter had to exist on voluntary contributions. Hence, it seems plausible that many tales of sexual immorality cited by the Senate in its persecutions were composed and spread by pagan priests.

This whole phenomenon soon would be repeated when Rome took sufficient note of the new religion come to Rome from Jerusalem.

Pagan "Monotheism"

PERHAPS STIMULATED BY THE presence of Jews in their midst and by contacts with Zoroastrianism, many Greek and Roman philosophers began to entertain monotheistic ideas, while several pagan groups attempted to transform one of their gods into as close an approximation of monotheism as was possible within the limiting assumptions of polytheism. The most extensive efforts in this direction were made on behalf of the goddess Isis.

When Isis came west, she soon shed her Egyptian role as responsible for the rise and fall of the Nile. Instead, she began to be hailed as the Goddess Supreme, the Queen of the Sky, the Mother of the Stars, and often was referred to as the savior goddess. As Plutarch explained: "Isis is the female principle in nature, which is the receiver of every act of creation; wherefore she is called 'nurse' and 'receiver of all' by Plato, and by mankind in general 'the goddess of ten thousand names.'"[73]

The many surviving inscriptions and scriptures in praise of Isis[74] include such claims as:

> It was Isis "who separated earth from heaven, showed the stars their courses, ordained the path of sun and moon."

> Isis is "sole ruler of eternity" and "all call me the highest goddess, greatest of all the gods in heaven," and "nothing happens apart from me."

> Isis is "ruler of the world . . . greatest of the gods, the . . . ruler of heavenly things and immeasurable. . . . You are the ruler of all forever."

But no matter how often Isis was referred to as the "one True and Living God,"[75] she could not escape the limitations of paganism. She could be recognized as a *supreme* god, but not as an *only* god because the existence of a whole pantheon of other gods, including her son Horus, could not be denied within the context of paganism. Moreover, hers was entirely an otherworldly tale, in contrast to the manifest historicity of Judaism. That is, Isis's "biography" took place entirely within the invisible world of the gods. It was there, within the womb of her mother Nut (Goddess of the Sky), that Isis had sex with her twin brother Osiris. It was in this same invisible world that Osiris was murdered by his evil brother Seth, his body torn into fourteen pieces and these flung throughout space. And it was in that nether world that Isis searched for these pieces in order to reassemble Osiris—finding everything but his penis. And so on. As Cyril Bailey (1871–1957) put it: "On the one side were the legendary figures, unhistorical and mere puppets in a story . . . [whereas] on the [Jewish] side there were indeed historical personages."[76] God was believed to have revealed himself to mortal Jews, and the Bible tells the history of a real people and occurs on this earth.

Conclusion

ON CHRISTMAS EVE, JUDAISM was the only fully developed monotheism available in the Roman West. It is well known that the Jews played a crucial role in preparing the way for the Christianization of Rome. But much too little has been made of the extent to which the Oriental religions also prepared the way: the geography of the spread of early Christianity through the empire closely followed the geography of the spread of temples devoted to Cybele and to Isis.[77] By the same token, the persecution of the Oriental faiths, and of the Jews, anticipated the later Roman attempts to destroy Christianity.

CHAPTER TWO

Many Judaisms

ALTHOUGH JUDAISM WAS THE ONLY fully developed monotheism within the Roman Empire, there was as much religious variety and conflict in Palestine as in Rome, despite the fact that everyone involved claimed to be a Jew. Samaritan claims to be Jewish were rejected by the other Jewish groups, all of whom treated the Samaritans with contempt and sometimes with bloody brutality. Jews living in the Hellenized cities founded in Palestine by Greeks following Alexander the Great's conquests also were locked in nasty struggles with other Jews. As for the rest of the Jewish groups, some demanded strict observance of the Law, while others were very lax in their observance. Some collaborated with Roman rule, others plotted rebellion, and still others anxiously awaited the Messiah who would restore Jewish independence and power.

On Christmas Eve there were about nine million Jews living in the Roman Empire (which had a total population of about sixty million), about 90 percent of them living in the larger Roman cities west of Palestine. In addition, at least several million Jews lived in cities to the east of Palestine; there was a large Jewish community in Babylon. These communities made up what is known as the Jewish Diaspora (or dispersion) and came to play a very significant role in the spread of Christianity. However, the story of Christianity begins in Palestine.

If we place Christmas Eve in 6 BCE,[1] King Herod's brutal reign was nearly over. His death two years later prompted an outbreak of bloody revolts by Jewish zealots. In response, the Romans crucified thousands of Jews and placed Judea under the rule of a Roman Procurator—a position eventually filled by Pontius Pilate.

Herod

ONLY BECAUSE ROMANS WROTE most of the history of the era is King Herod (73–04 BCE) typically remembered as "Herod the Great." Romans remarked on his immense building projects and his faithful service to Rome. Jewish history remembers his brutality, his immorality, his subservience to Rome, and his profanation of the Temple— even though he had also caused it to be rebuilt.

Herod was not born a Jew. His mother was the daughter of an Arabian sheik and his father, Antipater, was an Edomite—a pagan people living in what is now Jordan. Antipater was a gifted opportunist who backed the right Hasmonian prince in a succession struggle and managed to marry a Hasmonian princess and secure an appointment at court. Next, he displayed excellent political judgment in backing Julius Caesar in the civil war against Pompey. For backing Caesar, Antipater obtained the appointment of his twenty-five-year-old son Herod as governor of Galilee. Soon after taking office Herod suppressed an uprising led by Hezekiah (or Ezekias), and put him and a large number of his followers to death. Taking "the law into his own hands got him in grave trouble with the Jewish Council in Jerusalem,"[2] a conflict with religious Jews that was to continue throughout his life.

After Caesar was murdered, his assassins Brutus and Cassius took control of the East and demanded funding from the local rulers. Herod complied but eventually fled to Rome where he somehow gained the favor of Mark Antony and the Second Triumvirate, and they caused the Senate to elect him "King of the Jews." With this backing, in 37 BCE Herod gained the throne of Judea. To help secure his claim to the throne, he banished his wife and son and then married his teenage niece.

Herod claimed to be a Jew, but many Jews did not accept him as such. In an effort to gain support from the more traditional Jews, Herod undertook a massive rebuilding of the Temple in Jerusalem on a far more magnificent scale. Later he greatly compromised this achievement by placing a huge golden eagle over the main entrance to the Temple. This was hotly condemned by leading Pharisees as an idolatrous Roman symbol, and some young zealots smashed it during the night, for which they were arrested and burned to death by order of Herod.

As king, Herod was empowered to appoint the high priest. Being cautious about possible rivals, as his first selection he appointed "an obscure Jew from Babylonia."[3] This infuriated his mother-in-law and eventually Herod withdrew the appointment and gave the job to his mother-in-law's seventeen-year-old son Aristobulus. Soon after, Herod arranged a bathing party at Jericho, at which he had Aristobulus drowned. Subsequently, in an effort to overcome their angry opposition, Herod began to appoint Sadducees (the hereditary priestly class) to the high priesthood, each serving a short term and retaining his privileges after leaving office. This helped in building a base of influential religious supporters. But they were of little help in shielding him from growing religious antagonism, some of it based on his dreadful family life.

During his reign, Herod ran through ten wives and not only disinherited his sons from previous marriages, but had at least three of them murdered. Late in his reign he became very alarmed at the rapidly growing outbreak of messianic hopes and prophecies, and anyone he suspected of being the Messiah he had put to death. When he became suspicious that his current wife was involved with a group expecting the Messiah, he had her killed too.[4] Matthew 2:16 claims that, hoping to eliminate Jesus, Herod ordered the death of all the children under the age of two in Bethlehem. Whether or not this actually happened, it was utterly in character.

In any event, Herod was both a tyrant and a suspected pagan, and his long reign exacerbated conflict among the many Jewish religious groups and provoked even greater antagonism toward Rome.

Samaritans

NESTLED BETWEEN JUDEA IN the south and Galilee in the north lies Samaria. For nearly two centuries, the city of Samaria was the capital of Israel and the area around the city was home to the leading families. Then the Assyrians arrived in 597 BCE and took thousands of important Samarian Jews away to be held as captives in Babylon. Apparently, at this time the Assyrians also settled some of their own people in the Samarian region. Subsequently, these settlers requested teaching by Israelite priests and ever since have regarded themselves as Jews—as did all the Jews remaining in Samaria from before the invasion. However, when the descendents of the Jews taken to Babylon returned to Palestine, they refused to recognize the "Samaritans" as Jews and did not allow them to participate in the rebuilding of the Temple. In response, the Samaritans built their own temple at Nābulus, at the foot of Mount Gerizim.

Bitterness increased in 128 BCE when the Hasmonean (Maccabean) King John Hyrcanus had the Samaritan temple destroyed. There followed a long series of acts of reprisal and counter reprisal. "The hatred was such that to be called a Samaritan was a grievous insult . . . some rabbis said that to eat the bread of Samaritans was to eat pork, or to marry a Samaritan was to lie with a beast."[5] Thus the barbed irony of Jesus's parable of the "Good Samaritan" (Luke 10:30–37).

Hellenistic Judaism

SAMARITANISM WAS NOT THE only form of Judaism regarded as outside the acceptable sphere. Almost as bitter were the attacks on

Hellenized Jews who lived in the many Greek-speaking cities that had arisen in Palestine. They were accused of flirting with pagan gods and neglecting the Law. Moreover, the Hellenized Jews regarded themselves as culturally superior, and their haughtiness, their overt discrimination against more traditional Jews, and their presumed complicity in a campaign to eliminate Judaism entirely prompted the Maccabean Revolt.

The Hellenization of Judaism began with Alexander the Great's conquest of the entire Middle East, with the result that Palestine came under the control of Ptolemaic (Greek) Egypt. This soon led to the founding of twenty-nine Greek cities in Palestine—some of them in Galilee, the two largest of these being Tiberias (on the Sea of Galilee) and Sepphoris, which was only about four miles from Nazareth.[6] By early in the second century BCE, Jerusalem was so transformed into a Greek city that it was known as Antioch-at-Jerusalem.[7]

Soon the Hellenized Jews gained control of the high priesthood with the support of Antiochus IV Epiphanes (215–164 BCE), ruler of the Seleucid Empire, a portion of Alexander the Great's conquests that included Palestine. Antiochus assumed the right to appoint the high priest. When a conflict broke out between Hellenic factions over who should be the next high priest, Antiochus initiated a purge of Judaism. He "imposed the death sentence on any Jew who circumcised his children or observed the Sabbath. The authorities even forced the Jewish population to participate in pagan rites and eat forbidden foods, particularly pork, and the temple was desecrated and rededicated to Olympic Zeus."[8] Not surprisingly, these acts provoked the bloody Maccabean Revolt during which traditional Jews committed massacres in some of the Greek cities in Palestine and forced the Hellenized communities to conform to tradition—the sons of Hellenized Jews were "forcibly circumcised,"[9] for example.

Maccabean rule endured until 63 BCE when Pompey captured Jerusalem and placed Palestine under Roman rule, whereupon Greek influence strongly reasserted itself, if not in purely religious terms, then overwhelmingly in political terms: "Greek influence reached its height under King Herod . . . who built a Greek theatre, amphitheatre, and hippodrome in or near Jerusalem"[10] in addition to rebuilding the Temple.

Despite the bitterness of these disputes over *who* was an authentic Jew, they were in some ways overshadowed by disputes within the recognized Jewish community as to *how* to be a Jew.

Jewish Pluralism

AS DEMONSTRATED BY BOTH Romans and Jews, religious pluralism is the *natural* condition of any society (although, in the past it has not been the *usual* condition). That is, if the state permits religious diversity, there will come into being many religious groups spread across a spectrum of intensity. Even if the state suppresses all but an official, subsidized religious institution, as was the case in the classic pagan temple societies such as Greece, Egypt, and Persia, unauthorized religious groups will lurk on the periphery and exist on the sly. This follows from the existence in all societies of variations in individual religious tastes. These diverse tastes constitute a set of potential market niches ranging from groups with little or no interest in religion to ones with very intense religious concerns. This range of tastes has been observed even in primitive societies.[11] No single institution can serve this full spectrum of religious market niches, as no one institution simultaneously can be worldly and otherworldly or lax and strict. It follows that religious monopolies can exist only to the extent that coercion is able to keep dissenting groups tiny and circumspect and that whenever coercion falters, competing religious groups will arise.

Because erstwhile monopoly religions inevitably are relatively lax, lazy, and worldly, most of their opposition will come from groups promoting a far more intense faith—from *sects*, that being the name given to high-intensity religious groups. Monopoly religions slide into accommodation with their social surroundings even when they were first established by those committed to an intense faith. One reason that a monopoly religion drifts toward laxity is that religious intensity is never transmitted very efficiently from one generation to the next. Inevitably, many of the sons and daughters of sect members prefer a lower-tension faith than did their parents.[12] So long as leadership positions in a sect are restricted to those who are committed to the original standards, a sect can sustain a relatively high level of intensity. But when these positions are hereditary, and when they are highly rewarded as well (so that the less "religious" seldom depart for other careers), the institution will soon be dominated by those favoring a lower level of intensity.

This process has long been referred to as the *transformation of sects*, the social process that causes successful sects to become more moderate religious groups.[13] Transformation also is speeded by the involvement of the religious leaders in worldly affairs, both political and economic. Finally, if such a religious institution lacks the coercive power to muffle competitive impulses, it soon will be surrounded by sect movements mounted by those wanting a higher-tension faith. This is what happened in Israel, beginning soon after the return of the Jews from exile in Babylon.

The Judaism put in place by the Jewish leaders upon their return from exile required strict observance of the Law and absolute intolerance of polytheism. But authority over this new orthodoxy was centralized in Jerusalem and placed in the hands of a professional, hereditary priesthood, and the Temple was rebuilt. A universal tithe was imposed on the entire Jewish population to support the Temple and subsidize the hereditary priesthood.[14] Of perhaps even greater significance, the Temple became the dominant financial institution, housing money-changers as well as acting as the state treasury and even as an investment bank—"a depository for capital sums, such as money belonging to widows and orphans or to the rich, who feared for their capital under the often insecure conditions that prevailed."[15]

Soon the priests became "the wealthiest class and the strongest political group among the Jews of Jerusalem,"[16] given that Israel was ruled as a province by outsiders. Consequently, the high priest was not only "the religious head but also the political leader of the nation."[17] Membership in the priesthood was entirely hereditary and even the office of high priest often passed from father to son—and priests tended to only marry the daughters of other priests. Not surprisingly, the priests demanded and enjoyed a high level of public deference. Although many priests did not live in Jerusalem, they went there to serve in the Temple when their turn came, as well as for "the three festivals of Passover, Pentecost and Tabernacles."[18] Thus, the official Jewish religion was a centralized Temple religion, and the observance of any organized rites elsewhere was frowned upon. Centralization was also served by the fact that the tithes were gathered in Jerusalem and dispersed from there.

It was this combination of a rich, relatively worldly priesthood controlling a subsidized state Temple, on the one hand, and "outsider" political rulers reluctant to coerce religious conformity, on the other, that gave rise to the full range of Jewish religious groups (the Talmud notes twenty-four sects).[19] Unfortunately, all we know about most of the sects is their name, and often not that. And because so few of the many disputatious Jewish groups left much of anything in writing, most of what is known about the rest was composed by outsiders, many of them quite unfriendly.[20]

The most important source is the first-century Jewish adventurer-historian Josephus (ca. 37–100), who at least claimed to have spent time as a member of each of three leading Jewish groups: the Sadducees, the Pharisees, and the Essenes.[21] Members of each of these three groups kept themselves apart from other Jews and probably numbered no more than twenty thousand members altogether out of a population of perhaps one million.[22] But they played the determining influence on religious life, as the three spanned the spectrum of religious tastes from very low to very high intensity. All three were recruited primarily from among the wealthy and privileged.[23]

The *Sadducees* represented the "official" Temple Judaism and drew their support mainly from the aristocracy—primarily the hereditary priestly families.[24] Despite their conflicts with the more powerful

Pharisees, the Sadducees were able to maintain their monopoly on the right to serve as priests in the Temple (it was a Sadducee high priest who judged Jesus).[25] And, typical of all such temple priesthoods, their theology was quite worldly. For example, they denied both the immortality of the soul and the resurrection of the body and taught that God's rewards are gained only in this life. Perhaps their most controversial position was to assert that "only those laws written in the Pentateuch were to be regarded as binding, while those that were not written down [those that were only "oral" traditions] were not to be observed."[26]

The *Pharisees* believed in an immortal soul, in the resurrection of the good, and in the condemnation of the wicked to "eternal torment."[27] In their view the "good" were those who obeyed the Law, both written and oral. The Pharisees probably originated as a sect movement, generated by the increasing worldliness and accommodation of the restored Temple religion. If so, they too soon became a relatively lower-tension movement, the equivalent of a "mainstream" denomination, representing the large, moderate portion of the Jewish religious spectrum—having "the multitude on their side," according to Josephus.[28] In keeping with their moderate stance, the Pharisees "formulated the doctrine of two realms, secular and divine, with respect to the state." Consequently, when the first Roman Procurator initiated a census in order to fix the amount of Jewish taxes, "the Pharisees urged the people to cooperate, since the Romans were not interfering in the religious sphere,"[29] thereby anticipating Jesus's counsel to "render unto Caesar."

Perhaps the most significant single contribution of the Pharisees was the establishment of synagogues in Israel. The word *synagogue* refers both to a building used for local worship and to the congregation that gathers there to worship. Synagogues had of necessity existed in Babylon, but when they were instituted in Israel they posed a direct challenge to the centralized Temple Judaism. The Pharisees held that synagogues could "be established wherever there were enough men to constitute a *minyan* (quorum)," which was ten.[30] Initially this practice was opposed by the Sadducees, but having the numbers on their side, the Pharisees prevailed, and after the destruction of the Temple once again—this time by the Romans in the year 70—the synagogue became the primary institution of Jewish religious life.

The *Essenes* were typical of the many high-tension, ascetic sect movements that abounded in Israel. Josephus reported that the Essenes condemned "pleasures as evil," rejected marriage, and embraced abstinence, and that their piety was "very extraordinary."[31] Many authors suggest that the community at Qumran, from whose library the Dead Sea Scrolls probably came, were Essenes.[32] John the Essene was one of the Jewish generals in the Great Revolt against Rome (66–74), and Josephus indicated that rebellious Essenes were tortured by the Romans. Following the revolt, "the Essenes disappear from the stage of history,"[33] but there were many other high intensity groups to take their place.[34]

For many Jews, nationalism and piety were inseparable. They reasoned that because the Jews are God's chosen people, they are not subject to "foreign" rule, including Jews crowned as king by outsiders such as the Romans, and a pious Jew will violently resist all such iniquities. Although these sentiments were prominent throughout the history of the ancient Jews, as exemplified by Elijah, they became far more intense and organized in reaction against Herod and boiled over during the interregnum following his death in 4 BCE. Hence, it was at this time that pious Jewish rebels were called *Zealots*—proponents of the Fourth Philosophy, which held that only God should rule Israel.[35]

Perhaps the first of the Zealots was Judas of Galilee. He did not, however, raise his rebellion in Galilee, but in Jerusalem in 6 CE. The specific focus of the rebellion was a census instituted by the Roman authorities for tax purposes. The Zealots rejected paying any taxes to any ruler on grounds that it violated the First Commandment. In addition, the Roman emperors' pretentions to divinity aroused angry opposition among most Jews, who held it sacrilege to support such "pretenders." Judas's rebellion was brutally suppressed by the Romans; Josephus claimed that the Roman commander had two thousand crucified.[36] Nevertheless, it expressed a spirit and outlook that persisted—Judas's two sons continued their father's activities and were executed by the Procurator of Judea in 46 CE. Of course, the Zealots played the leading role in the Great Revolt of 66–73 CE—the bloody war with Rome that ended in the complete destruction of Jerusalem.

The most extreme Zealots were known as *Sicarii* because they concealed *sicae*, or small daggers, under their cloaks and used them to kill Jews who were not sufficiently opposed to Roman rule—primarily the Sadducee priestly aristocrats.[37] Josephus reported that the Sicarii "murdered people in broad daylight . . . mixing with the crowds, especially during the festivals . . . [they would] stealthily stab their opponents. Then, when the victims fell, the murderers simply melted into the outraged crowd. . . . [T]he first to have his throat cut was Jonathan the High Priest, after him many were murdered daily."[38] Remarkably, it is thought that the Sicarii "were probably a group of teachers, in membership as well as leadership."[39] This is consistent with their populism—when they "entered Jerusalem in 66, they burned the archives containing the records of debt."[40] In any event, this rash of murders helped bring on the Great Revolt, at the end of which about a thousand Sicarii (including wives and children) found martyrdom at Masada in 73.

Josephus also claimed that from age sixteen he had spent three years in the wilderness with a wandering holy man named Bannus (or Banus). Aside from the fact that Bannus lived off shrubs and plants and took frequent cold baths "in order to preserve his chastity,"[41] nothing more is known about him other than that the wilderness was full of such ascetic Jews. The most famous of them was, of course, John the Baptist—but on Christmas Eve he was still an infant. Some like Bannus were permanent residents of the wilderness, but more often Jews (both men and women) went on a short-term retreat, often for a period of forty days in memory of Moses's time on Sinai.[42]

Yet, amid all this pluralism, a remarkable number of Jews were agreed that the future of Israel was assured by the expected arrival of the Messiah.

Messianism

THE WORD *MESSIAH* DERIVES from the Aramaic word *meshiah* meaning "the Lord's anointed" (the Greek word is *christos*).[43] A constant theme in ancient Jewish thought through the centuries—especially when beset by powerful enemies—was that God would send a Messiah to reign over an era "of perfect happiness [when] the fulness of Israel's glory would be restored [and] God's justice would rule the world."[44] On this everyone agreed. But beyond this, as Jacob Neusner demonstrated, Judaism "presents no well-crafted doctrine of the Messiah."[45] Indeed, the Jews who wrote the scrolls found at Qumran even anticipated two Messiahs, "the Anointed Priest and the Anointed King."[46]

Hence, Jewish expectations about the Messiah were "a vast mass of confused, involved and even contradictory notions."[47] Some thought his would be an earthly reign lasting, some said, for sixty years, others said a thousand, still others said it would blend into eternity becoming Paradise. In fact, the coming of the Messiah often was linked to the end of time, to "the resurrection of the righteous dead; and the punishment of the wicked, past and present."[48] Some expected a serene and spiritual Messiah who would accomplish his mission in miraculous fashion. But many more expected a fierce and invincible warrior Messiah who would destroy the pagan nations. The apocryphal *Psalms of Solomon* prays that God will send the Messiah "to purge Jerusalem from gentiles . . . to smash the arrogance of sinners like a potter's jar . . . to destroy the unlawful nations with the word of his mouth."[49] There are even "far more savage passages in the other apocryphal books: they emphasized the warlike character of the messianic king and dwelt on the destruction of the heathen nations, the crushed heads, the piled-up bodies, the sharp arrows struck into the hearts of enemies . . . humiliated Israel awaited an avenger, or at all events a liberator who would give the nation back its place in the world."[50]

With the rise of the Zealots and their repeated rebellions against Rome, a number of leaders were identified as possible Messiahs—

some of them made that claim, others did not. This seems a rather reasonable development given the Jewish determination to drive away the Romans and their inadequate military resources to do so. As Josephus explained, "What more than all else incited them to war was an ambiguous oracle, likewise found in their sacred scriptures, to the effect that at that time one from their country would become ruler of the world."[51]

Despite the many disagreements concerning the expected Messiah, most Jews seem to have assumed that his would be a worldly kingdom. That the Christ story departed substantially from prophecies of a worldly rule is the sticking point that always has been offered as the reason that the Jews rejected Jesus.[52] Recent studies have revealed that there were in fact Jewish prophecies concerning a suffering rather than a conquering Messiah.[53] There may even have been a prophecy that the Messiah would die and rise again in three days. This resurrection prophecy is based on an interpretation of a newly discovered stone, three feet high and covered with writing in ink, now referred to as "Gabriel's Revelation."[54] Scholars date it as having been written either in the first century BCE or the first century CE.[55] If the former, then this could be interpreted as a prophecy fulfilled by Jesus. If the latter, it might have been inspired by the Christ story.

Conclusion

THIS WAS THE JEWISH world into which Jesus was born and raised, conducted his ministry, and was crucified. It was a society of monotheists dedicated to the importance of holy scripture. In addition to sustaining a remarkable number of scholars and teachers, it was also a world prolific in prophets and terrorists. Hence, this tiny society of Jews at the edge of the empire caused Rome far more trouble than did any other province. It even might be said that in the end, despite having been reduced to rubble by Titus in 70 CE, Jerusalem conquered Rome.

PART II

Christianizing the Empire

CHAPTER THREE

Jesus and the Jesus Movement

THE WORLD'S LARGEST RELIGION IS known as Christianity, not Je-
hovahism, because the Christ story is central to everything else. Consequently, Christians have always wanted to know as much as possible
about the life of Jesus during his time on earth. Hence, it is appropriate to assess what can be known about the human Jesus before turning
to the early days of the movement he inspired.

Jesus

UNFORTUNATELY, SECULAR HISTORIANS OF the time barely noticed Jesus. Writing in about the year 92, Josephus mentioned Jesus
only once, or possibly twice. The first mention tells how High Priest
Ananus had James, "the brother of Jesus who was called Christ,"
stoned to death.[1] The second passage, which might well have been
inserted by a later copyist, summarizes the Christ-story in five sentences, including the Crucifixion and Resurrection.[2] Even if we
accept both mentions as authentic, there is no evidence that Josephus
had sources independent of Christian teachings, such as Roman records or recollections. The same is true for Tacitus's report (probably
written in 117) that "Christus . . . had suffered the extreme penalty

during the reign of Tiberius at the hands of one of our procurators, Pontius Pilate."[3] Other mentions by classical authors were written significantly later and also offer no evidence of reporting an independent historical tradition.[4]

Consequently, most of those who have sought the historic Jesus have turned to inference—to assuming what Jesus *must have been* like, given the time and place in which he grew up and pursued his ministry. Keep in mind that "must have been" is one of the most suspect phrases in the scholarly vocabulary; usually it should be translated as "we don't really know, but perhaps."

In the case of Jesus, what mostly has gone on is to formulate generalizations about life in Galilee and then to apply them to Jesus: for example, most people in Galilee were illiterate so Jesus "must have been" illiterate too.[5] This approach ignores the obvious, that what might be true of most people does not tell us anything firm about any specific individual. Some people in Galilee could read. Was Jesus one of them? To assume he was not goes against extensive evidence in the Gospels that Jesus often read.[6] Similar problems arise when scholars infer what Jesus "must have been" like from the fact that he was a Jew. The results differ immensely depending on *what kind* of Jew the author assumes Jesus to have been,[7] and it remains quite possible that he was like none of them!

In the end, our knowledge of Jesus comes down to the Gospels; there isn't really anything else to go on. Matthew, Mark, Luke, and John are written in the form followed by Greco-Roman biographies.[8] Unlike modern biographies, this genre often focused on a major aspect of a life and could virtually ignore other biographical matters. This is certainly true of the Gospels. They barely mention Jesus's life before his baptism by John, and nearly all of the text of each Gospel is devoted to his ministry. Indeed, half or more of each Gospel is devoted to the last week of his life.[9] In any event, we know nothing of his appearance and little more about his personal style, although he clearly had no respect for the prevailing social distinctions, being quite willing to associate with stigmatized outsiders such as Samaritans, publicans, "fallen" women, beggars, and various other outcasts. We also know that he was not the meek, mild pacifist so popular with some modern writers, who place all their stress on Jesus's admonition to "turn the other cheek." They never mention, "Do not think that I have come to bring peace on earth; I have not come to bring peace, but a sword" (Matt. 10:34). And all sayings aside, the image of meekness is entirely incompatible with the Jesus who is reported to have "looked around at them with anger" (Mark 3:5), who often verbally skewered Pharisees, and who drove money-changers out of the Temple.

So, what do we really know about the human Jesus? First of all, his family knew him as Joshua—Jesus being the Greek form of that name. He probably was born in 6 BCE (and no later than 4 BCE), at the very end of the reign of Herod the Great. He grew up in the village of Nazareth. He was the son of a woman named Mary whose husband Joseph probably was a carpenter, although he might have been what today would be called a contractor.[10]

Was Jesus a carpenter too? That generally is assumed because in Mark 6:2–3, when Jesus began to teach in the synagogue, "many who heard him were astonished, saying, 'Where did this man get all this? . . . Is not this the carpenter, the son of Mary . . . ?'" However, the version in Matthew 13:55 does not call Jesus a carpenter. There, the people ask instead, "Is not this the carpenter's son?" Thus, the idea that Jesus was a carpenter is based only on one assertion in Mark that may not be consistent with the sentence in Matthew. Nothing else is said anywhere in the Gospels about Jesus being a carpenter nor is anything ever said about his education. However, throughout the Gospels, Jesus is addressed as rabbi or teacher—the two terms being synonymous and referring to one trained in the Law. It is worth noting the widespread Jewish practice that "a student of the Law always had a trade by which he could live."[11] It is very inviting to suppose that Rabbi Jesus was a carpenter only in that sense. Alternatively, Geza Vermes claimed that in "Talmudic sayings the Aramaic noun denoting carpenter or craftsman (*naggar*) stands for 'scholar' or 'learned man.'"[12] Both possibilities seem far more consistent with Jesus's knowledge of the Law than is the idea he spent his formative years sawing wood. So, with whom did Rabbi Jesus study? Where *did* he get all this? It is inappropriate to suggest that, being the son of God, he need not have studied. The human Jesus required educating.

Some have argued that he was a student of John the Baptist[13]; in fact they may have been cousins (Luke 1 and 2). But it is not clear that John was qualified for the role of rabbinical teacher. It seems more likely that Jesus studied with a local rabbi who was unknown outside of Galilee and, therefore, unlike the famous Gamaliel who taught Paul, no memory of him survived to inform the Gospel writers. But how could a carpenter's son become a rabbinical student? It appears that his family was sufficiently affluent to have supported him. For example, they could afford to go to Jerusalem every year for Passover (Luke 2:41), something most families could not do. Indeed, it is not unlikely that Jesus's brother James, who subsequently became head of the church, also was trained as a rabbi—given James's high standing with many Pharisees in Jerusalem who raised a tumult of protest at his execution.[14] But even if we suppose that Jesus's family could not or did not support him while he studied to be a rabbi, it was a central part of Jewish culture that young men of outstanding intellect were recruited as rabbinical students regardless of their background—after all, the famous Rabbi Akiva (ca. 50–135 CE) began as a shepherd. Perhaps the story of the twelve-year-old Jesus amazing the elders in the temple (Luke 2:42–51) was meant to convey how his talents were recognized and rewarded.

Of course, all this is conjecture. What we know for sure is that Jesus's followers and many others called him rabbi[15] and that in a "Jewish setting, an illiterate rabbi who surrounds himself with disciples, debating Scripture and halakhah with other rabbis and scribes, is hardly credible."[16] That we know nothing more of Jesus's education is unfortunate.

Jesus had brothers and sisters, but did not marry. At about age thirty he was baptized by John the Baptist and had a vision. It is entirely consistent with the doctrines concerning the human Jesus that this may have been when he first learned of his divine identity and his mission. According to the Gospels, Jesus then went into the wilderness and after forty days returned to Galilee and began his ministry, which lasted only for about a year according to Matthew, Mark, and Luke, while John extends it to at least two years, and possibly three. He usually preached in Aramaic, but in Hebrew to more sophisticated audiences.[17] Some scholars believe that he also spoke Greek,[18] since Nazareth is only about five miles from Sepphoris, then the capital of Galilee and a Greek-speaking city.[19] However, there is no hint in the Gospels that Jesus ever visited Sepphoris, or Tiberias, the other Greek city in Galilee, during his ministry;[20] seemingly he preferred the villages and countryside.

Even so, the emphasis on the homeless itinerancy of Jesus and his disciples[21] seems geographically naive. Although the Gospel of John has Jesus spending a substantial amount of time in Judea and Jerusalem, even John agrees he spent most of his time in Galilee, and the other three Gospels suggest that is where he spent nearly all his time, often preaching along the Sea of Galilee.[22] Although Galilee was "the richest, most populous . . . part of Palestine,"[23] it is so tiny that it is an easy two-day walk from north to south and only a day's walk from east to west at the widest point. Specifically, it is less than twenty-five miles from Nazareth to Capernaum, where most of Jesus's ministry took place (it was "his own city" according to Matt. 9:1), and only about two miles north from Capernaum to Chorazin, and less than five miles from Capernaum along the shore of the Sea of Galilee to Bethsaida, home of Simon, Peter, and Andrew. The "Sea" is, of course, a lake fed by the Jordan River and is only "about thirteen miles long and eight miles wide at its broadest point."[24] Shifting south, it is only about seven miles from Nazareth to Cana, and Nain is even closer. The only "long" trips reported in the Gospels were a journey from Capernaum to the Tyre area (about thirty miles) and one or several to Jerusalem, about seventy miles from Nazareth. Thus, almost nowhere Jesus is reported to have visited is even "a full day's journey away from either Nazareth or Capernaum and . . . it would have been quite feasible to regularly return to a home base in either town."[25] In fact, Peter had a house in Capernaum,[26] and perhaps Jesus did too (Mark 2:1–2). In any event, as E. P. Sanders noted, "After preaching elsewhere, Jesus would return [to Capernaum]."[27]

To sum up: according to the four Gospels, Jesus was a young teacher and miracle worker who spent most of his brief ministry in Galilee. We know nothing of his appearance and very little about his life before he was baptized by John. It seems unlikely that he was really a carpenter, and we probably can assume that he was trained as a rabbi, but we know nothing about who taught him, where, or when. We know that he aroused bitter opposition and was crucified by order of Pontius Pilate. We know that his disciples testified that he rose from the dead. We don't know much of anything else except, of course, that his teachings and his example changed the world.

But Can the Gospels Be Trusted?

FOR SEVERAL CENTURIES THERE has been a long and aggressive campaign to discredit as much of the "historical" content of the Gospels as possible. Some scholars dismiss the Gospels as "little more than a latter-day Christian fantasy that can tell us nothing reliable."[28] A leader in these efforts was Hans Conzelmann (1915–1989), who claimed, for example, that from beginning to end, Acts is fiction.[29] Paul's missionary voyages never happened! Paul's shipwreck is pure fantasy![30] In dismissing the Acts account of Paul's voyages and shipwreck, Conzelmann and others "proved" that the story must be a fantasy by demonstrating that it has the boat following "implausible" routes and otherwise goes against common sense. Knowledgeable as they might have been about many esoteric subjects, these historians knew nothing about sailing. To them the Mediterranean was like an indoor swimming pool, and one would, naturally, head directly to one's destination, giving no heed to currents or to the fact that it is impossible to sail directly into the wind. When it subsequently was shown that the Acts account is fully in accord with meteorological and nautical conditions and principles,[31] the response was to grudgingly accept the account in Acts as accurate, but to claim that it didn't happen to Paul; rather, since it was nautically correct, the account in Acts "must have been" lifted from another unknown, but unbiblical source![32]

As in the case above, the major result of the many unrelenting scholarly attacks on the historical reliability of the New Testament has been to frustrate the attackers because again and again scripture has stood up to their challenges. For one thing, the New Testament provides a very accurate geography, not only of Israel,[33] but of the Roman Empire. Places are where they are supposed to be. Reported travel times are consistent with the distances involved. The topography is accurately described and extends to tiny details such as the location of wells, streams, springs, gorges, cliffs, city gates, and the like.[34]

New Testament identifications and characterizations of a variety of individuals, both famous and obscure, also have frequently been confirmed. Commenting on the writings of Luke, the distinguished Frederick Fyvie Bruce (1910–1990) noted that a remarkable example of Luke's accuracy "is his sure familiarity with the proper titles of all the notable persons who are mentioned in his pages. This was by no means such an easy feat."[35] In fact, Luke used the term *politarchs* to identify the officers or magistrates in Thessalonica. If correct, this term would apply only in this city, as it is used nowhere else in ancient literature. That turns out to be the case, and Luke has been "completely vindicated by . . . inscriptions" in Thessalonica.[36] Many similar instances have been reported.

Turning to more specific identifications, an inscription discovered at Delphi in 1905 revealed that Gallio, a brother of Seneca the philosopher, was, in fact, proconsul of Achaia from July 51 to August 52 during which time Acts 18:12–17 says Paul was taken before him in Corinth.[37] Acts 19:22 identifies Erastus as one of Paul's helpers in

Corinth and Romans 16:23 identifies him further as "the city treasurer." That identification was deemed unlikely by scholars who were (mistakenly) certain that the early Christians were recruited from the lowest classes. But in 1929, archaeologists excavating a first-century street in Corinth unearthed an inscribed stone reading: "Erastus, Procurator and Aedile, laid this pavement at his own expense." Among the duties of an Aedile was to supervise the financial affairs of the city.[38] As might be expected, there have been many efforts to explain this discovery away; Justin J. Meggitt, for example, proposed that there probably were two Erastuses.[39]

A recently discovered ossuary identifies Caiaphas as the high priest who presided over the Sanhedrin when it condemned Jesus, just as the Gospels and Josephus maintained. An inscription found in Caesarea Maritima in 1961 identifies Pontius Pilate as governor of Judea precisely when the New Testament places him there. Moreover, accounts by both the Jewish historian Josephus and the Jewish philosopher Philo characterized Pilate as the callous figure depicted in scripture.[40] As a final example, Acts 18:2 tells that Paul met Aquila and his wife Priscilla in Corinth and that this couple had recently come from Rome because the emperor Claudius had ordered all Jews to leave. This is entirely consistent with Roman accounts that Jews were banished from Rome at this time because of conflicts among them over Christ, as discussed in chapter 1.

Over and above these and many other specific examples of accuracy is the more general aspect, noted so effectively by the great Harvard scholar Henry J. Cadbury (1883–1974). Referring to Acts he wrote: "In itself it often carries its own evidence of accuracy, of intelligent grasp of its theme, of fullness of information. Its stories are not thin and colorless but packed with variety and substance."[41] However, even though the New Testament has the proper feel for the places and the people of its time, and it is quite reliable as to geography, topography, and Roman and Jewish history, that does not mean, of course, that it is accurate as to the life of Jesus. But it does mean that efforts by Conzelmann and other "critical" scholars to disparage the

Gospels as nothing but ahistorical fantasies, are themselves revealed as wishful thinking.

As for the accounts of Jesus's ministry, at least Paul's letters were written and the early Gospels appeared while there still were active Christians who had heard and seen Jesus—including members of his own family. Followers of Jesus who had been in their twenties at the time of the Crucifixion would only have been in their sixties when Mark began to circulate. Nor is it likely that Gospels were written quickly just before they were circulated rather than having been drafted over a period of years and circulated in pieces. In fact, some of the early church fathers reported that Peter played a significant role in composing Mark.[42] Furthermore, the claim that the Gospel writers depended mainly on oral traditions now seems unlikely. Since some of the apostles could read and write, is it credible that they regularly heard Jesus teach and never wrote any notes? Indeed, Saul Lieberman (1898–1983) pointed out that it was the "general rabbinic practice" in those days for disciples to write down the teachings of their masters.[43] In fact, it appears that the Essenes wrote down the words of their Teacher of Righteousness on waxed tablets.[44] Why wouldn't the Christians have done so too? I agree with Claude Tresmontant (1927–1997) that to believe they did not is "simply absurd."[45] This issue is treated at length in chapter 5. Here, the obvious conclusion is that the Gospels are a quite reliable report of the Christ story *as it was believed and told* by the original eyewitnesses—members of what is now known as the Jesus Movement.

The Jesus Movement

IN THE WAKE OF the Crucifixion there were perhaps as many as several hundred Jews who had seen and heard Jesus and who believed that he was the Son of God.[46] Some of these followers organized to spread the "glad tidings," forming what has come to be known as the Jesus Movement.[47] The main group was in Jerusalem, and there probably were several subsidiary groups in Galilee.[48] Within the year, a tiny congregation also had been gathered in Damascus and possibly another in Rome.[49]

For much of the twentieth century it was generally assumed that the most remarkable thing about the Jesus Movement is that we know almost nothing about it—John Dominic Crossan called this era (from about 33 to 70 CE) the "lost years," "the empty years."[50] This claim was justified by learned exposés that Acts and other New Testament reports are unreliable fantasies, written for theological, not historical purposes.[51] Since the activities of the Jesus Movement were almost entirely ignored except by the authors of various books of the Bible, if these books are discredited the Jesus Movement has no history.

However, as the historical material in the Bible has regained credibility, it has become obvious once again that, although we know far less about the earliest days of Christianity than we would like to know (and there are some matters—such as Christian growth in the East—about which we know very little), some revealing information about the early days of the Jesus Movement has survived. These sources allow glimpses of early Christianity in Jerusalem—its leaders, its worship practices, and the unrelenting persecution directed against it.

Would that we knew a fraction as much about the mission effort devoted to the East. The initial activities of the Jesus Movement beyond Palestine probably were mainly directed eastward to Syria and Persia, which is consistent with the fact that following his conversion, Paul spent more than a decade as a missionary in that area. It is reflective of our ignorance that we know nothing about what Paul accomplished during these years or even where he actually went. Indeed, the conclusion that there were vigorous mission efforts to the East is mostly inferred from the impressive extent of Christianity in this area by the second century, for almost nothing survives about how this success was achieved, or by whom.

On the other hand, thanks to Acts, remarkably informative details have survived about how Paul went about conducting his missions in the West. Unfortunately, we know very little about the rapid spread of early Christianity across the empire in which Paul played no part, and we know almost nothing about what went on during the approximately twenty-year period between the Crucifixion and Paul's arrival in the West. For example, we probably shall never know how Christianity arrived in Rome. The celebrated Arthur Darby Nock (1902–1963) suggested that we know nothing of the formation of the earliest congregations in the West, including the one in Rome, because they were the result of "the migration of individuals,"[52] not of organized missions. All we know for certain is that the Romans still regarded Christians as Jews when they expelled them from the city in 49 for rioting over "Chrestus," and according to Suetonius these disturbances were chronic.[53] We also know that subsequent to this crisis the Christians probably ceased attempting to participate in the synagogues and withdrew into house churches. By the time that Paul wrote to the Romans (about 57 CE) there were "at least seven house churches in Rome,"[54] including one meeting in the home of Priscilla and Aquila, following their sojourn in Corinth.

Perhaps the most neglected aspect of the early days of the Jesus Movement is the important part played by Jesus's family, and on this there is far better information than might be expected.

The Holy Family

THE PRIMARY DIFFICULTY FACING all religious prophets and founders is credibility—how to get others to believe their claims. Consequently, *successful* religious innovators are not isolated loners, but are *well-respected members of primary groups* for the simple reason that it is far easier to convince people who love and trust you, than to convince strangers. Thus, contrary to Mark 6:4 that a prophet is without honor in his own country and among his own kin, the most famous religious innovators began by converting their immediate families and friends.[55] Moses began with his wife and father-in-law, followed by his brother and sister. Zoroaster's first converts were his wife and her uncle. Muhammad's first convert was his wife, then her cousin, and then his adopted son, four daughters, and assorted family retainers.

Contrary to the traditional teaching, but fully in keeping with the comments by Paul and many early church fathers, the same applies to Jesus. Matthew 13:55–56 and Mark 6:3 and 15:40–47 report that Jesus had four brothers (named James, Joses, Judas, and Simon according to the book of Mark) and an unknown number of sisters—one of them named Salome (Mark 15:40; 16:1). Paul (1 Cor. 9:5) asked: "Do we not have the right to be accompanied by a wife, as the other apostles and the brethren of the Lord and Cephas?" The clear implication here is that Jesus's brothers traveled with him, at least some of the time. This is supported by Acts 1:14 when not long before the Crucifixion the apostles gathered in Jerusalem, and "All these with one accord devoted themselves to prayer, together with . . . Mary the mother of Jesus, and with his brethren." It should be noted that here and elsewhere there is no mention of Joseph in Gospel accounts of Jesus's ministry. It is assumed that Joseph died sometime after he and Mary found Jesus in the temple at age twelve (Luke 2:41–46) and before Jesus began his ministry. Perhaps as a surrogate for Joseph, Jesus's uncle Clopas also was one of the disciples as was his wife Mary,[56] although neither was one of the twelve.[57]

Not only did his family often travel with Jesus; they were counted as equal to the apostles and remained well known and active in the early church.[58] Indeed, according to Clement of Alexandria (ca. 160–215), following the Ascension, none of the apostles claimed leadership of the church, but deferred to the Lord's brother, "James the Righteous."[59] After James was stoned by the Sanhedrin, Simeon, Jesus's cousin and the son of Clopas, succeeded to leadership in Jerusalem. Jesus's two grandnephews Zoker and James "were also leaders of the Palestinian Jewish Christian community around the end of the century."[60] In all, the early Jesus Movement was quite a family affair.

As for the famous denial of his family by Jesus as reported in Mark 3:33, the early church father Tertullian dismissed it as a misinterpretation. When told, "Your mother and your brethren are outside, asking for you," Jesus is quoted as responding, "Who are my mother and my brethren?" Then, gesturing to those who sat listening to him, Jesus added: "Here are my mother and my brethren! Whoever does the will of God is my brother, and sister, and mother" (Mark 3:32–35). Tertullian explained that Jesus used this device to stress the kinship of faith, not to deny family feelings.[61] In addition, Origen (ca. 185–251) dismissed as figurative the claim that "a prophet is not without honor, except in his own country, and among his own kin." If taken literally and generally, Origen noted, "it is not historically true," citing the many prophets of the Old Testament who were honored in their local communities. "But," he continued, "figuratively interpreted, it is absolutely true for we must think of Judea as their country, and . . . Israel as their kindred."[62] He then pointed out how different the history of Israel would have been had their "country" truly honored the prophets.

Although Jesus's family was prominent in the early church, the memory of them soon went into eclipse because of the developing tradition that not only was Mary a virgin when she bore Jesus, but that she remained one for life. As this doctrine of the perpetual virginity of Mary emerged in the second century,[63] the brothers and sisters of Jesus were at first transformed into cousins and eventually ignored altogether. But blood relatives or not, the Christian "holy family" played a significant role in the life of the early church, first in Jerusalem and then probably mainly in the East.

The Persecuted Church in Jerusalem

THE FIRST GENERATION OF Jesus's followers identified themselves as "Nazarenes,"[64] but everyone regarded the congregation in Jerusalem as the "mother church."[65] This was appropriate given that, as the location of the Temple, Jerusalem remained the authoritative center of Judaism, and the Nazarenes all still regarded themselves as devout Jews and continued to observe the Law. The leaders attended daily prayers in the Temple and afterward held evangelistic sessions in the outer court. This was a chronic source of conflict with other Jews, a clash that Paul and other missionaries also often aroused by continuing to teach the Christian message in the synagogues of the Diaspora. For doing this, Paul claimed to have been severely beaten eight times and stoned once (2 Cor. 11:24–25).

From the perspective of rank-and-file members, the life of the Jesus Movement was centered on gatherings in private homes, with "a focus on a common meal."[66] This probably had aspects of the "last supper" and, of course, allowed everyone to participate in the sacred, communal life. A vital part of the group's mission was to preserve and transmit the teachings and activities of Jesus, thus it seems "likely that the first written collections of Gospel traditions were produced in Jerusalem."[67] This also helps explain why the Gospels sometimes reflect both fear and antagonism toward Jews; the first writers were people directly affected by the embattled situation of the Jesus Movement in Palestine.[68]

An immense amount has been written about the Roman persecutions, but it is difficult to find more than a few lines here and there about the Jewish persecutions of the early church, whether in Palestine or in the Diaspora. Of the few studies written on this matter, some dismiss the claims that Jews persecuted Christians as fantasies and falsehoods.[69] According to James Everett Seaver, "the universal, tenacious, and malicious Jewish hatred of Christianity referred to by the church fathers and countless others has no existence in historical fact."[70] Others indict the *claims* about Jewish persecutions of the early Christians as further proof of Christian anti-Semitism.[71] Still others quibble that these conflicts were "intra-Jewish" and therefore cannot be identified as Jewish mistreatment of Christians.[72] But most writers simply ignore the entire matter. That may be *politique*, but it is irresponsible.

These very early persecutions not only happened; they probably were a far more dangerous threat to the survival of the faith than were those by the Romans, given how very few Christians there were when these events occurred. Even by the end of the first century there probably still were only about seven thousand Christians on earth, (see chapter 9) and the total number in Jerusalem in the 40s and 50s could not have exceeded several hundred. Given their lack of numbers and that they proclaimed that a man crucified for blasphemy was the promised Messiah, their persecution was inevitable.[73] And it began almost at once.

Caiaphas, who had presided over the trial of Jesus, remained high priest until 37 CE, and was as hostile to the Jesus Movement as he had been to its founder. As a result, in 34 or 35 CE, Stephen, one of the prominent members of the movement, was convicted by the Sanhedrin of blasphemy against Moses and God and stoned to death. According to Acts 8:1 Paul (Saul) was present and favored putting Stephen to death. At that time Paul was a Pharisee and an extremist in his opposition to Christianity. Consequently, "on that day [when Stephen was stoned] a great persecution arose against the church in Jerusalem; and they were all scattered throughout the region of Judea and Samaria. . . . Saul laid waste the church, and entering house after house, he dragged off men and women and committed them to prison" (Acts 8:1–3). Long after his conversion, Paul confessed in his letter to the Galatians: "For you have heard of my former life in Judaism, how I persecuted the church of God violently and tried to destroy it" (1:13). And in Acts 22:4–5 Paul is quoted as saying "I persecuted [Christians] to the death, binding and delivering to prison both men and women, as the high priest and the whole council of elders bear me witness."

We don't know more about the extent of this persecution or how long it took for the Jesus Movement to recover. What we do know is that the conversion of Paul did nothing to improve the circumstances of Christians in Jerusalem. Although the surviving accounts focus on especially significant executions, there are scattered hints that the antagonism against Jewish Christians was unrelenting and that only Roman pressures against disorder prevented them from being wiped out.[74] Keep in mind that this was an era of intense conflict and violence all across the spectrum of Jewish pluralism (see chapter 2). The

Sicarii lurked where crowds gathered and they even murdered high priests whom they deemed insufficiently zealous. It is silly to suppose that Christians would have been exempt.

The next to be martyred was James, son of Zebedee, and one of Jesus's first disciples. His death was ordered in 44 CE by King Herod Agrippa, perhaps in response to requests by the high priest, and this execution also seems to have been part of a more general persecution—"the king laid violent hands upon some who belonged to the church" (Acts 12:1). Peter also was arrested at this time. He subsequently escaped and fled (possibly to Antioch), and it was not until after the king's death that Peter returned to Jerusalem.

In about the year 56, Paul made his last visit to Jerusalem. His reputation as a missionary to the Gentiles who did not require converts to observe the Law was well known and resented, not only by most Jews, but seemingly by most Jewish Christians in Jerusalem. Thus it was that

> the Jews from Asia, who had seen him in the temple, stirred up all the crowd and laid hands on him, crying out "Men of Israel, help! This is the man who is teaching men everywhere against the people and the law and this place; moreover, he also brought Greeks into the temple and he has defiled this holy place." . . . Then all the city was aroused, and the people ran together; they seized Paul and dragged him out of the temple. . . . And as they were trying to kill him, word came to the tribune of the cohort that all Jerusalem was in confusion. He at once took soldiers and centurions, and ran down to them; and when they saw the tribune and the soldiers, they stopped beating Paul (Acts 21:27–28, 30–32).

The tribune had Paul bound with chains and took him back to the barracks. Eventually, of course, Paul was sent to Rome for trial—a right of all Roman citizens, Paul being one—and eventually he was executed there, probably by order of Nero.

Finally, in 62 CE the high priest Ananus had James, brother of

Jesus and head of the church (he sometimes is identified as the first pope), called before the Sanhedrin during a time when the Roman procurator had died and his replacement had not yet arrived. With no Roman presence to circumvent, Ananus had James convicted and pushed from a tower—he survived the fall to then be stoned and beaten to death. Although some prominent Pharisees vehemently protested James's death, as Josephus[75] noted, not only James, but also "certain others" were convicted on this occasion and then stoned. Again, we don't know the extent of the persecution, although Eusebius claimed that "as for the other apostles, countless plots were laid against their lives and they were banished from the land of Judea."[76] Nor do we know the fate of the Jesus Movement during the reign of terror when zealots purged Jerusalem and other cities during the late 60s at the start of the Great Revolt, but according to Eusebius,[77] at this time most members of the Jesus Movement probably relocated east of the Jordan River in Pella of the Decapolis.[78]

We do know that the revolt was long and bloody and that in 70 CE the Roman commander Titus destroyed Jerusalem down to its foundations, carted the Temple treasures back to Rome, and prohibited anyone but Roman soldiers from the ruins of the city. Whatever the impact of these events on the Jesus Movement, there still were settlements of Christians in Palestine to be persecuted by Bar Kokhba during the Second Revolt (132–135).[79]

Mission to the World

FOLLOWING HIS CONVERSION IN about the year 35, Paul appears to have devoted many years to missionary efforts in the East, with what results we do not know. That we don't is the telling detail. From earliest days, the Jesus Movement appears to have devoted its primary efforts to the East, as reflected in the rapid growth and spread of eastern Christianity, once stretching from Syria to China. But even though it endured for centuries, when the Asian church perished, most of the knowledge of this remarkable chapter in Christian history perished too. Recently, there have been some fine efforts to reclaim this lost era.[80] However, these accounts begin in the late second and third centuries because not even many legends survive about earlier times.

We know far more about Paul's missions to the West than those of anyone else because he happened to have been accompanied on two of his mission journeys by a competent historian who later spent two years with him in Rome, when Paul was under house arrest. Luke was a Gentile convert and in addition to writing Acts he also wrote the Gospel named for him. In fact, most Bible scholars believe that Luke and Acts are a single continued work—both dedicated to Theophilus (Luke 1:3; Acts 1:1), who probably was a Roman official.[81] Since he referred to his Gospel at the start of Acts, we know that Luke wrote it first—perhaps in about 60 or 61. Acts must have been written soon after since it does not include Paul's re-arrest and execution, which happened in about 66.

Although Paul is famous for his missionary journeys, he was, in fact, quite sedentary. His active mission efforts in the West began in about 47 CE and ended with his arrest in Jerusalem in 56 (after that he was under house arrest in Caesarea and Rome). Of this nine-year period, more than two years were spent in Ephesus, three years in Corinth, and at least a year in Antioch. That leaves about three years for his three long mission journeys.

Paul's journeys are well known, even if there is some confusion as to what happened where and when. The same applies to the "Council in Jerusalem" where Paul was given permission to convert Christians without requiring them to observe the Law or be circumcised. This was not unanimously accepted by the Jewish Christian community in Jerusalem, which seems to have been split between Hellenized Jews who favored it (Paul himself was, of course, a Hellenized Jew from Tarsus), and a more traditional faction—even though the very traditional James sided with Paul. Although this decision to liberate Christian members from the need to adopt Jewish ethnicity stirred up some bitter controversies, it was crucial to the eventual success of Christianity. All these things are so well-known as not to need retelling here, but what is little known is how Paul went about missionizing.

In the beginning Paul and Barnabas may have just walked into a town with several apprentices in tow and started preaching in the synagogue. If so, Paul soon learned better and refused to go anywhere without careful prior arrangements and some commitments of support. Typically, he began a visit to a new community by holding "privately organized meetings under the patronage of eminent persons . . . who provided him with . . . an audience composed of their dependents."[82] Paul did not travel alone, or even with a few supporters. Instead, he often was accompanied by a retinue of as many as forty followers, sufficient to constitute an initial "congregation,"[83] which made it possible to hold credible worship services and to welcome and form bonds with newcomers.

Among Paul's entourage there undoubtedly were scribes, as was typical in this day when even books had to be written by hand and copied the same way, one at a time. Most of the prolific early church fathers had remarkably large staffs to write down and copy their words.[84] We even know the name of one of Paul's scribes since he revealed himself at the end of Romans (16:22), where, after Paul's long list of individual greetings, he added "I Tertius, the writer of this letter, greet you in the Lord." Upon arrival, Paul would "gather any Christians already living in the city,"[85] attaching them to his "imported" congregation, and then use their social networks as the basis for further recruitment (see below). Finally, once the congregation was going and had adequately trained local leaders, Paul moved on, but maintained close contact through messengers and letters, and sometimes by making return visits. As Helmut Koester summed up: "Paul's missionary work, therefore, should not be thought of as the humble efforts of a lonely missionary. Rather, it was a well-planned, large-scale organization."[86]

In fact, it is not clear that Paul usually played any effective direct role in establishing new Christian congregations. As mentioned, Christians already were meeting in many of the cities Paul visited, and mission visits such as Paul's have little impact on the conversion of individuals to a new religious movement, because that's not how conversions occur.

On Conversion

FOR GENERATIONS IT WAS assumed that religious conversions were the result of doctrinal appeal—that people embraced a new faith because they found its teachings particularly appealing, especially if these teachings seemed to solve serious problems or dissatisfactions that afflicted them. Surprisingly, when sociologists[87] took the trouble to actually go out and watch conversions take place, they discovered that doctrines are of very secondary importance in the initial decision to convert. One must, of course, leave room for those rare conversions resulting from mystical experiences such as Paul's on the road to Damascus. But such instances aside, conversion is primarily about bringing one's religious behavior into alignment with that of one's friends and relatives, not about encountering attractive doctrines. Put more formally: *people tend to convert to a religious group when their social ties to members outweigh their ties to outsiders who might oppose the conversion, and this often occurs before a convert knows much about what the group believes.*

Of course, one can easily imagine doctrines so bizarre as to keep most people from joining. It also is true that successful faiths sustain doctrines that do have wide appeal. In that sense doctrines can facilitate or hinder conversion, but in the normal course of events, *conversion primarily is an act of conformity.* But then, so is nonconversion. In the end it is a matter of the relative strength of social ties pulling the individual toward or away from a group. This principle has, by now, been examined by dozens of close-up studies of conversion, all of which confirm that social networks are the basic mechanism through which conversion takes place.[88] To convert someone, you must be or become their close and trusted friend. Consequently, when someone converts to a new religion, then they usually seek to convert their friends and relatives, and consequently conversion tends to proceed through social networks.

Clearly, that's why we don't know the origins of the various Christian congregations as they began to appear even in the West. Mostly, the church spread as ordinary people accepted it and then shared it with their families and friends, and the faith was carried from one community to another in this same way—probably most often by regular travelers such as merchants. Such a process leaves few traces—it is seldom and only by chance that we know of people such as Priscilla and Aquila (Acts 18:2). Nor did the early church leave many physical traces. Archaeologists can dig in the ruins of synagogues from the first century, but only later were there any church buildings; in those days all Christian congregations were small and, as is evident in Paul's letters, most met in private homes.[89]

To say that doctrines play a quite secondary role in conversion is not to suggest that doctrines remain secondary. Once immersed in a religious group, people are instructed as to the significant implications of the doctrines, and most converts soon become very strongly attached to the doctrines—as are their friends.

Given how conversion actually occurs, it follows that Paul's visits were more like evangelistic campaigns, such as a Billy Graham crusade, than they were like a visit to a community by a missionary. Graham did not found churches, nor did he often bring the irreligious into faith. What he did was to greatly energize the participating local churches by intensifying the commitment of their members, which often led them to recruit new members. So it was with Paul's visits. When he spoke to the unconvinced as in Athens and Lystra, the results were meager, at best. But when he spoke mostly to the converted or to converts-in-process, as he usually did, he aroused them to far greater depths of commitment and comprehension.

To recognize these aspects of Paul's missions does not in any way reduce his stature. He not only strengthened many congregations; it seems likely that many who began in his entourage later became effective missionaries. But above all, Paul's contributions to Christian theology are what made him a giant.

Conclusion

AFTER ALL IS SAID and done, we still know very little about the Jesus Movement during the first century. We know that Jesus's family played a leading role in the church in Jerusalem—Paul clearly accepted the authority of James, the brother of Jesus, who headed this church until he was murdered in 62. Either in response to or in anticipation of the First Jewish Revolt, the Christian leadership left Jerusalem sometime in the late 60s and probably resettled in Pella. At this point their history ends—although it seems reasonable to assume that they played an active role in the rapid and remarkable Christianization of the East. As for the spread of Christianity in the West, it often is assumed we have substantial information on how this occurred, based on Acts and Paul's letters. But a closer look reveals that here too the story is quite lacking in details. That may well be because the spread of religious movements is not accomplished by dramatic events and persuasive preachers, but by ordinary followers who convert their equally anonymous friends, relatives, and neighbors.

CHAPTER FOUR

Missions to the Jews and the Gentiles

BECAUSE PAUL WON PERMISSION TO convert Gentiles without them becoming Jews, and because a substantial Jewish community remains, it long has been assumed that the mission to the Jews failed. But that is inconsistent with a great deal of evidence, including that Paul's mission efforts seem to have been devoted primarily to the Jews of the Diaspora. Of course, whatever the success of early efforts to convert Jews, the ultimate fate of Christianity depended upon a successful mission to the Gentiles. Oddly enough, important aspects of these efforts have been given little attention. How did pagan Gentiles perceive and respond to this very Jewish new religion? And why did they find it familiar and attractive? These are the matters to be pursued here.

The Diasporan Jews

IN 597 BCE, ISRAEL fell to the Babylonian king Nebuchadnezzar. To pacify his conquest, Nebuchadnezzar took somewhere between eight and ten thousand high officials, military commanders, priests, and other members of the Jewish upper classes, along with their families, back to Babylon as hostages. However, rather than imposing servile conditions upon them, Nebuchadnezzar made every effort to "assimilate the [exiles], and to cause them to strike roots in their new home-land."[1] Hence, Israelites soon were "serving in the royal court and attaining high rank."[2] Indeed, many exiles soon assimilated. They gave their children Babylonian names[3] and did not teach them to speak Hebrew.[4]

Seventy years after the Jews had been taken to Babylon, Cyrus the Great, founder of the Persian Empire, conquered Babylon and gave all exiles permission to return home. Most of the descendents of the exiles from Israel did not go! Some who stayed were still pious Jews, but had become so accustomed to life in Babylon that they had no desire to return to Israel.[5] But many who stayed were very lukewarm in their Jewishness or were no longer Jews at all.[6]

At the beginning of the Christian era, many Jews of the Diaspora resembled those Babylonian exiles who did not return. They had lived away from Israel far longer than had the exiles, and intermarriage with Gentiles was widespread.[7] Moreover, they read, wrote, spoke, thought, and worshipped in Greek. Of inscriptions found in the Jewish catacombs in Rome, fewer than 2 percent were in Hebrew or Aramaic, while 74 percent were in Greek and the remainder in Latin.[8] Most of the Diasporan Jews had Greek or Roman names; many of them "did not even hesitate to [adopt] names derived from those of Greek deities, such as Apollonius, Heracleides and Dionysus" or those of Egyptian gods—Horus was especially popular among the Diasporan Jews.[9] As early as the third century BCE the religious services held in Diasporan synagogues were conducted in Greek and so few Diasporan Jews could read Hebrew that it was necessary to translate the Torah into Greek—the Septuagint. In the process, not only Greek words, but Hellenic ideas crept into the sacred text. For example, Exodus 22:28 was rendered "You shall not revile *the gods*." Calvin Roetzel interprets this as a gesture of accommodation toward pagans.[10] This is quite consistent with the Jewish shrine in Elephantine in Egypt where not only was Yahweh worshipped, but so were two goddesses who were said to be Yahweh's consorts—Anath the goddess of war and Eshem, the sun.[11]

In addition to pagan influences, Greek philosophy also deeply affected the religious perspectives of Diasporan Jews. The most revered and influential Jewish leader and writer of the era, Philo of Alexandria (ca. 20 BCE–50 CE), described God in ways that Plato would have found familiar, but which would have been denounced in Jerusalem: "the perfectly pure unsullied Mind of the universe, transcending virtue, transcending knowledge, transcending good itself and the beautiful itself."[12] Philo was also very concerned to justify the Law on the basis of rational explanations. It was not sufficient for him that God had forbidden Jews to eat the flesh of birds of prey or of carnivores. The reason God had done so was to emphasize the virtue of peace. What portions of scripture Philo could not rationalize, he recast as allegories. Thus did Philo interpret the Law "exclusively through the filter of Greek philosophy." As a result, the clear religious and historical meaning of much of the Torah was "lost among the spiritual and moral sentiments by which Philo sought to demonstrate the harmony and rationality of the universe."[13] Philo's was not a lonely voice; he was the most celebrated leader of the Jewish Diaspora at this time. Thus did the image of God sustained by the influential Jews of the Diaspora shift from that of the authoritative Yahweh to a rather remote, abstract, and undemanding Absolute Being.

Socially, most of the Diasporan Jews found it degrading to live among Greeks and embrace Greek culture and yet to remain "enclosed in a spiritual ghetto and be reckoned among the 'barbarians.'"[14] Consequently, many failed to fully observe the Law, especially the prohibition against eating with Gentiles. It should be noted that, when faced with similar circumstances, the Jewish communities in China were slowly absorbed by Confucianism. Similarly, very high rates of conversion to Christianity broke out among European Jews when the many restrictions on them were removed during the late nineteenth and early twentieth centuries.[15] As for the Diasporan Jews, although some embraced paganism, for most of them paganism offered no real alternative—even most of the Greek philosophers had dismissed it. Thus it seems likely that many Jews in the Diaspora longed for "a compromise, a synthesis, which would permit a Jew to remain a Jew" and still be able to claim full entry into "the elect society of the Greeks."[16] Monotheism with deep Jewish roots, but without the Law, should have had wide appeal.

Cultural Continuity

ALTHOUGH SOCIAL NETWORKS PLAY the critical role in conversion, doctrine matters too, just not in the way that usually has been supposed. It is not so much a matter of what the doctrine promises to do for people as it is that bodies of doctrine, and the religious culture that surrounds them, represent *investments* of time, effort, and emotions. That is, any religion requires an adherent to master a lot of culture: to know the words and actions required by various rituals or worship activities, to be familiar with certain doctrines, stories, music, symbols, and history. Over time, people become increasingly attached to their religious culture ("It just wouldn't be Christmas for me without an angel at the top of the tree"). Expressed as a social scientific concept, one's *religious capital* consists of the degree of mastery of and attachment to a particular religious culture.[17]

It follows that, other things being equal, *people will attempt to conserve their religious capital.* This proposition has many implications. For one thing, people will tend not to change religions, and *the greater their religious capital, the less likely they are to change.* This is supported by a large research literature showing that converts overwhelmingly are recruited from the ranks of those having a very weak commitment to any other religion. In the United States, the group most likely to convert to a new religious movement consists of people raised in an irreligious or nonreligious home.[18] In addition, people are more likely to change faiths to the extent that they are presented with an option that allows them to conserve much of their religious capital. This explains why, in a Christian culture, people are more apt to convert to Mormonism than to Hinduism. To become a Mormon, a person of

Christian background need discard none of his or her religious capital (including Christmas tree decorations), but only add to it. In contrast, to become Hindus, Christians must discard all of their religious capital and start over.

Applied to new religious groups, this becomes the principle of *cultural continuity*. Other things being equal, a new religion is more likely to grow to the degree that it sustains continuity with the religious culture of those being missionized.

For all that many Diasporan Jews may have dabbled in paganism, rarely did they go all the way and convert. Those who did would have needed to undergo a great deal of religious re-education and to discard their Jewish religious capital. In fact, it is likely that those Jews who did become pagans had only modest amounts of Jewish religious capital at risk, probably having been raised by parents whose Judaism was nominal at best.

In contrast with paganism, Christianity offered Diasporan Jews a chance to preserve virtually all of their religious capital, needing only to add to it, since Christianity retained the entire Old Testament heritage. Although it made observance of many portions of the Jewish Law unnecessary, Christianity did not impose a new set of Laws to be mastered. In addition, services in Christian congregations were very closely modeled on those of the synagogue and, in early days, Christian services also were conducted in Greek, so a Hellenized Jew would have felt right at home. Finally, Christianity carefully stressed how its central message of salvation was the fulfillment of the messianic promises of orthodox Judaism.

Paul and the Diaspora

IT WASN'T, IN THE first instance, cultural continuity that led Christian mission efforts to the Hellenized Jews of the Diaspora. It was social networks. For missionaries headed out from Jerusalem, the pressing first question was where should they go? Who would receive them? The answer seemed obvious. All across the Greco-Roman world were relatively well-to-do communities of people to whom the missionaries had ties: those who were relatives (even if very distant), or friends of friends. Indeed, at least until the destruction of the temple in 70 CE the Diasporan communities were accustomed to visits by religious teachers from Jerusalem. So that's where the earliest Christian missionaries went, and Paul followed their example.

Although much has been made of Paul's breakthrough in gaining permission for Gentiles to become Christians without also becoming Jews, far too little has been made of the impact of his subsequent assertion that Jewish-Christians need no longer observe the Law (Gal. 3:15–29).[19] This had no consequences for Gentiles, but it would have had immense appeal to Hellenized Jews who wished to be free of the Law's social limitations. And for all the emphasis on Paul's mission being aimed at Gentiles, in fact nearly all of his efforts took place within the Diasporan Jewish communities. Except for Luke, of course, most of his entourage was Jewish. He was welcomed by Jews. He preached in Jewish homes and in the synagogues. And most of those greeted in his letters seem to be Jews. In addition, if Paul really was devoting his efforts to the pagans, why did he continue to receive so many severe beatings by local Jews?[20] Surely he would have been ignored by Diasporan Jewish leaders had he kept to pagan circles.

This raises the possibility that, despite the emphasis on missionizing to the Gentiles, Paul's efforts actually more often brought in Jewish converts. True enough, Paul's rejection of the Law created an even more profound gap between Christianity and orthodox Judaism. But, as a practical matter, devoutly orthodox Jews were not going to convert to Christianity anyway, which is why Palestine was not a rewarding mission area. Rather, as Nock explained, it was Hellenized Jews "who had lost their traditional piety . . . [who] were receptive of new convictions."[21]

In addition, W. H. C. Frend (1916–2005) pointed out that what Paul meant by a ministry to the Gentiles may have been limited to appeals to the "God-fearers," those Gentiles who already frequented the synagogues and even helped to build and support them, but who never became full converts to Judaism because they were unwilling to fully embrace the Law. Frend wrote: "When in Corinth Paul declared that henceforth he would go to the Gentiles, his progress was as far as the house of Titus Justice, 'a worshipper of God' who lived next door to the synagogue (Acts 18:7). Seen as a mission to the 'God-fearers,' Paul's activity and his successes become intelligible."[22] This is, of course, a far cry from attempting a ministry to real pagans, to people having no prior connection to Judaism. Indeed, when Paul made such an approach, as in Athens, he accomplished nothing. But being able to admit the God-fearers as full-fledged Christians gave Paul an immense recruiting advantage and should have rapidly swelled the ranks of non-Jewish Christians.

When Did Jewish Conversion Stop?

NEARLY EVERYONE BELIEVES THE mission to the Jews soon failed. Some suppose that an impervious barrier to Jewish conversion was erected during the Jewish Revolt of 66–74, when many Diasporan Jews supported the rebels and Christians did not. Others accept that substantial Jewish conversion continued until the Bar-Kokhba revolt in 132–135, which further alienated the church and the synagogue. But from then on, it is assumed that Jewish conversion was at an end. Perhaps so, but this conclusion seems contrary to a considerable variety of evidence and inference.

The first objection to the claim that the mission to the Hellenized Jews ended in failure early on is that the fundamental circumstances that led to its early success did not change—their weak attachment to Jewish culture and the Law persisted.

Of even greater significance is the abundant evidence of continuing Jewish influence within Christianity. Consider that, with the exception of Luke and Acts, the New Testament was written by Jews. Moreover, many of the early heretical movements such as Marcionism, as well as the bulk of writings identified as Gnostic, were remarkably anti-Jewish. These attacks, as well as the ease with which they were rejected as heretical, support an inference of continuing strong Jewish influence within the church. Turning to a later period, what are we to make of all the concern over Judaizing expressed by various Christian leaders as late as the fifth century? Historians agree that in this era large numbers of Christians showed such an affinity for Jewish culture that it could be characterized as "a widespread infatuation with Judaism."[23] It seems unlikely that this was but a lingering attraction, not if it had really been several centuries after Jewish conversion had ceased. On the other hand, this is precisely what one would expect to find in Christian communities containing many members of relatively recent Jewish origins, who retained ties of family and association with non-Christian Jews, and who therefore still retained a distinctly Jewish aspect to their Christianity. Moreover, this is consistent with Constantine's order early in the fourth century "that Jews be restrained from attacking members of their communities who converted to Christianity,"[24] as well as repeated Roman prohibitions against mixed marriages between Christians and Jews, one such statute being promulgated as late as 388 CE.[25] Governments seldom bother prohibiting things that are not taking place.

Consequently, what may have been at issue was not the Judaizing of Christianity, but that in many places a substantial Jewish Christianity persisted. And if that were the case, there is no reason to suppose that Jewish Christians had lost the ability to attract new converts from their network of Hellenized families and friends. Hence, rather than seeing the evidence as indicative of a sudden outbreak of Judaizing, it seems more plausible to interpret it as proof that Jewish conversion had never stopped. When John Chrysostom (349–407 CE) railed against Christians frequenting the synagogue, he addressed his remarks to an audience who knew whether he spoke the truth, so we can assume this was actually going on. The most reasonable interpretation of Chrysostom's polemic is that it aimed to separate a church and synagogue that were still greatly intertwined—and this at the start of the fifth century!

But probably the most fundamental assumption concerning the "failure" of the mission to the Jews is that after Christianity had overwhelmed Rome, there remained a substantial Diasporan Jewish population actively sustaining synagogues, and hence the Jews *must have* rejected the Christian mission efforts. But that overlooks that there were millions of Diasporan Jews, far more than enough to have provided large numbers of Christians while still sustaining synagogues. If the projections in chapter 9 are close to correct, there were only about a million Christians by the year 250, which means that only about one out of every five or even out of nine Diasporan Jews need have converted to fill that total without any Gentile conversions at all. And, of course, there were many Gentile converts.

Population data lend further support to the assumption of a very large number of Jewish converts. As noted, the Diasporan Jews constituted at least 10 percent of the total population of the empire, and perhaps as much as 15 percent. Medieval historians estimate that Jews made up only 1 percent of the population of Latin Europe in about the tenth century.[26] Granted that some of that percentage decline was caused by the Islamic conquest of areas having substantial Jewish populations. Nevertheless, the figures also suggest a considerable decline in the European Diasporan population during that millennium, and that is consistent with there having been a substantial rate of conversion. Indeed, a recent study suggests that there continued to be a high rate of Jewish conversions until about the seventh century.[27] Nor was the survival of strong synagogues inconsistent with that supposition. Indeed, by peeling away all of the tepid, Hellenized Jews, conversion to Christianity would have produced an increasingly orthodox, highly committed Jewish community, a community ideally constituted to sustain stout resistance to Christianization.

Finally, a wealth of archaeological findings in Italy (especially in Rome and Venosa) show that "Jewish and Christian burials reflect an interdependent and closely related community of Jews and Christians in which clear marks of demarcation were blurred until the third and fourth centuries C.E."[28] Similarly, excavations in Capernaum on the shores of the Sea of Galilee reveal "a Jewish synagogue and a Jewish-Christian house church on opposite sides of the street. . . . Following the strata and the structures, both communities apparently lived in harmony until the seventh century."[29]

It also is worth noting that Origen mentioned having taken part in a theological debate with Jews before "umpires" sometime during the first half of the third century.[30] This seems inconsistent with the assumption that church and synagogue had long been separated. Equally inconsistent is evidence that as late as the fourth century Christian theologians consulted "rabbis about the interpretation of difficult Scriptural verses."[31]

For all these reasons, it seems likely that the mission to the Jews was far more long-lasting and successful than has been assumed.

Gentile Yearnings

THE DIASPORAN COMMUNITIES WERE founded by Jews who migrated from Palestine. But neither continuing migration nor fertility could have produced the millions of Jews living in these urban settlements by the start of the first century CE. Rather, as Adolf von Harnack recognized, "it is utterly impossible to explain the large total of Jews in the Diaspora by the mere fact of the fertility of Jewish families. We must assume . . . that a very large number of pagans . . . trooped over to Yahweh."[32] Thus, Josephus was probably accurate when he claimed that "all the time they [the Jews] were attracting to their worship a great number of Greeks, making them virtually members of their own community."[33] By including the word *virtually*, Josephus acknowledged that many pagans embraced Jewish monotheism, but remained marginal to Jewish life because they were unwilling to fully embrace Jewish ethnicity—not only adult circumcision, but some other aspects of the Law as well.[34] As already has been noted, these "virtual" Jews were known as "God-fearers."

But it wasn't merely by converting to Judaism or by becoming

a God-fearer that Greco-Romans displayed a yearning for monotheism. That also was the basis for the remarkable success of the
Oriental religions that preceded Christianity in sweeping over the
Roman Empire. Indeed, in an earlier study I found statistical evidence that the Oriental faiths were effective forerunners of Christianity. For example, of seventeen major Greco-Roman cities having at
least one temple devoted to Isis, eleven had a Christian congregation
by the year 100 CE. Of the fourteen similar cities lacking a temple to
Isis, only two had a congregation by the year 100, and seven still had
no congregation in the year 180.[35] In similar fashion, of the ten cities
with a temple devoted to Cybele, eight had a Christian congregation by 100 CE, while only five of the twenty-one cities lacking such a
temple had a congregation that early.[36] Recall from chapter 1 that although followers of Isis, Cybele, and other such faiths acknowledged
the existence of many gods, they presented theirs as a Supreme God
and generated an exclusive commitment. And the key to it all was a
conception of God as loving, trustworthy, and all-powerful.

It is true that doctrine does not play the primary role in attracting
converts, but we must not forget that doctrine determines whether
or not the term *conversion* even applies to a shift in religious orienta-
tion. Where polytheism prevails, people add gods or easily switch
their patronage among them, whereas conversion means to make an
exclusive commitment to a particular divinity. That is, conversion implies monotheism (or something very close to it) and therefore rests
on doctrine. Indeed, the ability of monotheism to generate strong,
competitive organizations of people prepared to act on behalf of
their faith rests on doctrine—on the far greater value and credibility of exchanges with a God of maximum scope, power, virtue, and
dependability, as opposed to small gods whose intentions often are
not benign. It was this comparison that fueled the early success of the
Oriental faiths and that, by the same token, caused a supreme goddess
such as Isis to vacate her position to a One True God. Monotheism
prevails because it offers a God worth dying for—indeed, a God who
promises everlasting life. And that's why Christianity triumphed

among the pagans and why, even in the midst of a profoundly Christian world, Judaism has endured.[37] Indeed, had Judaism not been so tightly linked to Jewish ethnicity, it might have swept over the pagan world long before the birth of Jesus.

Pagan Cultural Continuity

A SERIOUS OBJECTION OFTEN raised against the entire Christ story is that it seems so fundamentally pagan. What purpose was served by the Crucifixion? Surely a God of miracles could simply have offered universal clemency to those who believed and thereby could have dispensed with any need for a "blood sacrifice." Although such a sacrifice may have seemed plausible to pagans, it rings quite false in our more enlightened times.

But that's the whole point. The message the Crucifixion sent to Greco-Roman pagans was: "Christ died for your sins!" Forget offerings of a hundred or even a thousand cattle! The Christian "God so loved the world that he gave his only Son, that whoever believes in him should not perish but have eternal life" (John 3:16). That message spoke powerfully and eloquently to a culture that took sacrifice, especially blood sacrifice, as fundamental to pleasing the gods—some of the Oriental faiths used blood from sacrificial animals to "wash away" an initiate's sins.

The same interpretation applies to the other aspects of the Christ story that so often have been condemned as derived from paganism. Mary's conception seems very like that of many women who were said to have been impregnated by pagan gods. Zeus was believed to have fathered "more than a hundred children by human mothers, most often, though not always, by virgins."[38] These half-gods, as Hesiod (700 BCE?) called them, include both Perseus and Dionysus as well as Helen of Troy. In similar fashion, dramatic signs and portents were to be expected at any celebrity birth, and always at the arrival of a future divinity. It was believed that many prodigies and portents accompanied the births of both Alexander the Great and Caesar Augustus. For some born of women to have ascended into godhood after gory deaths was a common belief—Fraser recounted many such "myths" in *The Golden Bough*.

But to claim that these similarities with pagan mythology discredit Christianity is to fail to see how these features played to the pagan world! There they were taken as compelling proof of Christ's divinity—the Christ story fulfilled every element of the classical hero, of how a human rose to become a god.[39] The early church fathers fully understood this. Having told the Christ story to a Roman magistrate, Tertullian (ca. 160–?) suggested that he "accept this story—it is similar to your own."[40] And as the early church fathers realized, these similarities can be interpreted as examples of *divine accommodation*.

The doctrine of divine accommodation holds that God's communications with humans are always limited to their current capacity to comprehend. As St. Gregory of Nyssa wrote in the fourth century, God is so "far above our nature and inaccessible to all approach" that he, in effect, speaks to us in baby talk, thereby giving "to our human nature what is it capable of receiving."[41] Hence, if the Christ story seems steeped in pagan conventions, this can be interpreted as having been the most effective way for God to communicate within the limits of Greco-Roman comprehension. These were "proofs" of Christ's divinity that pagans could most easily recognize. The perceptive Cyril Bailey (1871–1957) expressed this very well: At the time Christianity arose "men were looking in certain directions and couched their religious aspirations and beliefs in certain terms. Christianity spoke the language which they understood and set its theology and its ritual in the forms which to its own generation seemed natural. . . . [T]he Gospel [could not] have won its way if it had not found an echo in the religious searchings and even the religious beliefs of the time."[42]

Moreover, the "pagan elements" of the Christ story maximized cultural continuity between Greco-Roman paganism and Christianity. Pagan converts could retain many of their familiar conceptions about the gods and miracles, while embracing the far more intense levels of commitment, more comprehensive morality, and the far more compelling message of salvation. But unlike converts to Judaism, those who became Christians did not need to entirely abandon the more comprehensible, more familiar, more "human" aspects of the gods and embrace the remote, far less comprehensible, and forbidding Yahweh. Instead, Christians could have it *both* ways! Indeed, Jews and Muslims often object that Christianity is not monotheistic because it acknowledges Jesus as a divinity in his own right. Be that as it may, Christ gives a comfortable, reassuring, and more comprehensible aspect to Christianity than either Judaism or Islam can provide. Christ is regarded as an understanding, forgiving *person* who not only died that all may be saved, but who continues in the role of intercessor. Moreover, while Yahweh, Jehovah, and Allah are invisible and indescribable, Christ is plausibly *depictable*—consider the extraordinary impact of Christian art.[43] It is because Jesus so fully humanizes divinity that there has been little tendency for Christians to relapse into polytheism. But that, of course, forced the irrevocable break with Judaism.

Conclusion

THE INITIAL SUCCESS OF Christianity seems to have been based primarily on conversions among the Diasporan Jews. Our first knowledge of Christians in Rome comes from disorders reported within the Jewish community over "Chrestus." Paul was sent to Damascus to punish Jews for accepting Christ. The many other Christian congregations that preceded Paul's missions were most certainly Jewish since no exception had yet been made for the conversion of pagans without their becoming Jews too. No doubt Gentiles began to swell the ranks of converts as Paul spread the word about the new policy: the "God-fearers" probably quickly switched en masse from the synagogues to the churches. But since Paul continued to base his efforts within the Diasporan communities, Jewish Christians must have continued to dominate the church. This is consistent with my previous study in which I found strong statistical evidence that Greco-Roman cities with a significant Diasporan community had Christian congregations far sooner than did other cities. All nine of the larger Greco-Roman cities with Diasporan communities had a Christian congregation by the end of the first century. Only four of the twenty-two equally large Greco-Roman cities without such a community had a church that early; a third of them still lacked a church by 180.[44]

Eventually, of course, the rise of Christianity was accomplished by the mission to the Gentiles. This was greatly facilitated by the many aspects of the Christ story that made it familiar and convincing to pagans: the star in the East, the Virgin Birth, the visit by the Magi, the miracles, the blood sacrifice of the Crucifixion, the Resurrection, and the Ascension.

CHAPTER FIVE

Christianity and Privilege

TRADITION HAS IT THAT CHRISTIANITY recruited most of its initial supporters from among the very poorest and most miserable groups in the ancient world. Since early times, many ascetic Christians have claimed that poverty was one of the chief virtues of the "primitive" church, and by the nineteenth century this view was ratified by the radical Left as well. Karl Marx's collaborator Friedrich Engels (1820–1895) put it thus: "The history of early Christianity has notable points of resemblance with the modern working-class movement. Like the latter, Christianity was originally a movement of oppressed people: it first appeared as the religion of slaves and emancipated slaves, of poor people deprived of all rights, of peoples subjugated or dispersed by Rome."[1] Working from this assumption, Karl Kautsky (1854–1938), the German editor of Marx's works, built the case that Jesus may have been one of the first socialists and that the early Christians briefly achieved true communism.[2]

Although many Bible scholars rejected Kautsky's claims, the view that Christianity originated in lower-class bitterness and protest remained the received wisdom all across the theological spectrum. As Yale's Erwin Goodenough (1893–1965) summed up in a widely adopted college textbook: "Still more obvious an indication of the undesirability of Christianity in Roman eyes was the fact that its converts were drawn in an overwhelming majority from the lowest classes of society. Then as now the governing classes were apprehensive of a movement which brought into a closely knit and secret organization the servants and slaves of society."[3]

This view was further elaborated by the German sociologist Ernst Troeltsch (1865–1923) who claimed that *all* religious movements are the work of the "lower classes."[4] Troeltsch was echoed by the American Protestant theologian-turned-sociologist H. Richard Niebuhr (1894–1962), who wrote in an extremely influential book that a new religious movement is always "the child of an outcast minority, taking its rise in the religious revolts of the poor."[5] Subsequently, the most popular explanation of why people initiate new religious movements came to be known as *deprivation theory*, which proposes that people adopt supernatural solutions to their material misery when direct action fails or is obviously impossible.[6]

Recently, it has become apparent that deprivation theory fails to fit most, if not all, of the well-documented cases of new religious movements—whether Buddhism in the sixth century BCE[7] or the New Age Movement[8] in the twenty-first century CE. Contrary to prevailing sociological dogmas, *religious movements typically are launched by the privileged classes*. Why this occurs will be examined later in this chapter. First comes a detailed refutation of the claim that early Christianity was a lower-class movement, which I will replace with the recognition that, from the very beginning, Christianity was especially attractive to people of privilege—Jesus himself may have come from wealth or at least from a comfortable background.

Privileged Christians

ALL DISCUSSIONS OF THE social standing of the first Christians would seem to have been settled by Paul's "irrefutable" proof text, when he noted of his followers that "not many of you were wise according to worldly standards, not many were powerful, not many were of noble birth" (1 Cor. 1:26).

It is amazing how many generations of sophisticated people failed to see a very obvious implication of this verse. Finally, in 1960, the Australian scholar E. A. Judge[9] began an illustrious career by pointing out that Paul did not say "*none* of you were powerful, *none* of you were of noble birth." Instead, Paul said "not many" were powerful or of noble birth, which means that some were! Given what a miniscule fraction of persons in the Roman Empire were of noble birth, it is quite remarkable that *any* of the tiny group of early Christians were of the nobility. This raises the possibility that like the many other religious movements, Christianity also began as a movement of the privileged. In fact, several noted historians had expressed that view long before Judge pointed out the obvious. The immensely influential German historian Adolf von Harnack (1851–1930) remarked on the special appeal Christianity held for upper class women,[10] and the renowned Scottish classicist W. M. Ramsay (1851–1939) claimed that Christianity "spread at first among the educated more rapidly than among the uneducated; nowhere had it a stronger hold . . . than in the household and at the court of the emperor."[11] However, aside from a few specialists, these dissenting views have had little impact on the conventional wisdom that the early Christians were recruited mostly from the lower ranks of society. So, let us look more closely at the likely social position of Jesus, his disciples, Paul, and the early generations of Christians.

Many Bible scholars have been troubled by 2 Corinthians 8:9 wherein Paul remarks "For you know the grace of our Lord Jesus Christ, that though he was rich, yet for your sake he became poor, so that by his poverty you might become rich." Could this be true? Was Jesus once a rich man? Some have used this verse to "prove" that Paul knew nothing about the life of Jesus[12]—an obviously absurd claim. Most others have interpreted it metaphorically—claiming that the reference is to spiritual riches. But this interpretation is greatly compromised by the fact that the verse occurs within a context wherein

Paul is asking the Corinthians to contribute money, not prayers, for the poor in Jerusalem. He also cites the example of the Macedonians as setting a standard for giving money and assures the Corinthians that God's blessings will accrue to generous givers. To cite the example of Jesus in this context strongly suggests that Paul was talking about Jesus having given up material, not spiritual, riches. A careful examination of Jesus's biography, as well as the examples favored by Jesus in his teachings, suggests Paul may have known what he was talking about.

As noted in chapter 3, Jesus probably was not a carpenter, unless it was in keeping with the traditional Jewish practice that a rabbi always learned a trade to fall back on, since it seems extremely likely that Jesus was a well-educated rabbi. It appears that his parents "occupied a prominent place in the community" and were sufficiently well-off "to have had property in Capernaum as well as Nazareth."[13] They also were able to go to Jerusalem every year for Passover (Luke 2:41), something most families could not afford.[14]

In addition, among the immense number of analogies and metaphors used by Jesus in the Gospels, only three times[15] did he make any references to "building" or "construction," and these are so vague as to indicate nothing about his knowledge of carpentry. One surely need not be a carpenter to know it is better to build a foundation on rock than on sand (Luke 6:46–49). On the other hand, Jesus constantly used examples involving wealth: land ownership, investment, borrowing, having servants and tenants, inheritance, and the like. It has been noted that the "parable of the talents shows familiarity with banking practices."[16] These rhetorical tendencies may not reflect that Jesus was a son of privilege, but they surely do suggest a privileged audience. As the respected George Wesley Buchanan noted, many of Jesus's images and parables "would be pointless if told to people who had not enough wealth to entertain guests, hire servants, be generous with contributions, etc. The audiences, at least, were predominantly wealthy. . . . [A] teacher from the lower classes would have been less likely to have found his most attentive listeners among the upper classes than a teacher who, himself, had been reared in upper class conditions."[17] And, in fact, the Gospels are filled with clues that not only did Jesus address a privileged audience, but that he tended to draw his supporters from among them.

Consider the twelve apostles or disciples. It is widely assumed that they were all men of very humble origins and accomplishments. But is it true? We know almost nothing about some of them other than their names. But what the Gospels tell of others is inconsistent with their humble images. For example, when James and John abandoned their fishing boat to follow Jesus, "they left their father Zebedee in the boat with the hired servants" (Mark 1:20). It is not surprising that they employed servants; fishing was quite profitable and required a substantial investment. Since, according to Luke 5:10, Peter (Simon) and Andrew were partners of James and John, it can be assumed they too were somewhat affluent. In fact, it is quite possible that Peter owned two houses, one in Bethsaida and another in Capernaum. Mark's mother owned a house in Jerusalem that was sufficiently large to serve as a house church (Acts 12:12). Moreover, Andrew had previously had the leisure to be a disciple of John the Baptist. And then there was Matthew (or Levi) the tax collector. Tax collectors were hated; but they were powerful and affluent.

Among the people mentioned in the Gospels as involved with Jesus, a number can be identified as wealthy and even upper-class people. Zacchaeus was a chief tax collector and very rich. He was honored to have Jesus as his guest (Luke 19:1–10). Jairus, the ruler of the synagogue, came to Jesus seeking help for his daughter (Luke 8:40–56). Joseph of Arimathea was an early convert and very wealthy (Matt. 27:57). Joanna, the wife of Chuza who was steward of Herod Antipas, the tetrarch of Galilee, also was an early convert and a generous contributor to the support of Jesus and his disciples (Luke 8:3). Susanna was another wealthy woman who helped finance Jesus (Luke 8:3).

In Matthew 26:6–11, we learn that while Jesus was seated for dinner at the home of a leading Pharisee (see Luke 7:36) "a woman came up to him with an alabaster jar of very expensive ointment, and she poured it on his head" (v. 7). When his disciples become indignant because it could "have been sold for a large sum, and given to the poor" (v. 9), Jesus responds to them, "Why do you trouble the woman? For she has done a beautiful thing to me. For you always have the poor with you, but you will not always have me" (vv. 10–11). It should be noted that the value of the ointment was approximately equal to a year's wages for the average worker at that time.[18]

To quote Buchanan once again, "the majority of Jesus' teachings were directed toward the upper economic class with whom Jesus associated . . . [which] support[s] the possibility that Jesus may also have been reared in an upper class of society."[19]

Many will object that Jesus often advised that wealth was a barrier to salvation and that one should give one's wealth to the poor. But rather than interpreting this as a "poor man's" complaint against the rich, it would seem at least as plausible that these were the statements of someone in a position to say, "Do as I have done."

We come now to Paul and to the post-Crucifixion generation of Christians. Despite continuing and militant efforts to maintain that Paul was a pretentious nobody, truly a tentmaker,[20] it is certain that Paul was, as A. D. Nock put it, from a family "of wealth and standing."[21] He was born a Roman citizen when that was a very uncommon and meaningful badge of distinction in the East. Not only he, but his father, was a Pharisee (Acts 23:6). Paul left his home in the Greek city of Tarsus and went to Jerusalem in order to study under the famous Rabbi Gamaliel and then rapidly became so prominent that he was appointed to impose punishment on Jews who had taken up Christianity. His training as a tentmaker was in keeping with the long-standing tradition that every rabbi learn a trade "by which he could live."[22] That Paul later actually pursued this trade from time to time seems to have been a bit of an affectation. As C. H. Dodd (1884–1973) put it, "A man born to manual labour does not speak self-consciously of 'labouring with my own hands.' "[23] In addition, Paul did not preach to the masses, but "to those who, like himself, spoke and read Greek and knew their Septuagint; and he sought to interpret the mystery of God's purposes, for the relative few who could comprehend such concepts. . . . He moved easily among the upper reaches of provincial society."[24]

It should be no surprise, therefore, that Paul attracted many privileged followers, especially women. According to Gillian Cloke, "What is already evident is that women of the comfortably off and merchant classes of the empire were well-attested in the Christian movement from early on in its spread. . . . [Early Christianity] had substantial purchase amongst the classes of those capable of being patronesses to the apostles and their successors."[25] One of these was Lydia, a wealthy dealer in purple cloth, who was baptized by Paul—along with her family and servants—and who subsequently conducted the congregation in Philippi from her house. Several times she sent funds to Paul to support his mission in Thessalonica (Phil. 4:16). To a considerable extent, "Christianity was a movement sponsored by local patrons to their social dependents."[26] In fact, when Paul arrived in a new city, he usually stayed in a wealthy household and conducted his mission from there.[27] E. A. Judge identified forty persons who sponsored Paul and, not surprisingly, all were "persons of substance, members of a cultivated social elite."[28] Erastus, the city treasurer in Corinth, assisted Paul and may well have been one of his hosts. Another was Gaius who also had "a house ample enough not only to put up Paul, but also to accommodate all the Christian groups in Corinth meeting together. . . . The same is true of Crispus," who not only had "high prestige in the Jewish community" but probably was "well to do."[29] In addition, there is Theophilus to whom both Luke and Acts are dedicated and who most likely was a Roman official[30] who probably subsidized Paul—perhaps during his long period of house arrest in Rome.

Remarkable evidence of Paul's association with the privileged comes from Judge's calculation that, of ninety-one individuals named in the New Testament in connection with Paul, a third have names indicating Roman citizenship. Judge called this "a startlingly high proportion, ten times higher than in the case of a control group" based on epigraphic documents.[31] If this were not enough, there is evidence in Paul's letters that there already were significant numbers of Christians serving in the imperial household. Paul concluded his letter to the Philippians: "All the saints greet you, especially those of Caesar's household" (Phil. 4:22). And in his letter to the Romans (16:10–11), Paul sends greetings to "those who belong to the family of Aristobulus" and to "the family of Narcissus." Both Harnack and the equally authoritative J. B. Lightfoot (1828–1889), identified Narcissus as the private secretary of the emperor Claudius and Aristobulus as an intimate of the emperor.[32]

Finally, there is the First Epistle to Timothy. Whether or not Paul actually wrote this letter is not very important to the matters at hand. Everyone agrees that it was written no later than soon after Paul's ministry and that Timothy was engaged in a ministry in Ephesus. Thus it is instructive that the Epistle offered so much advice about what to preach to the rich members: "As for the rich in this world, charge them not to be haughty" (1 Tim. 6:17). Timothy was advised to tell his rich members not to cease being wealthy, but "to do good, to be rich in good deeds" (v. 18). In addition, 1 Timothy 2:9 advises that "women should adorn themselves modestly and sensibly in seemly apparel, not with braided hair or gold or pearls or costly attire." This advice is silly unless there were significant numbers of rich people in the congregation at Ephesus.

Did early Christianity also attract lower-class converts? Of course. Even when a wealthy household was baptized, the majority would have been servants and slaves, and surely some lower-status people found their way to the church on their own. The point is that early Christianity substantially over-recruited the privileged, not that it only recruited them, or even that most early Christians were well-off. This is entirely consistent with Gerd Theissen's reconstruction of the congregation in Corinth: it included many from the lower classes as well as a remarkable, if much smaller, number from the upper ranks of the city.[33]

In about 110 CE Ignatius, bishop of Antioch, was arrested by the

Romans and then set out on a long, leisurely walk to Rome in the company of ten soldiers. Along the way he wrote a famous series of letters to various congregations. Among those addressed or mentioned were people of high social status, including the wife of a procurator, and Alce, the wife of a police official. But the most telling revelation of the high status of some Christians came in Ignatius's letter to the congregation in Rome. Ignatius had made up his mind to die in the arena—to which he already had been sentenced—and his greatest fear was that well-meaning Christians in Rome would intervene and get him pardoned. So he wrote: "I am afraid that it is your love that will do me wrong. . . . [Let me] state emphatically to all that I die willingly for God, provided you do not interfere. I beg you, do not show me unseasonable kindness. Suffer me to be the food of wild beasts."[34]

The point is that Ignatius assumed that some members of the Roman congregation *could* get him pardoned, which required considerable, high-level influence. And there is every reason to believe that Ignatius was properly informed. Many historians now accept that Pomponia Graecina, a woman of the senatorial class who Tacitus reported as having been accused of practicing "foreign superstition" in 57 CE was a Christian. Nor was hers an isolated case. The distinguished Italian historian Marta Sordi noted: "We know from reliable sources that there were Christians among the aristocracy [in Rome] in the second half of the first century (Acilius Glabrio and the Christian Flavians) and that it seems probable that the same can be said for the first half of the century, before Paul's arrival in Rome."[35]

In 112 CE, Pliny the Younger wrote to the emperor Trajan for approval of his policies in persecuting Christians. He informed the emperor that the spread of "this wretched cult" involved "many individuals of every age and class."[36]

By the end of the second century, Tertullian claimed that Christians were present at every level in Rome, including the palace and the Senate.[37] Fifteen years later Tertullian mentioned in a letter to Scapula that there were many "women and men of the highest rank" known to be Christians.[38] At this same time, the noblewoman Perpetua was martyred at Carthage; Edmond Le Blant noted that a large number of the martyrs were rich.[39] During the reign of Commodus (180–192), according to Harnack, "in Rome especially a large number of wealthy people went over to this religion together with all their households and families."[40]

For more systematic evidence, in a sample of Romans of the senatorial class from late in the third century, 10 percent could be clearly identified as Christians—or at least twice the percentage of Christians in the empire.[41] A study of grave monuments in Phrygia from this same era found fourteen Christian city councillors and the son of a Christian city councillor. A city councillor was necessarily very rich since the office was imposed as a civic duty and required the expenditure of considerable personal funds for municipal benefits.[42]

Clearly, then, Paul told the truth when he implied that although not many Christians were powerful or of noble birth, *some* were! Indeed, as compared with the general population, it would seem that *many* were. Obviously, then, the early Christians were not a bunch of miserable underdogs. This always should have been obvious, not only from reading the Gospels, but from asking why and how a bunch of illiterate ignoramuses came to produce sophisticated written scriptures at a time when only the Jews had produced anything comparable; several of the Oriental faiths had brief scriptures, but the dominant Greco-Roman paganism had none.

Christian Literacy

As with all the other "scholarly" attacks on the credibility of the Gospels and the early church, claims that Jesus was illiterate, that Paul's Greek was "vulgar," and that the Gospels are written in a crude, artless style, originated with German professors during the late nineteenth and early twentieth centuries. The most prominent among them was Adolf Deissmann (1866–1937), who began with the assumption that Christianity was "a movement among the weary and heavy-laden, men without power and position, 'babes' as Jesus himself calls them, the poor, the base, the foolish."[43] Building on this foundation, Deissmann used the term *Kleinliteratur* (low or small literature) to distinguish Christian writings from those of educated ancient authors who wrote *Hochliteratur* (high literature). According to Deissmann, early Christian writings used "just the kind of Greek that simple, unlearned folk of the Roman Imperial period were in the habit of using."[44] And the letters of Paul show that "Christianity in its earliest creative period was most closely bound up with the lower classes and had as yet no effective connexion with the small upper class possessed of power and culture."[45] As Deissmann's colleague Martin Dibelius (1883–1947) summed up, early Christianity "gave no place to the artistic devices and tendencies of literary and polished writing. . . . [Christians were an] unlettered people [who] . . . had neither the capacity nor the inclination for the production of books."[46] Unfortunately, for most of the twentieth century even highly committed Christian scholars accepted these claims.[47]

But, as with all the other attacks on the early Christians by German academics in this era, this was mostly arrogant nonsense. Paul wrote letters, not plays or epic poems. It would have been bizarre had his (or anyone else's) letters been highly literary—one supposes that even James Joyce's letters were much less "literary" than his novel *Finnegans Wake*. As for Paul's Greek, it now is recognized that it was a "Jewish Greek," much like that used in the Septuagint (the Greek translation of the Hebrew Bible), and no one denies that Paul was a Jew, not an Athenian. Nock dismissed Deissmann's claims, arguing that "Paul is not writing peasant Greek or soldier Greek; he is writing the Greek of a man who has the Septuagint in his blood."[48] As for the Gospels lacking literary merit, the writing style is like that of the great Greek scientific works (such as Ptolemy's astronomy)—works written primarily to convey information and therefore presented in "straightforward, factual prose."[49] The authors of the Gospels were not writing fiction or art; they had material to convey and their style was in keeping with "the professional prose of the day."[50]

As scholars have finally turned away from the German claims that Christians were an ignorant and illiterate lot, there has been a growing awareness that the history of early Christian writing and texts reveals an unusually sophisticated group of writers and readers. One of the earliest proponents of this "privileged Christian audience" thesis was the distinguished Yale professor Abraham J. Malherbe. After analyzing the language and style of the early church writers he concluded that they were addressing a literate, educated audience.[51] Indeed, who else could they have been writing for? Deissmann seems to have forgotten that in those days the poor, the base, and the foolish couldn't read.[52]

Since Malherbe's book appeared, there have been some superb studies published of early Christian writing and literacy.[53] All of these scholars stress the Jewish origins of Christianity, which not only makes it likely that early Christians shared the unusually high levels of literacy enjoyed by the ancient Jews, but also would have encouraged Christians to regard scripture as essential to their religious life.

Clearly, the early Christians placed immense importance on Jewish scripture. As Harry Y. Gamble explained: "One of the most urgent tasks of the Christian movement in its infancy was to support its convictions by showing their consistency with Jewish scriptures. . . . [Hence they] necessarily developed scriptural arguments."[54] To this end, Gamble suggests, they would have assembled "anthologies of proof texts . . . extracted from Jewish scriptures."[55] Collections of proof texts were found in the scrolls surviving from the sect at Qumran, and it seems virtually certain that Christians would have assembled similar works. The existence of such collections is further supported by the fact that many of the quotations from Jewish scriptures that appear in early Christian writing vary from the wording in the Septuagint or from the Masoretic texts; hence they must have been copied from another source. As Gamble put it, "There is, then, at least a strong circumstantial probability that collections of testimonies were current in the early church and should be reckoned among the lost items of the earliest Christian literature."[56]

Alan Millard agreed with Gamble that from its earliest days Christianity was a written religion: "This is not to say the Evangelists began to compose the Gospels in Jesus' lifetime, but that some, possibly much, of their source material was preserved in writing from that period, especially accounts of the distinctive teachings and actions of Jesus."[57] Graham N. Stanton thought it unbelievable that Christians would have waited a generation or two before they began to write things down: "The widely held view that the followers of Jesus were illiterate or deliberately spurned the use of notes and notebooks for recording and transmitting Jesus traditions needs to be abandoned."[58] The use of notebooks in this era is lucidly examined in detail by Richard Bauckham who demonstrated that "such notebooks were in quite widespread use in the ancient world (2 Tim 4:13 refers to parchment notebooks Paul carried on his travels). It seems more probable than not that early Christians used them."[59]

Thus the evidence strongly suggests that the Gospels were the end product of a faith that was set down in writing from the very start. It seems nearly certain that at least some of Jesus's words were written down when they were spoken. It seems even more certain that the early evangelists, including Paul, possessed and often referred to written materials—far more of them than merely the postulated Q—which helps to explain the variations and differences across the Gospels. As for the latter, they were written to be read, not only by the emerging clergy, but by rank-and-file Christians!

Finally comes the persistent claim that Jesus was illiterate: This snide assertion flies in the face of the immense familiarity with Jewish Scriptures displayed by Jesus throughout the Gospels[60] and the near certainty that he was a well-trained rabbi. It also ignores statements such as in Luke 4:16–17: "and he went to the synagogue, as his custom was, on the sabbath day. And he stood up to read; and there was given to him the book of the prophet Isaiah. He opened the book and found the place where it was written." In addition is the frequency with which Jesus prefaces an exchange with the rhetorical question, "have you not read?"[61] Granted that this evidence comes only from the Gospels; but that is true of *everything* we know about Jesus.

It seems inescapable that early Christianity was not an exception to the rule that religious innovation is primarily the work of the privileged. This recognition has caused considerable anxiety among many recent historians of the early church. Why, they ask almost incredulously, would privileged people feel driven to form and embrace a new religious movement? This has led to many confused and rigid discussions of various social scientific notions such as status inconsistency and cognitive dissonance.[62] But the reason the privileged turn to religion is neither so complex nor so convoluted.

Privilege and Religious Innovation

To set the stage, consider that Buddha was a prince, that fifty-five of his first sixty converts were from the nobility, and the other five might have been nobles too (we simply don't know their backgrounds).[63] For another major example, after many years of effort and only two converts, Zoroaster built a successful movement after converting the king, queen, and then the court of a nearby kingdom. The early Taoists as well as the Confucianists were recruited from among the Chinese elite, and, of course, Moses was a prince. Or consider two small sects that appeared in ancient Greece: the Orphics and the Pythagoreans. According to Plato, both movements were based on the upper classes: their priests "come to the doors of the rich . . . and offer them a bundle of books."[64]

Nor is it true that most, let alone all, of the Christian sect movements arose from the lower classes. With the possible exception of some Anabaptist Movements, the great Christian religious movements that occurred through the centuries were very obviously based on persons of considerable wealth and power: on the nobility, the clergy, and the well-to-do urbanites.[65] For example, the Cathars enrolled a very high proportion of nobility[66] and so did the early

Waldensians.[67] Luther's Reformation was not supported by the poor, but by princes, merchants, professors, and university students (see chapter 18). At the outbreak of the first French War of Religion in 1562, it is estimated that 50 percent of the French nobility had embraced Calvinism,[68] but very few peasants or urban poor had done so.[69] Indeed, of 482 medieval ascetic Roman Catholic saints, three-fourths were from the nobility—22 percent of them from royalty.[70]

Many sociologists continue to cite the Methodists as a classic proletarian movement,[71] seemingly ignorant of the fact that John Wesley and his colleagues did not depart from the Church of England and found Methodism because they were lower-class dissidents seeking a more comforting faith. They were themselves young men of privilege who began to assert their preference for a higher intensity faith while at Oxford. By the same token, the prophets of the Old Testament all belonged "to the landowning nobility"[72] and, contrary to most sociologists, so did most members of the Jewish sect known as the Essenes.[73] If they thrive, nearly all religious movements attract many lower class adherents—as, of course, the Methodists did. But like the Methodists, these movements originate in the religious concerns of the privileged, not in lower class dissatisfaction.

Clearly, then, based on history the correct generalization ought to be that religious movements are not "revolts of the poor," but are spiritual ventures of the privileged. But why?

Insufficiencies and Opportunities of Privilege

HAVING NEVER BEEN RICH, let alone born into privilege, most scholars share with the vast majority of persons many unfounded illusions about what it is like to be at the top of the social pyramid. Although popular rhetoric abounds in adages minimizing the importance of wealth and status, most people don't really mean it and their perceptions are clouded by envy as well as by rampant materialism. Oh, to be born a Rockefeller! That Laurence Rockefeller played an active role in founding and funding various New Age groups such as Esalen seems mystifying.[74] But the fact is that wealth and power do not satisfy all human desires. Abraham Maslow (1908–1970) wrote at length about the need for self-actualization,[75] and the Nobel laureate economist Robert William Fogel linked this to privilege: "throughout history . . . freed of the need to work in order to satisfy their material needs, [the rich] have sought self-realization."[76]

In earlier times, the route to self-realization quite obviously was a spiritual journey; hence the remarkable propensity of the privileged to found or join religious movements. In modern times this quest has often led the privileged to leftist politics, as in the case of late-nineteenth-century participants in the British Fabian Society or in the instance of the many sons and daughters of privilege who sustained American radical movements during the 1960s.[77] In both cases, however, for many, the worldly, materialist quest proved unsatisfactory, whereupon substantial numbers dropped out and turned to religious movements. Many '60s radicals joined intense religious groups,[78] and many Fabians became Spiritualists.[79] Indeed, a large proportion of Muslim terrorists who have attacked the West have come from highly privileged backgrounds. What this reflects is that while worldly Utopias inevitably fail to deliver,[80] spiritual salvation does not. Buddha could not find satisfactory purpose and meaning when living in a palace; he found it under a Banyan tree.

Clearly it is necessary to add a fundamental extension to deprivation theory as it originally was formulated. It is not merely that people will adopt supernatural solutions to their thwarted material desires, but that people will pursue or initiate supernatural solutions to their thwarted existential and moral desires—a situation to which the privileged are especially prone, since they are not distracted by immediate material needs.[81]

It also must be recognized that the privileged are in a position to act on their spiritual dissatisfactions and desires in a way that the poor are not: they have visibility, influence, experience, and means. That the prophets Jeremiah and Ezekiel were both born into wealth and the priesthood gave them initial credibility. As he founded the Waldensians, Waldo, a rich merchant of Lyon, had the funds to commission a French translation of the Gospels and the experience needed to administer an ascetic movement that attracted many other rich followers. John Wycliff launched the Lollard movement without stirring from his rooms at Oxford; it was enough that he published an English translation of the Bible and proposed that the church pursue "apostolic poverty." Merchants and members of the nobility took it from there.[82] Jan Hus was the personal chaplain of the Queen of Bohemia and thus able to recruit followers from the nobility on a face-to-face basis. Martin Luther was a professor and so prominent in church affairs that he was sent to Rome to make appeals on behalf of the Augustinian Vicar-General. Ulrich Zwingli's parents bought him a parish. During his youth in Noyon, John Calvin enjoyed the sponsorship of the local nobleman, and while a student in Paris he was assigned the income from several ecclesiastical posts.[83] The University of Paris not only trained Calvin as a theologian, but perfected the rhetorical skills that enabled him to achieve political power in Geneva from whence he mounted religious campaigns in many parts of Europe. No matter how otherworldly their outlook, to succeed, religious movements must deal effectively with complex worldly affairs.

Finally, growing up in privilege often generates the conviction that one has the superior wisdom needed to transform the world and the right, perhaps even the duty, to do so.

Conclusion

KARL MARX WAS MERELY reflecting the conventional wisdom of the day when he wrote that "religion is the sigh of the oppressed creature . . . the opium of the people."[84] But he might better have said that "religion often is the opium of the dissatisfied upper classes, the sigh of wealthy creatures depressed by materialism." Of course, given his relentless intellectual as well as personal materialism, Marx couldn't conceive of such a thing. Neither can far too many social scientists. Fortunately, most New Testament historians no longer believe that the early Christians were a motley crew of slaves and the downtrodden. Had that really been the case, the rise of Christianity would most certainly have required miracles.

CHAPTER SIX

Misery and Mercy

EVEN IF IT IS THE affluent who usually initiate new religions, it is obvious that rich and poor alike often turn to Christianity in response to the widespread need to be comforted for the miseries of life—not merely poverty, but disease, the deaths of loved ones, and all the other misfortunes and disappointments humans face. The central idea is, of course, that Christian faith offers a sedative for suffering in this life by promising that we will be fully compensated in the next, when "many that are first will be last, and the last first" (Matt. 19:30). Atheists like to ridicule this aspect of faith as "pie in the sky."[1]

What is almost always missed is that Christianity often puts the pie on the table! It makes life better here and now. Not merely in psychological ways, as faith in an attractive afterlife can do, but in terms of concrete, worldly benefits. Consider that a study[2] based on ancient tombstones has established that early Christians outlived their pagan neighbors! What that demonstrates is that Christians enjoyed a superior quality of life. They did so because of their commitment to what was an unusual virtue in ancient times: "the quality of mercy," as Portia put it in *The Merchant of Venice*, played a major role in the growth of early Christianity.

Urban Misery

JESUS'S MINISTRY WAS MAINLY in the rural areas of Galilee, but his disciples soon transformed the Jesus Movement into an urban phenomenon.[3] Not only was the church headquartered in Jerusalem, but the earliest congregations were in the larger cities.[4] Of course, what were "larger" cities in those days were very small by today's standards. Even so, they were far more crowded, crime-infested, filthy, disease-ridden, and miserable than are the worst cities in the world today.

Size and Density

Ancient history has long suffered from very exaggerated numerical claims offered in the original sources.[5] Many armies of perhaps ten thousand were said to number in the hundreds of thousands or even as many as a million.[6] Similar exaggerations distort city sizes. For example, Josephus reported that in the first century CE there were more than 204 villages in Galilee, and that the smallest of these had a population of fifteen thousand.[7] In fact, Sepphoris, the largest *city* in Galilee probably did not have as many as five thousand residents, and most villages probably had fewer than one hundred. Consider that in this era Jerusalem's population probably exceeded twenty-five thousand only when it was crowded with refugees fleeing Roman armies—and even then it is unlikely to have contained more than forty or fifty thousand people, despite ancient claims that more than a million Jews were slaughtered when Jerusalem fell to Titus in 70 CE.[8]

Ancient cities had small populations! When Paul visited, Corinth probably had fifty thousand residents, Thessalonica thirty-five thousand, and Athens seventy-five thousand. Even Rome, then the largest city in the world (Loyang, China, was second), probably only had a population of about 450,000,[9] although many historians still cling to outdated figures in excess of a million.[10] But despite having small populations, ancient cities were remarkably crowded because they covered such small areas. Rome probably suffered from the greatest density. John Stambaugh[11] estimates it to have had 302 people per acre (compared with 122 in modern Calcutta and 100 in Manhattan). I have estimated the density of Antioch as 195 per acre.[12] Most other "major" cities of the day had densities comparable to Antioch. To get some feel for what such density was like, imagine yourself living on a popular beach in mid-summer.

To squeeze everyone in, it was necessary to jam all the buildings together and build them higher than was safe. Even so, most streets were so narrow that we would consider them to be mere footpaths. Although Roman law required that all streets be at least 9.5 feet wide, many were narrower.[13] In fact, the famous roads leading out of Rome such as the *Via Appia* or the *Via Latina*, were only fifteen to twenty feet wide! The main thoroughfare of Antioch was celebrated throughout the classical world for its spaciousness—it was only thirty feet wide[14] (streets in modern residential areas usually are forty feet wide). In most parts of ancient cities, streets were so narrow that if people leaned out of their windows they could chat with someone living across the street without having to raise their voices. Such crowding, combined with the fact that everything except a few temples and palaces was constructed of wood (covered with stucco), and that all heating and cooking was done over open braziers, explains why "dread of fire was an obsession among rich and poor alike."[15]

There was a nearly equal obsession with the collapse of buildings. In Rome it was illegal to construct a building higher than sixty-five feet. Nevertheless, buildings fell down all the time. Rome "was constantly filled with the noise of buildings collapsing or being torn down to prevent it; and the tenants of an *insula* [tenement] lived in constant expectation of its coming down on their heads."[16] The tenements collapsed because they were too lightly built[17] and because the less desirable upper floors (there being no elevators) housed the poor, who so subdivided them that the upper floors became heavier than the lower floors and beyond what the beams and foundations could carry.

Housing

Not only were the buildings squeezed together; inside them people were crowded into tiny cubicles.[18] Private houses were rare; in Rome there was "only one private house for every 26 blocks of apartments."[19] Tenements lacked both furnaces and fireplaces. As noted, cooking was done over wood or charcoal braziers, which also were the only source of heat; since everyone lacked chimneys (it was still many centuries before they were invented), the rooms were always smoky in winter. Because windows could only be "closed" by "hanging cloths or skins,"[20] the tenements were sufficiently drafty to prevent frequent asphyxiation. But, of course, the drafts increased the danger of rapidly spreading fires. Given these living conditions, people tended to live their lives in public places, and the "home" of the average person "must have served only as a place to sleep and to store possessions."[21]

Filth

Soap had not yet been invented. Because water had to be carried home in jugs from public fountains, there could have been little water for scrubbing floors or washing clothes. Nor could there have been much for bathing—although many people could go to the public baths. But even at the baths the water was quite contaminated because, whether it came to a city by way of an aqueduct or from local wells, all the larger Greco-Roman cities had to store water in cisterns, awaiting use. And "untreated water[,] . . . when left stagnant, encourages the growth of algae and other organisms, rendering the water malodorous, unpalatable, and after a time, undrinkable."[22] No wonder Pliny (23–79 CE) advised that "all water is the better for being boiled."[23]

One thing is certain: when human density is high, urgent problems of sanitation arise. Granted that an underground sewer carried water from the major baths of Rome through public latrines next door and on out of the city (to be dumped untreated into the Tiber River which could, therefore, be smelled for many miles). But few people jogged off to public latrines each time nature called. Like all cities until very modern times, people used chamber pots and pit latrines—and for lack of open spaces most Greco-Roman cities were entirely dependent on pots.[24] Of course pots needed to be emptied, and often the only option was to dump them in the open ditches running down streets that served as sewers. Too often the pots were emptied out of upper-story windows at night. As the great French historian Jerome Carcopino (1881–1970) described it:

> There were other poor devils who found their stairs too steep and the road to the dung pits too long, and to save themselves further trouble would empty the contents of their chamber pots from the heights above the streets. So much the worse for the passer-by who happened to intercept the unwelcome gift! Fouled and sometimes even injured, as in Juvenal's satire, he had no redress save to lodge a complaint against the unknown assailant; many passages in the *Digest* indicate that Roman jurists did not disdain to take cognisance of this offense.[25]

Given limited water and means of sanitation and the incredible density of humans and animals (narrow as they were, the streets were constantly traversed by horses, donkeys, and oxen, as well as by flocks on their way to be butchered, all making their own contributions to the mess), it must have been a remarkably filthy existence. The tenement cubicles were smoky, dark, often damp, and always dirty. The smell of sweat, urine, feces, and decay permeated everything. Outside: mud, open sewers, manure, and crowds. In fact, human corpses—adult as well as newborns—were sometimes just pushed into an open sewer.[26] And even if the wealthiest households could provide ample space and personal cleanliness, the rich could not prevent the stench of general filth from penetrating their homes—no wonder everyone was so fond of incense. Worse yet, flies, mosquitoes, and other insects flourish where there is stagnant water and filth—and like stinks, insects are very democratic.

Crime and Disorder

Amid all the concern that modern cities lack community, being filled with newcomers and strangers, it is forgotten that ancient cities were even more so. Had that not been true, ancient cities would quickly have become empty ruins. A constant and substantial influx of newcomers was required to offset the extremely high mortality rates of ancient cities.[27] Consequently, ancient cities had a quite high proportion of residents who were very *recent* newcomers, and Greco-Roman cities were therefore communities of strangers. Wherever such conditions prevail, crime abounds since people are attached to the moral order primarily by their ties to others. Consequently, Greco-Roman cities were far more crime-ridden than are the worst of modern cities. As Carcopino described Rome:

> Night fell over the city like the shadow of great danger, diffused, sinister, menacing. Everyone fled to his home, shut himself in, and barricaded the entrance. The shops fell silent, safety chains were drawn behind the leaves of the doors. . . . If the rich had to sally forth, they were accompanied by slaves who carried torches to light and protect them on their way. . . . Juvenal sighs that to go out to supper without having made your will was to expose yourself to reproach for carelessness. . . . [W]e need only to turn to the leaves of the *Digest* [to discover the extent to which criminals] abounded in the city.[28]

More specifically, "most criminals in Rome followed traditional pursuits, and the city was plagued with housebreakers, pickpockets, petty thieves, and muggers."[29] There also were very high levels of interpersonal violence[30]—there even were professional murderers for hire.[31]

In addition to crime, the constant influx of strangers into Greco-Roman cities caused a great deal of disorder, including riots—some involving ethnic conflicts, some involving political disputes.[32] Riots not only cost many lives and ruined immense amounts of property (major fires often resulted), but the political riots aroused such extreme anxiety among the ruling elite that secret police proliferated, generating a huge network of informants. Subsequently, "no class, high or low, could escape their prying. . . . [T]hey [also] were commissioned to carry out political assassinations."[33] All this added to the miseries of everyday life.

Disease

The constant companion of filth, insects, and crowding is disease. Consequently, people were far more likely to die during the summer than when the chill of winter mitigated the effects of filth and insects.[34] Even so, illness and physical afflictions probably were dominant features of daily life. A recent analysis of decayed human fecal remains in an ancient Jerusalem cesspool found an abundance of tapeworm and whipworm eggs, indicating that almost everyone had them.[35] Although being infected with one or both of these parasites is not fatal, both can cause anemia and make victims more vulnerable to other illnesses. Given their living conditions and lack of medications, the majority of persons living in Greco-Roman cities must have suffered from chronic health problems that caused them pain and some degree of disability, and of which many would soon die. Compared with modern cities, sickness was highly visible: "Swollen eyes, skin rashes and lost limbs are mentioned over and over again in the sources as part of the urban scene."[36] Roger Bagnall reported that in this age before photography and finger-printing, written documents offered descriptive information to help identify the parties, and these very often relied on "their distinctive disfigurements, mostly scars."[37] Bagnall cited a fourth-century papyrus that lists a number of persons owing debts, *all* of whom were scarred.[38] Finally, as will be discussed in chapter 7, women were especially susceptible to health problems due to childbirth and to widespread abortion by means of unsanitary and crude methods.

Christian Mercy

IN THE MIDST OF the squalor, misery, illness, and anonymity of ancient cities, Christianity provided an island of mercy and security.

Foremost was the Christian duty to alleviate want and suffering. It started with Jesus: "for I was hungry and you gave me food, I was thirsty and you gave me drink, I was a stranger and you welcomed me, I was naked and you clothed me, I was sick and you visited me, I was in prison and you came to me. . . . Truly, I say to you, as you did it to one of the least of these my brethren, you did it to me" (Matt. 25:35–36, 40).

James 2:15–17 expresses a similar idea: "If a brother or sister is ill-clad and in lack of daily food, and one of you says to them, 'Go in peace, be warmed and filled,' without giving them the things needed for the body, what does it profit? So faith by itself, if it has no works, is dead."

In contrast, in the pagan world, and especially among the philosophers, mercy was regarded as a character defect and pity as a pathological emotion: because mercy involves providing *unearned* help or relief, it is contrary to justice. As E. A. Judge explained, classical philosophers taught that "mercy indeed is not governed by reason at all," and humans must learn "to curb the impulse"; "the cry of the undeserving for mercy" must go "unanswered." Judge continued: "Pity was a defect of character unworthy of the wise and excusable only in those who have not yet grown up."[39]

This was the moral climate in which Christianity taught that mercy is one of the primary virtues—that a merciful God requires humans to be merciful. Moreover, the corollary that *because* God loves humanity, Christians may not please God unless they *love one another* was even more incompatible with pagan convictions. But the truly revolutionary principle was that Christian love and charity must extend beyond the boundaries of family and even those of faith, to all in need. As Cyprian, the martyred third-century bishop of Carthage explained, "there is nothing remarkable in cherishing merely our own people with the due attentions of love. . . . Thus the good was done to all men, not merely to the household of faith."[40]

It wasn't just talk. In 251 the bishop of Rome wrote a letter to the bishop of Antioch in which he mentioned that the Roman congregation was supporting fifteen hundred widows and distressed persons.[41] This was not unusual. In about the year 98 CE, Ignatius, bishop of Antioch, advised Polycarp, the bishop of Smyrna, to be sure to provide special support for widows.[42] As the distinguished Paul Johnson put it: "The Christians . . . ran a miniature welfare state in an empire which for the most part lacked social services."[43] Tertullian (155–222) explained how this welfare system functioned:

> There is no buying or selling of any sort of things of God. Though we have our treasure chest, it is not made up of purchase money, as of a religion that has its price. On the monthly day, if he likes, each puts in a small donation; but only if it be his pleasure, and only if he is able; for there is no compulsion; all is voluntary. These gifts are, as it were, piety's deposit fund. For they are not taken thence and spent on feasts, and drinking bouts, and eating houses, but to support and bury poor people, to supply the wants of boys and girls of destitute means and parents, and of old persons confined now to the house; such, too, as have suffered shipwreck; and if there happen to be any in the mines, or banished to the islands, or shut up in prisons, for nothing but their fidelity to the cause of God's Church, they become the nurslings of their confession.[44]

These charitable activities were possible only because Christianity generated congregations, a true community of believers who built their lives around their religious affiliation. And it was this, above all else, that insulated Christians from the many deprivations of ancient life. Even if they were newcomers, they were not strangers, but brothers and sisters in Christ. When calamities struck, there were people who cared—in fact, there were people having the distinct responsibility to care! All congregations had deacons whose primary job was the support of the sick, infirm, poor, and disabled. As outlined in *Apostolic Constitutions*, deacons "are to be doers of good works, exercising a general supervision day or night, neither scorning the poor nor respecting the person of the rich; they must ascertain who are in distress and not exclude them from a share in church funds; compelling also the well-to-do to put money aside for good works."[45]

Nothing illustrates the immense benefits of Christian life better than responses to the two great plagues that struck the empire.

Plagues and Faith

IN THE YEAR 165, during the reign of Marcus Aurelius, a devastating epidemic swept through the Roman Empire. Some medical historians suspect this was the first appearance of smallpox in the West.[46] Whatever the actual disease, it was lethal—as many contagious diseases are when they strike a previously unexposed population. During the fifteen-year duration of the epidemic, a quarter to a third of the population probably died of it.[47] At the height of the epidemic, mortality was so great in many cities that the emperor Marcus Aurelius (who subsequently died of the disease) wrote of caravans of carts and wagons hauling out the dead.[48] Then, a century later came another great plague. Once again the Greco-Roman world trembled as, on all sides, family, friends, and neighbors died horribly.

No one knew how to treat the stricken. Nor did most people try. During the first plague, the famous classical physician Galen fled Rome for his country estate where he stayed until the danger subsided. But for those who could not flee, the typical response was to try to avoid any contact with the afflicted, since it was understood that the disease was contagious. Hence, when their first symptom appeared, victims often were thrown into the streets, where the dead and dying lay in piles. In a pastoral letter written during the second epidemic (ca. 251), Bishop Dionysius described events in Alexandria: "At the first onset of the disease, they [pagans] pushed the sufferers away and fled from their dearest, throwing them into the roads before they were dead and treated unburied corpses as dirt, hoping thereby to avert the spread and contagion of the fatal disease; but do what they might, they found it difficult to escape."[49]

It must have caused most people considerable pain and grief to abandon loved ones in this manner. But what else could they do? What about prayers? Well, if one went to a temple to pray, one discovered that the priests were not there praying for divine aid, but that all of them had fled the city. They had done so because there was no belief that the gods cared about human affairs. It was thought that they sometimes could be "bribed" to grant wishes, but the idea of a merciful or caring God was utterly alien. As Thucydides explained about an earlier plague that had struck Athens:

> Useless were prayers made in the temples, consultation of oracles, and so forth; indeed, in the end people were so overcome by their sufferings that they paid no further attention to such things. . . . [T]hey died with no one to look after them; indeed there were many houses in which all the inhabitants perished through lack of attention. . . . The bodies of the dying were heaped one on top of the other, and half-dead creatures could be seen staggering about in the streets or flocking around the fountains in their desire for water. The temples in which they took up their quarters were full of the dead bodies of people who had died inside them. For the catastrophe was so overwhelming that men, not knowing what would happen next to them, became indifferent to every rule of religion and law. . . . No fear of god or law of man had a restraining influence. As

for the gods, it seemed to be the same thing whether one worshipped them or not, when one saw the good and the bad dying indiscriminately.[50]

By the same token the classical philosophers had nothing useful to say except to blame it all on fate. As Canadian historian Charles Norris Cochrane (1889–1945) put it: "while a deadly plague was ravaging the empire . . . the sophists prattled vaguely about the exhaustion of virtue in a world growing old."[51]

But Christians claimed to have answers and, most of all, they took appropriate actions. As for answers, Christians believed that death was not the end and that life was a time of testing. This is how Cyprian, bishop of Carthage, explained to his people that the virtuous had nothing to fear during the second great plague.

> How suitable, how necessary it is that this plague and pestilence, which seems horrible and deadly, searches out the justice of each and every one and examines the mind of the human race; whether the well care for the sick, whether relatives dutifully love their kinsman as they should, whether masters show compassion for their ailing slaves, whether physicians do not desert the afflicted. . . . Although this mortality had contributed nothing else, it has especially accomplished this for Christians and servants of God, that we have begun gladly to seek martyrdom while we are learning not to fear death. These are trying exercises for us, not deaths; they give to the mind the glory of fortitude; by contempt of death they prepare for the crown. . . . [O]ur brethren who have been freed from this earth by the summons of the Lord should not be mourned, since we know that they are not lost but sent before; that in departing they lead the way; that as travelers, as voyagers are wont to be, they should be longer for not lamented . . . and that no occasion should be given to pagans to censure us deservedly and justly, on the ground that we grieve for those who we say are living.[52]

As for action, Christians met the obligation to care for the sick rather than desert them, and thereby saved enormous numbers of lives!

Toward the end of the second plague, Bishop Dionysius of Alexandria wrote a pastoral letter to his members, extolling those who had nursed the sick and especially those who had given their lives in doing so:

> Most of our brothers showed unbounded love and loyalty, never sparing themselves and thinking only of one another. Heedless of danger, they took charge of the sick, attending to their every need and ministering to them in Christ, and with them departed this life serenely happy; for they were infected by others with the disease, drawing on themselves the sickness of their neighbors and cheerfully accepting their pains. Many, in nursing and curing others, transferred their death to themselves and died in their stead. . . . The best of our brothers lost their lives in this manner, a number of presbyters, deacons, and laymen winning high commendation so that in death in this form, the result of great piety and strong faith, seems in every way the equal to martyrdom.[53]

Should we believe the bishop? Certainly, given that he was writing to his local members who had independent knowledge of the events. But what difference could it really have made? A huge reduction in the death rate!

As William H. McNeill pointed out in his celebrated *Plagues and Peoples*, under the circumstances prevailing in this era, even "quite elementary nursing will greatly reduce mortality. Simple provision of food and water, for instance, will allow persons who are temporarily too weak to cope for themselves to recover instead of perishing miserably."[54] It is entirely plausible that Christian nursing would have reduced mortality by as much as two-thirds! The fact that most stricken Christians survived did not go unnoticed, lending immense credibility to Christian "miracle working." Indeed, the miracles often included pagan neighbors and relatives. This surely must have produced some conversions, especially by those who were nursed back to health. In addition, while Christians did nurse some pagans, being so outnumbered, obviously they could not have cared for most of them, while all, or nearly all, Christians would have been nursed. Hence Christians as a group would have enjoyed a far superior survival rate, and, on these grounds alone, the percentage of Christians in the population would have increased substantially as a result of both plagues.

What went on during the epidemics was only an intensification of what went on every day among Christians. Because theirs were communities of mercy and self-help, Christians did have longer, better lives. This was apparent and must have been extremely appealing. Indeed, the impact of Christian mercy was so evident that in the fourth century when the emperor Julian attempted to restore paganism, he exhorted the pagan priesthood to compete with the Christian charities. In a letter to the high priest of Galatia, Julian urged the distribution of grain and wine to the poor, noting that "the impious Galileans [Christians], in addition their own, support ours, [and] it is shameful that our poor should be wanting our aid."[55] But there was little or no response to Julian's proposals because there were no doctrines and no traditional practices for the pagan priests to build upon. It was not that the Romans knew nothing of charity, but for them it was not based on service to the gods. Since pagan gods required only propitiation and beyond that had no interest in what humans did, a pagan priest could not preach that those persons lacking in the spirit of charity risked their salvation. There was no salvation! The gods did not offer any escape from mortality. We must keep that in mind when we compare the reactions of Christians and pagans in the shadow of death. Christians believed in life everlasting. At most, pagans believed in an unattractive existence in the underworld. Thus, for Galen to have remained in Rome to treat the afflicted during the first great plague would have required far greater bravery than was needed by Christian deacons and presbyters to do so. Faith mattered.

Conclusion

SOME WILL OBJECT THAT to stress the importance of tangible, worldly benefits for Christian conversion is to wrongly downplay the religious motivations for the rise of Christianity. This objection overlooks that these worldly benefits were *religious* in the fullest sense. "Truly, I say to you, as you did it to one of the least of these my brethren, you did it to me" (Matt. 25:40). It was by imitation of Christ that Christians were able to live longer and enjoy more comfortable lives.

Chapter Seven

Appeals to Women

Because Jesus, the twelve apostles, Paul, and the prominent leaders in the early church in Jerusalem were all men, the impression prevails that early Christianity was primarily a male affair. Not so. From earliest days women predominated.

In his Epistle to the Romans, Paul begins with personal greetings to fifteen women and eighteen men who were prominent members of the Roman congregation.[1] If we may assume that sufficient sex bias existed so that men were more likely than women to hold positions of leadership, then this very close sex ratio suggests a Roman congregation that was very disproportionately female. Indeed, the converts of Paul "we hear most about are women," and many of them "leading women."[2] Thus, the brilliant Cambridge church historian Henry Chadwick (1920–2008) noted, "Christianity seems to have been especially successful among women. It was often through the wives that it penetrated the upper classes of society in the first instance."[3] In this he echoed the formidable Adolf von Harnack (1851–1930): "Christian preaching was laid hold of by women in particular. . . . [T]he percentage of Christian women, especially among the upper classes, was larger than Christian men."[4] This was recently confirmed by a sample of senatorial class Romans who lived between 283 and 423 CE, in which 50 percent of the men and 85 percent of the women were Christians.[5]

The question persists: Why? The answer consists of two parts. First, unless they specifically prohibit or at least discourage women from joining, religious movements *always* attract more women than men. Indeed, all around the world, data show that women are more religious than men, in terms of both belief and participation.[6] Recently, a debate has sprung up as to why this is so[7]—but that is of no significance here. Far more important is the second part of the answer, which suggests that Christianity was attractive to women far beyond the usual level of gender differences. Women were especially drawn to Christianity because it offered them a life that was so greatly superior to the life they otherwise would have led. After examining this matter in detail, the chapter then examines how the situation of Christian women had important consequences for the speed of Christian growth.

Pagan and Jewish Women

IN NO ANCIENT GROUP were women equal to men, but there were substantial differences in the degree of inequality experienced by women in the Greco-Roman world. Women in the early Christian communities were considerably better off than their pagan and even Jewish counterparts.

It is difficult to generalize about the situation of pagan women in the ancient West because there were marked differences between Hellenes and Romans. Hellenic women lived in semi-seclusion, the upper classes more than others, but all Hellenic women had a very circumscribed existence; in privileged families the women were denied access to the front rooms of the house. Roman women were not secluded, but in many other ways they were no less subordinated to male control. Neither Hellenic nor Roman women had any significant say in who they married, or when. Typically, they were married very young—often before puberty—to a far older man. Their husbands could divorce them with impunity, but a wife could only gain a divorce if a male relative sought it on her behalf. However, a Hellenic wife's father or brother could obtain her divorce against her wishes! Both Roman and Hellenic husbands held the absolute power to put an unwanted infant to death or to force a wife to abort, but Roman husbands were not allowed to kill their wives. Roman wives had very limited property rights; Hellenic women had none. Neither could be a party to contracts. Many upper-class Roman women were taught to read and write; Hellenic women were not.[8] These differences may have played a role in the fact that Christianity grew more rapidly in the Hellenic than in the Roman cities (see chapter 9). Finally, only in a few temples devoted to goddesses were either Roman or Hellenic women allowed to play any significant role in religious life.

The situation of Jewish women varied considerably, not only between the Diaspora and Palestine, but also across—and even within—the Diasporan communities. In some Diasporan communities, many women were semi-secluded. According to Philo of Alexandria, the most authoritative Jewish voice in the Diaspora, "The women are best suited to the indoor life which never strays from the house, within which the middle door is taken to the maidens in their boundary, and the outer door by those who have reached full womanhood. . . . A woman, then, should not be a busybody, meddling with matters outside her household concerns, but should seek a life of seclusion."[9] There is no evidence of female seclusion in Palestine, and clearly many Jewish women in the Diaspora were not secluded either. However, everywhere Jewish girls were married very young to whomever their father chose, although in many settings they could request to remain at home until puberty. To the extent that Deuteronomy 22:13–21 was followed, brides who turned out not to be virgins were to be stoned to death at their father's door, but such events must have been rare. On the other hand, Jewish wives were easily and quite often divorced by their husbands, but wives could not seek a divorce except under very unusual circumstances, such as the husband being impotent or a leper. Jewish women could not inherit unless there were no male heirs. They "had no right to bear witness, and could not expect credence to be given to anything [they] reported."[10] As Rabbi Eliezer is quoted in the *Babylonian Talmud* (ca. 90 CE), "Better burn the Torah than teach it to a woman." Indeed, elsewhere the Talmud advises: "Everyone who talketh much with a woman causes evil to himself."[11]

Even so, Exodus 20:12 demands: "Honor your father and your mother," and Leviticus 19:3 even reverses the order: "Every one of you shall revere his mother and his father." Moreover, Jewish women were said "to have a *right* to sexual pleasure."[12] In keeping with Rabbi ben Azzai's opinion that "a man ought to give his daughter knowledge of the Law,"[13] some Jewish women were well educated and, in some Diasporan communities (beyond the reach of patriarchs in Palestine), women held leadership roles in some synagogues, including "elder," "leader of the synagogue," "mother of the synagogue," and "presiding officer," as is supported by inscriptions found in Smyrna and elsewhere.[14] However, men and women were seated separately in the synagogues and women were not allowed to read the Torah to the assembly. In general, Jewish women were better off than pagan women, but had less freedom and influence than did Christian women.

Christian Women

CHRISTIAN WRITERS HAVE LONG stressed that Jesus's "attitude toward women was revolutionary. . . . For him the sexes were equal."[15] Many feminist critics have dismissed the inclusive statements and actions of Jesus as having had no impact on the realities of gender relations within the early Christian community, where rampant sexism continued.[16] But recent, objective evidence leaves no doubt that early Christian women did enjoy far greater equality with men than did their pagan and Jewish counterparts. A study of Christian burials in the catacombs under Rome, based on 3,733 cases, found that Christian women were nearly as likely as Christian men to be commemorated with lengthy inscriptions. This "near equality in the commemoration of males and females is something that is peculiar to Christians, and sets them apart from the non-Christian populations of the city."[17] This was true not only of adults, but also of children, as Christians lamented the loss of a daughter as much as that of a son, which was especially unusual compared with other religious groups in Rome.[18]

Of course, there is overwhelming evidence that from earliest days, Christian women often held leadership roles in the church and enjoyed far greater security and equality in marriage.

Church Leadership

OUR PERCEPTIONS OF THE role of women in the early church has long been distorted by a statement attributed to Paul: "the women should keep silence in the churches. For they are not permitted to speak" (1 Cor. 14:34). There are solid grounds for dismissing these lines since they are inconsistent with everything else Paul had to say about women: he was "the only certain and consistent spokesman for the liberation and equality of women in the New Testament."[19] Robin Scroggs has made a good case that the statement that women should keep silence was inserted by those who composed the deutero-Pauline and Pastoral Epistles—those letters wrongly attributed to Paul.[20] Laurence Iannaccone has made the interesting suggestion that this statement about women was being made by some members of the church at Corinth to whom Paul was opposed, and that this distinction was lost somehow.[21] Be that as it may, it surely is the case that these lines are absurd given Paul's acknowledgement, encouragement, and approval of women in positions of religious leadership.

In Romans 16:1–2 Paul introduces and commends to the Roman congregation "our sister Phoebe" who is a deaconess "of the church at Cenchreae, that you may receive her in the Lord as befits the saints, and help her in whatever she may require from you, for she has been a helper of many and of myself as well." Deacons were important leaders in the early church, with special responsibilities for raising and dispersing funds. Clearly, Paul saw nothing unusual in a woman filling that role. Nor was this an isolated case or limited to the first generation of Christians. In 112, Pliny the Younger noted in a letter to Emperor Trajan that he had tortured two young Christian women "who were called deaconesses."[22] Clement of Alexandria (150–216) wrote of "women deacons," and Origen (185–254) wrote this commentary on Paul's letter to the Romans: "This text teaches with the authority of the Apostle that . . . there are, as we have already said, women deacons in the Church, and that women . . . ought to be accepted in the diaconate."[23] As late as 451 the Council of Chalcedon determined that in the future a deaconess must be at least forty and unmarried.[24]

Prominent historians now agree that women held positions of honor and authority in early Christianity. Thus, Peter Brown noted that Christians differed in this respect not only from pagans, but from Jews: "The Christian clergy . . . took a step that separated them from the rabbis of Palestine. . . . [T]hey welcomed women as patrons and even offered women roles in which they could act as collaborators."[25] As Wayne Meeks summed up: "Women . . . are Paul's fellow workers as evangelists and teachers. Both in terms of their position in the larger society and in terms of their participation in the Christian communities, then, a number of women broke through the normal expectations of female roles."[26]

Infanticide

THE SUPERIOR SITUATION OF Christian women vis-à-vis their pagan sisters began at birth. The exposure of unwanted infants was "widespread" in the Roman Empire,[27] and girls were far more likely than boys to be exposed. Keep in mind that legally and by custom, the decision to expose an infant rested entirely with the father as reflected in this famous, loving letter to his pregnant wife from a man who was away working: "If—good luck to you!—you should bear offspring, if it is a male, let it live; if it is female, expose it. You told Aphrodisias,

'Do not forget me.' How can I forget you? I beg you therefore not to worry."[28] Even in large families, "more than one daughter was hardly ever reared."[29] A study based on inscriptions was able to reconstruct six hundred families and found that of these, only six had raised more than one daughter.[30]

In keeping with their Jewish origins, Christians condemned the exposure of infants as murder.[31] As Justin Martyr (100–165) put it, "we have been taught that it is wicked to expose even new-born children . . . [for] we would then be murderers."[32] So, substantially more Christian (and Jewish) female infants lived.

Marriage

AS MARRIAGE APPROACHED THE Christian advantage continued. Pagan girls were married off at very young ages, usually to much older men, and they rarely had any choice in the matter. Here the evidence is both statistical and literary. As for the latter, silence offers strong testimony that Roman girls married at a tender age, often before puberty. The Cambridge historian Keith Hopkins (1934–2004) found that it was possible to calculate that many famous Roman women had been child brides: Octavia (daughter of Emperor Claudius) married at eleven. Nero's mother Agrippina married at twelve. Quintilian, the famed rhetorician must have married a twelve-year-old since we know she bore him a son when she was thirteen. The historian Tacitus married a thirteen-year-old, and so on. But in none of these instances was this fact seen as sufficiently interesting to be mentioned in the women's biographies. Beyond such silence, the historian Plutarch (46–120) reported that Romans "gave their girls in marriage when they were twelve years old, or even younger."[33] The historian Dio Cassius (155–229) agreed: "Girls are considered to have reached marriageable age on completion of their twelfth year."[34]

A pioneering study of age at marriage, based on Roman funerary inscriptions, was able to distinguish Christian from pagan women.

The data show very substantial differences. Twenty percent of the pagan women were twelve or younger when they married (4 percent were only ten). In contrast, only 7 percent of Christians were under thirteen. Half of pagan women were married before age fifteen, compared with 20 percent of Christians—and nearly half of Christian women (48 percent) had not married until they were eighteen or older.[35] These data alone would not settle the matter since the results are based on only a few hundred women. But given that they fully support the extensive "literary" evidence, it seems certain that Roman pagan girls married very young, and much younger than did most Christians.

It must be noted that marriages involving child brides were not marriages in name only. They usually were consummated at once, even when the girl had not yet reached puberty. There are reports of the defloration of wives as young as seven![36] This practice caused Plutarch to condemn Roman marriage customs as cruel, reporting "the hatred and fear of girls forced contrary to nature."[37] Very few Christian girls suffered similar fates. Most married when they were physically and emotionally mature; most had a say in whom they married and enjoyed a far more secure marriage.

Divorce

THE CHRISTIAN POSITION ON divorce was defined by Jesus: "And I say to you: whoever divorces his wife, except for unchastity, and marries another, commits adultery" (Matt. 19:9). This was a radical break with past customs. A survey of marriage contracts going all the way back to ancient Babylon found that they always contained a divorce clause specifying payments and divisions of property and the cause of divorce need be nothing more than a husband's whim.[38] Jewish law specifically stated that a divorced wife was now free "to go to be the wife of any Jewish man that you wish."[39] But the early church was unswerving in its commitment to the standard set by Jesus, and this soon evolved into the position that there were no grounds for remarriage following divorce.[40] In addition, although like everyone else early Christians prized female chastity, unlike anyone else they rejected the double standard that gave men sexual license. As Henry Chadwick explained, Christians "regarded unchastity in a husband as no less serious a breach of loyalty and trust than unfaithfulness in a wife."[41]

Sexuality

FREQUENTLY, THE REJECTION OF divorce and of the double standard has been dismissed as incidental to a Christian revulsion against sexuality and a strong bias in favor of celibacy. Often this is illustrated by reference to Paul's statement that it is "better to marry than to burn" (1 Cor. 7:9 KJV), which is taken as a very grudging acknowledgement of sexual drives. In fact, even Paul was very supportive of marital sexuality as is entirely evident in the verses leading to the one quoted above: "The husband should give to his wife her conjugal rights, and likewise the wife to her husband. For the wife does not rule over her own body, but the husband does; likewise the husband does not rule over his own body, but the wife does. Do not refuse one another except perhaps by agreement for a season, that you may devote yourselves to prayer; but then come together again, lest Satan tempt you through lack of self-control" (1 Cor. 7:3–5).

In fact, devout Christian married couples may have had sex more often than did the average pagan couple, because brides were more mature when they married and because husbands were less likely to take up with other women.

Sex Ratios and Fertility

ONE REASON ROMAN MEN so often married very young girls was their concern to be sure of getting a virgin. But an even more important reason was a *shortage of women.*[42] A society cannot routinely dispose of a substantial number of female newborns and not end up with a very skewed sex ratio, especially when one adds in the high mortality rate associated with childbirth in all ancient societies. Thus, writing in the second century, the historian Dio Cassius noted the extreme shortage of Roman women. In a remarkable essay, Gillian Clark pointed out that among the Romans, unmarried women were so rare that "we simply do not hear of spinsters. . . . There is not even a normal word for spinster."[43] As further evidence of the acute shortage of women, it was common for them to marry again and again, not only following the death of a husband, but also after their husbands had divorced them. In fact, state policy penalized women under fifty who did not remarry, so "second and third marriages became common,"[44] especially since most women married men far older than themselves. Tullia, Cicero's daughter "was not untypical . . . married at 16 . . . widowed at 22, remarried at 23, divorced at 28; married again at 29, divorced at 33—and dead, soon after childbirth, at 34."[45] Another woman was said to have married eight times within five years.[46] Apparently, there always was a considerable surplus of marriageable men.

The best estimate is that there were 131 males per 100 females in Rome, rising to 140 males per 100 females in the rest of Italy, Asia Minor, and North Africa.[47] In contrast, the growing Christian communities did not have their sex ratios distorted by female infanticide, on top of which they enjoyed an excess of women to men based on the gender difference in conversion.

This would have resulted in very substantial differences in overall fertility between pagans and Christians even had the average woman in each group had the same number of children. If women made up 43 percent of the pagan population of Rome (assuming a ratio of 131 males to 100 females), and if each bore four children, that would be 172 infants per 100 pagans, making no allowance for exposure or infant mortality. But if women made up, say, 55 percent of the Christian population (which may well be low), that would be 220 infants per 100 Christians—a difference of 48 infants. Such differences would have resulted in substantial annual increases in the proportion of the population who were Christians, even if everything else were equal.

But there are compelling reasons to accept the testimony of ancient historians, philosophers, senators, and emperors that everything else was *not* equal, that the average fertility of pagan women was so low as to have resulted in a declining population, thus necessitating the admission of "barbarians" as settlers of empty estates in the empire and especially to fill the army.[48] The primary reason for low Roman fertility was that men did not want the burden of families and acted accordingly: many avoided fertility by having sex with prostitutes rather than with their wives,[49] or by engaging in anal intercourse.[50] Many had their wives employ various means of contraception which were far more effective than had been thought until recently;[51] and they had many infants exposed.[52]

Pagan husbands also often forced their wives to have abortions—which also added to female mortality and often resulted in subsequent infertility.[53] Consider the instructions the famous Roman medical writer Aulas Cornelius Celsus offered to surgeons in the first century. Having warned that an abortion "requires extreme caution and neatness, and entails very great risk," he advised that the surgeon first kill the fetus with a long needle or spike and then force his "greased hand" up the vagina and into the uterus (there was no anesthesia). If the fetus is in a headfirst position, the surgeon should then insert a smooth hook and fix it "into an eye or ear or the mouth, even at times into the forehead, and then this is pulled upon and extracts the foetus." If the fetus was positioned crosswise or backward, then Celsus advised that a blade be used to cut up the fetus within the womb so it could be taken out in pieces. Afterward, Celsus instructed surgeons to tie the woman's thighs together and to cover her pubic area with "greasy wool, dipped in vinegar and rose oil."[54]

Given that this was the recommended technique used in an age before soap, let alone any effective treatment of infections, little wonder that abortions killed many women and left many survivors sterile. So why did they do it? Probably mainly because it usually was a man, not a pregnant woman, who made the decision to abort. It is hardly surprising that a culture that gave husbands the right to have babies exposed also gave them the right to order abortions. Roman law did advise husbands not to order their wives to abort without good reason, but there were no penalties specified. Moreover, the weight of classical philosophy fully supported abortion. In his *Republic*,[55] Plato made abortions mandatory for all women who conceived beyond the age of forty (in order to limit population growth) and Aristotle agreed, writing in his *Politics*, "There must be a limit fixed to procreation of offspring, and if any [conceive] in contravention of these regulations, abortion must be practiced."[56]

In contrast, consistent with its Jewish origins, the early church condemned abortion. The second chapter of the *Didache* (an early Christian text probably written in the first century) orders: "Thou shalt not murder a child by abortion nor kill them when born."

Both Plato and Aristotle linked their positions on abortion to threats of overpopulation, but that was not the situation in the Roman Empire in the days of early Christianity. Rome was threatened by a declining population and, consequently, there was much concern to increase fertility. In 59 BCE Julius Caesar secured legislation giving land to fathers of three or more children (he himself had only one legitimate child, but many bastards, one with Cleopatra). Cicero proposed that celibacy be outlawed, but the Senate did not support him. In 9 CE Augustus promulgated laws giving political advantages to men who fathered three or more children and imposing political and financial penalties on childless couples, unmarried women over the age of twenty, and upon unmarried men over the age of twenty-five. Most subsequent emperors continued these policies and Trajan even provided substantial subsidies for children.[57] But nothing worked. By the start of the Christian era, Greco-Roman fertility had fallen below replacement levels[58] so that by the third century CE there is solid evidence of decline in both the number and the populations of Roman towns in the West.[59]

Recently Bruce Frier contested the claim that Roman fertility was low, asserting that "no general population" has ever limited its fertility prior to modern times.[60] That contradicts considerable anthropological evidence, dismisses Roman concerns to increase fertility as groundless, ignores weighty evidence of "manpower" shortages, and ultimately misses the point. Perhaps even more remarkable is that following a great deal of discussion as to why powerful demographic methods such as Coale-Trussell models and the Gompertz relational fertility model need to be brought to bear, Frier then applied these sophisticated techniques to data based on *172 women* living in *rural Egypt* "during the first three centuries AD." He found that their fertility was high and then confidently extended this finding to "the Roman world."

Even if that were the case, even if Roman women had lots of kids, the fact that there was such a shortage of women in the empire seems sufficient to have produced the apparent population decline. And it most certainly gave Christians a significant advantage, not only in fertility, but also in producing substantial rates of conversion through marriage.

Secondary Conversions

As explained in chapter 4, conversion flows through social networks. Most people convert to a new religion because their friends and relatives already have done so—when their social ties to the religious group outweigh their social ties to outsiders. One such social tie is, of course, marriage. Some people convert after their spouses have done so or when they marry someone who already belongs to the religious group. However, the special intimacy of the marriage tie has given rise to a distinction between *primary* and *secondary conversion*. Those involved in *primary* conversions take a relatively active role in their shift of religious identity. Although their decision is supported and influenced by their attachments to others who already belong, in the end their choice is relatively freely made. *Secondary* conversion involves yielding to considerable pressure and having sufficient reluctance to convert so that the choice is not nearly so freely made. Secondary conversions are very common in Latin America today: wives join a Pentecostal Protestant congregation and eventually, after much effort, many of them succeed in getting their husbands to join as well. These men are secondary converts. Once they are active members of a Pentecostal church, many of these men become highly committed to their new faith, but the fact remains that they never would have joined had their wives not done so and then managed to bring them along.[61]

Secondary conversions of husbands were very common in early Christianity. And the major reason was the great prevalence of mixed marriages due to the great surplus of Christian women in a world suffering from a considerable scarcity of pagan brides. Many Christian girls had to marry pagan men or remain single, and for many pagan men, it was either a Christian bride or bachelorhood.

Both Peter and Paul accepted intermarriage. Peter advised women with unconverted husbands: "be submissive to your husbands, so that some, though they do not obey the word, may be won without a word by the behavior of their wives, when they see your reverent and chaste behavior" (1 Pet. 3:1–2). Paul put it this way: "If any woman has a husband who is an unbeliever, and he consents to live with her, she should not divorce him. For the unbelieving husband is consecrated through his wife, and the unbelieving wife is consecrated through her husband" (1 Cor. 7:13–14). Although Paul addresses both Christian husbands and wives, as Harnack reported, instances "in which the husband was a Christian, while his wife was a pagan . . . must have been infrequent."[62] And, although both passages suggest marriages made before the conversion of a spouse, there is abundant evidence that "marriages between Christians and pagans were common. . . . The church did not at first discourage this practice, which had its advantages: it might bring others into the fold."[63]

In fact, even if the spouse did not convert, there were the children! Even men who firmly remained unconverted seem usually to have agreed to having the children raised in the faith. The case of Pomponia Graecina, the aristocratic early convert mentioned in chapter 6, is instructive. It is uncertain whether her husband Plautius (who served as the first Roman governor of Britain) ever became a Christian, although he carefully shielded her from gossip, but there is no doubt that her children were raised as Christians. According to Marta Sordi, "in the second century [her family] were practicing Christians (a member of the family is buried in the catacomb of St. Callistus)."[64]

Had the church opposed mixed marriages it risked either a substantial rate of defection by women willing to give up their religion in order to marry, or accumulating a substantial number of unwed, childless Christian women who could contribute nothing to church growth. Moreover, everyone involved seems to have been very confident that the secondary conversions would be to Christianity, not to paganism. This confidence seems justified on the basis of plentiful evidence of Christian steadfastness even in the face of martyrdom. It also is consistent with modern evidence on the consequences of mixed marriages involving a spouse belonging to an intense religious group. For example, female Jehovah's Witnesses frequently marry outside their faith, but rarely does this involve their defection and often it results in the conversion of the spouse.[65] In fact, because there is so much religious intermarriage in the United States, Andrew Greeley has proposed the rule that in the case of mixed marriages, most often the less religious person will become a secondary convert by joining the faith of the more religious person.[66] The same rule applies even more fully to the religious upbringing of the children—that they will be raised in the faith of the more religious parent.

It would require extremely complex calculations to project the rise of Christianity solely on the basis of superior fertility, but the outcome of such a projection is easily seen: everything else staying the same, eventually, but inevitably, Christianity would have become the majority faith.

Conclusion

THE RISE OF CHRISTIANITY depended upon women. In response to the special appeal that the faith had for women, the early church drew substantially more female than male converts, and this in a world where women were in short supply. Having an excess of women gave the church a remarkable advantage because it resulted in disproportionate Christian fertility and in a considerable number of secondary conversions.

CHAPTER EIGHT

Persecution and Commitment

DURING THE SUMMER OF THE year 64, the emperor Nero sometimes lit up his garden at night by setting fire to a few fully conscious
Christians who had been covered with wax and then impaled high on
poles forced up their rectums. Nero also had Christians killed by wild
animals in the arena, and he even crucified a few. According to the
Roman historian Tacitus, Nero did these atrocities to escape blame
for the great fire that had destroyed parts of the city of Rome: "Nero
fastened the guilt and inflicted the most exquisite tortures on a class
hated for their abominations, called Christians by the populace."[1]
Among the victims may have been the apostle Peter and his wife,[2] as
well as the apostle Paul.

This chapter begins with brief descriptions of the major persecutions and explains why they occurred. Then it considers why so
many Christians knowingly and willingly accepted brutal martyrdom
rather than deny their faith. Finally, attention is given to why and
how, rather than destroy the church or even retard its growth, Roman
persecutions probably sped the rise of Christianity as the fortitude of
the martyrs amazed and deeply impressed many wavering Christians
as well as pagans.

Episodic Persecutions

NERO'S PERSECUTION OF CHRISTIANS lasted for several years and may have extended to other parts of the empire.[3] In the end it might have resulted in nearly a thousand deaths,[4] although Marta Sordi thought there were only "a few hundred"[5] victims, which seems more consistent with the very small total number of Christians at that time (see chapter 9). In any case, it was but the first episode of intermittent Roman attacks on Christians that continued to erupt in various places—"between 64 and 250 there were only isolated, local persecutions."[6]

A generation after Nero's excesses it is believed that the emperor Domitian (ruled: 81–96) murdered a number of Christians, including several members of his own family. Under the emperor Trajan (ruled: 98–117) Christianity was regarded as illicit, and we know that at least some provincial governors engaged in persecutions. Thus in 112, Pliny the Younger, governor of Bithynia, wrote to Trajan:

> For the moment, this is the line I have taken with all persons brought before me on charges of being Christians. I have asked them in person if they are Christians, and if they admit it, I repeat the question a second and third time, with a warning of punishment awaiting them. If they persist, I order them to be led away for execution; for, whatever the nature of their admission, I am convinced that their stubbornness and unshakeable obstinacy ought not go unpunished. . . . Now that I have begun to deal with the problem, as so often happens, the charges are becoming more widespread . . . for a great many individuals of every age and class, both men and women, are being brought to trial, and this is likely to continue.[7]

The emperor responded that Pliny had followed the right course, but that Christians "must not be hunted out; if they are brought before you and the charge against them is proved, they must be punished," but anonymous accusations should be ignored.[8]

Obviously, when Pliny wrote to Trajan, the complaint against Christians was not that they merely violated the law against unlicensed organizations. Rather, Pliny took it for granted that there was a specific law, or at least an imperial policy, that defined simply being a Christian as a capital offense—and Trajan concurred. Clearly this rule remained in force until it was repealed in about 260 by Gallienus, but nothing is known about when it was first promulgated. We do know it already was in force in about 95, when Domitian attacked Christians. The distinguished Harold Mattingly (1884–1964) thought it likely that the ban on Christianity originated with Nero and remained in force because "Romans of character and position continued to speak of Christianity as a horrible superstition and have no doubt that mere persistence in it merit[ed] death."[9] The equally admired G. E. M. de Ste. Croix (1910–2000) agreed, but suggested there never actually was a law against being a Christian, merely a precedent begun under Nero, which would have carried nearly as much weight as a specific law.[10]

Some admirers of the philosopher-emperor Marcus Aurelius (ruled: 161–180) deny that he was directly involved in persecutions of Christians.[11] In fact, he personally directed executions of Christians when consulted by provincial officials. Of course, it ought to be noted that during his reign a devastating plague swept through the Empire killing millions (see chapter 6). Searching for an explanation, the emperor came to agree with those who advocated that the plague was sent by the gods or at least condoned by them because they had been affronted and neglected. It was a very bad time to belong to a group notorious for refusing to sacrifice to the gods.

Thus in 177 a vicious persecution broke out in Lyons. Some historians think it may have been prompted in part by officials seeking to cut costs in obtaining victims for death in the arena.[12] In any event, mob attacks on Christians broke out and a number were beaten and then dragged before the magistrate. Since some of the accused were Roman citizens and therefore exempt from being killed by animals in the arena, the local officials wrote to Marcus Aurelius for guidance.

He responded that those who persisted in their Christianity were to be executed—the Roman citizens should be beheaded, the rest delivered to the wild beasts in the arena.[13] Thus did the "martyrs of Lyons" die, including the celebrated young woman Blandina. Initially she was "suspended from a stake, exposed as food to wild beasts." When the beasts ignored her she was taken down and subsequently subjected to "every torture, again and again." Then, "after the scourging . . . after the frying pan, she was at last thrown into a basket and presented to a bull. . . . Then she too was sacrificed, and even the heathen themselves acknowledged that never in their experience had a woman endured so many and terrible sufferings."[14]

In 202, a twenty-two-year-old Carthaginian noblewoman with a nursing infant fell victim to an edict by Emperor Septimus Severus (ruled: 192–211) that no new conversions to Christianity or Judaism would be tolerated, under pain of death. Along with four others, Perpetua was taken to the arena and scourged, then set upon by wild animals, and, when she still survived, was put to the sword.

These were sideshows compared with the bloody anti-Christian riot that broke out in Alexandria in 248. Over the previous several centuries, riots had resulted in the death of many Jews, and this was at least the third riot in the city's history during which pagan mobs "rampaged through the streets looting, burning, and destroying property belonging to Christians."[15] This seems to have gone on "for some time; whenever Christians appeared in public, night or day, they were liable to seizure, torture, and death."[16] Apparently the Roman officials did nothing to prevent the disorder.

Finally, the stage was set for empire-wide persecutions.

Imperial Persecutions

TOO OFTEN, HISTORIANS HAVE ignored the sincerity of pagans, misreading their casual forms of worship for indifference. But Rome was far more religious than other societies in the ancient world, and large numbers of Romans, especially those making up the political elite, sincerely believed that the gods had made Rome the great empire that it had become. That being the case, Christianity was an obvious affront to the gods, given that the church denied the existence of the gods and charged that to worship them was blasphemy. It was entirely logical to assume that for Rome to tolerate Christianity was to risk bringing down the displeasure of the gods upon its affairs. This might not have been an urgent matter during the heyday of the empire (except during a disaster such as a plague), but as Rome began to experience lasting bad times—economic recessions, political instability, and military misfortunes—it became a matter that no conscientious emperor could ignore. Even so, when the first major, empire-wide, Roman persecution of Christianity erupted in the middle of the third century, the initial concern did not merely reflect intolerance of Christianity, but a perceived need for a universal expression of pagan piety.

Persecution by Decius and Valerian

IN 249 GAIUS MESSIUS Decius was hailed as emperor of Rome by his army and, after he defeated his predecessor Philip in battle (in which Philip died), the Senate ratified Decius's claim to the crown. It could hardly have been a worse time to take the throne.[17] Invaders were making inroads all along the European frontiers, and the army, no longer manned by citizen soldiers, was becoming increasingly expensive and less effective.[18] The Roman army had never had superiority in terms of weapons or armor, but triumphed due to far superior training and discipline in battle.[19] This advantage had largely disappeared with the recruitment of "barbarian" troops. In addition, the economy was falling apart. Trade had collapsed and the prices of basic commodities were high and rising rapidly.[20] Taxes were soaring.[21] What was wrong and how could it be fixed?

Decius came to the conclusion that all Rome's troubles were of religious origin. His reasoning was as follows. For centuries the gods had smiled on and sustained an expansive and invincible Rome. But with the arrival of the many new religions, the traditional gods had been considerably neglected, and consequently they had in turn been neglecting Rome. The solution was obvious: a religious revival to regain the favor of the gods who had made Rome great!

The method was equally obvious: stage an unprecedented display of piety. So the famous edict was issued requiring that "all inhabitants of the Empire sacrifice to the gods, taste the sacrificial meat, and swear that they had always sacrificed"[22]—or that they regretted past neglect and promised future observance. In addition to seeking divine aid, Decius hoped that by returning to the traditional gods he also could reestablish a religious basis for a renewal of patriotism and civic-mindedness, persuading the people to be more willing to pay taxes and otherwise support the state.

Decius was not content to send a message to the Senate or even to circulate an edict to the appropriate provincial governors. In a remarkable break with custom, he directed his edict to all the people of the empire. Nor was he content with expressing his wishes; he demanded proof of fulfillment by requiring local magistrates to issue certificates to all persons and households verifying that the required sacrifice had been accomplished in their presence. Notice that Decius did not ask the people to pray, or to fast, or to confess, or to attend a praise meeting. In keeping with traditional Roman religious conceptions, his idea of a revival involved nothing but a quick, unemotional, ritual—as is obvious when one reads this certificate of compliance, typical of the dozens that have survived from Roman Egypt:[23]

> To the Superintendents of Sacrifices, from Aurelius Akis, from the village of Theadelphia, with his children Aion and Heras, all being of the village of Theadelphia. It was always our practice to sacrifice to the gods and now in your presence, in accordance with the regulations, we have sacrificed, have made libations, and have tasted the offerings, and we request you certify this.

[Below]

We, Aurelius Serenus and Aurelius Hermas, saw you sacrificing.

[Signed and dated]

Although the ban on Christianity was still in force, it would seem that initially Decius did not intend to persecute Christians. He did not seize church property. He did not ban worship services. He even allowed Christians to perform their religious rites while in prison awaiting trial. He simply "failed to understand why Christians could not offer a normal sacrifice in addition to worshipping their god in their own fashion."[24] It was only when Christians refused this "simple" request, and did so very loudly and in public, that the persecution began. At that point, Decius may well have come to hate Christians. Following the execution of Pope Fabian, Decius is quoted as saying, "I would far rather receive news of a rival to the throne, than another bishop in Rome."[25]

It should be noted that apparently the Jews were not persecuted although they surely did not comply with the edict either. Romans believed that one was forever obligated to honor the religion of one's ancestors, hence Jews were usually given an exemption from actions in violation with their ancestral faith. But the Romans were contemptuous of all who had abandoned their ancestral faith as, of course, all Christians had done, making their refusal to comply with the edict doubly offensive. So the round-ups began.

Clearly, the Roman prosecutors paid primary attention to church leaders.[26] The bishops of Rome and Antioch were tortured and executed almost at once. The bishops of Jerusalem and of Antioch died in prison. Efforts to arrest Dionysius in Alexandria and Cyprian in Carthage failed when both went underground. But some ordinary Christians also were seized, including harmless elderly women such as Apolonia of Alexandria, who had all of her remaining teeth smashed out before being burned alive.[27]

But for all of the ferocity of both officials and pagan onlookers, the persecution was a very hit or miss affair, probably in part because

Decius soon had to lead his army out to head off another serious invasion by Goths. In the subsequent battle, Decius was killed and his army was annihilated. His successor Valerian continued the persecution, again concentrating on the Christian elite. Some members of the imperial household were exposed as Christians and were sent in chains to do forced labor. Pope Sixtus was discovered in the catacombs beneath Rome and put to death. More bishops were executed—Cyprian of Carthage was found and martyred.[28] But no Christian victim came to a worse end than did Valerian himself, who led forces east to Edessa, lost a battle, and was taken prisoner by Persians who humiliated him, tortured him at great length, and after he died stuffed his skin with straw and kept it in a temple as a trophy.

With the death of Valerian, his son Gallienus, who had been serving with his father as co-emperor, took over. Historians disagree as to whether Gallienus was an effective emperor (like so many emperors, he was murdered by the army), but he earned a significant place in history by repealing all of the anti-Christian policies. Amazingly, dozens of accounts of this action written by modern historians of the early church offer no explanation of why he did it. Apparently few are aware that his wife, the empress Salonia, was a Christian![29] In any event, Gallienus inaugurated a long period of toleration during which the church expanded rapidly and many Christians rose to positions of power. Of this era, Eusebius wrote: "It is beyond our powers to describe in a worthy manner the measure and nature of that honor as well as freedom which was accorded [the church] by all men."[30] Then, in "about AD 296 a purge of Christians from army and Civil Service began—an ominous sign for the future; in 303 the Great Persecution broke out."[31]

The "Great Persecution"

HISTORIANS (MYSELF INCLUDED) HAVE long blamed the emperor Diocletian for initiating the "Great Persecution." That may be somewhat unwarranted. Both Diocletian's wife and daughter were Christians.[32] In addition, Diocletian had allowed Christians to build a large new church directly facing his palace (Diocletian resided in Nicomedia). Finally, he did nothing to upset the "peace of Gallienus" during his first twenty years on the throne.

The evidence would seem conclusive that this last bloody persecution mainly originated with Galerius as he rose to power; he succeeded Diocletian in 305. Galerius was "a fanatical pagan" and Diocletian "feared him."[33] In any event, Diocletian did give in to demands that Christians pay for the ills that had befallen the empire. Indeed, it was an era of more rapid imperial decline and even greater peril than had been faced by Decius. Large areas had been lost to barbarian invaders. As for internal affairs, Michael Rostovtzeff (1870–1952) offered this pithy summary:

> Hatred and envy reigned everywhere: the peasants hated the landowners and the officials, the city proletariat hated the city *bourgeoisie*, the army was hated by everybody. . . . Work was disorganized and productivity was declining; commerce was ruined by the insecurity of the sea and the roads; industry could not prosper, since the market for industrial products was steadily contracting and the purchasing power of the population was diminishing; agriculture passed through a terrible crisis. . . . Prices constantly rose, and the value of the currency depreciated at an unprecedented rate. . . . The relations between the state and the taxpayer were based on more or less organized robbery: forced work, forced deliveries, forced loans and gifts were the order of the day. The administration was corrupt and demoralized. . . . The most terrible chaos thus reigned throughout the ruined Empire.[34]

What could be done? Like Decius, Diocletian decided that the salvation of Rome lay in the hands of the gods. And, guided by Decius's prescription for revival, he too issued an edict requiring a general sacrifice. Of course, the Christians refused. So it was that on

February 23, 303, imperial soldiers marched into the church across from the palace, looted the altar plates and chalices, burned all sacred scriptures, and then demolished the building.[35] Then an edict was issued, perhaps by Galerius in Diocletian's name since it is thought that at this moment Diocletian was incapacitated "by a severe nervous breakdown, no doubt brought on by the strain of action that struck so many near to him."[36] This edict banned all Christian gatherings, ordered the seizure or destruction of all churches, required that all Christian scriptures be burned, barred Christians from public office or from appearing in court, and prohibited anyone from freeing a Christian slave. However, even if Diocletian did not originate this edict, eventually he did "preside over many trials and tortures in person."[37] In the case of a member of the imperial household named Peter, who was discovered to be a Christian, Diocletian had him "stripped, raised high, and scourged all over." Then salt and vinegar were poured on his wounds and he was "slowly roasted" alive.[38]

All told, approximately three thousand leaders and prominent members were executed, and thousands of others were sentenced to slavery and sent to the mines.[39] Even so, the edicts against Christians were ignored in some cities and, even more remarkably, rapid Christian growth continued! In fact, the large size of the Christian population by this time probably accounts for the fact that there was very little popular support for the persecutions. No mobs took part; no flood of informants came forth. Christianity had become "respectable."[40]

On his deathbed in 311, Galerius revoked all the decrees he had caused to have been issued against the Christians. He grumbled that the persecutions had been ineffective anyway, but he also ordered the Christians to pray for his recovery. The persecutions were over.

The total number of Christian fatalities resulting from the Roman persecutions is unknown. Frend's claim that the *total* killed in *all* anti-Christian persecutions amounted only to "hundreds, not thousands"[41] is surely wrong. Eusebius's *Martyrs of Palestine* is not a sound basis for estimating deaths even in that area, because it is primarily a memorial

Eusebius wrote about his friends who had died. Local tradition has it that the number of Christians martyred in the city of Alexandria between 303 and 311 came to 660.[42] Whatever the grand total, clearly the number who died was not sufficient to make any dent in the rapid growth of the Christian population. In 250 at the onset of Decius's persecution, Christians probably already made up nearly 20 percent of the populations of the major cities and in 303 when the "Great Persecution" began, at least 10 percent of the whole empire had become Christian, and Christians probably were a majority in the major cities. It would have required a gigantic bloodbath to destroy the church.

Christian Intransigence

FROM EARLIEST DAYS THROUGH the present, accounts of the persecutions focus on the martyrs, on those who displayed extraordinary courage to stand firmly in their Christian commitment through the most abominable tortures. These martyrs will take center stage here as well. But first it seems appropriate to acknowledge that very substantial numbers of Christians denied or renounced their faith when faced with such ordeals.[43] As Eusebius noted, "some indeed, from excessive dread, broken down and overpowered by their terrors, sunk and gave way."[44] It could hardly have been otherwise. Thus, during the persecution by Decius, many Christians performed the required sacrifice, and many others paid bribes to obtain certificates that they had sacrificed. Many more did these same things during the Great Persecution.

In the eyes of the church leaders the two acts were equivalent and both of them placed the individual outside the Christian community. But even if they had lacked the courage needed to stand firm, the overwhelming majority wanted to regain the kingdom and asked to be readmitted. This was achieved by a "judicious blend of severity and mercy. . . . Forgiveness, after repentance attested by heavy penance, was the rule."[45]

In any event, primary attention must be paid to those many Christians whose incredible intransigence has stood as a beacon of inspiration to Christians ever since. However, given the snippets of brutality included thus far, there is little point in offering more examples of martyrdom. It seems sufficient to point out that a few were beheaded, that being regarded as the humane sentence, but the rest were put through such an amazing array of tortures that it seems beyond credibility that *anyone* persisted—especially since most could have escaped at any point along the way simply by defecting. But again and again they bore it all. In fact, the church fathers were forced to frequently forbid voluntary martyrdom in an effort to prevent zealous members from presenting themselves to the authorities. Even so, surviving documents reveal "an astonishingly large number of volunteers."[46]

The Basis of Martyrdom

FOR CENTURIES CHRISTIAN MARTYRS were revered for their faith and courage. Then along came social scientists to reassure us that normal people never would have done such things, that the martyrs were mentally ill and their apparent feats of courage were rooted in *masochism*—the love of pain. Hence, their capacity to endure "the most excruciating torments . . . can only be explained as the result of the building up of a pathologically intense, ecstatic mental state. . . . The masochistic phenomena are the most remarkable characteristic of the early martyrdoms."[47] Subsequently, a study produced at the prestigious University of Chicago Divinity School drew very favorable reviews by claiming: "One of the elements of the morbid desire for martyrdom was the abnormal enjoyment of the pain which it involved. This phenomenon is known as 'masochism.' . . . Clearly, the voluntary surrender of one's self to the experience of martyrdom, when it is known that the most exquisite tortures were involved, is *prima facie* evidence of the presence of the tendency towards masochism."[48] Other psychologists and psychiatrists have offered different explanations of martyrdom, including self-hypnosis and sensory overload,[49] but all of them persist in seeing voluntary martyrdom as proof of irrationality if not outright psychosis. In doing so, they fail to recognize that there were substantial rewards attached to martyrdom. While these were not sufficient to motivate most Christians to endure torture, they seem to have been the primary motivation of those Christians who did.

Early in the rise of Christianity there developed a "cult of saints" that offered amazing rewards for martyrdom—not all of them postponed until the life after death. Extraordinary fame and honor were achieved by the martyrs. They often were lionized before they even were sentenced, let alone put to the test. Consider Bishop Ignatius of Antioch. In about 110 CE, he was arrested and sentenced to die in the arena at Rome. Then began his long, leisurely journey to Rome, accompanied by ten Roman soldiers. All along the way, local Christians came out to meet and greet him as a "conquering hero,"[50] to shower him with food and gifts, and to display their admiration for his steadfast refusal to compromise. Hence, as noted in chapter 6, his only real fear was that influential Christians in Rome would arrange to have him pardoned. For, as he wrote in his letter asking them not to interfere: "Suffer me to be the food of wild beasts, which are the means of making my way to God."[51]

But for all his eagerness to make his way to God, Ignatius anticipated glory in this life as well because martyrs were carefully remembered and their feats of endurance were constantly retold and celebrated by the living. Consider the example of Polycarp, bishop of Smyrna, who was burned alive in about 156. Afterward his charred bones were retrieved by local Christians and each year thereafter they gathered where his bones were buried "to celebrate with great gladness and joy the birthday of his martyrdom."[52] Indeed, we know the names of so many of the early Christian martyrs precisely because their stories were carefully recorded for posterity.

Finally, of course, the martyrs usually suffered their agonies in public settings and that too helped to fulfill their hopes of making a lasting contribution to their faith. Eugene and Anita Weiner have presented this compelling portrait of the "rewards" of martyrdom:

> Every effort was made to ensure that the group would witness the events leading up to the martyrdom. It was not uncommon for fellow Christians to visit the accused in their cells and to bring food and clothing to make the imprisonment more bearable. There even were celebrations to dramatize the forthcoming test of faith. These supportive efforts brought comfort and help in a most trying situation, and had a latent message for the martyr-designate, "what you do and say will be observed and recorded." In a word, it will be significant and passed down in ritual form and celebration.
>
> All martyrs were on stage. Some suffered remorse and recanted but those who could take the pressure were assured of eternity, at least in the memories of the survivors. What was distinctive about martyrdom was not only the promise of reward in the hereafter, but the certainty of being memorialized in this world. The martyr saw before dying that he or she had earned a place in the memories of the survivors and the liturgy of the church.[53]

Notice that many Christians made their identity as such obvious by flocking to meet or to serve those facing martyrdom and that the authorities seem to have ignored them. This was in keeping not only with the usual policy to not seek out Christians—as Trajan told Pliny—but also with the primary Roman tactic of persecuting the church top-down. The Romans assumed that the bishops and clergy were the active elements of the church and should they be destroyed, the masses of ordinary Christians would simply drift away. This was no doubt true of the pagan temples and perhaps for the Oriental faiths. But it was a misreading of Christianity where behind each bishop, priest, and deacon there was a line of lay persons ready and able to replace them. Indeed, the church was an independent social sphere wherein high status was entailed by positions within the group, whatever one's status outside—a separate world wherein a high city official and a slave could meaningfully call one another "brother." And within this Christian status sphere, no higher rank could be accorded than that of a "holy martyr."

Martyrdom and Credibility

LET US NOW SHIFT our attention from the martyrs to their audiences. The fundamental problem facing all religions is one of credibility. Ultimately, all religions require an act of faith—that adherents be willing to believe in a supernatural realm that is not directly observable. Hence many religions feature testimony from those who have had a personal experience that supports the claims about the supernatural. Typically these involve an appeal for supernatural help that appears to have been answered: tales of miraculous survival, of recovery from injury or illness, sometimes even of victory in battle. In this way people offer others proof that their religion "works," and hence that its fundamental premises must be true.

Of all the proofs and all of the testimonials, nothing approaches the credibility inherent in martyrdom. How could mere mortals remain defiant after being skinned and covered with salt? How could anyone keep the faith while being slowly roasted on a spit? Such performances seemed virtually supernatural in and of themselves. And that was the effect they often had on the observers. Christian viewers could "see" that the hand of God was on the martyrs. Many pagans also were amazed: the distinguished physician Galen wrote of Christians that "their contempt of death . . . is patent to us every day."[54] Accounts of martyrdom make frequent mention of pagans having gained respect for the faith from having observed, or even having taken part in, the torture of martyrs. The pagan onlookers knew full well that they would not endure such tribulations for their religion. Why would so many Christians do so? Were they missing something about this strange new faith? This sort of unease and wonderment often paved the way for new conversions.

Conclusion

IT SEEMS FITTING TO quote the introductory sentences written by Eusebius in *The Martyrs of Palestine*[55]—his account of some who suffered during the Great Persecution. "These holy martyrs of God . . . accounted a horrible death more precious than a fleeting life, and won all the garlands of victorious virtue. . . . And the spirits of the martyrs, counted worthy of the kingdom of heaven, are come to the assembly of the prophets, and are precious."

Thus were the Roman authorities overmatched.

CHAPTER NINE

Assessing Christian Growth

THROUGH THE CENTURIES, MANY HISTORIANS have supposed that in order to achieve the size that it must have reached by the fourth century, Christianity had to grow at an incredible rate. The authoritative German historian Adolf von Harnack (1851–1930) agreed with St. Augustine (354–430) that "Christianity must have reproduced itself by means of miracles, for the greatest miracle of all would have been the extraordinary extension of the religion apart from any miracles."[1] Can that be true?

As with nearly all discussions of Christian growth, no actual numbers were offered by Harnack and he made no attempt to calculate what rate of growth actually would have been required to achieve this "miracle." Had he done so, he would have discovered that no miracle was needed, albeit exponential growth curves often seem miraculous to those unfamiliar with this form of arithmetic.

In any event, it seems appropriate to pause here to create a plausible statistical model of Christian growth in the Roman Empire. It is impossible to extend such a model to include growth in the East since there is far too little to go on, but it must be kept in mind that there probably were *substantially more Christians in the East than in the West* at all points in time until after the Muslim conquests (see chapter 12). The validity of the model of

Christian growth in the empire is tested in various ways and then the geography of Christian growth is examined: how did it spread across the empire? When geography is combined with the model of growth, it is possible to estimate the probable size of the Christian population in the city of Rome over time and thereby to more fully appreciate the emergence of Christians as a powerful political force.

Ancient Statistics

ONE OF THE MAJOR impediments to writing ancient or medieval history is the lack of reliable statistics. Not only are numbers very seldom provided in the sources, the few that are given usually are absurd. For example, Josephus (37–100 CE) claimed that when the Romans conquered Jerusalem in 70 CE, 1,100,000 residents of the city were killed and another 97,000 were enslaved.[2] In truth, there probably never were even 40,000 people in Jerusalem, and many of them are known to have escaped. To further confuse matters, some numbers in the ancient sources probably are accurate: Josephus may well have been correct in reporting that 960 Jewish zealots, including men, women, and children, perished at Masada.[3]

One reason ancient statistics are so few and implausible is that although "[officials] actually were interested in statistics . . . the literary-minded persons who wrote history . . . were not interested."[4] A second reason is that until modern times, writers often did not mean for their numbers to be taken literally, but simply used them to suggest "many" or "few"—Fulcher of Chartes (1059–1127), for example, surely knew that six million French knights had not set out on the First Crusade (a number larger than the entire population of France).

It is impossible to know how many people actually saw Jesus or heard him preach. Although one prominent scholar has claimed that everyone in Palestine had been evangelized by Jesus during his ministry, or more than eight hundred thousand Jews,[5] the total could not have been more than a fraction of that number since Jesus spent nearly his entire ministry in and around the tiny villages of a small portion of Galilee, itself a small province. Of course, the issue is not how many heard, or even heard of Jesus, but how many accepted him as Christ. Fortunately, we do have a very plausible report of the total number of Christians soon after the Crucifixion. Acts 1:15 reads: "In those days Peter stood up among the brethren (the company of persons was in all about a hundred and twenty)."

That total is consistent with the early days of most new religious movements since it seems that conversion is a person-by-person phenomenon that only slowly gains momentum through social networks. Sudden, mass conversions simply don't happen. It is true that a generation ago many social scientists believed in the reality of mass conversions—they wrote of "mass hysteria," "herd instincts," "mob psychology," "collective madness," and the like. But no one could cite a certified example of such phenomena. Consequently, even social scientists have relegated such notions to the dustbin of useless concepts.[6] Thus the claim in Acts 2:41 that in response to a public sermon by Peter, "about three thousand souls" were baptized that day and added to the community of Christians, must be dismissed as hyperbole. Even had so many come forward (which is extremely unlikely), the primary result would have been three thousand wet Jews and pagans—far more was involved in becoming an authentic Christian than hearing a sermon and getting a quick dunk in the river. Ignoring this claim of a mass baptism, and giving credence only to Acts 1:15, is consistent with Howard Clark Kee's estimate "that participation in the Jesus movement in Gentile cities during the first generation numbered in dozens, or scores at most."[7] I propose that there were a total of about a thousand Christians in the empire in the year 40.

There are no other relevant numbers, plausible or not, offered in the New Testament. Still, it is possible to infer that the total number of Christians grew slowly until late in the second century from the fact that there are no indications of any church structures.[8] "The earliest church building in the city of Rome that can be dated [was] built in the mid-third century."[9] Instead, Christians still met in one another's homes: "there might be several meeting places in a city, but the space for each congregation cannot have been large."[10] Thus the distinguished Robert Wilken suggested that by about the year 150 "Christian groups could be found in perhaps forty or fifty cities within the Roman Empire. Most of these groups were quite small, some numbering several dozen people, others as many as several hundred. The total number of Christians within the empire was probably less than fifty thousand."[11]

A century later, the Christian population may have amounted to about 2 percent of the population of the empire, or slightly more than a million members, according to Robert Lane Fox.[12] Many historians have proposed an estimate of the size of the Christian population for the year 300, and all are in close accord at about 6 million.[13] And it is generally agreed that by the year 350, Christians were in the majority—if barely— amounting to somewhat more than 30 million who were at least nominal Christians. These milestone estimates appear in table 9.1.

A Model of Growth

IS IT POSSIBLE TO discover a simple model of Christian growth that fits this set of milestones? Yes. Starting with a thousand Christians in the year 40, and assuming that Christianity grew at a rate of 3.4 percent per year, the result is a projected model of growth that hits each milestone nearly exactly, as can be seen in table 9.1.

Table 9.1: Christian Growth in the Roman Empire
(Growth Projected at an Annual Rate of 3.4 Percent)

Year	Number of Christians	Milestone	Percent of Population* Estimates
40	1,000	—	—

Year	Number of Christians	Milestone	Percent of Population* Estimates
50	1,397	—	—
100	7,434	—	—
150	39,560	(-50,000)	0.07
180	107,863	—	0.18
200	210,516	—	0.35
250	1,120,246	(1 million)	1.9
300	5,961,290	(6 million)	9.9
312	8,904,032	—	14.8
350	31,722,489	(+30 million)	52.9

Based on a stable imperial population of 60 million.

It would be hard to imagine a closer matchup between the various historical estimates and this model. Of course, were it available, the actual Christian growth curve probably would be somewhat lumpy, some years falling a bit below 3.4 percent and some other years exceeding that rate. But the extraordinary overall fit suggests that any departures must have been very modest and short-lived. Keep in mind that this is a growth rate, not a conversion rate. It is made up of conversions and fertility, minus deaths and defections.

This projection shows that there need not have been anything miraculous about Christian growth. Rather, many contemporary religious bodies, including the Jehovah's Witnesses and the Mormons, have sustained well-documented growth rates as high as or higher than 3.4 percent a year for many decades.[14] As for objections that there were far more than a thousand Christians in the year 40,[15] if there were more, then the needed rate of growth would have been substantially lower. For example, had there been ten thousand Christians in the year 40, a rate of growth of only 2.65 percent would have sufficed to pass the thirty million mark by 350. But that rate produces a model that is extremely out of line with the intervening milestones, making it far less plausible. In any event, there was plenty of time for Christianity to achieve its growth by way of the conventional network process.

In addition to meeting the milestones, this model based on 3.4 percent growth so closely matches several available bodies of actual data that it must be granted considerable credibility. For example, the projections agree very closely with estimates made by Roger S. Bagnall of the percent of Christians in the population from the year 239 through 315 based on an analysis of the percentage of Christian names among those appearing in Egyptian documents.[16] A second basis of comparison is even more compelling. Carlos R. Galvao-Sobrinho[17] has published data on the number of Christian epigraphs appearing on gravestones in the city of Rome, broken down into twenty-five-year groupings.[18] A time series analysis using the Roman data and the projections of the Christian population of the empire, beginning in the year 200 and ending at 375 resulted in an incredibly close matchup. As can be seen in the graphed Z scores shown in figure 9.1, the two curves are virtually identical and produce an almost perfect correlation of .996.

It should be noted that, of course, this curve could not have kept rising indefinitely, and it soon must have decelerated as the number of potential converts declined. Furthermore, not only is it impossible to convert more than 100 percent of a population, in this instance significant numbers of residents of the empire never converted to Christianity. Many Jews did not; organized paganism lingered for centuries; and millions of people in rural areas seem never to have gone beyond merely adding Jesus to their pantheon of gods (see chapter 15). Consequently, the complete growth curve would resemble the S-shaped curve that has been found to so typically apply to the diffusion of various phenomena through a population.

The Geography of Christian Growth

ALTHOUGH JESUS PREACHED IN the villages and from the hillsides in Galilee, within twenty years after the Crucifixion, early Christianity had become overwhelmingly an urban movement. Paul's mission-

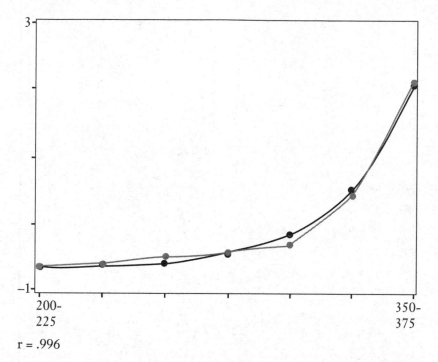

Figure 9.1: Christian Epigraphs in Rome and Membership Projections
Z Scores

• PROJECTION   • EPIGRAPHS

r = .996

ary journeys took him to major cities such as Antioch, Corinth, and Athens, with occasional visits to smaller communities such as Iconium and Laodicea, but no mention is made of him ever preaching in the countryside. In fact it was centuries before the Christians devoted much effort to converting the rural peasantry. By then, of course, many rural people had been Christianized by friends and neighbors who had returned from a sojourn in a city where they had become Christians. However, for the first several centuries it is important to assess the Christian growth curve as heavily weighted to the cities, for that fact maximized the visibility as well as the local impact of Christian communities. Both factors would have been enhanced by the intense congregational nature of Christianity—whatever their numbers, they gathered regularly and coordinated their participation in civic life.

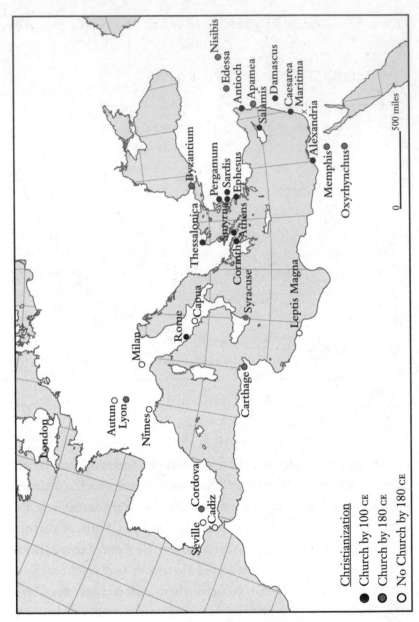

Map 9.1: Christianization

The model of Christian growth applies to the empire overall, but even among the cities Christianity did not spread at the same rate everywhere. There was a Christian group in Damascus before 34 CE since Paul was on his way there to persecute them when he had his roadside conversion experience. But there was no Christian congregation in Carthage until the second century and none in Milan or Capua until the third. These differences reflect that Christianity radiated from Jerusalem and its spread was greatly influenced by how far a place was from there. The exception was Rome, which may have had Christians as soon as Damascus (see chapter 4).

As noted, we have little or nothing to go on to plot the spread of Christianity to the East. Fortunately, von Harnack devoted immense effort to tracing the arrival of Christianity across the West, assembling all available evidence of Christian activity in the empire, province by province and city by city. He prepared two lists. The first includes all places that had a Christian community by the end of the first century; the second includes those places that had a Christian community by 180 CE—with the complete sources carefully reported for each. Von Harnack's work remains unsurpassed and all of the atlases mapping the spread of Christianity rely on him. As might be expected, his lists are quite complete for the larger cities, while necessarily being far more hit or miss for the smaller places. Consequently, map 9.1 is limited to all thirty-one cities of the empire having estimated populations of thirty thousand or more as of the year 100 CE[19] (having been razed by the Romans in 70, Jerusalem barely existed at this time). The following characteristics of cities influenced when they first gained a Christian congregation.

As is obvious, *cities closer to Jerusalem* (see X on map) tended to have a Christian congregation sooner than did those farther away. Of the seventeen cities within a thousand miles of Jerusalem, twelve (71 percent) had a church by the year 100 and all of them did by the year 180, while of the fourteen cities more than a thousand miles from Jerusalem, only one (7 percent) had a church by 100 and eight (57 percent) had none by 180 (gamma = .950).

Port cities tended to be the first to gain a Christian group. The reason is that in those days travel by boat on the Mediterranean was far faster than was travel by land, and in this sense port cities were much closer to Jerusalem than were inland cities. Consequently, of the fourteen port cities, nine (64 percent) had a congregation by the year 100, and only two had no congregation by 180. Of the seventeen nonport cities, only four (24 percent) had a congregation by 100 and six had no congregation by the year 180 (gamma = .598).

As noted in chapter 7, Christian growth was more rapid in the *Hellenic* than in the Roman cities, in part, perhaps, because Hellenic women had far more to gain from becoming Christians than did Roman women. Of nineteen Hellenic cities, twelve (63 percent) had a congregation by 100 and all of them did by 180, while only one (8 percent) of the twelve non-Hellenic cities had a congregation that soon and eight (67 percent) had none by 180 (gamma = .928). It is true, too, that Hellenic cities were closer to Jerusalem, but even when that factor is controlled statistically, a very strong Hellenic effect remains.

As noted in chapter 4, cities also had Christian congregations earlier if they had a temple devoted to Cybele or Isis, as the Oriental faiths seem to have prepared the way. As also noted in chapter 4, Christianity established a local congregation sooner in cities having a substantial Jewish Diasporan community.

Finally, the *larger* the city, the sooner it was likely to have had a Christian congregation. Of the eight larger cities, six (75 percent) had a congregation by 100 CE, and all did so before 180. Of the twenty-three smaller cities, seven (30 percent) had a congregation by 100 CE and eight (35 percent) still had no Christian congregation by 180.

Christianizing the City of Rome

THE GROWTH OF URBAN Christianity is best illustrated by the case of Rome, which was by far the largest Roman city and was among the first to have a Christian congregation. By making some additional assumptions, it is possible to very roughly estimate the number of Christians in the city of Rome over time, as shown in table 9.2. Keep in mind that the population of the empire was overwhelmingly rural—the best assumption is that only about 4.5 million (7.5 percent) of the 60 million residents of the empire lived in places having populations of a thousand or more.[20] Given the estimated population of Rome was about 450,000,[21] that means that 10 percent of the urban population lived in Rome, which is consistent with the fact that even most major Roman cities had fewer than fifty thousand residents. According to all historians, in early years nearly all Christians were urbanites. For the calculations shown in the table, it was assumed that 90 percent of Christians were urban until the year 200. For the year 250 it was assumed that 75 percent of Christians were urban, and the calculation for the year 300 assumed that 50 percent were urban. The Christian population of the city of Rome was then calculated by assigning the appropriate portion of Christians from table 9.1 (see p. 156) under these assumptions. To avoid giving a false impression of precision, the totals have been rounded, and it should also be understood that these statistics are offered only as illustrative since they are far less trustworthy than the overall growth curve.

Table 9.2: Estimated Christian Population of the City of Rome

Year	Number	Milestone	Percentage of Rome's Estimated Population
100	700	<1,000	0.15
150	3,600	—	0.8
200	19,000	20,000	4.2
250	78,000	—	17.3
300	298,000	—	66.2

The historical literature offers only two estimates of the Christian population of Rome to serve as milestones in table 9.2. L. William Countryman suggested that the Christians in Rome "could not have numbered much less than 1,000" at the end of the first century,[22] which is entirely consistent with the estimate of seven hundred. Robert M. Grant proposed that the Christians numbered about twenty thousand in Rome the year 200,[23] which is very close to the projection of nineteen thousand for that year. The more important point is that even if the estimates in table 9.2 were reduced by half, the Christian presence in Rome would still have loomed very large by the year 300.

In about the year 200, the early church father Tertullian boasted that "nearly all the citizens of the cities are Christians."[24] This was an exaggeration, but only by about a century since by the year 300 Christians were a substantial majority in Rome and probably in many other cities as well. But even by 200, Christianity was not just another insignificant sect in Rome! Unlike pagans, Rome's nineteen thousand Christians were well organized. They belonged to relatively small, intense congregations and they may even have had their own neighborhoods. Christians could easily be mobilized vis-à-vis local affairs, which greatly amplified their numbers. Thus the size and effectiveness of the Christian communities may well have been a factor in the persecution that fell upon them in 250 and again a half a century later. Keep in mind too that the Great Persecution took place mainly in the East—Diocletian's capital was Nicomedia (now Izmit in northwestern Turkey)—and there was little or no effort to confront what by then may have been a Christian majority in the city of Rome.

Conclusion

THE FUNDAMENTAL PURPOSE OF this chapter was to impose needed discipline on the subject of Christian growth—to substitute an arithmetic of the plausible and possible for unfounded speculations and wild assumptions. It certainly is not "proven" that Christianity grew at a rate of 3.4 percent a year, but a growth curve based on that rate is very *plausible* because it matches the credible milestones available on the matter and is in extremely close agreement with known measurements such as the increasing percentage of Christian gravestones in Rome. The rate also is quite *possible* in that it has been achieved or exceeded by some contemporary religious movements for which very accurate data are available.

Possession of these estimates of the Christian population for the first three centuries brings needed discipline to the history of this era. If nothing else, it forces recognition of how tiny and fragile the church was for such a long time. Thus, for example, the concern and antagonism expressed in the Gospels about "the Jews" must be interpreted as the sentiments of a group totaling no more than three thousand (in 70 CE) and who had reason to fear a group numbering in the millions—too often critics have anachronistically reversed the relative sizes.

Conversely, too often histories of Roman politics late in the third and early fourth centuries have tended to ignore the very large and rapidly growing Christian communities, especially in the major cities—both as they caused anxiety in ruling circles and as they offered a potential source of powerful political support. Hence, although a great deal has been written about how much the church benefitted from Constantine's favor, far too little been written about how the support of millions of Christians benefitted Constantine by solidifying his power and ending decades of constantly changing rule.

PART III

Consolidating Christian Europe

CHAPTER TEN

Constantine's Very Mixed Blessings

FLAVIUS VALERIUS AURELIUS CONSTANTINUS—COMMONLY known as Constantine I—was emperor of Rome from 306 until his death in 337. The Orthodox Catholic Church recognizes Constantine as a saint, the Roman Catholic Church does not. While this reflects substantial differences in evaluation, both Eastern and Western Catholics have long esteemed the emperor's contributions to the security, prosperity, and power of Christianity, and writers in both traditions routinely refer to him as "Constantine the Great."

However in later, more skeptical centuries, many historians echoed the attack on Constantine made by the emperor Julian the Apostate (331–363) during his quixotic and brief effort to reestablish paganism: Julian denounced Constantine as an insincere and self-indulgent tyrant. Thus generations of scholars rejected the authenticity of Constantine's conversion, dismissed his support of Christianity as cynical, and condemned the unity he attempted to impose on the church. A leading critic was Jacob Burckhardt (1818–1897), who wrote: "Attempts have been made to penetrate the religious consciousness of Constantine and to construct a hypothetical picture of the changes in his religious convictions. Such efforts are futile. In a genius driven without surcease by ambition and lust for power there can be no question of religiosity; such a man is essentially unreligious, even if he pictures himself standing in the midst of a churchly community. . . . [A]ll of his energies, spiritual as well as physical, are devoted to the great goal of domination."[1] Then Burckhardt summed up Constantine as "a calculating politician who shrewdly employed all available physical resources and spiritual powers to the end of maintaining himself and his rule."[2]

This chapter opens by noting the reasons why recent historians have returned to a more complimentary view of Constantine's conversion and his commitment to Christianity. It then assesses the benefits Constantine heaped upon the church—his massive church-building program all across the empire, as well as the privileges and power he conferred upon the clergy. Then it will be seen that Constantine's imposition of doctrinal unity on Christianity created a tradition of crushing dissent. Remarkably, all the while he led religious intolerance within Christianity, he extolled tolerance of paganism. Finally, Constantine's embrace of Christianity was interpreted in Persia to mean that all local Christians were potential traitors during wars with the empire, thus initiating decades of bloody persecution.

Constantine

AFTER GENERATIONS OF SKEPTICISM, it is now widely accepted once again that Constantine did appeal to the Christian God for aid in his battle at Milvian Bridge against Maxentius, his rival for the throne. It also is accepted that his subsequent conversion was real,[3] not pretended, as too many historians claimed for too many years. If Constantine delayed his baptism until shortly before his death, that was not proof of his previous lack of piety, but was such a common practice that even St. Ambrose had done so. The reason for such delays was that, since baptism washed away all prior sins, with death close at hand there would be little time to pile up a new set of infractions requiring a lengthy period of atonement after death. But if Constantine's sincerity has been restored, it remains that historians have been lacking in curiosity as to why Constantine appealed to the Christian God in the first place, rather than to Jupiter or another of the traditional gods of Rome.

One reason Constantine did so is that at this time everyone must have been very aware of Christianity since it probably was the faith of the majority of residents of Rome and many other major cities. Few could have failed to notice the thousands of conversions taking place as the exponential curve of Christian growth accelerated. But of perhaps even greater importance is that Constantine's mother Helena, to whom he was very close and who often shared his household, was a Christian—probably of long standing. Few historians are willing to accept T. G. Elliott's[4] claim that she actually raised Constantine as a Christian, but neither do most any longer accept Eusebius's claim that Constantine converted Helena.[5] No one knows when Helena became a Christian, but it was well before her son won at the bridge since while Constantine was still holding court at Trier, she donated her house to the archbishop for use as a church. For a long time this gift was denied by scholars, but recent archeological work has confirmed it.[6] Moreover, in light of Helena's remarkable Christian activism during her son's reign, it must be supposed that Constantine was well versed in Christianity when he decided to have his soldiers place the Chi-Rho sign (the monogram for Christ) on their shields. To then have won a smashing victory cinched it.

It also is very suggestive that prior to the battle, as Constantine's troops approached, the people of Rome "became restless and hostile," causing Maxentius to fear treachery.[7] If the calculations in chapter 9 are anywhere near the truth, it may well be that it was the Christians of Rome whose "restlessness" was an expression of their support for Constantine; they probably knew his mother was a Christian and they most certainly knew that he had long since ended the Great Persecution and provided restitution for Christian losses in the area he controlled.[8] What is perhaps even more surprising is that Constantine seems to have been the first to recognize what powerful political support the Christians could provide.

All of this fits with reports that when Constantine entered Rome following his victory, crowds surged into the streets to greet him "with a joy almost all genuinely felt," not only because he came in triumph, but also "as a Christian."[9] Moreover, Constantine's refusal to honor tradition by ascending the Capitol to perform the expected sacrifices to the pagan gods must have exhilarated the Christian throngs in the city.

In light of Constantine's subsequent personal involvement in Christian affairs, it is obvious that he "believed sincerely that God had given him a special mission."[10] The depth and extravagance of this conviction was fully displayed in his funeral—all carefully scripted by Constantine himself. As his health was failing, Constantine had an extraordinary shrine built to "perpetuate for all mankind the memory of the Saviour's Apostles."[11] Inside, he built twelve monuments, one for each of the twelve, with a space reserved in the middle to receive his coffin. Thus, his funeral was conducted with Constantine's remains situated with memorials to six apostles on each side of his coffin—symbolic of his self-conception as being the Thirteenth Apostle.[12]

Perhaps the two most important things to remember about Constantine are that he was among the most powerful of all the emperors and that he took his "obligations" to Christianity as God-given and necessitating his personal attention and leadership.

Building the Church

THE CLAIM THAT CONSTANTINE "built" the church must be taken literally, in that he immediately launched an immense church-building program all across the empire. When Constantine came to power, Christians had very few churches as such, and most of those they did have were "private dwellings converted for the purpose," many of them having been apartment houses.[13] Within two weeks after the battle of Milvian Bridge, Constantine donated an imperial villa just outside

Rome to the church and began work to transform it into the great hall that came to be known as the Church of St. John Lateran. Soon imposing churches, modeled on imperial throne halls, had been erected all across Rome—including St. Peter's Basilica[14] (in the sixteenth century, Constantine's original St. Peter's was rebuilt). According to tradition, Constantine had St. Peter's placed above the grave of the saint for whom it is named. Although this claim was, of course, dismissed in more "enlightened" times, it has turned out to be true.[15]

When Constantine constructed his new capital on the site of the old city of Byzantium on the Bosporus, he was equally prolific in constructing great churches. But nowhere was his building more extensive than in the Holy Land, once his mother Helena had explored Jerusalem. At the age of eighty, Helena went on a pilgrimage to Jerusalem in about 326 where she interviewed local residents concerning their traditions as to the location of important sacred sites. Thus she learned that it was believed that Christ's tomb had been buried beneath a temple of Venus, built by the emperor Hadrian in 130. What followed was one of the very earliest archeological undertakings, well told by the church historian Eusebius (ca. 263–339) in his *Life of Constantine*.[16]

Eusebius began by noting that apparently Hadrian's engineers had been "determined to hide" the tomb "from the eyes of men. . . . After expending much labor in bringing in earth from outside, they covered up the whole place; then having raised the level of the terrain, and after paving it with stone, they entirely concealed the sacred grotto beneath a great mound." On top of this the Romans had constructed "a dark shrine of lifeless idols."

Eusebius continued: "Constantine gave orders that the place should be purified. . . . And as soon as he issued the orders, these deceitful constructions were torn down . . . images and demons and all, were overthrown and utterly destroyed . . . one layer after another was laid bare . . . then suddenly, contrary to all expectation, the venerable and sacred monument to our Savior's resurrection became visible, and the most holy cave." What the excavators seem to have uncovered was a tomb carved into the rock that fit the New Testament description.

Constantine's response was to have the great Church of the Holy Sepulcher constructed over the site, and Eusebius, by then bishop of Caesarea, was present at its consecration. Constantine also had great churches built in Bethlehem and on the Mount of Olives. In response to all of this, it soon became popular all across the empire to make a pilgrimage to Jerusalem, and Helena became a saint in both the Orthodox and Roman churches.

Constantine's building program was not limited to Rome, Constantinople, and the Holy Land. In Italy he also built large churches in Ostia, Albinum, Capua, and Naples, and he built churches at Cirta (in Africa), at Trier, at Antioch, and at Nicomedia as well.[17]

In addition to building so many imposing churches, Constantine donated "an extraordinary amount of property" to the church.[18] Thus, "massive grants of land and property were made . . . [and an] avalanche of precious metals."[19] For example, Constantine granted the churches in Rome all the rent from various landed estates, amounting to "more than four hundred pounds of gold per year."[20] Eventually his gifts to the church were so immense that they "laid the foundations for the church's enduring wealth in later centuries."[21]

But Constantine's major contribution was to elevate the clergy to high levels of wealth, power, and status. Keep in mind that, contrary to popular belief, Constantine did not make Christianity the official religion of the empire. "What he did was to make the Christian church the most-favoured recipient of the near-limitless resources of imperial favour."[22] Legal privileges and powers were lavished on the clergy. Episcopal courts were given official status. The clergy were exempted from taxes and civic duties. And bishops "now became grandees on a par with the wealthiest senators . . . [and were] expected to take on the role of judges, governors, great servants of state."[23] As a result there was a sudden influx of men from aristocratic families into the priesthood which transformed the church into a far more worldly and far less energetic institution, as will be seen in chapter 17. Such a transformation may well have happened anyway once Christianity had become the dominant religion. But Constantine made this shift occur very rapidly and to a remarkable degree.

Unity and Conformity

FROM EARLIEST DAYS, CHRISTIANITY was marked by theological disputes, some of them of sufficient importance as to produce schismatic movements. For example, after having been excommunicated from the church in about the year 144 for proposing to dispense with all Jewish aspects of the faith, Marcion successfully led a dissenting church that lasted for about another three hundred years. At almost the same time, Montanus founded an extremely ascetic variation on traditional Christianity. It achieved a considerable following in the East and seems not to have fully died out until the eighth century. Another such movement was Manichaeism, founded by the "prophet" Mani around the middle of the third century. It had the remarkable distinction of having been declared a heresy by both the conventional Christian church and by the Zoroastrian state church of Persia. In addition to these three major schismatic groups, there were a number of minor "Gnostic" groups such as the Valentinians. But although these groups were rejected by the Christian establishment, they were not persecuted at that time—except, perhaps, by Roman officials who mistook them for conventional Christians (although the Gnostics were never unwilling to make the required sacrifices to the gods).

Perhaps the early church did not persecute heresy only because it lacked the means to do so. If so, Constantine provided the means in his unrelenting efforts to create unity within the church. As Eusebius reported: "to the Church of God he paid particular attention. When some were at variance with each other in various places, like a universal bishop appointed by God he convoked councils of the ministers of God. He did not disdain to be present and attend during their proceedings. . . . Then such as he saw able to be prevailed upon by argument and adopting a calm and conciliatory attitude, he commended most warmly, showing how he favored general unanimity, but the obstinate he rejected."[24] Indeed, for them, persecution loomed. It all began within six months after Constantine's great victory at Milvian Bridge.

The Donatist Controversy

At the beginning of his reign, Constantine assumed there "was one united body of Christians."[25] Events in North Africa soon challenged that assumption. At issue was the status of clergy, including bishops, who were *traditores* who had deserted the faith and collaborated with Roman officials during the Great Persecution—the many who had handed over their copies of scripture to be burned and some who had even betrayed other Christians to the oppressors. A major group of North African bishops held that these men were expelled from the church and that any and all sacraments performed by these clerics were therefore invalid. Of central concern here was the consecration of new bishops. The leader of this faction was Donatus (315–355), the bishop of Carthage, and hence the group became known as the Donatists. In opposition were church leaders, including *traditores*, who held that penance was available for all sins and therefore, having undergone the required acts of penance, the *traditores* were not only forgiven, but restored to full communion, and thus to office.

Seeking to settle this dispute, Constantine called a council at Arles. At this point Constantine only ruled in the West, so only Western bishops attended—including three from Britain. In addition to passing many measures, including a ban on gladiatorial matches, the bishops excommunicated Donatus. This was ignored in Africa where the Donatists continued to dominate. So, in 317 Constantine sent troops to Carthage to enforce the council's verdict. But the Donatists stood firm and in 321 Constantine withdrew his forces. Eventually, it was left to St. Augustine, as bishop of Hippo, to propel Roman forces to crush the Donatists. Even so they continued in the more remote communities into the seventh century.

By far the most important aspect of the case of the Donatists is that it marked the first use of repressive state power on behalf of the church. Constantine's proclamation against the persecution of Christians would now apply only to *some* Christians. The affair also acknowledged the state as a legitimate arbiter of church policies. Constantine wanted to settle disputes within the church and maintain unity. But, just as he did not tolerate disobedience to his political rule, he was quite willing to destroy those who opposed the religious positions he decided to favor. All of these negative aspects of the new relationship between church and state were greatly reinforced during the battle over Arianism.

Arianism

A theological dispute had long been brewing among church intellectuals, especially in North Africa and the East. Was Jesus equal to God, having always existed? Or was he created by God, and hence there was a time when Jesus did not exist? Tradition stood with the always existing Son. But there were a number of dissenters, many of them bishops who had studied under Lucian of Antioch (240–312), a renowned theologian who was martyred at the end of the Great Persecution. Eventually Arius (250–336), a priest in Alexandria, emerged as the intellectual leader of this group who believed in the creation of Jesus, and as the matter became a major dispute within the church, the doctrine became known as Arianism. Eventually the conflict became so intense (somewhat inflamed by antagonisms concerning priests and bishops who had collaborated during the persecution) that Constantine took the matter in hand.

In 325 the emperor assembled a council at Nicaea (near Constantinople). Having been urged to do so by Constantine, the council adopted a formal creed, or statement of orthodox belief. Known as the Nicene Creed, it is still repeated in many Christian churches, and it explicitly rejects Arianism, if in somewhat convoluted form. In addition, Arius and several of his supporters were denounced and exiled and all copies of Arius's writings were ordered to be burned. In 336, with Constantine's concurrence, church officials decided to re-admit Arius to communion, but he died on the way to Constantinople (some believe he was poisoned).

Thus the position was adopted that there could be no dissent and only one Christianity. This was a legal, not a sociological, position—as the latter holds that there never is complete agreement on religious matters and dissent is inherent in the variation in religious tastes that exists among members of any population (see chapter 2). Hence Constantine's interference ensured a future of nasty persecutions of dissenting Christians.

Pagan Coexistence

ALTHOUGH CONSTANTINE PLAYED A central role in repressing all Christian dissent, he was remarkably tolerant of paganism throughout his reign. Constantine neither outlawed paganism nor did he condone persecution of non-Christians. In fact, although Constantine subsidized and gave official standing to the Christian church, he continued some funding of pagan temples.[26] As for charges that he encouraged Christian mobs to destroy pagan temples, a claim that originated with the early Christian historian Eusebius who used it to show how "the whole rotten edifice of paganism" rapidly came crashing down as part of God's plan, "it is very likely that Eusebius report[ed] everything he knew of temple destruction," yet he could offer only four instances[27] and only one of these seems a legitimate case. The other three involved temples of Aphrodite, which featured ritual prostitution.

More significant even than his toleration of pagan temples, Constantine continued to appoint pagans to the very highest positions, including those of consul and prefect (see chapter 11). In addition, pagan philosophers played a prominent role in his court,[28] and depictions of the sun god appeared on his coins. Indeed, "Constantine directed his most ferocious rhetoric" not against pagans, but against Christian dissidents: Donatists, Arianists, Valentinians, Marcionites, and the "Gnostic" schools.[29] Partly for these reasons, ever since Gibbon's time, leading historians have dismissed Constantine's conversion as an insincere political gambit. But, the most recent historians[30] now regard Constantine's conversion as genuine and cite the persistence of pagan elements in his reign as examples of his commitment to religious harmony. Of critical importance are two edicts issued by Constantine soon after he defeated Licinius to reunite the empire. Both stressed peaceful pluralism.

The *Edict to the Palestinians* is notable for the pluralism of its language. In it, Constantine repeatedly referred to God, but never mentioned Christ, using "phrases common to Christians and pagans alike [which] is consistent with the search for a common denominator that was the hallmark of his religious policy."[31] But, it is the *Edict to the Eastern Provincials* that fully expresses Constantine's commitment to accommodation and his rejection of coercive forms of conversion. He began with a prayer, invoking "the most mighty God" on behalf of "the common benefit of the world and all mankind, I long for your people to be at peace and to remain free from strife." He went on: "Let those who delight in error alike with those who believe partake of the advantages of peace and quiet. . . . Let no one disturb another, let each man hold fast to that which his soul wishes, let him make full use of this." He continued, "What each man has adopted as his persuasion, let him do no harm with this to another. . . . For it is one thing to undertake the contest for immortality voluntarily, another to compel it with punishment." Finally, Constantine condemned "the violent opposition to wicked error . . . immoderately embedded in some souls, to the detriment to our common salvation."[32]

Thus, in both word and deed Constantine supported religious

pluralism, even while making his own commitment to Christianity explicit. In fact, during Constantine's reign, "friendships between Christian bishops and pagan grandees" were well known, and the many examples of the "peaceful intermingling of pagan and Christian thought may . . . be thought of as proof of the success of [Constantine's] . . . policy" of consensus and pluralism.[33]

The Persian Massacres

THUS FAR THE FOCUS has been on the role of Constantine vis-à-vis Christianity and paganism within the empire—a subject that has received lavish scholarly coverage. But hardly any attention has been paid to his role in provoking an extraordinary slaughter of the Christians in Persia. Oddly, although the number who died in these massacres probably greatly exceeded the number who died in all the persecutions by the Romans put together, this aspect of Christian history has been almost totally ignored. *Encyclopedia Britannica* covers the Persian massacres in one sentence in its biography of the Persian ruler Shāpūr II and in two sentences in its history of Iran. In his magisterial *Martyrdom and Persecution in the Early Church*, W. H. C. Frend gave the Persian martyrs no mention at all. John Fox (1517–1587) devoted half a page of his *Book of Martyrs* to "Persecutions of the Christians in Persia," but told nothing of the events involved and is content to fill most of his space with a letter supposedly sent to the King of Persia by Constantine, urging him to embrace his local Christians. If the letter is authentic, it was odd of Constantine to have written it since Rome and Persia had been bitter enemies for centuries. In any event, Constantine's embrace of Christianity was the primary factor prompting the Persians to massacre Christians. It happened like this.

Shāpūr II was proclaimed as King of Persia at his birth in 309, and after a period of regency, he took command and ruled until his death in 379. In 337, the year that Constantine died, Shāpūr sent his forces across the Tigris River to attempt to reconquer Armenia and Mesopotamia from the Romans. Shāpūr was fully aware of the special status Constantine had conferred upon Christianity, and consequently he feared that the Persian Christians were potential traitors in conflicts with Rome. These fears were exploited by Zoroastrian priests who whispered to Shāpūr "that there is no secret" that the Christian bishops do not reveal to the Romans.[34]

As a response, the king imposed a double tax on Christians, but it did not cause the flood of defections he had anticipated. So, on Good Friday 344, Shāpūr had five bishops and one hundred Christian priests beheaded outside the walls of the city of Susa, and the massacres began.[35] For the next several decades "Christians were tracked down and hunted from one end of the empire to the other."[36] Before it ended, soon after Shāpūr died, tens of thousands had been killed— one source estimated that thirty-five thousand were martyred,[37] and another that "as many as 190,000 Persian Christians died."[38] Nevertheless, substantial numbers of Persian Christians survived and the faith soon reestablished itself as a major presence.

Conclusion

THE CREATION OF A rich, powerful, and intolerant Christian church was the primary legacy of the conversion of Constantine. Far better that he had remained a pagan who opposed religious persecution, while allowing Christian diversity to flourish.

Chapter Eleven

The Demise of Paganism

RECENTLY, IT HAS BECOME FASHIONABLE to admire the old pagans and to wish they had managed to withstand the rise of Christianity. Jonathan Kirsch began his recent book, *God Against the Gods*, with a brief catalogue of lurid episodes of religious intolerance, and then proceeded to regret that the emperor Julian failed to undo Constantine's boost of Christianity and restore the empire to paganism: "it is tantalizing to consider how close he [Julian] came to bringing the spirit of respect and tolerance back into Roman government and thus back into the roots of Western civilization, and even more tantalizing to consider how different our benighted world might have been if he had succeeded."[1] Similarly, in his prizewinning study of Hellenism, Glen Bowersock wrote that "polytheism is by definition tolerant and accommodating."[2] And Ramsay MacMullen claimed that paganism was "no more than a spongy mass of tolerance and tradition."[3]

This view of religious history was initiated during the so-called Enlightenment by Edward Gibbon (1737–1784), who claimed that the triumph of Christianity was produced by "intolerant zeal."[4] Pagans were unable to survive this militant Christian onslaught because they were, in Gibbon's oft-quoted phrase, imbued with "the mild spirit of antiquity."[5] Should anyone object to this claim by citing pagan persecutions of Christians, Voltaire (1684–1778) confided that the persecution of Christians had never amounted to much[6] and Gibbon agreed, charging that Christian "writers of the fourth and fifth centuries" exaggerated the extent of the persecutions because they "ascribed to the magistrates of Rome the same degree of implacable and unrelenting zeal which filled their own breasts against heretics." In truth, Gibbon continued, the Roman magistrates "behaved like men of polished manners . . . [and] respected the rules of justice."[7] There is not a hint here about Christians being burned on poles to light up Nero's garden.

Even many generations of Christian writers, going as far back as Eusebius (275–339), proudly claimed that once armed with the authority of the state the church had quickly smashed all the pagan temples and crushed all opposition. Until recently, not even major Christian historians have objected to Gibbon's conclusion that the Christianization of Rome was due to "the irresistible power of the Roman emperors"[8] in concert with the repressive nature of the Roman Catholic Church. As the distinguished historian Peter Brown summed up: "From Gibbon and Burckhardt to the present day, it has been assumed that the end of paganism was inevitable, once confronted by the resolute intolerance of Christianity; that the interventions of the Christian emperors in its suppression were decisive."[9]

But it isn't true!

As Peter Brown continued: large, active pagan communities "continued to enjoy, for many generations, [a] relatively peaceable . . . existence." All that really happened is that they slowly "slipped out of history."[10]

During the past generation many distinguished historians[11] not only have reaffirmed the reality of the pagan persecutions of Christians; they also have greatly qualified and minimized claims concerning the Christian coercion of pagans. To this has been added renewed interest in the political aspects of Constantine's rule (especially through the remarkable studies by H. A. Drake). Consequently, we now know that a period of relative tolerance and tranquility prevailed between Christians and pagans during Constantine's reign. The

Christians were, of course, growing rapidly in this era, but without substantial recourse to coercive methods. Enter Julian the Apostate. An examination of Emperor Julian's anti-Christian efforts reveals how it fully rekindled Christian fears of renewed persecutions and thereby empowered the most militant elements in the early church. Even so, post-Julian efforts by this Christian faction to settle "old scores" with pagans resulted in only sporadic and scattered efforts at coercion and reprisal—far less extensive, much less severe, and not nearly as effective as had been thought. Nor was coercion of pagans backed by the state. Consider this clause from the Code of Justinian (529–534): "We especially command those persons who are truly Christians, or who are said to be so, that they should not abuse the authority of religion and dare to lay violent hands on Jews and pagans, who are living quietly and attempting nothing disorderly or contrary to law."[12] As this suggests, there had been some attacks by Christians on pagans, but the overall record shows that in this same era pagan mobs also had attacked Christians from time to time. Far more surprising is how few attacks of either kind seem to have occurred.[13]

Consequently, and despite the prevailing historical view, paganism wasn't quickly obliterated. Instead, it seeped away very slowly. The Academy at Athens did not close until 529, and "even in most Christian Eddessa . . . organized communities of pagans were still sacrificing to Zeus-Hadad in the last quarter of the sixth century."[14] When early Muslim forces threatened Carrhae (Harran) in 639, pagans still so outnumbered Christians in the city that all members of the delegation sent to negotiate with the Arabs were pagans.[15] In fact, there were still many active pagans and functioning temples to the gods in Greece and further east as late as the tenth century.[16] Moreover, for a considerable time in many parts of the empire, including some major cities, the prevailing religious perspectives and practices consisted of a remarkable amalgam of paganism and Christianity. Finally, paganism never fully died out in Europe; it was assimilated by Christianity. For example, many pagan festivals continued to be celebrated and many of the gods lingered under very thin Christian overlays. Although the medieval church went to extreme lengths to stamp out various Christian heresies such as the Cathars, it essentially ignored the persistence of paganism.

Now for the details.

Coexistence

CONSTANTINE WAS NOT RESPONSIBLE for the triumph of Christianity. By the time he gained the throne, Christian growth already had become a tidal wave of exponential increase.[17] If anything, Christianity played a leading role in the triumph of Constantine, providing him with substantial and well-organized urban support. And although historians long reported bitter outcries by pagans against Constantine's support of Christianity, the best recent scholars now agree that there is no evidence of such protests[18] and propose that even those pagans most directly involved regarded the emperor's favors to the church as a "bearable evil."[19]

Well they might have, for as was recounted in the previous chapter, Constantine was very tolerant of paganism. Not only did he fail to suppress the temples, he continued to appoint some pagans to high office (see table 11.1, p. 193) while repeatedly advocating religious tolerance. This policy was continued by "the refusal of his successors for almost fifty years to take any but token steps against pagan practices."[20] And a public culture emerged that mixed Christian and pagan elements in ways that seem remarkable, given the traditional accounts of unrelenting repression. A newly famous example is a calendar prepared in 354 for an upper-class Roman.[21]

The calendar was created by a prominent artist who later fulfilled commissions for Pope Damasus, and it is likely that many such calendars were circulated. As with Catholic calendars ever after, this one noted all of the festivals of the church and commemorated the burial dates of important popes. But it also included illustrated sections consisting of "representations of those rites of the Roman public cult associated with each month." Careful examination of the calendar confirms that the Christian and pagan elements are not discordant elements, but, as Peter Brown put it, "form a coherent whole; they sidle up to each other."[22]

Indeed, a sort of Christo-paganism was prevalent well into the fifth century, and probably later. In Ravenna during the 440s, the bishop expressed his dismay that "the new birth of the year is blessed by outworn sacrilege" in reaction to the participation of "the most Catholic princes" of the city in pagan rites involving their dressing as "the gods of Rome" and comporting themselves before a huge audience in the Hippodrome.[23] In similar fashion, not even St. Augustine could convince his flock in Hippo that such matters as bountiful crops and good health were not, in effect, subcontracted to pagan gods by the One True God,[24] as Christians in Hippo continued to regard it as both legitimate and valuable to perform pagan rites. In many parts of Europe, the use of paganism as magic has continued into the modern era.[25]

Unfortunately, the era of toleration that existed under Constantine was misrepresented by early Christian writers, particularly Eusebius, who wanted to show that the emperor was the chosen instrument to achieve God's will that all traces of paganism be quickly stamped out and the One True Faith established as the Church Triumphant. It may have been an effective polemic, but it was spurious history and, worst of all, as we have seen, it has been avidly seized upon by those eager to place the church in the worst possible light. In truth it was not Constantine or his immediate successors who reinstituted religious persecution, but the last pagan emperor—the one whom Jonathan Kirsch wishes had won out.

Julian's Folly

FLAVIUS CLAUDIUS JULIANUS, NOW known as Julian the Apostate, had only a brief (361–363) and quite disastrous rule as emperor. Despite that, he has become a virtual saint among antireligious intellectuals. Edward Gibbon complained[26] that Julian's many virtues have been "clouded" by the "irreconcilable hostility" of his Christian enemies who despised him for his "devout and sincere attachments to the gods of Athens and Rome."[27] Two centuries later, Gore Vidal turned Julian's life into an heroic novel. Throughout, the central theme has been that while Julian did seek to revive the vigor of paganism, he did so in a tolerant spirit. The truth is quite different.

Julian was ostensibly raised as a Christian, but some of his prominent tutors were pagans and they steeped him in the Greek classics.[28] Under their tutelage, Julian became a puritanical,[29] ascetic, and fanatical[30] pagan, who had been initiated into several of the mystery cults, including the Eleusinian mysteries[31] and probably Mithraism[32] as well. Julian was careful to comport "himself publicly as a Christian while worshipping the pagan gods,"[33] until he took the throne. Once installed as emperor, Julian loudly revealed his contempt for those he reviled as "Galileans" whose "haughty ministers," according to Gibbon, "neither understood nor believed their religion"[34] and at once set about trying to restore paganism as the state-supported, dominant faith.

Not wanting to create new martyrs, Julian did not initiate the bloody persecution of Christians à la Nero or Diocletian, but he did condone the torture of several bishops, exiled others, and ignored the "summary executions that seem to have taken place in large numbers in central and southern Syria during [his] reign."[35] Thus there was no imperial response when the "holy virgins [in Heliopolis] were rent limb from limb and their remains thrown to the pigs."[36] When knowledge that a pagan emperor now ruled prompted pagans in Alexandria to torture the city's Christian bishop, to tear him limb from limb, and to then crucify "many Christians," Julian's main concern was to obtain the dead bishop's library for himself.[37]

In a gesture that H. A. Drake compared to "a schoolboy thumbing his nose at his teachers,"[38] Julian revived the widespread celebration of blood sacrifices, sometimes involving a hundred cattle at a time, a practice that had long been outlawed in response to Christian influence. In addition, Julian cut off state funding of the churches and subsidized the temples. He replaced Christians with pagans in high imperial offices (see table 11.1). In an action that was far more significant than it might appear to modern readers, Julian made it illegal for Christians to teach the classics. This meant that upper-class parents had to choose between sending their offspring to be instructed by pagans or deny them the opportunity to acquire "the language, the looks, the innumerable coded signals that were absorbed unconsciously with classical *paideia* [or education, without which] Christian children would not have been able to compete in the elite culture of classical antiquity, as Julian knew full well."[39]

But, as Drake noted, the deepest of all the "wounds [Julian] was able to inflict, despite a relatively short tenure," was to revive Christian anxieties that another era of vicious persecution lay ahead. "Christians at the time . . . had no assurance that another Julian was not in the offing, and they could plausibly fear that worse was yet to come."[40] Consequently, "Julian was a blessing" for those Christians who opposed pluralism. As Drake summed up: "The effect of Julian's efforts was to polarize Christians and pagans, to remove the middle ground that traditional culture had previously provided, while at the same time lending credence to militant fears of a revival of persecution."[41] Julian's friend and admirer Liabius agreed that Julian "refused the use of force, but still the threat of fear hung over [the Christians], for they expected to be blinded or beheaded: rivers of blood would flow in massacres, they thought, and the new master would devise new-fangled tortures, the fire, sword, drowning, burial alive, hacking and mutilation seemed child's play. Such had been the behaviour of his predecessors and they expected his measures to be more severe still."[42]

Persecution and Persistence

ALTHOUGH HE RULED FOR only eighteen months and was killed during battle in a foolish campaign against the Persians, Julian's name still terrorized Christians a generation later.[43] However he was not replaced by another pagan emperor, although his favorite Procopius tried to take the throne, naming himself emperor at Constantinople late in 365. But Procopius was deserted by the army and executed as a rebel, so it was Jovian who managed to take the throne. Jovian was a Christian who undid some of Julian's anti-Christian actions, but he ruled for only a year before being succeeded by Valentinian in the West and by his brother Valens, who ruled in the East. Although Valentinian was a devoted Christian, he also was quite tolerant[44] and continued to appoint many pagans to high office. Valens was a rather fanatical Arian Christian who persecuted non-Arian Christians from time to time, but who also appointed many pagans.

Nevertheless, in the wake of Julian's campaign for paganism, the church was able to obtain statutes forbidding certain pagan activities. In three edicts issued during 391–392, Theodosius I banned public and private sacrifices to the gods, not only blood sacrifices, but also "such pagan devotions as sprinkling incense on altars, hanging sacred fillets on trees and raising turf altars."[45] However these prohibitions were so widely ignored that each of the next two emperors, Arcadius and Justinian, reasserted the ban. Pagans obeyed to the extent of no longer conducting massive public animal slaughters, but commitment to paganism remained open and widespread.[46]

It is important to recognize that paganism was not merely a set of superficial practices and only half-believed myths—or, as Lactantius put it, "no more than worship by the fingertips."[47] In past work I have been as guilty as most early church historians of underestimating the depth of paganism. Indeed, late fourth and fifth century pagans often are portrayed as little more than "nostalgic antiquarians." But, in fact, theirs was an active faith "premised upon the conviction that the world was filled with the divine, and that proper sacrifice brought the human into intimate communion with the divine."[48] Although the rapid and extensive Christianization of the empire showed that pagans were very susceptible to conversion by their friends and relatives, the failure of legal prohibitions to dent paganism demonstrated that coercion was no greater deterrent to commitment to the gods than it had been when used against commitment to the One True God. Moreover, imperial efforts to actually suppress paganism by force were far less sustained and far less vigorous than has long been claimed. Consider that well into the fifth century, men who were openly pagans were still being appointed as consuls and prefects as were many more who kept their religious preference obscure—something Christians had no reason to do (see table 11.1). As late as the sixth century, temples remained open in many parts of the empire,[49] and some survived into the tenth century.[50]

In the post-Julian era, the public persistence of paganism did not reflect imperial tolerance, so much as imperial pragmatism. Emperors often grumbled that their edicts against paganism were ignored. One imperial letter complained that "Provincial governors set aside imperial commands for the sake of private favors, and they openly allow the [Christian] religion which we [emperors] properly venerate to be openly disturbed, perhaps because they themselves are negligent."[51] The emperor Honorius charged that laws against paganism were not enforced because of the "sloth of the governors . . . [and] the connivance of their office staffs."[52] However the emperors carefully did not crack down on those provincial governors who justified their inaction on grounds that enforcement of edicts against paganism would create levels of public discontent that "would seriously disrupt the collection of taxes in the province."[53] Hence, in 400 CE the emperor Arcadius rejected a proposal to destroy the temples in Gaza, remarking "I know that the city is full of idols, but it shows [devotion] in paying its taxes. . . . If we suddenly terrorize these people, they will run away and we will lose considerable revenues."[54] Roger Brown suggests that persistent paganism served the emperor especially well, as cities would "have been all the more punctual in paying their taxes, if they needed to preserve . . . their ancestral religious practices" from imperial intervention.[55]

It even is questionable whether most emperors expected their various edicts involving Christianity and paganism to be fully observed. For example, when urged to do so by the bishops, Constantine outlawed gladiatorial combats. But when some Umbrian towns petitioned him for permission to celebrate the imperial cult with a festival that would include gladiatorial combats, Constantine granted their request. In similar fashion, Constantius issued an edict to close all pagan temples immediately. Then, in virtually the same breath he advised the prefect of Rome to care for and sustain the temples around the city. During a subsequent visit to Rome, Constantius toured these temples and expressed his admiration for them.[56] For the fact was that even well into the fifth century "a considerable section of the population of the Roman empire, at all social levels, remained unaffected" by Christianity. "They [remained] impenitently polytheistic, in that the religious common sense of their age, as of all previous centuries, led them to assume a spiritual landscape rustling with invisible presences—with countless divine beings and their ethereal ministers."[57]

In the end, of course, the pagan temples did close and Christianity became, for many centuries, the only licit faith, although most peasants and members of the urban lower classes seem never to have been fully Christianized. Even so, to the extent that Europe was Christianized, it didn't happen suddenly nor did it involve substantial bloodshed; the latter was mainly limited to conflicts *among* Christians which sometimes resulted in military action against various heretical movements.[58]

The Decline of Paganism

GIBBON DATES THE "FINAL destruction of Paganism" to the reign of Theodosius (379–395), noting that this "is perhaps the only example of the total extirpation of any ancient and popular superstition; and may therefore deserve to be considered, as a singular event in the history of the human mind." And, of course, this extirpation occurred because "Rome submitted to the yoke of the Gospel."[59] But as with so much else reported by Gibbon, it simply isn't so. Consider one fact alone: Theodosius, the emperor who, according to Gibbon, extirpated paganism, appointed nearly as many men who were openly pagans as he did Christians to the positions of consuls and prefects, as can be seen in table 11.1.

Table 11.1: Religious Affiliations of Men Appointed as Consuls and Prefects, 317–455

Reign	Christians	Pagans	Unknown	Number
Constantine (317–337)*	56%	18%	26%	55
Constantinus & Constans (337–350)*	26%	46%	28%	43
Constantius (351–361)*	63%	22%	15%	27
Julian (361–363)**	18%	82%	0%	17
Valentinian (364–375)**	31%	38%	31%	32
Valens (364–378)**	39%	25%	36%	36
Gratian (375–383)	50%	11%	39%	44
Valentinian II (383–392)**	32%	32%	36%	19
Theodosius (379–395)	27%	19%	54%	83

Reign	Christians	Pagans	Unknown	Number
Arcadius & Honorius (395–423)**	34%	12%	54%	161
Theodosius II & Valentinian III (408–455)**	48%	4%	48%	157

* Computed from Barnes, "Statistics and the Conversion of the Roman Aristocracy" (1995).
** Computed from von Haehling (1978) in Barnes, 1995.

This table has often been referred to earlier in the chapter, but here is the appropriate place to consider it in detail. The initial coding was done by Raban von Haehling in 1978. Subsequently, T. D. Barnes corrected von Haehling's statistics through the reign of Constantius (351–361) to eliminate some duplications when the same man was appointed several times. Although Barnes's figures are undoubtedly more accurate, they resulted in no fundamental reinterpretations, and there are no grounds not to use von Haehling's original findings for the reign of Julian and later.

Reading across the table, there seem to be three major patterns. First, except narrowly during the reign of Constantine and by a greater margin among those appointed by Constantius, men known to be Christians were not in the majority, and this held for the first half of the fifth century as well. Second, Julian did discriminate against Christians, although not entirely. Third, if it can be assumed that men whose religious affiliation is unknown were unlikely to have been Christians, then the decline of pagan influence and power was very slow indeed.

Many have argued that paganism held its own far longer among the upper classes and the educated than among persons of lesser rank.[60] But that is mostly inferred from the known paganism of many persons of rank and the assumption that Christianity's primary appeal was to the lower classes. However since it is now recognized that Christianity had as much or more appeal to the upper classes as to the lower, that inference is unjustified.[61] Rather, what table 11.1 more likely demonstrates is that paganism died slowly in all classes and, as it did, the upper classes became increasingly discreet about their religious identity, seeking to maintain their positions and their access to imperial favor.

And that brings into view a major factor in the Christianization of the empire: *opportunism*. From the time of Constantine, with the very brief exception of Julian's reign, the imperial throne was in Christian hands and very likely to remain there. Although identifiable pagans continued to be appointed to high political offices, their prospects were on the downward trend. In addition, the many powerful and increasingly lucrative positions in the church were closed to them. Understandably, many ambitious individuals and families chose to convert. As Roger Brown put it, "A groundswell of confidence that Christians enjoyed access to the powerful spelled the end of polytheism far more effectively than did any imperial law or the closing of any temple."[62] Even many pagan philosophers broke ranks, some of them becoming leading bishops of the church.[63]

Assimilation

THE WORD PAGAN DERIVES from the Latin word *paganus*, which originally meant "rural person," or more colloquially "country hick." It came to have religious meaning because after Christianity had triumphed in the cities, most of the pagans were rural people. However, even in the cities, as already noted, an elaborate mixture of Christianity and paganism flourished for centuries. As for rural people, most of them seem never to have been fully Christianized, in that they transplanted their familiar gods, sacred places, rites, and holidays into Christianity. As MacMullen put it: "The triumph of the church was not one of obliteration but of widening embrace and assimilation."[64]

The assimilation of paganism reflected several things. First of all, once established as the official faith of the empire, Christian leaders soon adopted a "trickle down" theory of conversion.[65] It was sufficient that the upper classes in an area acknowledged the authority of the church and then to wait for their example to eventually trickle down the ranks until the peasants were Christians too. But the peasants tended to respond to Christianity as they always had to the appearance of various new gods within paganism—to add the new to the old, rather than to replace it. Hence Jesus and various saints were simply added to the local pantheon. As was written in the Icelandic *Landnánabók*, Helgi the Lean "believed in Christ, but invoked Thor in matters of seafaring and dire necessity."[66]

A second basis for the assimilation of paganism was overt church policy. In a letter dated 601 and preserved by the Venerable Bede,[67] Pope Gregory the Great advised Abbot Mellitus, who was setting out to missionize Britain: "[I] have come to the conclusion that temples of the idols among that people should on no account be destroyed. . . . For it is certainly impossible to eradicate all errors from obstinate minds at one stroke." Instead, the pope recommended that altars and sacred relics should be placed in the pagan temples which would transform them into Christian edifices. The same policy was applied to the other pagan sites. "The hundreds of magical springs which dotted the country became 'holy wells,' associated with a saint, but they were still used for magical healing and for divining the future."[68] The famous healing shrine just outside Alexandria, dedicated to the goddess Isis, underwent an elaborate transformation into a Christian healing site when the remains of two martyrs were placed inside. The same process of assimilation was applied to the plentiful sacred groves, rock formations, and other pagan sites. People continued to visit these traditional sites for the original reasons, even if these sites now took on Christian coloration, although many of the visitors continued to direct their supplications to the old gods.[69]

Traditional pagan ways for celebrating holidays also were quickly assimilated by the church and in this way a great deal of festive dancing, bell-ringing, candle-lighting, and especially singing became "Christian."

As MacMullen noted, "Among Christians, singing was at first limited to psalms, as had always been the custom among Jews. After the mid-fourth century, however, more is heard of a different sort of music not only at private parties . . . but in the very churches as well. . . . The intrusion of music into a sacred setting must obviously be credited to the old cults."[70]

The early church fathers also were careful to assimilate the primary pagan festivals by Christianizing them. This was noted by Augustine (354–430): "[when] crowds of pagans wishing to become Christians were prevented from doing this because of their habits of celebrating feast days to their idols with banquets and carousing . . . our ancestors thought it would be good to make a concession . . . and permit them to celebrate other feasts."[71] May Day became the feast day for Saints Philip and James; Midsummer Eve became the Nativity of St. John.[72] Easter occurs at the time of the Spring Equinox and the name itself may have come from the Saxon goddess Eostre.[73] All Saints Eve seems to have been introduced to overlie the traditional harvest festival. It also has been generally accepted that some minor local saints are overlays of equally minor, local pagan deities.

Thus several respected historians insist that "pre-Christian ceremonial," and a "persistent pagan mentality"[74] have lived on among rural and small-town Europeans, among whom "pagan antiquity . . . never disappeared."[75] "Many pre-Christian practices intended to ensure good harvests or safe childbirth, to predict the weather, or to ward off evil [were] . . . not abandoned until well into the modern period."[76] As a report written by the leader of an official Lutheran visitation to the district of Wiesbaden in 1594 put it: "The use of spells is so widespread among the people here that not a man or a woman begins, undertakes, does or refrains from doing anything . . . without employing some particular blessing, incantation, spell or other such heathenish means."[77] Other Lutheran visitation reports from the sixteenth century report the same thing and all stress that very, very few people ever went to church (see chapter 15). Finally, a remarkable amount of paganism lingers in modern forms of New Age and esoteric spiritualism.[78]

Conclusion

IN ONE OF HIS thousands of letters, this one written around 420, the Christian monk Isidore of Pelusium remarked: "The pagan faith, made dominant for so many years, by such pains, such expenditure of wealth, such feats of arms, has vanished from the earth."[79] More than fifteen hundred years later, the prominent Oxford historian E. R. Dodds (1893–1973) agreed: "In the fourth century paganism appears as a kind of living corpse, which begins to collapse from the moment when the supporting hand of the State is withdrawn."[80]

But it wasn't true. In the fourth and early fifth centuries, paganism was still quite robust. But to recognize that fact it is necessary, as Peter Brown put it, to attend to "tantalizing fragments" of historical evidence that can be "glimpsed through the chinks in a body of evidence which claims to tell a very different story." That false story being that "this one short period of time (under a century) witnessed the 'death of paganism' . . . as a succession of Christian emperors . . . played out their God-given role in abolishing . . . the old gods."[81]

Granted that the early church fathers were certain that theirs was the Only True Faith, and therefore they could not, and did not, commit themselves to ideals of religious freedom. Nevertheless, the church did not exploit its official standing to quickly stamp out paganism, nor did the emperors accomplish this on behalf of the new faith. Instead, paganism survived relatively unmolested for centuries after the conversion of Constantine, only slowly sinking into obscurity, meanwhile managing to create niches for some of its traditions within Christianity and to live on among the only slightly Christianized European masses.

CHAPTER TWELVE

Islam and the Destruction of Eastern and North African Christianity

CHRISTIANITY DID NOT START OUT as a European religious movement; in early days far more missionary activity was devoted to the East than to the West. Thus, following his conversion, Paul devoted his initial missionary efforts to Arabia[1] (Gal. 1:17). Subsequently, when the Great Revolt brought Roman vengeance unto Israel, the leaders of the church in Jerusalem appear to have taken shelter in the East. Although we know precious little about how Christianity was spread in the East, we know that it was extremely successful there, soon becoming a major presence in Syria, Persia, parts of Arabia, Mesopotamia, Turkestan, Armenia, and on into India and even with several outposts in China.[2] As for North Africa, it was "the most Christianized region of the Western empire,"[3] home to "such great early leaders as Tertullian, Cyprian, and Augustine."[4] By the year 300, it is plausible that more than half of all Christians lived in the East and Africa; in 325, 55 percent of the bishops invited to the Council of Nicaea were from the East and this did not, of course, include Montanists, Marcionites, Manichaeists, or other Eastern "heretical" Christians. By the year 500, probably more than two-thirds of Christians were outside of Europe,[5] and if we can identify "a Christian center of gravity" at this time, it would be in "Syria rather than Italy."[6]

Christianity became a predominately European faith "by default"[7] when it was destroyed in Asia and North Africa. The destruction began in the seventh and early eighth century when these areas were over-run by Islam. The number of Eastern bishops (as measured by council attendance) fell from 338 in 754 to 110 in 896.[8] However, following the initial Muslim conquests, for centuries Christians persisted as a large, if repressed, majority. Then, in the fourteenth century came a relentless and violent Muslim campaign of extermination and forced conversions. After centuries of gradual decline, the number of Christians in the East and North Africa suddenly was reduced to less than 2 percent of the population by 1400.[9] With the fall of Constantinople in 1453, Christianity had been essentially restricted to Europe. That is the story to be told in this chapter.

Muslim Conquests

THERE WERE MANY CHRISTIAN and Jewish tribes and communities in Arabia in 570 when Muhammad was born. A large area in north-ern Arabia was fully Christianized, and there also were a number of Christian towns in the south (modern Yemen). As for Jews, in addi-tion to several large communities within Mecca and Medina, there were at least six Jewish towns on the Arabian Peninsula.[10]

Initially, Muhammad expected that Jews and Christians would accept him as the prophet who fulfilled both faiths. Frustrated when they rejected him, as soon as he possessed sufficient means to do so, Muhammad attacked the Jews in Mecca and Medina; and eventually he forced the male members of the last Jewish clan in Medina to dig their own mass grave, whereupon all six to nine hundred of them were beheaded and the women and children were sold into slavery.[11] Then Muhammad also sent his army to seize the Jewish towns.

Most of the Christians in Arabia were Nestorians, named for Nestorius, the archbishop of Constantinople, who was condemned as a heretic in 431, but whose followers soon dominated the entire Christian movement in the East. For a time, the Christian communities in Arabia were too strong to be easily overcome, so Muhammad allowed them to exist so long as they paid an annual protection fee. However, Caliph Umar (*caliph* means successor and Umar was Muhammad's second successor) possessed overwhelming military power and easily expelled all non-Muslims from the Arabian Peninsula.

Shortly before his death in 632, Muhammad's forces began probing attacks into Byzantine Syria as well as into Persia. These attacks were in keeping with what came to be known as Muhammad's farewell address, during which he said: "I was ordered to fight all men until they say 'There is no god but Allah.' "[12] That was entirely consistent with the Qur'an (9:5): "slay the idolaters wherever ye find them, and take them (captive), and besiege them, and prepare for them each ambush." In this spirit, Muslim armies launched a century of successful conquests.

First to fall was Syria, in 636 after three years of fighting. The defeat of the Byzantine force in Syria was ensured by the defection of its Arab mercenaries—sometimes they changed sides during an actual battle. Meanwhile, other Arab forces had moved against the Persian area of Mesopotamia, known today as Iraq. The problem of unreliable Arab troops also beset the Persians just as it had the Byzantines: in several key battles whole units of Persian cavalry, which consisted exclusively of Arab mercenaries, joined the Muslim side, leading to an overwhelming defeat of the Persians in the Battle of al-Qādisyyah in 636. Subsequently, Caliph al-Mansur built his capital city on the Tigris River. Its official name was Madina al-Salam (City of Peace), but everyone called it Baghdad (Gift of God). Eastern Persia, the area that is today Iran, soon fell to Muslim invaders as well.

Having conquered Persia, Muslim forces ventured north to conquer Armenia and also moved east, eventually occupying the Indus Valley (modern Pakistan). From this base, over many centuries the Muslims eventually expanded far into India. Meanwhile, Muslim forces also moved west.

First up was the Holy Land, at that time the most western part of Byzantine Syria. Muslim forces entered it in 636 and in 638, after a long siege, Jerusalem surrendered to Caliph Umar. In 639 Caliph Umar began the invasion of Egypt, a major center of Christianity and also a Byzantine colony. Because the major Egyptian cities were strongly fortified, the Arabs could only resort to massacres of the villages and rural areas in hopes that Christian forces would be drawn into open battles. That occurred from time to time, but following each engagement, the Christians were able to withdraw to their fortifications in good order. Moreover, since Alexandria (the second largest city in Christendom) and several other major Egyptian cities were seaports and easily supplied and reinforced by sea, sieges were ineffective. In 641 a new Byzantine governor of Egypt was appointed. For reasons that remain unknown, a month after his arrival by sea in Alexandria he arranged to meet the Muslim commander and surrendered the city and all of Egypt to him.

But this wasn't the end. Four years later a Byzantine fleet of about three hundred vessels suddenly arrived in the harbor at Alexandria and disembarked a substantial army that quickly dispatched the Muslim garrison of about a thousand. Once again the Greeks had an impregnable position behind the great walls of the city, but their arrogant and foolish commander led his forces out to meet the Arabs and was routed. Even so, enough Byzantine troops made it back to Alexandria to adequately man the fortifications and once again they were secure against attack—but for the treachery of an officer who opened a gate to the Arabs. Some reports say he was bribed; others claim he was a Coptic Christian who was getting even with the Byzantines for having persecuted people of his faith (the Orthodox Byzantines were militantly intolerant). In any event, having burst into the city, the Muslims engaged in "massacre, plunder, and arson . . . [until] half the city was destroyed."[13] They also tore down the city walls to prevent any repetition of the problem.

The need to take Alexandria twice made the Muslims fully aware of the need to offset Byzantine sea power. Turning to the still-functioning Egyptian shipyards they commissioned the construction of a fleet and then hired Coptic and Greek mercenaries to do the navigation and sailing. In 649 this new fleet was adequate to sustain an invasion of Cypress, and Sicily and Rhodes were pillaged soon after. A major Muslim Empire now ruled most of the Middle East and was free to continue spreading along the North African Coast.

But at this moment the Muslim conquests halted because a brutal civil war broke out within Islam and lasted for years. At issue were conflicting claims to be the true successor to Muhammad, which pitted Muhammad's cousin and son-in-law Ali against Muawiyah, cousin of Caliph Uthman, who had just been murdered. After much bloodshed, Ali was also murdered and Muawiyah became Caliph, with the result that Islam was forever divided into the Sunnis and the Shiites (who had backed Ali). It was not until 670 that a Muslim army advanced further along the North African coast.

As Egypt had been, the entire north coast of Africa also was under Byzantine rule. Since all the major cities were ports and well garrisoned, the Arab commander moved west over desert routes, established an inland base, and built a huge mosque in what became the city of Kairouan—now regarded as the third holiest Muslim city (after Mecca and Medina).[14] From this base in the Maghreb (as the Arabs called North Africa), the Muslim force first made war on the desert-dwelling Berbers, many of whom had long ago converted to Judaism.[15] Despite bitter resistance, especially by tribes from the Atlas Mountain area led by a charismatic Jewish woman named Kahina, the Muslims eventually prevailed and then succeeded in enlisting the Berbers as allies.[16] Meanwhile, a new Muslim army of perhaps forty thousand swept over the coastal cities, taking Carthage in 698. But, as had happened with Alexandria, the Byzantines managed to land troops in the Carthage harbor and retake the city. In response, the Muslims assembled a fleet and another army, including large numbers of Berbers, and in 705 Carthage was "razed to the ground and most of its inhabitants killed."[17] Possession of an adequate fleet by the Muslims sealed the fate of all the remaining African coastal towns.[18]

All of Christian Africa was now under Muslim rule as was all of the Middle East and the Christian portions of Asia, except for the area that now is modern Turkey, which still was ruled from Constantinople. Then, in 711 Muslim forces from Morocco invaded Spain and soon pushed the Christian defenders into a small area in the North, from which they never could be dislodged. A century later Sicily and Southern Italy fell to Muslim forces.

Conversion

IT WAS A VERY long time before the conquered areas were truly Muslim in anything but name. The reality was that very small Muslim elites long ruled over non-Muslim (mostly Christian) populations in the conquered areas. This runs contrary to the widespread belief that Muslim conquests were quickly followed by mass conversions to Islam.

In part this belief in rapid mass conversions is rooted in the failure to distinguish "conversions by treaty" from changes in individual beliefs and practices. Tribes that took arms for Muhammad often did so on the basis of a treaty that expressed acceptance of Muhammad's religious claims, but these pacts had no individual religious implications—as demonstrated by the many defections of these tribes following the prophet's death. Similar "conversions by treaty" continued during the Muslim conquests, the Berbers being a notable case. When attacked by the Muslim invaders of North Africa, some of the Berber tribes were pagans, some were Jews, and some were Christians. But after the defeat of Kahina and her forces, the Berbers signed a treaty declaring themselves to be Muslims. Perhaps some of them were. But even though Marshall Hodgson wrote that the Berbers "converted en mass,"[19] theirs was mainly a conversion by treaty that qualified them to participate in subsequent campaigns of conquest and share in the booty and tribute that resulted. The actual conversion of the Berbers in terms of individual beliefs was a slow process that took many centuries.

The second source of mistaken belief in mass conversions is the failure to recognize compelled or opportunistic conversions as opposed to those involving an authentic change of heart. Muslims sometimes confronted nonbelievers with the choice between conversion on the one hand, and death or slavery on the other. Thus, in 1292 the Coptic Christian scribes serving the Mamlūk sultan in Cairo were given the option of conversion or death. Not too surprisingly, they chose to convert although even the sultan knew their conversions "were not taken very seriously."[20] In addition, non-Muslims living in Muslim societies had to endure many humiliations and hardships, including far higher tax rates. Moreover, just as many pagans embraced Christianity because of the financial and social benefits, so too did many embrace Islam for similar motives. The more surprising fact is not that many such conversions resulted, but that so many people chose to remain steadfast Christians or Jews (pagans usually not being tolerated at all).

Aside from confusing these varieties of conversions for the real thing, historians also have erred by assuming that once a people came under Muslim occupation, there "must have been" mass conversions. As previously noted, "must have been" is one of the most untrustworthy phrases in the scholarly vocabulary. In this case, social scientists who have studied conversion would respond that there "must not have been" mass conversions, since it is very doubtful that a mass conversion has ever occurred, anywhere! All observed instances of conversion have revealed them to be individual acts that occur relatively gradually as people are drawn to a particular faith by a network of family and friends who already have converted.[21] In the instances at hand, the network model gains credibility from the fact that it took centuries for as many as half of the population of conquered societies to become Muslims.

Richard W. Bulliet[22] has provided superb data on conversion to Islam in the various conquered regions. For whatever reason, from earliest times, Muslims produced large numbers of very extensive biographical dictionaries listing all of the better-known people in a specific area, and new editions appeared for centuries. Eventually Bulliet was able to assemble data on more than a million persons. The value of these data lies in the fact that Bulliet was able to distinguish Muslims from non-Muslims on the basis of their names. Then, by merging many dictionaries for a given area and sorting the tens of thousands of people listed by their year of birth, Bulliet was able to calculate the proportion of Muslims in the population at various dates and thus create curves of the progress of conversion in five major areas. Because only somewhat prominent people were included in the dictionaries, these results overestimate both the extent and the speed of conversions vis-à-vis the general populations in that elites began with a higher proportion of Muslims and Muslims would have continued to dominate. Consequently, Bulliet devised a very convincing procedure to convert these data into conversion curves for whole populations.

Table 12.1 shows the number of years required to convert 50 percent of the population to Islam in five major areas. In Iran it took 200 years from the date of the initial conquest by Muslim forces to the time when half of Iranians were Muslims. In the other four areas it took from 252 years in Syria to 264 years in Egypt and North Africa.

Table 12.1: Estimated Number of Years Required to Convert 50 Percent of the Population to Islam

Syria	252 years
Western Persia (Iran)	253 years
Eastern Persia (Iran)	200 years
Egypt and North Africa	264 years
Spain	247 years

Source: Calculated from Bulliet, Conversion to Islam in the Medieval Period, *(1979a); and Bulliet, "Conversion to Islam and the Emergence of Muslim Society in Iran" (1979b).*

As to why things happened somewhat more rapidly in Iran, two things set it apart from the other areas. Probably the most important is that for more than a century after falling to Islamic invaders, the

Iranians frequently revolted again Muslim rule and did so with sufficient success so that many very bloody battles ensued as did brutal repressions. These conflicts would have resulted in substantial declines in the non-Muslim population, having nothing to do with conversion. Secondly, the climate of fear that must have accompanied the defeats of these rebellions likely would have prompted some Iranians to convert for safety's sake and caused others to flee.

In any event, despite the onerous conditions imposed upon them, the conquered peoples only slowly converted to Islam. Even as late as the thirteenth century, very substantial segments of the populations of the Muslim Empire outside of Arabia (where non-Muslims were not permitted) were Christians or Jews.

Dhimmis *and Muslim "Tolerance"*

A GREAT DEAL OF nonsense has been written about Muslim tolerance—that, in contrast with Christian brutality against Jews and heretics, Islam showed remarkable tolerance for conquered people, treated them with respect, and allowed them to pursue their faiths without interference. This claim probably began with Voltaire, Gibbon, and other eighteenth-century writers who used it to cast the Catholic Church in the worst possible light. The truth about life under Muslim rule is quite different.

It is true that the Qur'an forbids forced conversions. However, that recedes to an empty legalism given that many subject peoples often were "free to choose" conversion as an alternative to death or enslavement. That was the usual choice presented to pagans, and often Jews and Christians also were faced with that or with an only somewhat less extreme option.[23] In principle, as "People of the Book," Jews and Christians were supposed to be tolerated and permitted to follow their faiths, but only under quite repressive conditions—death was (and remains) the fate of any Muslim who converted to either faith. Nor could any new churches or synagogues be built. Jews and

Christians also were prohibited from praying or reading their scriptures aloud, not even in their homes or in churches or synagogues, lest Muslims should accidentally hear them. And, as the remarkable historian of Islam Marshall G. S. Hodgson (1922–1968) pointed out, from very early times Muslim authorities often went to great lengths to humiliate and punish *dhimmis*—these being Jews and Christians who refused to convert to Islam. It was official policy that *dhimmis* should "feel inferior and to know 'their place' . . . [imposing laws such as] that Christians and Jews should not ride horses, for instance, but at most mules, or even that they should wear certain marks of their religion on their costume when among Muslims."[24] In some places non-Muslims were prohibited from wearing clothing similar to that of Muslims, nor could they be armed.[25] In addition, non-Muslims were invariably severely taxed compared with Muslims.[26]

These were the normal circumstances of Jewish and Christian subjects of Muslim states, but conditions often were far worse, as will be seen. This is *not* to say that the Muslims usually were more brutal or less tolerant than were Christians or Jews, for it was a brutal and intolerant age. It *is* to say that efforts to portray Muslims as enlightened supporters of multiculturalism are at best ignorant.

What is true is that many Muslim rulers depended almost entirely on *dhimmis* to provide them with literate bureaucrats. Indeed, as late as the middle of the eleventh century, the Muslim writer Nasir-i Khrusau reported "Truly, the scribes here in Syria, as is the case of Egypt, are all Christians . . . [and] it is most usual for the physicians . . . to be Christians."[27] In Palestine under Muslim rule, according to the monumental history by Moshe Gil, "the Christians had immense influence and positions of power, chiefly because of the gifted administrators among them who occupied government posts despite the ban in Muslim law against employing Christians [in such positions] or who were part of the intelligentsia of the period owing to the fact that they were outstanding scientists, mathematicians, physicians and so on."[28] The prominence of Christian officials was also acknowledged by Abd al-Jabbār, who wrote in about 995 that "kings in Egypt, al-Shām, Iraq, Jazīra, Fāris, and in all their surroundings, rely on Christians in matters of officialdom, the central administration and the handling of funds."[29] The many riots against Christians in Cairo and other Egyptian cities and towns during the fourteenth century were prompted by the extraordinary wealth of Copts who dominated the Sultan's bureaucracy and who, despite repeated purges, always returned to power because Muslim replacements could not be found.[30]

Stamping Out the "Unbelievers"

JUST AS LITTLE IS known about the spread of Christianity in the East, the final destruction of the *dhimmi* communities of Eastern Christians is lacking in detail. It was not prompted by the Crusades. As will be seen in chapter 13, at the time Muslims paid little attention to the Crusades, and current anger about them originated in the twentieth century. Apparently, sustained attacks on the *dhimmis* began in Cairo in 1321, when Muslim mobs began destroying Coptic churches. These anti-Christian riots "were carefully orchestrated throughout Egypt"[31] until large numbers of churches and monasteries were destroyed. Although the mobs eventually were put down by Mamlūk authorities, small-scale anti-Christian attacks, arson, looting, and murder became chronic and widespread. Then, in 1354 once again mobs "ran amok, destroying churches . . . and attacking Christians and Jews in the streets, and throwing them into bonfires if they refused to pronounce the *shadādatayn*"[32] (to acknowledge Allah as the One True God). Soon, according to Al-Maqrizi's (1364–1442) account, in "all the provinces of Egypt, both north and south, no church remained that had not been razed. . . . Thus did Islam spread among the Christians of Egypt."[33]

The massacres of Christians and the destruction of churches and monasteries were not limited to Egypt. Having converted to Islam, the Mongol rulers of Mesopotamia, Armenia, and Syria took even more draconian measures than did the Mamlūks. When Ghāzān took the Mongol throne of Iran in 1295, in pursuit of increased public support he converted to Islam (he had been raised a Christian and then became a Buddhist), and yielded to "popular pressure which compelled him to . . . persecute Christians."[34] According to an account written by Mar Yaballaha III (1245–1317), the Nestorian patriarch, in keeping with his aim of forcing all Christians and Jews to become Muslims, Ghāzān issued this edict:

> The churches shall be uprooted, and the altars overturned, and the celebrations of the Eucharist shall cease, and the hymns of praise, and the sounds of calls to prayer shall be abolished; and the heads of the Christians, and the heads of the congregations of the Jews, and the great men among them, shall be killed.[35]

Within a year Ghāzān changed his mind and attempted to end the persecutions of Christians, but by now the mobs were out of control and it was widely accepted "that everyone who did not abandon Christianity and deny his faith should be killed."[36]

Meanwhile, similar events were taking place in Mongol Armenia. In an effort to force Christians into Islam, church services were forbidden and a crushing tax was imposed on each. In addition, local authorities were ordered to seize each Christian man, to pluck out his beard and to tattoo a black mark on his shoulder. When few Christians defected in response to these measures, the Khān then ordered that all Christian men be castrated and have one eye put out—which caused many deaths in this era before antibiotics, but did lead to many conversions.[37]

In 1310 there was "a terrible massacre in Arbil" in Mesopotamia.[38] Things were no better in Syria. In 1317 the city of Āmid was the scene of an anti-Christian attack. The bishop was beaten to death, then churches were all burned, the Christian men were all murdered, and twelve thousand women and children were sold into slavery.[39] Similar events occurred all across the East and North Africa.[40] Then came Tamerlane.

Tamerlane, also known as Timur, was born near the Persian city of

Samarkand in 1336 and died while campaigning in China in 1405. Although he made Samarkand his capital, Tamerlane never spent more than a few days there at a time, remaining a nomadic conqueror his entire life. A Muslim of Turkic-Mongol origins, Tamerlane is remembered mainly for his barbarity, earning the sobriquet the "Scourge of God," as Christopher Marlowe put it in his great play (1587). Again and again Tamerlane perpetrated huge massacres—perhaps as many as two hundred thousand captives (men, women, and children) were slaughtered during his march on Delhi[41]—and had towering pyramids built from the heads of his victims. And while he killed huge numbers of Muslims, Hindus, and Buddhists, he virtually wiped out the Christians and Jews in the East. In Georgia alone, Tamerlane "destroyed seven hundred large villages, wiped out the inhabitants, and reduced all the Christian churches . . . to rubble."[42] Any Christian communities that survived Tamerlane were destroyed by his grandson, Ulugh Beg.[43]

Conclusion

BY THE END OF the fourteenth century only tiny remnants of Christianity remained here and there in the East and North Africa, having been almost completely wiped out by Muslim persecution. Thus, as Philip Jenkins put it, Christianity became a European faith because Europe was the only "continent where it was not destroyed."[44]

Chapter Thirteen

Europe Responds

The Case for the Crusades[1]

In the immediate aftermath of the destruction of the World Trade Center by Muslim terrorists, frequent mention was made of the Crusades as a basis for Islamic fury. It was argued that Muslim bitterness over their mistreatment by the Christian West can be dated back to 1096 when the First Crusade set out for the Holy Land. Far from being motivated by piety or by concern for the safety of pilgrims and the holy places in Jerusalem, it is widely believed that the Crusades were but the first extremely bloody chapter in a long history of brutal European colonialism.[2] More specifically: that the crusaders marched east, not out of idealism, but in pursuit of lands and loot; that the Crusades were promoted "by power-mad popes" seeking to greatly expand Christianity through conversion of the Muslim masses[3] and thus the Crusades constitute "a black stain on the history of the Catholic Church"; that the knights of Europe were barbarians who brutalized everyone in their path, leaving "the enlightened Muslim culture . . . in ruins."[4] As Akbar Ahmed, chair of Islamic studies at American University in Washington, DC, suggests: "the Crusades created a historical memory which is with us today—the memory of a long European onslaught."[5]

Two months after the attack on New York City, former president Bill Clinton informed an audience at Georgetown University that "Those of us who come from various European lineages are not blameless" vis-à-vis the Crusades as a crime against Islam, and then summarized a medieval account about all the blood that was shed when Godfrey of Bouillon and his forces conquered Jerusalem in 1099. That the Crusades were a crime in great need of atonement was a popular theme even before the Islamic terrorists crashed their hijacked airliners. In 1999, the *New York Times* had solemnly proposed that the Crusades were comparable to Hitler's atrocities or to the ethnic cleansing in Kosovo.[6] Also in 1999, to mark the nine hundredth anniversary of the crusader conquest of Jerusalem, hundreds of devout Protestants took part in a "Reconciliation Walk" that began in Germany and ended in the Holy Land. Along the way the walkers wore T-shirts bearing the message "I apologize" in Arabic. Their official statement explained the need for a Christian apology:

> Nine hundred years ago, our forefathers carried the name of Jesus Christ in battle across the Middle East. Fueled by fear, greed, and hatred . . . the Crusaders lifted the banner of the Cross above your people. . . . On the anniversary of the First Crusade . . . we wish to retrace the footsteps of the Crusaders in apology for their deeds. . . . We deeply regret the atrocities committed in the name of Christ by our predecessors. We renounce greed, hatred and fear, and condemn all violence done in the name of Jesus Christ.[7]

These are not new charges. Western condemnations of the Crusades originated in the "Enlightenment," that utterly misnamed era during which French and British intellectuals invented the "Dark Ages" in order to glorify themselves and vilify the church (see chapter 14). Voltaire (1694–1778) calls the Crusades an "epidemic of fury which lasted for two hundred years and which was always marked by every cruelty, every perfidy, every debauchery, and every folly of which human nature is capable."[8] According to David Hume (1711–1776) the Crusades were "the most signal and most durable monument to human folly that has yet appeared in any age or nation."[9] Denis Diderot (1713–1784) characterized the Crusades as "a time of the deepest darkness and of the greatest folly . . . to drag a significant part of the world into an unhappy little country in order to cut the inhabitants' throats and seize a rocky peak which was not worth one drop of blood."[10] These attacks reinforced the widespread "Protestant conviction that crusading was yet another expression of Catholic bigotry and cruelty."[11] But the notion that the crusaders were early Western imperialists who used a religious excuse to seek land and loot probably was originated by Edward Gibbon (1737–1794), who claims that the crusaders really went in pursuit of "mines of treasures, of gold and diamonds, of palaces of marble and jasper, and of odoriferous groves of cinnamon and frankincense."[12]

During the twentieth century, Gibbon's thesis was developed into a quite elaborate "materialist" account of why the Crusades took place.[13] As summed up by Hans Mayer, the Crusades alleviated a severe financial squeeze on Europe's "knightly class." According to Mayer and others who share his views, at this time there was a substantial and rapidly growing number of "surplus" sons, members of noble families who would not inherit and whom the heirs found it increasingly difficult to provide with even modest incomes. Hence, as Mayer put it, "the Crusade acted as a kind of safety valve for the knightly class . . . a class which looked upon the Crusade as a way of solving its material problems."[14] Indeed, a group of American economists recently proposed that the crusaders hoped to get rich from the flow of pilgrims (comparing the shrines in Jerusalem to modern amusement parks) and that the pope sent the crusaders east in pursuit of "new markets" for the church, presumably to be gained by converting people away from Islam.[15] The prolific Geoffrey Barraclough wrote: "our verdict on the Crusades [is that the knightly settlements established in the East were] centers of colonial exploitation."[16] It is thus no surprise that a leading college textbook on Western Civilization informs students that "From the perspective of the pope and European monarchs, the crusades offered a way to rid Europe of contentious young nobles . . . [who] saw an opportunity to gain territory, riches, status, possibly a title, and even salvation."[17] Or, as the popular writer Karen Armstrong confided, these "were our first colonies."[18]

Thus, it is the accepted myth that during the Crusades *an expansionist, imperialistic Christendom brutalized, looted, and colonized a tolerant and peaceful Islam.* These claims have been utterly refuted by a group of distinguished contemporary historians.[19] They propose that the Crusades were precipitated by Islamic provocations, by many centuries of bloody attempts to colonize the West, and by sudden new attacks on Christian pilgrims and holy places. Although the Crusades were initiated by a plea from the pope, this had nothing to do with hopes of converting Islam. Nor were the Crusades organized and led by surplus sons, but by the heads of great families who were fully aware that the costs of crusading would far exceed the very modest material rewards that could be expected. Most went at immense personal cost, some of them knowingly bankrupting themselves to go. For example, Godfrey of Bouillon sold the entire province of Verdun and also heavily mortgaged his province of Bouillon to finance his participation. Moreover, the crusader kingdoms that the knights established in the Holy Land, and which stood for two centuries, were not sustained by local exactions, but required immense subsidies from Europe. In addition, it is utterly unreasonable to impose modern notions about proper military conduct on medieval warfare—both Christians and Muslims observed quite different rules of war. Even so, the crusaders were not nearly as brutal or bloodthirsty as they have been portrayed. Finally, claims that Muslims have been harboring bitter resentments about the Crusades for a millennium are nonsense: Muslim antagonism about the Crusades did not appear until about 1900 in reaction against the decline of the Ottoman Empire and the onset of actual European colonialism in the Middle East.

Now for the details.

Provocations

As described in chapter 12, Muslims began raiding Christian areas in the lifetime of Muhammad. Then, a year after his death, Muslim invasions began in earnest when their forces entered Syria, then a Christian province of the Eastern Roman Empire. Muslim forces soon won a series of battles, taking Damascus and some other cities in 635, and by 636 the Byzantine army was forced to abandon Syria. Next the Arabs marched into the Holy Land: Jerusalem was taken in 638, Caesarea Maritima in 640. From there Muslim armies invaded Christian Egypt, taking Cairo; Alexandria fell to them in 642. A major Muslim empire now ruled most of the Middle East and was spreading along the North African Coast—then a major Christian region. Thirty years later the empire stretched past Tangier and reached the Atlantic. By 714 much of Spain was occupied. Soon major thrusts were made into France before the Franks managed to repel the Muslim forces at Tours (or Poitiers) in 732. In 831 Muslim forces invaded Sicily and held it until 1072, and in 846 they sacked Rome and then withdrew to rule over southern Italy for the next two centuries. Thus, by the time of the First Crusade, Christendom had been fighting a defensive war with Islam for more than 450 years!

It seems very odd that those who are so vociferous about the misery and injustice imposed by Europeans on their former colonial empires fail to admit any such consequences of Muslim imperialism. But as was clarified in chapter 12, Muslims were brutal and intolerant colonialists. Thus the fact remains that the Crusades were fundamentally defensive, and it is against this general background of chronic and long-standing Western grievances that the very specific provocations for the Crusades must be considered. These involved the destruction of, and threat to, holy places in Jerusalem and the murder, torture, enslavement, robbery, and general harassment of Christian pilgrims.

In 1009, at the direction of Fatimid Caliph al-Hakim, Muslims destroyed the Church of the Holy Sepulcher in Jerusalem—the splendid basilica that Constantine had erected over what was believed to be the site of the tomb where Christ lay before the Resurrection. Worse yet, the Muslims attempted to destroy the tomb itself, leaving only traces of the hollow in the rocks. As word of the desecration of the holiest of all Christian shrines reached Europe, it prompted considerable anger and concern among the informed elites. But the crisis soon passed because al-Hakim was assassinated and some semblance of religious tolerance was restored in Jerusalem, thus permitting resumption of the substantial flow of Christian pilgrims. Indeed, the value of the pilgrim traffic probably was the primary factor in the very liberal policies that had prevailed in Muslim-controlled Jerusalem through the centuries. Despite the great distances involved and the limited means of transportation, pilgrimages to Jerusalem were surprisingly common. In the first of his famous three volumes on the Crusades, Sir Steven Runciman (1903–2000) reported that "an unending stream of travellers poured eastward, sometimes travelling in parties numbering thousands, men and women of every age and every class, ready . . . to spend a year or more on the [journey]."[20] A major reason for going to the Holy Land was the belief that a pilgrimage would absolve even the most terrible sins. Thus, many pilgrims came all the way from Scandinavia—some even from Iceland. As Runciman explained, the Norse "were violent men, frequently guilty of murder and frequently in need of an act of penance."[21]

But then, later in the eleventh century, everything changed again. The Seljuk Turks, recent converts to Islam, became the new rulers of Asia Minor, pushing to within a hundred miles of Constantinople. Perhaps because they were new to Islam, or perhaps because they were still seminomadic tribesmen untainted by city dwelling, the Turks were unflinchingly intolerant. There was only One True God and his name was Allah, not Yahweh or Jehovah. Not that the Turks officially prohibited Christian pilgrimages, but they made it clear that Christians were fair game. Hence, every Anatolian village along the route to Jerusalem began to exact a toll on Christian travelers. Far worse, many pilgrims were seized and sold into slavery while others were tortured, often seemingly for entertainment. Those who survived these perils "returned to the West weary and impoverished, with a dreadful tale to tell."[22]

Anger and anxiety about the Holy Land continued to grow. It is important to understand just how vivid was the image of the Holy Land to sincere medieval Christians (if not to the barely Christian masses). It was where Christ and the disciples had lived, and to an almost palpable degree still did. In the words of Robert Payne (1911–1983), in Palestine Christians "expected to find holiness in a concrete form, something that could be seen, touched, kissed, worshipped, and even carried away. Holiness was in the pathways trodden by Christ, in the mountains and valleys seen by Christ, in the streets of Jerusalem where Christ had wandered."[23] In Jerusalem, a Christian could even climb the hill on which the cross had borne the Son of God. But no longer.

It was in this climate of opinion that Alexius Comnenus, Emperor of Byzantium, wrote from his embattled capital to the Count of Flanders requesting that he and his fellow Christians in the West come to the rescue. In his letter, the emperor detailed gruesome tortures of pilgrims and vile desecrations of churches, altars, and baptismal fonts. Should Constantinople fall to the Turks, not only would thousands more Christians be murdered, tortured, and raped, but "the most holy relics of the Saviour," gathered over the centuries, would be lost. "Therefore in the name of God . . . we implore you to bring this city all the faithful soldiers of Christ . . . in your coming you will find your reward in heaven, and if you do not come, God will condemn you."[24]

When Pope Urban II read this letter he was determined that it be answered in deeds. He arranged for a great gathering of clergy and laity in the French city of Clermont on November 27, 1095. Standing on a podium in the middle of a field, and surrounded by an immense crowd that included poor peasants as well as nobility and clergy, the pope gave one of the most effective speeches of all time. Blessed with an expressive and unusually powerful voice, he could be heard and understood at a great distance. Subsequently, copies of the speech (written and spoken in French) were circulated all across Europe.[25]

The pope began by graphically detailing the torture, rape, and murder of Christian pilgrims and the defilement of churches and holy places:

> Many of God's churches have been violated. . . . They have ruined the altars with filth and defilement. They have circumcised Christians and smeared the blood on the altars or poured it into baptismal fonts. It amused them to kill Christians by opening up their bellies and drawing out the end of their intestines, which they then tied to a stake. Then they flogged their victims and made them walk around and around the stake until their intestines had spilled out and they fell dead on the ground. . . . What shall I say about the abominable rape of women? On this subject it may be worse to speak than to remain silent.

At this point Pope Urban raised a second issue to which he already had devoted years of effort: the chronic warfare of medieval times. The pope had been attempting to achieve a "Truce of God" among the feudal nobility, many of whom seemed inclined to make war, even on their friends, just for the sake of a good fight. After all, it was what they trained to do every day since early childhood. Here was their chance! "Christian warriors, who continually and vainly seek pretexts for war, rejoice, for you have today found a true pretext. . . . If you are conquered, you will have the glory of dying in the very same place as Jesus Christ, and God will never forget that he found you in the holy battalions. . . . Soldiers of Hell, become soldiers of the living God!"

Now, shouts of "*Dieu li volt!*" (God wills it!) began to spread through the crowd and men began to cut up cloaks and other pieces of cloth to make crosses and to sew them on their shoulders and chests. Everyone agreed that next spring they would march to Jerusalem. And they did.

It has often been suggested that we should not trust the pope or the emperor on what was taking place in the Holy Land. Perhaps they were misinformed. Perhaps they were lying to arouse a military venture for reasons of their own. James Carroll has even suggested that the pope cynically used the Muslims as threatening outsiders in order to unite the European princes "against a common enemy."[26] But as Runciman pointed out, Europeans, especially the nobility, had trustworthy independent information on the brutalization of the Christian pilgrims—from their own relatives and friends who had managed to survive. Even had the pope and emperor been cynical propagandists, that would not alter the motivation of the crusaders, for that depended entirely on what the knights believed.

Economic Aspects of the Crusades

HAD THERE BEEN A financial squeeze on the knightly class, about the last thing they would have done was march off on a Crusade to the Holy Land. As Peter Edbury explained, "Crusading was expensive, and the costs were borne by the crusaders themselves, their families, their lords and, increasingly from the end of the twelfth century, by taxes levied on the Church in the West."[27] Even the many crusader castles and the garrisons by which Christians held portions of the Holy Land for two centuries were not built or sustained by local exactions, but by funds sent from Europe. Indeed, the great wealth of the knightly crusading orders was not loot, but came from donations and legacies in Europe.[28] All told, "large quantities of Western silver flowed into the crusader states."[29] The Crusades were possible only because this was not a period of economic decline, but one of *growth*, "which put more resources and money into the hands of the ruling elites of Western Europe."[30]

Moreover it was not "surplus" sons who went. Because the "cost of crusading was truly enormous"[31] only the heads of upper-class households could raise the money to go: it was kings, princes, counts, dukes, barons, and earls who enrolled, led, and paid the expenses for companies of knights and infantry.[32] Even so, they raised the needed funds at a very great sacrifice. Many sold all or substantial amounts of their holdings, borrowed all they could from relatives, and impoverished themselves and their families in order to participate.[33] As for making up their losses by looting and colonizing in the Holy Land, most of them had no such illusions—indeed, most of them had no plans to remain in the East once the fighting was done, and all but a small garrison did return home.

Why They Went

THE KNIGHTS OF EUROPE sewed crosses on their breasts and marched East for two primary reasons, one of them generic, the other specific to crusading. The generic reason was their perceived need for penance. The specific reason was to liberate the Holy Land.

Just as it has today, the medieval church had many profound reservations about violence, and especially about killing. This created serious concerns among the knights and their confessors because war was chronic among the medieval nobility, and any knight who survived for very long was apt to have killed someone. Even when victims were evil men without any redeeming worth, their deaths were held to constitute sins,[34] and in most instances the killer enjoyed no obvious moral superiority over the victim—sometimes quite the reverse. Consequently, knights were chronically in need of penance and their confessors imposed all manner of acts of atonement. Confessors sometimes required a pilgrimage to a famous shrine, and for particularly hideous sins, a journey all the way to the Holy Land.

As already noted, pilgrimages to Jerusalem were remarkably common for several centuries before the First Crusade. Thousands went every year, often in large groups. For example, in 1026 a group of seven hundred persons from Normandy made a pilgrimage to the Holy Land, and along the way they were joined by many other groups of Western pilgrims.[35] A major reason pilgrimages were so common was because the knights of Europe were both very violent and very religious. Thus, when Count Thierry of Trier murdered his archbishop in 1059, his confessor demanded that he undertake a pilgrimage, and he went.[36] Perhaps the most notorious pilgrim was Fulk III, Count of Anjou (972–1040), who was required to make four pilgrimages to the Holy Land, the first as penance for having his wife burned to death in her wedding dress, allegedly for having had sex with a goatherd. All things considered, four pilgrimages may have been far too few, given that Fulk was a "plunderer, murderer, robber, and swearer of false oaths, a truly terrifying character of fiendish cruelty. . . . Whenever he had the slightest difference with a neighbor he rushed upon his lands, ravaging, pillaging, raping and killing; nothing could stop him."[37] Nevertheless, when confronted by his confessor Fulk "responded with extravagant expressions of devotion."[38]

Thus the call to crusade was not a call to do something novel—no doubt many knights had long been considering a pilgrimage. Indeed, the pope himself had assured them that crusading would wash away all their sins and, at the same time, they could rescue the Holy Land, including Christ's tomb, from further damage and sacrilege at the hands of the enemies of God. It was an altogether noble and holy mission, and the knights treated it as such. The Burgundian Stephen I of Neublans put it this way: "Considering how many are my sins and the love, clemency and mercy of Our Lord Jesus Christ, because when he was rich he became poor for our sake, I have determined to repay him in some measure for everything he has given me freely, although I am unworthy. And so I have decided to go to Jerusalem, where God was seen as man and spoke with men and to adore the place where his feet trod."[39]

Had the crusaders not been motivated by religion, but by land and loot, the knights of Europe would have responded earlier, in 1063, when Pope Alexander II proposed a crusade to drive the infidel Muslims out of Spain. Unlike the Holy Land, Moorish Spain was extremely wealthy, possessed an abundance of fertile lands, and was close at hand. But hardly anyone responded to the pope's summons. Yet only about thirty years later, thousands of crusaders set out for the dry, impoverished wastes of faraway Palestine. What was different? Spain was not the Holy Land! Christ had not walked the streets of Toledo, nor was he crucified in Seville.

So finally, on June 7, 1099, and against all odds, the crusaders arrived at Jerusalem. Of the original forces numbering perhaps a hundred and thirty thousand, disease, privation, misadventure, desertion, and fighting had so reduced their ranks that the crusaders now numbered only about fifteen thousand, although Muslim historians placed their numbers at three hundred thousand.[40] Those who reached Jerusalem were starving—having long since eaten their horses. Nevertheless, following a brief siege, on July 15, 1099, the badly outnumbered crusaders burst into the city. Thus, after about 460 years of Muslim rule, Jerusalem was again in Christian hands, although it was nearly destroyed and depopulated in the process.

The Crusader Kingdoms

WITH JERUSALEM IN THEIR possession, and having defeated a large Egyptian army sent to turn them out, the crusaders had to decide what to do to preserve their victory. Their solution was to create four kingdoms—independent states along the Mediterranean Coast (see map 13.1). These were the County of Edessa, named for its major city; the Princedom of Antioch, which surrounded the city of Antioch in what is now southern Turkey; the County of Tripoli, just south of the Princedom and named for the Lebanese coastal city of that name; and the Kingdom of Jerusalem, an enclave on the coast of Palestine roughly equivalent to modern Israel.[41]

Unlike the other three kingdoms, Edessa was landlocked. When the main body of crusaders marched south in 1098 to attack Antioch, Baldwin of Boulogne led a smaller force east to Edessa and managed to convince Thoros, the ruler of the city (who was a Greek Orthodox Christian), to adopt him as his son and heir! When Thoros was assassinated by angry subjects, Baldwin took over. Edessa was the first crusader state (founded in 1098) and the first to be retaken by Islam (1149).

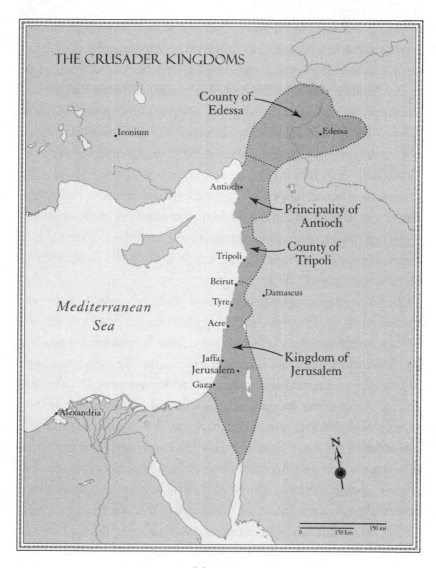

THE CRUSADER KINGDOMS

County of Edessa

Iconium

Edessa

Antioch

Principality of Antioch

County of Tripoli

Tripoli

Beirut

Damascus

Tyre

Mediterranean Sea

Acre

Jaffa

Kingdom of Jerusalem

Jerusalem

Gaza

Alexandria

N

0 150 km 150 mi

Map 13.1

Crusaders captured the city of Antioch in 1098 after a long siege during which the knights ran so short of supplies that they ate many of their horses. Almost immediately after the crusaders had taken the city, a new Muslim army appeared and laid siege to the knights. Against staggering odds, Bohemond of Taranto led his troops out from the city **and** somehow defeated the Muslims—subsequent accounts claim that an army of saints had miraculously appeared to help the knights. Following this victory, Bohemond named himself prince. The area remained an independent state until 1119 when it was joined to the Kingdom of Jerusalem. In 1268 Antioch fell to an army led by Baybars, Sultan of Egypt, whose troops killed every Christian they could find (see below).

The County of Tripoli was the last of the four crusader states to be established—in 1102. It came into being when Count Raymond IV of Toulouse, one of the leaders of the First Crusade, laid siege to the port city of Tripoli. When Raymond died suddenly in 1105, he left his infant son as heir so when the knights finally took the city the County became a vassal state of the Kingdom of Jerusalem. It was captured by Mameluke forces in 1289.

By far the most important and powerful of the crusader states was the Kingdom of Jerusalem, which was also known at Outremer, the French word for "overseas" (*outre-mer*). Initially that term applied to all the crusader states, but it came to refer primarily to the Kingdom of Jerusalem. Like the other states, Outremer was never a European colony, it being fully independent. Godfrey of Bouillon, who led the capture of Jerusalem, was installed as the first ruler, with the title Defender of the Holy Sepulcher. Godfrey was chosen not only for his integrity, but also for his military talent, which was just as well since no sooner was he in command than he was confronted by a very large Egyptian army intent on recapturing Jerusalem. Rather than shelter his outnumbered forces behind the walls of the city, Godfrey marched them out for a night attack that found the Egyptians sleeping and defeated them with a great loss of life.

This terrible defeat long deterred Muslim leaders from mounting new attacks. The Muslim historian Ibn Zafir recorded "reproachfully": "He [the Egyptian vizier] had given up hope of the Syrian coastline remaining in Muslim hands and he did not personally wage war against them after that."[42] This was fortunate for the crusaders, since following their victory over the Egyptians, nearly all of the forces of the First Crusade boarded ships and sailed home, leaving the Outremer to be protected by a small company of about three hundred knights and perhaps two thousand infantry.[43] Eventually their ranks were substantially reinforced by two knightly religious orders in which "monastic discipline and martial skill were combined for the first time in the Christian world."[44] The Knights Hospitaller were founded initially to care for sick Christian pilgrims to the Holy Land. Eventually the order kept its "medical" name, but in about 1120 expanded its vows from chastity, poverty, and obedience to include the armed protection of Christians in Palestine. The Knights Templar originated as a military religious order in about 1119. Hospitallers wore black robes with a white cross on the left sleeve, while the Templars wore a white robe with a red cross on the mantel. The two orders hated one another quite intensely, but together they provided the Kingdom of Jerusalem with a reliable force of well-trained soldiers who built and garrisoned a chain of extremely well-sited castles along the frontiers of the kingdom.

Nevertheless, the existence of the kingdoms remained perilous, surrounded as they were by a vast and populous Muslim world. For many years, whenever the Muslim threat loomed especially large, new Crusades were mounted in Europe bringing fresh troops east in support of the crusader kingdoms—and then went home again. Eventually, Europeans lost their fervor to defend the "Holy Land" and Islamic forces began to eat away at the crusader areas. Still, that the Kingdom of Jerusalem lasted until 1291, when its last fortress at Acre fell to a huge Mameluke army, seems a remarkable achievement.

As already noted, not only the defenders, but most of the funds for all of this came from Europe.[45] Both of the knightly orders established many religious houses in Europe from which they sent not only young recruits, but a constant, substantial flow of cash. Some of the funds were raised by the productive activities of the houses—each owned great estates including some towns and villages—but most of it was donated by wealthy Europeans. About seventy years after the conquest of Jerusalem, the trade routes from Asia shifted to pass through the kingdom's ports. This seems to have enriched Genoa and

Pisa (and perhaps Venice), since these cities controlled maritime trade on the Mediterranean, but it had little impact on the general economy of the kingdom and surely played no role in motivating crusaders.[46] Thus the crusader states "remained dependent on Christendom for men and money, endured as long as Christendom retained enough interest to keep supplying them, and withered and collapsed when that interest was lost."[47] Since a colony is normally defined as a place that is politically directed and economically exploited by a homeland, the crusader states were not colonies[48]—unless one places a high material value on spiritual profits.

Nevertheless, the crusaders made no attempt to impose Christianity on the Muslims. In fact, "Muslims who lived in crusader-won territories were generally allowed to retain their property and livelihood, and always their religion."[49] Consequently the crusader kingdoms always contained far more Muslim residents than Christians. In the thirteenth century some Franciscans initiated conversion efforts among Muslims, but these were based on peaceful persuasion, were quite unsuccessful, and soon abandoned.[50] In fact, the church generally opposed any linkage between crusading and conversion until the issue arose during the "Crusades" against Christian heretics in Europe (chapter 17).[51]

Crusader "War Crimes"

IN THE LAST PARAGRAPH of his immensely influential three-volume work on the Crusades, Sir Steven Runciman regretted this "tragic and destructive episode." The "high ideals" of the crusaders "were besmirched by cruelty and greed . . . by a blind and narrow self-righteousness."[52] In the wake of Runciman's huge work, many more historians adopted the tradition that the Crusades pitted a barbarian West against a more sophisticated and more civilized East. Thus, the emphasis has been given to evidence that the crusaders were brutal, bloodthirsty, religious zealots.

It is the massacre subsequent to the fall of Jerusalem that is taken as certain proof that the crusaders were brutal even for their era and especially so in comparison with their Muslim opponents. Following a short siege the Christian knights took the city by storm and this is said to have been followed by an incredibly bloody massacre of the entire population. Unfortunately, these claims were written by Christian chroniclers "eager to portray a ritual purification of the city."[53] Did it really happen? The chroniclers' accounts seem farfetched—streets don't run knee-deep in blood—but it seems likely that a major massacre did occur. However, it is important to realize that according to the norms of warfare at that time, a massacre of the population of Jerusalem would have been seen as justified because the city had refused to surrender and had to be taken by storm, thus inflicting many casualties on the attacking forces. Had Jerusalem surrendered as crusaders gathered to assault the walls, it is very likely that no massacre would have occurred. But, mistakenly believing in their own military superiority, the Muslims held out. In such cases commanders (Muslims as well as Christians) believed they had an obligation to release their troops to murder, loot, and burn as an example to other cities that might be tempted to hold out excessively long in the future. Thus, Muslim victories in similar circumstances resulted in wholesale slaughters too.

The remarkable bias of so many Western histories of the Crusades could not be more obvious than in the fact that massacres by Muslims receive so little attention. As Robert Irwin pointed out, "In Britain, there ha[s] been a long tradition of disparaging the crusaders as barbaric and bigoted warmongers and of praising the Saracens as paladins of chivalry. Indeed, it is widely believed that chivalry originated in the Muslim East. The most perfect example of Muslim chivalry was, of course, the twelfth-century Ayyubid Sultab Saladin."[54] In fact, this is not a recent British invention. Since the Enlightenment, Saladin has "bizarrely" been portrayed "as a rational and civilized figure in juxtaposition to credulous barbaric crusaders."[55] For example, in 1898, Germany's Kaiser Wilhelm visited Damascus and placed a bronze laurel wreath on Saladin's tomb. The wreath was inscribed, "From one great emperor to another."[56]

Much has been made of the fact that Saladin did not murder the Christians when he retook Jerusalem in 1187. Writing in 1869, the English historian Barbara Hutton claimed that although Saladin "hated Christians . . . when they were suppliants and at his mercy, he was never cruel or revengeful."[57] But neither Hutton nor most other modern, Western sympathizers with Islam have had anything to say about the fact, acknowledged by Muslim writers, that Jerusalem was an exception to Saladin's usual butchery of his enemies. Indeed, Saladin had planned to massacre the knights holding Jerusalem, but offered a safe conduct in exchange for their surrender of Jerusalem without resistance (and unlike many other Muslim leaders, he kept his word). In most other instances Saladin was quite unchivalrous. Following the Battle of Hattin, for example, he personally participated in butchering some the captured knights and then sat back and enjoyed watching the execution of the rest of them. As told by Saladin's secretary, Imad ed-Din: "He [Saladin] ordered that they should be beheaded, choosing to have them dead rather than in prison. With him was a whole band of scholars and sufis and a certain number of devout men and ascetics; each begged to be allowed to kill one of them, and drew his sword and rolled back his sleeve. Saladin, his face joyful, was sitting on his dais; the unbelievers showed black despair."[58] It thus seems fitting that during one of his amazing World War I adventures leading irregular Arab forces against the Turks, T. E. Lawrence "liberated" the Kaiser's wreath from Saladin's tomb and it now resides in the Imperial War Museum in London.

Not only have many Western historians ignored the real Saladin; they have given little or no coverage to Baybars (also Baibars), Sultan of Egypt, although he is much more celebrated than Saladin in Muslim histories of this period. When Baybars took the Knights of the Templar fortress of Safad 1266, he had all the inhabitants massacred even though he had promised to spare their lives during negotiations.[59] Later that same year his forces took the great city of Antioch.

Even though the city surrendered after four days, Baybars ordered all inhabitants, including all women and children, killed or enslaved. What followed was "the single greatest massacre of the entire crusading era"[60]—it is estimated that seventeen thousand men were murdered and tens of thousands of women and children were marched away as slaves.[61]

Since Count Behemund VI, ruler of Antioch, was away when this disaster befell his city, Baybars sent him a letter telling him what he had missed: "You would have seen your knights prostrate beneath the horses' hooves, your houses stormed by pillagers. . . . You would have seen your Muslim enemy trampling on the place where you celebrate Mass, cutting the throats of monks, priests and deacons upon the altars, bringing sudden death to the Patriarchs and slavery to the royal princes. You would have seen fire running through your palaces, your dead burned in this world before going down to the fires of the next."[62]

The massacre of Antioch is seldom reported in the many apologetic Western histories of the Crusades. Karen Armstrong did report this massacre, but attributes it to "a new Islam" that had developed in response to the dire crusader threat and with a "desperate determination to survive." Armstrong also noted that because Baybars was a patron of the arts, he "was not simply a destroyer . . . [but also] a great builder."[63] Even so, Armstrong's evaluation of Baybars is faint praise compared with that of the Muslims. An inscription from about 1266 calls him "the pillar of the world and religion, the sultan of Islam and the Muslim, the killer of infidels and polytheists, the tamer of rebels and heretics . . . the Alexander of the age."[64] Many other inscriptions also compare him with Alexander the Great.

Of course, even though most of the crusaders went to war for reasons of faith and at considerable personal cost, few of them adopted a religious lifestyle. They ate and drank as well as they were able, and most of them routinely violated many commandments, especially those concerned with murder, adultery, and coveting wives. Moreover, they did not disdain the spoils of battle and looted as much as they were able—which wasn't much when balanced against the costs of crusading. And of course they were often cruel and bloodthirsty—after all they had been trained from childhood to make war, face to face, sword to sword, and Pope Urban II called them "Soldiers of Hell." No doubt it was very "unenlightened" of the crusaders to be typical medieval warriors, but it strikes me as even more unenlightened to anachronistically impose the Geneva Convention on the crusaders while pretending that their Islamic opponents were either UN Peacekeepers or hapless victims.

Rediscovering the Crusades

KAREN ARMSTRONG WOULD HAVE us believe that the Crusades are "one of the direct causes of the conflict in the Middle East today."[65] That may be so, but not because the Muslim world has been harboring bitterness over the Crusades for the past many centuries. As Jonathan Riley-Smith explained: "One often reads that Muslims have inherited from their medieval ancestors bitter memories of the violence of the crusaders. Nothing could be further from the truth. Before the end of the nineteenth century Muslims had not shown much interest in the crusades . . . [looking] back on [them] with indifference and complacency."[66] Even at the time they took place, Muslim chroniclers paid very little attention to the Crusades, regarding them as invasions by "a primitive, unlearned, impoverished, and un-Muslim people, about whom Muslim rulers and scholars knew and cared little."[67] Moreover, most Arabs dismissed the Crusades as having been attacks upon the hated Turks, and therefore of little interest.[68] Indeed, in the account written by Ibn Zafir at the end of the twelfth century, it was said that it was better that the Franks occupied the Kingdom of Jerusalem as this prevented "the spread of the influence of the Turks to the lands of Egypt."[69]

Muslim interest in the Crusades seems to have begun in the nineteenth century, when the term itself[70] was introduced by Christian

Arabs who translated French histories into Arabic—for it was in the West that the Crusades first came back into vogue during the nineteenth century. In Europe and the United States "the romance of the crusades and crusading" became a very popular literary theme, as in the many popular novels of Sir Walter Scott.[71] Not surprisingly, this development required that, at least in Britain and America, the Crusades be "de-Catholicized."[72] In part this was done by emphasizing the conflict between the Knights Templar and the pope, transforming the former into an order of valiant anti-Catholic heroes. In addition, there developed a strong linkage between the European imperial impulse and the romantic imagery of the Crusades "to such an extent that, by World War One, war campaigns and war heroes were regularly lauded as crusaders in the popular press, from the pulpit, and in the official propaganda of the British war machine."[73]

Meanwhile in the East, the Ottoman Empire was fully revealed as "the sick man of Europe," a decrepit relic unable to produce any of the arms needed for its defense, which highlighted the general backwardness of Islamic culture and prompted "seething anger"[74] against the West among Muslim intellectuals, eventually leading them to focus on the Crusades.

Thus, current Muslim memories and anger about the Crusades are a twentieth century creation,[75] prompted in part by "post–World War I British and French imperialism and the post–World War II creation of the state of Israel."[76] It was the last Sultan of the Ottoman Empire to rule with absolute authority, Abdulhamid II (reign: 1876–1909), who began to refer to European Crusades. This prompted the first Muslim history of the Crusades, published in 1899. In the introduction, its author, Sayyid Ali al-Hariri, noted that "the sovereigns of Europe nowadays attack our Sublime Empire in a manner bearing great resemblance to the deeds of those people in bygone times [the crusaders]. Our most glorious sultan, Abdulhamid II, has rightly remarked that Europe is now carrying out a Crusade against us."[77]

This theme was eagerly picked up by Muslim nationalists. "Only Muslim unity could oppose these new crusades, some argued, and the crusading threat became an important theme in the writings of the pan-Islamic movement."[78] Even within the context of Muslim weakness in the face of the modern West, Islamic triumphalism flourished; many proposed that through the Crusades the "savage West . . . benefited by absorbing [Islam's] civilized values." As for crusader effects on Islam, "how could Islam benefit from contacts established with an inferior, backward civilization?"[79]

Eventually, the brutal, colonizing crusader imagery proved to have such polemical power that it eventually drowned out nearly everything else in the ideological lexicon of Muslim antagonism toward the West, except, of course, for Israel and paranoid tales about the worldwide Jewish conspiracy.

Conclusion

THE CRUSADES WERE NOT unprovoked. They were not the first round of European colonialism. They were not conducted for land, loot, or converts. The crusaders were not barbarians who victimized the cultivated Muslims. The Crusades are not a blot on the history of Christianity. No apologies are required.

PART IV

Medieval Currents

CHAPTER FOURTEEN

The "Dark Ages" and Other Mythical Eras

LET US NOW RETURN TO earlier times and the fall of Rome. For centuries it has been the common wisdom that after the fall of Rome came the *Dark Ages*—many centuries during which ascendant Christianity imposed an era of ignorance and superstition all across Europe. In her long-admired study of medieval philosophers, Anne Fremantle (1909–2002) wrote of "a dark, dismal patch, a sort of dull and dirty chunk of some ten centuries, wedged between the shining days of the golden Greeks . . . and the brilliant galaxy of light given out jointly by those twin luminaries, the Renaissance and the Reformation."[1]

The Italian humanist Petrarch (1304–1374) may have been the first to call "the period stretching from the fall of the Roman Empire until his own age as a time of 'darkness,'"[2] an anti-Christian judgment that has echoed down the centuries. Voltaire (1694–1778) described this long era as one when "barbarism, superstition, [and] ignorance covered the face of the world."[3] According to Rousseau (1712–1778), "Europe had relapsed into the barbarism of the earliest ages. The people of this part of the world . . . lived some centuries ago in a condition worse than ignorance."[4] Edward Gibbon (1737–1794) also proclaimed that the fall of Rome was the "triumph of barbarism and religion."[5] More recently, Bertrand Russell (1872–1970) lent his authority to the matter, writing in the illustrated edition of his famous college textbook: "As the central authority of Rome decayed, the lands of the Western Empire began to sink into an era of barbarism during which Europe suffered a general cultural decline. The Dark Ages, as they are called . . . it is not inappropriate to call these centuries dark, especially if they are set against what came before and what came after."[6]

As Russell suggested, the prevailing ignorance during the Dark Ages seems magnified by contrast with the Renaissance. Being the French word for "rebirth," Renaissance identifies the era beginning at the end of the fourteenth century when Europeans rediscovered long-forgotten classical learning, thereby causing new light to break through the prevailing intellectual darkness. According to the standard historical account, the Renaissance occurred because a decline in church control over major northern Italian cities such as Florence[7] allowed a revival of classical Greco-Roman culture. Furthermore, this new appreciation for knowledge, especially for scientific knowledge not hobbled by theology, led directly from the Renaissance to the Enlightenment. Also known as the "Age of Reason," the Enlightenment is said to have begun in the sixteenth century when (aided by the Reformation) secular thinkers freed themselves from clerical control and revolutionized both science and philosophy, thereby ushering in the modern world. To quote Bertrand Russell once more: "Enlightenment was essentially a revaluation of independent intellectual activity, aimed quite literally at spreading light where hitherto darkness had prevailed."[8]

To sum up: Western history consists of four major eras: 1) classical antiquity, then 2) the Dark Ages when the church dominated, followed by 3) the Renaissance-Enlightenment which led the way to 4) modern times.

For several centuries that has been the fundamental organizing scheme for every textbook devoted to Western history,[9] despite the fact that serious historians have known for decades that this scheme is a complete fraud—"an indestructible fossil of self-congratulatory Renaissance humanism."[10] It is appropriate to use the term *renaissance* to identify a particular period in the arts when there was renewed interest in classical styles, and to distinguish this period from the Gothic or the Baroque. But it is inappropriate to apply this term to identify the rebirth of progress following the Dark Ages because there *never were any Dark Ages*!

The Myth of the "Dark Ages"

IRONICALLY, THE MOST BENEFICIAL factor in the rise of Western civilization was the fall of Rome! Like all of the ancient empires, Rome suffered from chronic power struggles among the ruling elite, but aside from that and chronic border wars and some impressive public works projects, very little happened—change, whether technological or cultural, was so slow as to go nearly unnoticed. This prompted the distinguished Roman engineer Sextus Julius Frontinus (40–103 CE) to note that "Inventions have long since reached their limit, and I see no hope for further developments."[11] Instead, as the centuries passed most people continued to live as they always had, "just a notch above barest subsistence . . . little better off than their oxen."[12] Of course, as much as half of the population of the empire consisted of slaves who, in effect, were oxen. But even most free Romans lived at a bare subsistence level, not because they lacked the potential to achieve a much higher standard of living, but because a predatory ruling elite extracted every ounce of "surplus" production. If all production above the bare minimum needed for survival is seized by the elite, there is no motivation for anyone to produce more. Consequently, despite the fabulous wealth of the elite, Rome was very poor. As E. L. Jones noted, "emperors amassed vast wealth but received incomes that were nevertheless small relative to the immensity of the territories and populations governed."[13]

When the collapse of the Roman Empire "released the tax-paying millions . . . from a paralysing oppression,"[14] many new technologies began to appear and were rapidly and widely adopted with the result that ordinary people were able to live far better, and, after centuries of decline under Rome, the population began to grow again. No longer were the productive classes bled to sustain the astonishing excesses of the Roman elite, or to erect massive monuments to imperial egos, or to support vast armies to hold Rome's many colonies in thrall. Instead, human effort and ingenuity turned to better ways to farm, to sail, to transport goods, to conduct business, to build churches, to make war, to educate, and even to play music. But because so many centuries later a number of examples of classical Greek and Roman public grandeur still stand as remarkable ruins, many intellectuals have been prompted to mourn the loss of these "great civilizations." Many who are fully aware of what this grandeur cost in human suffering have been quite willing even to write-off slavery as merely "the sacrifice which had to be paid for this achievement."[15] To put it plainly, for too long too many historians have been as gullible as tourists, gaping at the monuments, palaces, and conspicuous consumption of Rome, and then drawing invidious comparisons between such "cosmopolitan" places and "provincial" communities such as medieval merchant towns.

In any event, there was no "fall" into "Dark Ages." Instead, once freed of the bondage of Rome, Europe separated into hundreds of independent "statelets."[16] In many of these societies progress and increased production became profitable, and that ushered in "one of the great innovative eras of mankind," as technology was developed and put into use "on a scale no civilization had previously known."[17] In fact, it was during the "Dark Ages" that Europe took the great technological and intellectual leap forward that put it ahead of the rest of the world.[18] How could historians have so misrepresented things?

In part, the notion that Europe fell into the "Dark Ages" was a hoax perpetrated by very antireligious intellectuals such as Voltaire and Gibbon, who were determined to claim that theirs was the era of "Enlightenment." Another factor was that intellectuals too often have no interest in anything but literary matters. It is quite true that after the fall of Rome, educated Europeans did not write nearly as elegant Latin as had the best Roman writers. For many, that was sufficient cause to regard this as a backward time. In addition, during this era only limited attention was paid to classical thinkers such as Plato and Aristotle, and that too was taken as proof of widespread ignorance.

Another factor contributing to the myth of the "Dark Ages" is that in this era there no longer were large cities having hundreds of thousands of residents, as had ancient Rome and Alexandria.[19] It seemed obvious that high culture could not have been sustained in the small communities of Medieval Europe—in the year 1000 there were only twenty thousand inhabitants in Paris, not many more in London, and Rome had shrunk to fewer than thirty thousand.[20] But perhaps the most important factor in the myth of the "Dark Ages" is the inability of intellectuals to value or even to notice the nuts and bolts of real life. Hence, revolutions in agriculture, weaponry and warfare, nonhuman power, transportation, manufacturing, and commerce went unappreciated. So too did remarkable moral progress. For example, at the fall of Rome there was very extensive slavery everywhere in Europe; by the time of the "Renaissance" it was long gone. But what is truly difficult to explain is how the creators of the "Dark Ages" myth could have overlooked what would seem to have been their chief interest: high culture. Nevertheless, they missed or dismissed the enormous progress that took place in music, art, literature, education, and science.

I have written at length elsewhere[21] on what truly took place during the mythical era of the "Dark Ages." Here a summary will suffice.

Progress in Technology

THE ROMANS MADE LITTLE use of water or wind power, preferring manual labor performed by slaves. In contrast, an inventory conducted in the ninth century found that one-third of the estates along the Seine River in the area around Paris had water mills, the majority of them on church-owned properties.[22] Several centuries later there was one mill every seventy feet along this stretch of the river![23] Meanwhile across the channel, the *Domesday Book*, compiled in 1086 as a forerunner of the modern census, reported that there were at least 5,624 water-powered mills already operating in England, or one for every fifty families, and this is known to be an undercount.[24] Among many other things, mills such as these mechanized the manufacture of woolen cloth and soon enabled England to dominate the European market.[25] Many dams also were constructed during the "Dark Ages"; one at Toulouse, built around 1120, was more than thirteen hundred feet across and was constructed by driving thousands of giant oak logs into the riverbed to form a front and rear palisade, which then was filled with dirt and stone.[26] In similar fashion, "Dark Age" Europeans excelled at bridge building. Recently, underwater archeologists discovered the timbers that once had supported a bridge more than five hundred feet long across the Shannon River in Ireland. Tree ring evidence revealed that all of these timbers had been felled in 803.[27]

During this era, Europeans also harnessed the wind. They not only used windmills to power the same equipment as did water mills; they also used them to reclaim huge portions of what are now Belgium and the Netherlands by pumping out the sea. Tens of thousands of windmills devoted to this task worked day and night throughout most of the "Dark Ages." Indeed, by late in the twelfth century, western Europe had become so crowded with windmills that owners began to file lawsuits against one another for blocking their wind.[28] (Europeans in this era sustained well-organized courts and a host of lawyers, although the latter may not have amounted to progress.)

Meanwhile, agriculture was revolutionized.[29] First came the shift to a three-field system wherein one third of the productive land was left unplanted each year while continuing to be cultivated (to remove weeds) and fertilized. The result of this renewal of the land was far greater production. In addition, the invention of the heavy plow permitted far better cultivation of the wetter, denser soils north of Italy, and the introduction of the horse-collar permitted the replacement of slow oxen teams with teams of horses, thus at least doubling the speed of cultivation. Selective plant breeding also began in the monasteries resulting in more productive and hardy crops. Altogether these "Dark Ages" achievements fed a larger population much better.

Also of immense importance was the invention of chimneys, which allowed buildings and homes to be heated without needing holes in the roof to let out smoke while letting in rain, snow, and cold air. Another revolutionary innovation was eyeglasses, which were invented in about 1280 and almost immediately went into mass production thus allowing huge numbers of people to lead productive lives who otherwise could not have done so.[30] In 1492, when Columbus set out on his first voyage west, eyeglasses still were known only in Europe.

Prior to the "Dark Ages," there was no heavy cavalry. Mounted troops did not charge headlong at a gallop, putting the full weight of horse and rider behind a long lance. The reason was the lack of stirrups and a proper saddle. Without stirrups to brace against, a rider attempting to drive home a lance will be thrown off his horse. The ability of a rider to withstand sudden shocks is also greatly increased by a saddle with a very high pommel and cantle—the latter being curved to partly enclose the rider's hips. It was not Rome or any other warlike empire that produced heavy cavalry: their mounted troops rode on light, almost flat, pad saddles, or even bareback, and they had no stirrups. Consequently, these mounted warriors could only fire bows, throw spears, or swing swords. They could not bowl over their opponents. It was the "barbarous" Franks who, in 732, fielded the first armored knights astride massive horses, and who slaughtered invading Muslim forces on the battlefield of Tours when they charged them behind long lances, secure in their high-backed Norman saddles and braced in their revolutionary stirrups.[31] Nearly four centuries later, when the knights of Europe confronted Muslim armies in the Holy Land, nothing had changed. The crusaders still were the only ones with stirrups and adequate saddles. They also were the only ones with crossbows.

Roman sea power was based on galleys powered by oars and having only an auxiliary sail. They fought by ramming one another and then by engaging in hand-to-hand combat with swords and spears. But well before the end of the "Dark Ages," Europeans had invented true sailing ships and armed them with cannons.[32] That gun powder was not invented in the West is immaterial. What matters is that within a decade of the arrival of gunpowder from China, church bell manufacturers all over Europe were casting effective cannons that were adopted by every army and navy, transforming the nature of war.[33] In contrast, the Chinese cast only a few, ineffective cannons, mostly being content to use gunpowder in fireworks.[34]

These are only a few of the important technological innovations achieved during the "Dark Ages." What is clear is that so much important technological progress occurred during this era that classical Greece and Rome had been left far behind. In fact, even though they did not yet possess gunpowder, the crusader knights who marched off to the Holy Land in 1097 would have made short work of the Roman legions.

Inventing Capitalism

HISTORIANS OF THE RISE of Western civilization agree that the development of capitalism was of immense importance—even Karl Marx (1818–1883) supports this view, writing that "[capitalism has] created more massive and more colossal productive forces than all the preceding generations together."[35] Although many sociologists still echo Max Weber's (1864–1920) claim that capitalism originated in the Protestant Reformation, capitalism actually originated in the "depths" of the "Dark Ages." Beginning in about the ninth century, many of the large, prosperous, and growing monastic estates developed into well-organized and stable firms involved in complex commercial activities that generated a sophisticated banking system within a developing free market, thereby achieving capitalism in all its glory.[36] Many secular capitalist firms were soon founded, especially in major Italian city-states, and capitalism began to spread rapidly. By the thirteenth century, there were 173 major Italian banks having hundreds of branches all over western Europe—even in England and Ireland.[37]

Because capitalism had originated within the great religious orders, Christian theologians were prompted to rethink traditional doctrines opposed to profits and interest.

St. Albertus Magnus (1206–1280) proposed that the "just price" to charge for something is not what it cost, but what "goods are worth according to the estimation of the market at the time of sale."[38] That is, a price is just if that's what uncoerced buyers are willing to pay. Echoing his teacher, but using many more words, St. Thomas Aquinas (1225–1274) began his analysis of just prices by posing the question, "Whether a man may lawfully sell a thing for more than it is worth?"[39] He answered by first quoting St. Augustine (354–430) that it is natural and lawful for "you to wish to buy cheap, and sell dear." Next, Aquinas excluded fraud from legitimate transactions. Finally, he recognized that worth is not really an objective value—"the just price of things is not absolutely definite"—but is a function of the buyer's desire for the thing purchased and the seller's willingness or reluctance to sell, so long as the buyer was not misled, or under duress. To be just, a price had to be the same for all potential buyers at a given moment, thus barring price discrimination.

As to interest on loans, Aquinas was unusually confusing. In some writings he condemned all interest as the sin of usury, while in other passages he accepted that lenders deserve compensation, although he was fuzzy as to how much and why.[40] However, prompted by the realities of a rapidly expanding commercial economy, many of Aquinas's contemporaries, especially the Canonists, were not so cautious, but began "discovering" many exceptions wherein interest charges were not usurious.[41] For example, if a productive property such as an estate is given as security for a loan, the lender may take all of the production during the period of the loan and not deduct it from the amount owed.[42] Many other exclusions involved the "costs" to the lender of not having the money available for other commercial opportunities such as buying goods for resale or acquiring new fields. Since these alternative opportunities for profit are entirely licit, it is licit to compensate a lender for having to forgo them.[43] Thus, while the "sin of usury" remained on the books, so to speak, "usury" had become essentially an empty term.

Thus, by no later than the thirteenth century, the leading Christian theologians had fully debated the primary aspects of emerging capitalism—profits, property rights, credit, lending, and the like. As Lester K. Little summed up: "In each case they came up with generally favorable, approving views, in sharp contrast to the attitudes that had prevailed for six or seven centuries right up to the previous generation."[44] Capitalism was fully and finally freed from all fetters of faith.[45]

It was a remarkable shift. These were, after all, theologians who had separated themselves from the world. Most of them had taken vows of poverty. Most of their predecessors had held merchants and commercial activities in contempt. Had asceticism truly prevailed in the religious orders, it seems most unlikely that Christian disdain for and opposition to commerce would have mellowed, let alone have been radically transformed. This theological revolution was the result of direct experience with worldly imperatives. For all their genuine acts of charity, monastic administrators were not about to give all their wealth to the poor or to sell their products at cost. It was the active participation of the great houses in free markets that caused monastic theologians to reconsider the morality of commerce. Nothing of the sort took place among Islamic theologians, with the result that capitalism could not develop, which had obvious consequences for Muslim economic progress.

Moral Progress

ALL CLASSICAL SOCIETIES WERE slave societies—both Plato and Aristotle were slave-owners, as were most free residents of Greek city-states. In fact, all known societies above the very primitive level have been slave societies—even many of the Northwest American Indian tribes had slaves long before Columbus's voyage.[46] Amid this universal slavery, only one civilization ever rejected human bondage: Christendom. And it did it twice!

Elsewhere I have told the story of how slavery reappeared and then was prohibited in the Western Hemisphere.[47] But the very first time slavery was eliminated anywhere in the world was not during the "Renaissance" or the "Enlightenment," but during the "Dark Ages." And it was accomplished by clever church leaders who first extended the sacraments to all slaves, reserving only ordination into the priesthood. Initially, the implications of the Christianization of slaves went unnoticed, but soon the clergy began to argue that no true Christian (or Jew) should be enslaved.[48] Since slaves were Christians, priests began to urge owners to free their slaves as an "infinitely commendable act" that helped ensure their own salvation.[49] Many manumissions were recorded in surviving wills. Soon there was another factor: intermarriage. Despite being against the law in most of Europe, there is considerable evidence of mixed unions by the seventh century, usually involving free men and female slaves. The most celebrated of these unions took place in 649 when Clovis II, King of the Franks, married his British slave Bathilda. When Clovis died in 657, Bathilda ruled as regent until her eldest son came of age. Bathilda used her position to mount a campaign to halt the slave trade and to redeem those in slavery. Upon her death, the church acknowledged Bathilda as a saint.

At the end of the eighth century Charlemagne opposed slavery, while the pope and many other powerful and effective clerical voices echoed St. Bathilda. As the ninth century dawned, Bishop Agobard of Lyons thundered: "All men are brothers, all invoke one same Father,

God: the slave and the master, the poor man and the rich man, the ignorant and the learned, the weak and the strong. . . . [N]one has been raised above the other . . . there is no . . . slave or free, but in all things and always there is only Christ."[50] Soon, no one "doubted that slavery in itself was against divine law."[51] Indeed, during the eleventh century both St. Wulfstan and St. Anselm successfully campaigned to remove the last vestiges of slavery in Christendom.[52]

Progress in High Culture

EVEN IF VOLTAIRE, GIBBON, and other proponents of the "Enlightenment" could be excused for being oblivious to engineering achievements and to innovations in agriculture or warfare, surely they must be judged severely for ignoring or dismissing the remarkable achievements in "high culture" accomplished by medieval Europeans: in music, art, literature, education, and science.

Music: The Romans and Greeks sang and played monophonic music: a single musical line sounded by all voices or instruments. It was medieval musicians who developed polyphony, the simultaneous sounding of two or more musical lines, hence harmonies. Just when this occurred is unknown, but "it was an established practice when it was described in *Musica enchiriadis*," published around 900.[53] And, in about the tenth century, an adequate system of musical notation was invented and popularized so that music could be accurately performed by musicians who had never heard it.

Art: Unfortunately, the remarkable artistic era that emerged in eleventh century Europe is known as "Romanesque," despite the fact that it was quite different from anything done by the Romans. This name was imposed by nineteenth century professors who "knew" that Europe only recovered from the "Dark Ages" by *going back* to Roman culture. Hence this could only have been an era of poor imitations of things Roman. In fact, Romanesque architecture, sculpture, and painting were original and powerful in ways that "even the late

Roman artists would never have understood."[54] Then, in the twelfth century, the Romanesque period was followed by the even more powerful Gothic era. It seems astonishing, but Gothic architecture and painting were scorned by critics during the "Enlightenment" for not conforming to "the standards of classical Greece and Rome: 'May he who invented it be cursed.'"[55] These same critics mistakenly thought the style originated with the "barbarous" Goths, hence the name, and, as anyone who has seen one of Europe's great Gothic cathedrals knows, the artistic judgment of these critics was no better than their history, to say nothing of their disregard for the architectural inventions, including the flying buttress, that made it possible for the first time to build very tall buildings with thin walls and large windows, thus prompting major achievements in stained glass. It also was thirteenth-century artists in northern Europe who were the first to use oil paint and to put their work on stretched canvass rather than on wood or plaster. This "allowed the painter to take his time, to use brushes of amazing delicacy, to achieve effects . . . which seemed close to miracles."[56] Anyone who thinks that great painting began with the Italian "Renaissance" should examine the work of the Van Eycks. So much, then, for notions that the millennium following the collapse of Rome was an artistic blank or worse.

Literature: Gibbon wrote *The Decline and Fall of the Roman Empire* in English, not Latin. Voltaire wrote exclusively in French, Cervantes in Spanish, and Machiavelli and Da Vinci in Italian. This was possible only because these languages had been given literary form by medieval giants such as Dante, Chaucer, the nameless authors of the *chansons de geste*, and the monks who, beginning in the ninth century, devoted themselves to writing lives of saints—"the first known pages of French literature . . . belong to this genre."[57] Thus was vernacular prose formulated and popularized. So much for "Dark Age" illiteracy and ignorance.

Education: The university was something new under the sun—an institution devoted exclusively to "higher learning." This Christian invention was quite unlike Chinese academies for training Mandarins or a Zen master's school. The new universities were not primarily concerned with imparting the received wisdom. Rather, just as is the case today, faculty gained fame and invitations to join faculties elsewhere by innovation. Consequently, during the "Dark Ages" university professors—now known as the Scholastics—gave their primary attention to the pursuit of knowledge.[58] And they achieved many remarkable results, as will be outlined in chapter 16. The world's first two universities were founded by Catholic scholars in Paris and Bologna in about 1160. Forty years later came Oxford and Cambridge and by the end of the thirteenth century another twenty universities had been founded all across Europe, enrolling thousands of students.

Science: For generations, historians claimed that a "Scientific Revolution" began in the sixteenth century when Nicolaus Copernicus proposed a heliocentric model of the solar system. But recently, specialists in the history of science have concluded that what occurred was an evolution, not a revolution.[59] Just as Copernicus simply took the next implicit step in the cosmology of his day, so too the flowering of science in that era was the culmination of the gradual progress that had been made over previous centuries. This evolution will be properly traced in chapter 16.

This, then, was the era that the intellectual proponents of the "Enlightenment" described as a tragic decline into ignorance and superstition. Little wonder that many contemporary historians become incensed by use of the term *Dark Ages*. As the distinguished medievalist Warren Hollister (1930–1997) put it in his presidential address to the Pacific Historical Association, "to my mind, anyone who believes that the era that witnessed the building of Chartres Cathedral and the invention of parliament and the university was 'dark' must be mentally retarded—or at best, deeply, deeply, ignorant."[60]

The Myth of the "Renaissance"

OBVIOUSLY, IF THE "DARK AGES" are a ridiculous myth, so too must be the "Renaissance" since it proposes that Europe was saved from ignorance when intellectuals in various Northern Italian city-states broke sufficiently free from church control to allow the "rebirth" of classical knowledge. Had there really been a return to classical knowledge, it would have created an era of cultural decline since Christian Europe had long since surpassed classical antiquity in nearly every way. Unfortunately, many creators of the "Renaissance" myth had no knowledge of the immense progress of the "Dark Ages" and seem to have based their entire assessment on the extent to which scholars were familiar with Aristotle, Plato, Euclid, Sophocles, Aristophanes, and other stalwarts of classical learning and literature. But even this legacy of classical culture was fully restored long before the "Renaissance." The key development was the translation of these writers into Latin, since Greek was no longer the intellectual language of Christendom. And these translations were not made during the "Renaissance," but centuries earlier, by pious monastic scholars. Indeed, "between 1125 and 1200, a veritable flood of translations into Latin, made Greek . . . [writing] available, with more to come in the thirteenth century."[61] This is fully supported by surviving monastery library catalogues from as far back as the twelfth century which reveal extensive holdings of classical authors.[62]

As for the famous "Italian Renaissance," it was not a rebirth of classical learning at all! It was a period of cultural emulation during which people of fashion copied the classical styles in manners, art, literature, and philosophy. Out of this passion for their own ancient days of glory, northern Italians recast history to stress "the achievements of modern Italy and their dislike and contempt for the barbarians of the north."[63] Thus they imposed the "Dark Ages" between themselves and their past. But it wasn't so. The Scholastics knew of, and often knew more than, the ancient Greek and Roman authors.

The Myth of Secular "Enlightenment"

THE SINGLE MOST REMARKABLE and ironic thing about the "Enlightenment" is that those who proclaimed it made little or no contribution to the accomplishments they hailed as a revolution in human knowledge, while those responsible for these advances stressed continuity with the past. That is, Voltaire, Rousseau, Diderot, Hume, Gibbon, and the rest were literary men, while the primary revolution they hailed as the "Enlightenment" was scientific. Equally misleading is the fact that although the literary men who proclaimed the "Enlightenment" were irreligious, the central figures in the scientific achievements of the era were deeply religious.[64] So much then for the idea that suddenly in the sixteenth century, enlightened secular forces burst the chains of Christian thought and set the foundation for modern times. What the proponents of "Enlightenment" actually initiated was the tradition of angry secular attacks on religion in the name of science—attacks like those of their modern counterparts such as Carl Sagan, Daniel Dennett, and Richard Dawkins. Presented as the latest word in sophistication, rationalism, and reason, these assaults are remarkably naive and simplistic—both then and now.[65] In truth, the rise of science was inseparable from Christian theology, for the latter gave direction and confidence to the former, as will be seen in chapter 16.

Claims concerning the revolutionary character of the "Renaissance" and the "Enlightenment" have seemed plausible because remarkable progress was made in these eras. But rather than being a revolutionary break with the past, these achievements were simply an extension of the accelerating curve of progress that began soon after the fall of Rome. Thus, the historian's task is not to explain why so much progress has been made since the fifteenth century—that focus is much too late. The fundamental question about the rise of the West is: What enabled Europeans to begin and maintain the extraordinary and enduring period of rapid progress that enabled them, by the end of the "Dark Ages," to have far surpassed the rest of the world? Why was it that, although many civilizations have pursued alchemy, it led to chemistry only in Europe? Or, while many societies have made excellent observations of the heavens and have created sophisticated systems of astrology, why was this transformed into scientific astronomy only in Europe?

Several recent authors have discovered the secret to Western success in geography. But, that same geography long sustained European cultures that were well behind those of Asia. Others have traced the rise of the West to steel, or to guns and sailing ships, and still others have credited a more productive agriculture. The trouble is that these answers are part of what needs to be explained: *Why* did Europeans excel at metallurgy, ship-building, or farming? I have devoted a book to my answer: that the truly fundamental basis for the rise of the West was an extraordinary faith in *reason* and *progress* that was firmly rooted in Christian theology, in the belief that God is the rational creator of a rational universe.[66]

Conclusion

WHEN ONE EXAMINES THE conventional outline of Western history one encounters some truly fabulous inventions of great historical eras that never really happened: the "Dark Ages," the "Renaissance," the "Enlightenment," and the "Age of Reason." We turn next to an equally fictitious era: the "Age of Faith."

Chapter Fifteen

The People's Religion

MEDIEVAL TIMES HAVE FREQUENTLY BEEN described as the "Age of Faith"[1] or the "Age of Belief"[2] because in this era "everyone believed what religious authority told them to believe."[3] In his bestseller *A World Lit Only by Fire*, the distinguished William Manchester (1922–2004) proclaimed that "there was no room in the medieval mind for doubt; the possibility of skepticism simply did not exist."[4]

It would be hard to discover a more glaring instance of historical bias and ignorance. As will be seen, the masses of medieval Europeans not only were remarkably skeptical, but very lacking in all aspects of Christian commitment—often militantly so! To attempt to explain why medieval Christianity had made so little headway among the peasants and lower classes, this chapter examines the local clergy, finding them almost universally ignorant, often lazy, and frequently dissolute. The discussion then turns to how the church long neglected the rural population in an era when nearly everyone was a peasant, and how both the Catholic and Protestant hierarchies, in contrast with the early church, failed to offer the general public an appealing model of Christian life. Finally, the chapter examines the actual religion pursued by most people in the Middle Ages and how it was misinterpreted by Christian theologians—with tragic results.

Popular Christian Commitment

THERE ARE VERY FEW statistics on religious life in medieval times, but there are a surprising number of trustworthy reports from many times and places, and they are in amazing agreement that the great majority of ordinary people seldom if ever went to church. As Michael Walzer put it, "Medieval society was largely composed of non-participants [in the churches]."[5]

Alexander Murray's assessment of medieval Italian religious life is confirmed again and again: "Substantial sections of thirteenth-century society hardly attended church at all."[6] The Dominican prior Humbert of Romans (1200–1277) admitted that people in Italy "rarely go to church."[7] When the Blessed Giordano of Rivalto (1260–1311) arrived in Florence to preach, he suggested to a local woman that she take her daughter to church at least on feast days, only to be informed: "It is not the custom."[8] In about 1430, St. Antonio noted that Tuscan peasants seldom attended mass, and that "very many of them do not confess once a year, and far fewer are those who take communion."[9] St. Bernardino of Siena (1380–1444) also reported that even the few parishioners who came to mass, usually were late and hastened out at the elevation of the Host, "as though they had seen not Christ, but the Devil."[10]

Meanwhile, in England the anonymous authors of *Dives and Pauper* (ca. 1410) complained that "the people these days . . . are loath to hear God's Service. [And when they are forced to attend] they come late and leave early."[11] According to G. G. Coulton (1858–1947), medieval church attendance was "still more irregular in Wales, Scotland, and Ireland than in England."[12]

Extraordinary reports on the lack of popular religious participation are available for Lutheran Germany based on the regular visitations by higher church officials to local communities, beginning in 1525. These have been extracted by the distinguished American historian Gerald Strauss who noted, "I have selected only such instances as could be multiplied a hundredfold."[13] It is true that these German reports postdate the medieval era, but there is nothing whatever to suggest that they reveal a decline from earlier times—the factors responsible for low levels of popular support and participation had remained constant.

Strauss offered several of these reports of low attendance. In Saxony (1574): "You'll find more of them out fishing than at service. . . . Those who do come walk out as soon as the pastor begins his sermon."[14] In Seegrehna (1577): "A pastor testified that he often quits his church without preaching . . . because not a soul has turned up to hear him."[15] In Barum (1572): "It is the greatest and most widespread complaint of all pastors hereabouts that people do not go to church on Sundays. . . . Nothing helps; they will not come . . . so that pastors face near-empty churches."[16] In Braunschweig-Grubenhagen (1580s): "many churches are empty on Sundays."[17] In Weilburg (1604): "Absenteeism from church on Sundays was so widespread that the synod debated whether the city gates should be barred on Sunday mornings to lock everyone inside. Evidence from elsewhere suggests that this expedient would not have helped."[18]

Nevertheless, it is not clear that having a large turnout at Sunday services would have been desirable. That's because when people did come to church so many of them misbehaved! The eminent historian Keith Thomas combed the reports of English church courts and clerical diaries finding not only constant complaints that so few came to church, but that "the conduct of many church-goers left so much to be desired as to turn the service into a travesty of what was intended. . . . Members of the congregation jostled for pews, nudged their neighbors, hawked and spat, knitted, made course remarks, told jokes, fell asleep, and even left off guns. . . . A Cambridgeshire man was charged with indecent behaviour in church in 1598 after his 'most loathsome farting, striking, and scoffing speeches' had occasioned 'the great offence of the good and the great rejoicing of the bad.'"[19]

Visitation reports from Lutheran Germany abound in similar accounts of misbehavior. In Nassau (1594): "Those who come to service are usually drunk . . . and sleep through the whole sermon, except sometimes they fall off the benches, making a great clatter, or women drop their babies on the floor."[20] In Wiesbaden (1619): "[during church] there is such snoring that I could not believe my ears when I heard it. The moment these people sit down, they put their heads on their arms and straight away they go to sleep."[21] In addition, many bring their dogs inside the church, "barking and snarling so loudly that no one can hear the preacher."[22] In Hamburg (1581): people make "indecent gestures at members of the congregation who wish to join in singing the hymns, even bringing dogs to church so that due to the loud barking the service is disturbed."[23] In Leipzig (1579–1580): "they play cards while the pastor preaches, and often mock or mimic him cruelly to his face; . . . cursing and blaspheming, hooliganism, and fighting are common. . . . [T]hey enter church when the service is half over, go at once to sleep, and run out again before the blessing is given. . . . [N]obody joins in singing the hymn; it made my heart ache to hear the pastor and the sexton singing all by themselves."[24]

In addition, the locals often misused the church itself. In 1367, John Thoresby, the archbishop of York, fulminated against holding markets in churches, especially on Sunday. Indeed, between "1229 and 1367 there are eleven such episcopal injunctions recorded. . . . Bishop after bishop thundered in vain . . . against those who 'turned the house of prayer into a den of thieves.' "[25] The same thing occurred again and again across the continent, as higher church officials complained against using churches, even cathedrals, for storing crops, sheltering livestock, and for indoor market days.[26]

Given their attitudes and their lack of church attendance, it is hardly surprising that most medieval Europeans were completely ignorant of the most basic Christian teachings.[27] Interviews in Spain during the fourteenth and fifteenth centuries with persons so pious that they reported having had a religious vision (usually of Mary) revealed that most were ignorant of the Ten Commandments and the Seven Deadly Sins. It was not merely that they could not recite them, but that they were entirely ignorant of their contents—some even failing to identify murder as a sin.[28]

In Saxony (1577 and 1589): "In some villages one could not find a single person who knew the Ten Commandments."[29] In Brandenburg (1583) "A random group of men was . . . asked how they understood each of the Ten Commandments, but we found many who could give no answer at all. . . . [N]one of them thought it a sin to get dead drunk and curse using the name of God."[30] In Notenstein (1570): parishioners "including church elders, could remember none of the Ten Commandments."[31] In Salzliebenhalle (1590): no one knows "who their redeemer and savior is."[32] In Nuremberg (1626): many could not name Good Friday as the day of the year when Jesus died.[33] And from Catholic Salzburg (1607): according to the bishop, "the common man cannot even say the Lord's Prayer or the Ave Maria with the right words and does not know the Apostles' Creed, to say nothing of the Ten Commandments."[34] And the pastor at Graim (1535) summed up: "Since they never go to church, most of them cannot even say their prayers."[35]

As for the English, the fourteenth-century preacher John Bromyard asked a shepherd if he knew who were the Father, Son, and Holy Ghost. He replied, "The father and son I know well for I tend their sheep, but I know not that third fellow; there is none of that name in our village."[36] In 1606 Nicholas Bownd remarked that the stories in the Bible are "as strange to them [the public] as any news that you can tell them."[37] Indeed, one English bishop lamented that not only did the people know nothing from the scriptures, but "they know not that there *are* any Scriptures."[38]

Perhaps not surprisingly, the lifestyles of ordinary people in this era seem exceedingly dissolute even by modern standards. The sources abound in charges of general misconduct, agreeing with the Margrave of Brandenburg, who in 1591 noted widespread "blaspheming, sorcery, adultery and whoring, excessive drinking and other vices, all practiced openly [by] the common man."[39] This is entirely consistent with Pieter Breughel's (1525–1569) paintings of Dutch peasant life, especially *The Wedding Dance* (1566), which shows that all the men dancing in the foreground have full erections pushing out their tights (albeit these protrusions are removed in the reproductions shown in most college textbooks). Breughel's depiction of peasants was not unusual. In Dutch painting at this time "peasants are invariably associated . . . with base impulses,"[40] and are depicted as drunken, lustful, and obscene. Given that several generations of a family often lived crowded together in one small room with absolutely no privacy, it is little wonder that their lifestyle was crude and their sensibilities rather gross.

Defective Clergy

NOT ONLY WAS THE medieval public lacking in Christian commitment; the same was true of the rank-and-file clergy. In fact, given how ignorant the clergy were, it is no surprise that their parishioners knew so little.

In 730 the Venerable Bede advised the future bishop Egbert that because so few English priests and monks knew any Latin, "I have frequently offered translations of both the [Apostles'] Creed and the Lord's Prayer into English."[41] In 1222 the Council of Oxford described the parish clergy as "dumb dogs,"[42] and Archbishop Pecham wrote in 1287: "The ignorance of the priests casteth the people into a ditch."[43] Subsequently, William Tyndale reported in 1530 that hardly any of the priests and curates in England knew the Lord's Prayer. When the bishop of Gloucester systematically tested his diocesan clergy in 1551, of 311 pastors, 171 could not repeat the Ten Commandments, and 27 did not know the author of the Lord's Prayer.[44] The next year, Bishop Hooper found "scores of parish clergy who could not tell who was the author of the Lord's Prayer, or where it was to be found."[45] At this same time, it was reported that in Wales "there were thousands of people who knew nothing of Christ—'yea almost that never heard of him.' "[46]

Matters were no better in Italy. In 1417, Bishop Niccolò Albergati of Bologna visited his diocese and discovered many priests who were "unable to identify the seven deadly sins."[47] St. Bernardino of Siena (1380–1444) observed a priest who "knew only the Hail Mary, and used it even at the elevation during mass."[48] In France, St. Vincent de Paul discovered in 1617 that his local priest knew no Latin, not even the words of absolution, and simply mumbled nonsense syllables.[49] So too the Lutheran clergy. In Bockenem (1568): "not one of the fourteen pastors examined could name the [books] of the New Testament."[50] In Kalenberg (1584): a pastor was asked, "Which person of the Trinity assumed human form?" and answered, "The Father."[51] Keep in mind that there were "virtually no seminaries," and that most priests picked up what little they knew as an apprentice to "a priest who had himself little or no training."[52]

Not only did the clergy resemble the laity in terms of ignorance; they also often led similarly dissolute lives as was noted in the preceding chapter. As Eamon Duffy reported: "Concubinage was widespread: impecunious clergy with a houseful of children, presiding over a half-coherent liturgy on Sundays . . . were common all over Europe."[53] Nor was dissolute living concentrated in the lower clergy. As is documented in chapter 17, there were many notorious popes, including Alexander VI (served 1492–1503), a member of the Borgia family, who flaunted his many mistresses, fathered nine illegitimate children by three women, and is widely believed to have poisoned a number of cardinals in order to seize their property.[54] As for Rome itself, in 1490 more than 15 percent of its resident adult females were registered prostitutes, and the Venetian ambassador described it as the "sewer of the world."[55]

However, "it is a mistake to suppose that the corruption of the clergy was worse in Rome than elsewhere," according to Roman Catholic historian Ludwig Pastor (1854–1928). Pastor continued: "there is documentary evidence of the immorality of the priests in almost every town in the Italian peninsula."[56] Duffy reported an abbot in southern Italy who had a concubine and five children, who told his bishop he could not end the affair because "he was fond of the children, and his physician had prescribed sexual intercourse for his gallstones!"[57] Humbert of Romans reported that many clergy "spent so much of their time in gaming, pleasure and 'worse things,' [that they] scarcely come to church."[58] As for Spain, consider that an examination of priests in the archdiocese of Braga found that an astounding seventeen hundred were the sons of priests![59] Early in the sixteenth century, Erasmus charged that "many convents of men and women differ little from public brothels."[60] In fact, after visiting the monasteries and convents in Tuscany, the pope's representative Ambrogio Traversari (1386–1436) reported that one convent was openly a brothel.[61] Meanwhile, in England, visitations from as early as the fourteenth century regularly reported local priests keeping mistresses (some of them more than one)[62] while clerical drunkenness and absenteeism were widespread.[63]

Rural Neglect

IF MOST MEDIEVAL EUROPEANS did not attend church, a primary reason was that for many centuries only the nobility and those living in towns and cities had a local church to attend! Most churches in rural areas were not located in peasant villages, but were private chapels, each maintained by a local nobleman for his family and retainers, being only about the size of "a moderately large living room in a modern house."[64] Until the thirteenth century and later, most peasants could have contact with the church only by travelling a considerable distance for baptism or marriage, and by occasional visits by an itinerant friar. This was consistent with the antirural outlook of the early Christian movement which, in turn, reflected the urban snobbery of Rome—the term *pagan* comes from the Latin word for rustic or rural-dweller (*paganus*). As Richard Fletcher explained: "The peasantry of the countryside were beyond the pale"; hence urban Christians made little or no effort to evangelize them. Rather, for early Christians "the countryside did not exist as a zone for missionary enterprise. After all, there was nothing in the New Testament about spreading the Word to the beasts of the field."[65]

Even when rural parishes did begin to appear, they suffered from neglect and most of them probably lacked a pastor, even an ignorant one, most of the time. Eamon Duffy has estimated that during the sixteenth century, for example, as many as 80 percent of the churches in the diocese of Geneva had no clergy. To make matters worse, even when there was an assigned pastor, "absenteeism was rife."[66] Thus the bishop's visitation of 1520 found that of 192 parishes in Oxfordshire, 58 pastors were not in residence.[67] The same was often reported in Italy—absent clergy, many villages with "no services at all."[68]

How then could the peasants be expected to possess any Christian culture? Where should they have learned the Lord's Prayer or who preached it, especially since even if they had a local priest, he probably didn't know either? What seems most remarkable is that the rural populace even knew who Jesus was, at least to the extent that he was one of the divine beings who could be called upon for blessings.

Eventually, of course, subsequent to the Reformation, Protestants in northern Europe and Counter-Reformation Catholics in the south (and Anglicans in Britain) initiated vigorous campaigns to educate and activate the peasant masses and the rapidly expanding urban underclasses. Thus, Martin Luther had optimistically launched massive programs to inform and energize the Lutheran parishes in Germany. But before he died, he recognized that these efforts had failed, as demonstrated by the reports from Lutheran visitations mentioned earlier in this chapter.

Inappropriate Expectations

THE PRIMARY REASONS THAT even vigorous efforts failed to reach the peasantry and urban lower classes was the failure by both Protestant and Catholic clerics to propose a Christian lifestyle that was appropriate and attractive to ordinary people,[69] and their failure to present Christian doctrines in simple, direct language rather than as complex theology.

Even though many clergy were dissolute, the medieval church presented only one model of the proper Christian life, and that was the ascetic lifestyle followed by devout monks and nuns. There was no acknowledgement by the church that this was not an appropriate model for the laity; instead they were merely "exhorted to imitate clerical piety."[70] Hence, although the church fathers certainly knew that celibacy was not to be expected of the laity, they continued to present it as the *ideal* and to teach that sexual intercourse was always sinful even within marriage,[71] never mentioning Paul's admonition to couples that they should "not refuse one another" (1 Cor. 7:5). In similar fashion, monastic commitments to fasting, to extensive prayer sessions, and even to poverty were prominent in the model of Christian life proposed by the church. But asceticism only appeals to those for whom it is a *choice*. Fasting has little appeal to those for whom hunger is an actual threat; hours of prayer presuppose having considerable leisure; and poor people never chose to increase their poverty. Hence, most medieval Europeans disdained the moral expectations of the church, thereby remaining alienated from sincere Christian commitment.

In contrast, early Christianity was attractive to the laity because it offered a model of Christian virtue that improved their quality of life by urging attractive family norms, a tangible love of neighbors, and feasible levels of sacrifice, along with a clear message of salvation. When these aspects of the early Christian faith were preached in medieval times, as they often were by various reform and dissident movements, they continued to appeal—at least to *some people*. Thus we encounter the most significant aspect of medieval Christianity, both heretical and conventional; its appeal was primarily to people of at least some privilege, to the burghers of the towns and cities as well as to the nobility. As Keith Thomas noted: "Preaching was popular with the educated classes, but aroused the irritation of the others."[72] Even so, most peasants seldom had contact with any form of Christianity, and what little contact they did have was with a Christianity that urged an unsuitably otherworldly lifestyle and the prompt payment of tithes.

As for the ignorance of the laity, it must be recognized that until the Reformation, church services (with the exception, sometimes, of brief homilies) were in Latin, a language that almost no one in the pews and many in the pulpit could understand. Not surprisingly, mass attendance was neither edifying nor educational. Thus, it was widely anticipated that Protestant preaching in the local vernaculars would end these centuries of ignorance. Not so! Why? Because when a well-trained clergy did emerge at this time, they so "often pitched their discourse far above the capacity of most of their listeners."[73]

The English philosopher John Locke (1632–1704) noted that a preacher "may as well talk Arabic to a poor day-labourer as the notions"[74] that the Anglican clergy preferred as the basis for their sermons. By the same token, Martin Luther's efforts to provide religious education for the German peasants and urban lower classes failed so completely because the lessons were conceived by a university professor primarily far more concerned with intricate theological nuances than with basic themes. The heart of Lutheran religious education was Luther's Catechism, which provides a very lengthy explication of basic Christian doctrines such as the Ten Commandments and the Lord's Prayer. Thus, it devotes many pages of convoluted text to interpreting each of the commandments. The local Lutheran clergy were supposed to preach from the Catechism every Sunday afternoon and hold classes for young people during the week. In most villages these sessions were never or rarely held because no one came.

Luther's error was not unique. All across Europe, the established churches failed to convert and arouse the "masses," by failing to recognize that it was a job for preachers, not professors. But the clergy seemed unable to grasp the point that sophisticated sermons on the mysteries of the Trinity neither informed nor converted. Thus the Oxford theologian William Pemble (1591–1623) reported on a man of sixty who had faithfully attended church twice on every Sunday and often on other days of the week, thus hearing as many as three thousand sermons in his lifetime, who when questioned on his death-bed as to "what he thought of God, he answers that he was a good old man; and what of Christ, that he was a towardly young youth; and of his soul, that it was a great bone in his body; and what should become of his soul after he was dead, that if he had done well he should be put into a pleasant green meadow."[75]

As James Obelkevich explained, "what parishioners understood as Christianity was never preached from a pulpit or taught in Sunday school, and what they took from the clergy they took on their own terms. . . . Since the clergy were incapable of shaping a more popular version of the faith, villagers were left to do so themselves."[76]

The People's Religion

DESPITE THEIR IGNORANCE OF Christianity and their alienation from the local clergy, Europe's peasants and lower classes had a ful-some supply of religion of which they made constant use. As Gerald Strauss put it, they "practiced their own brand of religion, which was a rich compound of ancient rituals, time-bound customs, a sort of un-reconstructable folk Catholicism, and a large portion of magic to help them in their daily struggle for survival."[77] Notice that Strauss did not include a list of popular divinities, neither pagan nor Christian. Although the people's religion did often call upon God, Jesus, Mary, and various saints, as well as upon some pagan gods and goddesses (and even more frequently invoked minor spirits such as fairies, elves, and demons), it did so only to invoke their aid, having little interest in matters such as the meaning of life or the basis for salvation. Instead, the emphasis was on pressing, tangible, and mundane matters such as health, fertility, weather, sex, and good crops. Consequently, the centerpiece of the people's religion was, as it had always been, magic.

Magic and Misfortune

The word *magic* initially identified the arts and powers of the magi,[78] the Zoroastrian priests of Persia who were discussed in chapter 1. The magi were especially admired in the classical world for their command of astrology, but also for their repertoire of spells and occult ceremonies that claimed to *enlist or compel supernatural forces to provide some desired outcome*, that becoming the general definition of magic. The purpose of magic is the same as that of technology and science: to allow humans to control nature and events in a reality permeated with misfortune.

Like everyone else, medieval peasants felt most threatened by ill health, and hence medical magic was paramount. Indeed, the Roman scholar Pliny the Elder (23–79 CE), claimed that magic "first arose from medicine."[79] In medieval times, medical magic coexisted with nonmagical remedies and treatments, and practitioners seldom distinguished between the two. Thus, the application of an herb thought to have medicinal properties was almost always accompanied by attempts to cast various spells and often by charms or amulets. The same was true of other "healing" efforts such as inserting a charm when binding up wounds, and "amulets of various kinds were used to aid in childbirth"[80] by experienced midwives. Thus the success of a treatment confirmed both the magical and the nonmagical efforts. A particularly vital aspect of early medical magic was the widely held belief that evil supernatural forces such as demons were the cause of most medical problems and that a cure was to be obtained by driving them away, which generated an extensive catalogue of appeals and threats used to expel demons, many of them of pre-Christian origin. As will be seen, eventually this led to the witch hunts since in every hamlet and village there were "Wise Ones" whose treatments for illness and injury included the invocation of supernatural agencies.

Second most important was weather magic used to quiet storms and bring rain for the crops. As would be expected, there were many specialists offering weather magic, but few details have survived compared with those who specialized in bringing bad weather, especially hail and drought to destroy a neighbor's crops.

Love and sex magic probably was the third most common form of magic, with revenge magic close behind. Love magic took many forms. Often it was used to cause a particular person to fall in love with the individual who purchased or performed the magic in order to gain a spouse. Often too, it was used for purposes of seduction. Sex magic was mainly the erectile dysfunction treatment of the times, purchased by men suffering from impotence, or by their wives. Not surprisingly there also was an extensive store of magic meant to cause impotence or to suppress sexual desires. Indeed, St. Hildegard of Bingen wrote extensive instructions about how to use mandrake root to suppress sexuality—oddly enough mandrake was far more often used to cause sexual desire and fertility, as in Genesis 30:14–16.

Revenge magic was widely known as *maleficia* or "evil doings" and consisted of attempts to harm others directly by causing death or injury, or indirectly by damaging crops or livestock. Archeology has turned up many magical curses scratched on lead tablets, one of which reads: "I curse Tretia Maria and her life and mind and memory and liver and lungs mixed up together, and her words, thoughts, and memory." Seven nails had been pounded through the sheet of lead on which this curse was written.[81] Lawsuits brought against malefactors often presented evidence that "magical amulets" had been discovered under the plaintiffs' thresholds or even under their beds, placed there by the accused in order to do them harm.[82] There also are many recorded cases, especially in medieval Switzerland, of lawsuits filed against persons accused of causing storms to destroy their neighbor's crops.

Sometimes magic was used in pursuit of wealth, including a variety of efforts to turn base metals into gold. And, of course, there were various magical efforts to read the future, not only via astrology, but also through study of various arcane texts such as the *kabbalah*. However none of these kinds of magical activities involved the general population. Finally, there were all manner of minor magical techniques used by everyone to bring them good luck.

Church Magic

The Christian hierarchy objected to popular magic not because it was superstitious nonsense (in fact they believed it worked), but because it was rooted in paganism and competed with the church for support. Hence massive efforts were made not merely to suppress it, but to replace it.[83] As would be expected, the greatest emphasis was placed on providing church forms of medical magic.

As already noted in chapter 11, from early days the church transformed the thousands of healing springs, wells, and shrines into Christian sites, often associated with a saint or martyr. The church also sanctioned and promulgated many magical procedures for the treatment of specific health problems. However, unlike the treatments offered by the village Wise Ones, medical church magic very seldom was combined with herbs or physical procedures, but usually consisted entirely of Christianized spells and incantations. For example, a recommended treatment for someone with a speck in her or his eye was for the priest to pray:

> Thus I adjure you, O speck, by the living God and the holy God, to disappear from the eye of the servant of God (name of victim), whether you are black, red, or white. May Christ make you go away. Amen. In the name of the Father, and of the Son, and of the Holy Spirit. Amen.[84]

When a woman suffered from menstrual problems, the cure was to write these words on a slip of paper, "By Him, and with Him, and in Him," and then to place the slip of paper on the woman's forehead.[85]

The church also provided a great deal of weather magic. Weather crosses, blessed by a local priest, were erected in fields as far back as the sixth century, to protect against hail and high winds,[86] and church bells often were rung to drive away thunderstorms.[87] And, of course, it was common to have a local priest pray for rain, as needed.

Although the church made vigorous efforts to provide medical and weather magic, it entirely rejected both love and revenge magic. The former was resoundingly condemned as bordering on rape when used to charm women and as violating the individual free will of both men and women. Of course, condemnation did not eliminate it. In fact, given the intensity of market demand, Christian variants of love magic arose—albeit they were forbidden—and even Christian clergy sometimes were involved in their use. For example, a priest in Modena confessed in 1585 that he had acceded to the request of a local noblewoman to baptize a piece of magnet thus giving it the power to attract her husband away from promiscuous women.[88] Revenge magic also was condemned as unchristian as well as antisocial, giving an uncontested market to those laypersons willing to deal in *maleficia*. An additional advantage enjoyed by lay magical practitioners was proximity—at a time when many places lacked a priest, there were Wise Ones in every village and hamlet, since they were local people, very often midwives, on whom their neighbors depended for medical as well as magical services.

Not surprisingly, popular magic soon was infused with elements of church magic. Many spells and formulations made use of holy water taken from church fonts. "People said the Lord's Prayer while casting lead to tell fortunes. They . . . invoked the names of the Father, the Son, and the Holy Ghost to protect chickens from hawks and humans from the evil eye. . . . Village healers cured cattle of worms by spitting three times in appeal to the Trinity. . . . They concocted infusions of baptismal water against bed-wetting."[89] The mixture of church and nonchurch magic was so extensive that people even bound amulets into the swaddling clothes of infants, to ward off enchantments when they took them to be baptized.[90]

Theology and Tragedy

All magic works some of the time. Many magical medical treatments and other uses of church magic often seemed successful—the desired outcome was gained. But because the nonchurch magic also succeeded (probably more often than church magic because it was usually associated with herbal and other physical treatments, some of which were effective), it could not be dislodged by church magic. That raised a dangerous question.

Christianity is a theological religion. It isn't satisfied with mystery and meditation, but relentlessly seeks to ground its entire system of beliefs in logic and reason. This has many admirable features, including the way the Christian commitment to rationalism provided a model for the development of Western science. But when confronted with magic, this aspect of Christianity turned out to have tragic consequences. In other cultural settings magic is usually taken for granted. Thus, the ancient Romans and Greeks devoted little or no effort to explaining why magic works—as it appears to do, at least some of the time. But Christian thinkers demanded to know *why* magic works. A clear answer could easily be provided for why church magic worked. God, Jesus, the Holy Ghost, sometimes Mary, and various saints and angels were the active agents; when church magic failed it was because these supernatural beings had decided it should not work in a given instance. Clearly, however, these hallowed figures did not cause nonchurch magic to work. *Who* then? The answer seemed equally obvious: evil supernatural beings, especially Satan. From there it was a short, obvious step to deducing that thousands of Wise Ones all across Europe were involved in satanic dealings. The witch hunts were born.[91]

The European conception of witchcraft was entirely the product of theological reflection; there was no basis for it in the popular magical culture. As the celebrated Norman Cohn (1915–2007) reported: "Nowhere, in the surviving [medieval] books on magic, is there a hint of Satanism. Nowhere is it suggested that the magician should ally himself with the demonic hosts, or do evil to win the favour of the Prince of Evil."[92] As the equally celebrated Richard Kieckhefer put it: "The introduction of diabolism . . . [resulted] from a desire of the literate elite to make sense of [magic]."[93] Thus it was university professors who played the leading roles in generating and sustaining the terrible witch hunts that stormed across Europe.[94] And it was the continuing magical activities of the peasants and urban lower classes in particular that gave substance to the witch hunts.[95] Ironically, despite the nearly universal belief to the contrary, the earliest, most vigorous, and most effective opposition to the witch hunts came from the Spanish Inquisition (see chapter 19). It was the inquisitors who never lost sight of the fact that the Wise Ones were performing magic in good conscience and were not knowingly involved in pacts with the devil.

Conclusion

MEDIEVAL TIMES WERE NOT the "Age of Faith." For the vast majority of medieval Europeans, their "religious" beliefs were a hodgepodge of pagan, Christian, and superstitious fragments; they seldom went to church; and they placed greater faith in the magic of the Wise Ones than in the services of the clergy. The frequent claims that empty churches and low levels of religious activity in Europe today reflect a steep decline in piety are wrong—it was always thus. As Martin Luther summed up in 1529, after recognizing the failure of his campaign to educate and arouse the general public: "Dear God help us. . . . The common man, especially in the villages, knows absolutely nothing about Christian doctrine; and indeed many pastors are in effect unfit and incompetent to teach. Yet they all are called Christians, are baptized, and enjoy the holy sacraments—even though they cannot recite either the Lord's Prayer, the Creed or the Commandments. They live just like animals."[96]

CHAPTER SIXTEEN

Faith and the Scientific "Revolution"

EVERYONE KNOWS THAT IT TOOK Columbus years to raise the funds needed to launch his famous voyage of discovery because of the unanimous opposition by church scholars and officials, all of whom were certain that the world must be flat. Hence if anyone sailed west to reach the Far East, they would simply fall off the edge of the earth. As reported by the famous Andrew Dickson White (1832–1918), founder and first president of Cornell University, and author of the extremely influential two-volume study *A History of the Warfare of Science with Theology in Christendom:*

> The warfare of Columbus [with religion] the world knows well: how the Bishop of Ceuta worsted him in Portugal; how sundry wise men of Spain confronted him with the usual quotations from Psalms, from St. Paul, and from St. Augustine; how even after he was triumphant, and after his voyage had greatly strengthened the theory of the earth's sphericity . . . the Church by its highest authority solemnly stumbled and persisted in going astray. . . . [T]he theological barriers to this geological truth yielded but slowly. . . . Many conscientious [religious] men oppose the doctrine for two hundred years longer.[1]

Unfortunately, nearly every word of White's account is a lie—as are so many of the other stories he wrote about conflicts between religion and science in his now discredited, but long-esteemed, work. Long before the fifteenth century, every educated European, including Roman Catholic prelates, knew the earth was round.[2] *Sphere* was the title of the most popular medieval textbook on astronomy, written early in the thirteenth century. The opposition Columbus encountered was not about the shape of the earth, but about the fact that he was wildly wrong about the circumference of the globe. He estimated it was about 2,800 miles from the Canary Islands to Japan. In reality it is about 14,000 miles. His opponents knew how far it was and opposed his voyage on grounds that Columbus and his men would all die at sea. Had the Western Hemisphere not been there, and no one knew it existed, the *Niña*, *Pinta*, and *Santa Maria* might as well have fallen off the earth, for everyone aboard would have died of thirst and starvation.

Amazingly enough, there is no hint about Columbus having to prove that the earth is round in any contemporary accounts, not in his own *Journal* nor in his son's *History of the Admiral*. The story was entirely unknown until more than three hundred years later when it suddenly appeared in a biography of Columbus published in 1828. The author? Washington Irving (1783–1859), best known for his fiction: in *The Legend of Sleepy Hollow* he introduced the Headless Horseman.[3] Although the tale about Columbus and the flat earth is equally fictional, Irving presented it as fact. Almost at once the story was eagerly embraced by historians who were so certain of the wickedness and stupidity of the medieval church that they felt no need to seek any additional confirmation, although some of them must have realized that the story had appeared out of nowhere. Anyway, that's how the tradition that Columbus proved the world was round got into all the textbooks.

Far more serious is that many similar falsehoods about the conflict between science and religion were made up by famous writers such as Voltaire and Gibbon during the "Enlightenment"—the same folks who invented the "Dark Ages"—and these fabrications have been repeated and added to ever since by militant atheists such as A. D. White, Bertrand Russell, and Richard Dawkins. The truth is that not only did Christianity not impede the rise of science; it was essential to it, which is why science arose only in the Christian West! Moreover, there was no sudden "Scientific Revolution"; the great achievements of Copernicus, Newton, and the other stalwarts of the sixteenth and seventeenth centuries were the product of normal scientific progress stretching back for centuries. But first it will be clarifying to define science.

What Is Science?

SCIENCE IS NOT JUST technology, nor is it simply knowledge. Many societies have known how to build dams and bridges, but have had no understanding of physics. The same can be said about the extensive knowledge of animal and plant life possessed by many societies that had no glimmer of the science of biology. For example, all but the most primitive societies can identify the seeds of many plants and know how to plant them and make them grow. But only societies having advanced science know why and how seeds are formed and how they develop into new plants.

Science is a *method* utilized in *organized efforts* to formulate *explanations of nature*, always subject to modifications and corrections through *systematic observations*. Thus science consists of two components: *theory* and *research*. Theorizing is the explanatory aspect of science. Scientific theories are *abstract statements* about why and how some portion of nature (including human social life) fits together and works. Of course, not all abstract statements, not even those offering explanations of nature, qualify as scientific theories; otherwise theology would be a science. Instead, abstract statements are scientific only if it is possible to deduce from them some definite predictions and prohibitions about what will be observed. Scientific research consists of making observations that are relevant to the predictions and prohibitions from a theory. If the observations contradict what has been deduced from the theory, then we know that the theory is wrong and must be rejected or modified. By "organized efforts" it is recognized that science is not merely random discovery. Instead, scientists pursue their efforts systematically, intentionally, and collectively—even scientists who work alone do not do so in isolation. From earliest days, scientists have constituted networks and have been very communicative.

This definition of science excludes all efforts through most of human history to explain and control the natural world. Most of these prior efforts are not science because until more recent times "technical progress—sometimes considerable—was mere empiricism," as the revered Marc Bloch (1886–1944) put it.[4] That is, progress was the product of observation and of trial and error, but was lacking in explanations—in theorizing. These prescientific funds of information are best described as lore, skills, wisdom, techniques, crafts, technology, engineering, learning, or simply knowledge. But, until such observations are linked to testable theories, they remain merely "facts." Charles Darwin put it very well: "About thirty years ago there was much talk that geologists ought to observe and not theorize; and I well remember someone saying that at that rate a man might as well go into a gravel-pit and count the pebbles and describe the colors. How odd it is that anyone should not see that all observation must be for or against some view if it is to be of any service."[5] Of course, Darwin was a man of very narrow interests since many observations are of great value without having any scientific implications (one can enjoy a full moon without scrambling to see if it fits with modern astronomical predictions). But Darwin was correct about what is a scientific observation: its purpose is to test a theory.

Clearly, then, science is limited to statements about natural and material reality, about things that are at least in principle observable. Hence there are entire realms of discourse that science is unable to address, including such matters as the existence of God. Nor can there be a physics of miracles.

For all the intellectual achievements of the classical Greeks or Eastern philosophers, their work was not scientific since their observations were without regard for theories and their theorizing ignored observational tests. For example, Aristotle (384–322 BCE) taught that the speed at which objects fall to earth is proportional to their weight, heavy things falling much faster than light things. Had he taken a stroll to any nearby cliff, taking along a big rock and a little one, he could have observed that this is false. But Aristotle was not a scientist. Nobody was until a few Europeans slowly evolved the scientific method in medieval times.

The Scholastic Origins of Science

JUST AS THERE WERE no "Dark Ages," there was no "Scientific Revolution." Rather, the notion of a Scientific Revolution was invented to discredit the medieval church by claiming that science burst forth in full bloom (thus owing no debts to prior Scholastic scholars) only when a weakened Christianity no longer could suppress it. This claim usually is illustrated by a number of stories of discovery and repression that are as false as the story of Columbus and the flat earth. A first step was to discredit the achievements of the Scholastics or school men of the medieval era. John Locke (1632–1704) condemned the Scholastics as lost in trivial concerns, as great "mintmasters" of useless terms as an "expedient to cover their ignorance."[6] Others accused them of pursuing absurd interests such as how many angels can dance on the head of a pin. Eventually the word *scholastic* became an epithet defined as "pedestrian and dogmatic" according to most dictionaries. But in fact the great scientific achievements of the sixteenth and seventeenth centuries were produced by a group of scholars notable for their piety, who were based in Christian universities, and whose brilliant achievements were carefully built upon an invaluable legacy of centuries of brilliant Scholastic scholarship.[7]

Copernicus and Normal Science

Since the start of the "Scientific Revolution" is usually attributed to Nicolaus Copernicus (1473–1543) it is appropriate to examine him and his intellectual predecessors to demonstrate that his was a work of "normal" science.

According to the fashionable account, Copernicus was an obscure Catholic canon in far-off Poland, an isolated genius who somehow discovered that, contrary to what everyone believed, the earth revolves around the sun. Moreover, the story goes, the church made unrelenting efforts to suppress this view.

There is far more fiction than fact in this account. Rather than being some obscure Pole, Copernicus received a superb education at the best Italian universities of the time: Bologna, Padua, and Ferrara. The idea that the earth circles the sun did not come to him out of the blue; he was taught the essential fundamentals leading to the heliocentric model of the solar system by his Scholastic professors. What Copernicus added was not a leap, but the implicit next step in a long line of discovery and innovation stretching back for centuries.

Because the Greeks thought vacuums could not exist, they assumed that the universe was a sphere filled with transparent matter. If so, the movement of all heavenly bodies would need to constantly overcome friction. To solve this problem, many Greek philosophers transformed the sun, moon, stars, and other bodies into living creatures having the capacity to move on their own, and others imagined various sorts of pushers in the form of gods and spirits. Early Christian scholars assumed that angels pushed the heavenly bodies along their courses. It was the famous English Franciscan monk William of Ockham (1295–1349)—he of Ockham's razor—who did away with the pushers by recognizing that space is a frictionless vacuum. He then anticipated Newton's First Law of Motion by proposing that once God had set the heavenly bodies in motion, they would remain in motion ever after since there was no force to counter their motion.

The next vital step toward the heliocentric model was taken by

Nicole d'Oresme (1325–1382), the most brilliant (and sadly neglected) of the Scholastic scientists, who, among many other major achievements, firmly established that the earth turns on its axis, thus giving the illusion that the other heavenly bodies circle the earth. D'Oresme served for many years as rector of the University of Paris and ended his career as bishop of Lisieux. The idea that the earth rotates had occurred to many people through the centuries, but two objections had always made it seem implausible. First, if the earth turns, why wasn't there a constant and powerful wind from the east, caused by the rotation of the earth in that direction? Second, why did an arrow shot straight up into the air not fall well behind (or in front of) the shooter? Since this does not happen, since the arrow comes straight back down, the earth cannot turn. Building on the work of Jean Buridan (1295–1358), his predecessor as rector of the University of Paris, d'Oresme proposed that there is no wind from the east because the motion of the earth is imparted to all objects on the earth or close by, including the atmosphere. This also explains why arrows fall straight back down: they not only have vertical impetus imposed on them by the bow, but they also have horizontal impetus conferred on them by the turning earth.

Then came Nicholas of Cusa (1401–1464), a German who became bishop of Brixen and then was elevated to cardinal in 1448. He was educated at the great Italian University of Padua, where he learned that the earth turns in response to "an impetus conferred upon it at the beginning of time." Having noted that "as we see from its shadow in eclipses . . . the earth is smaller than the sun" but larger than the moon, Nicholas went on to observe that "whether a man is on the earth, or the sun, or some other star, it will always seem to him that the position he occupies is the motionless center, and that all other things are in motion."[8] It followed that humans need not trust their perceptions that the earth is stationary.

All of this prior theorizing was well known to Copernicus—having been carefully summed-up in Albert of Saxony's *Physics*, the first edition of which was published at Padua in 1492, just prior to Copernicus's becoming a student there.

So what did Copernicus contribute? He put the sun in the middle of the solar system and had the earth circling it as one of the planets. What gave such special luster to his work was that he expressed it all in mathematics[9] and worked out the geometry of his system so as to permit the calculation of future positions of the bodies involved, which was essential for setting the dates of Easter, the solstices, and the like. However these calculations were no more accurate than those based on the prior Ptolemaic system dating from the second century CE because Copernicus failed to realize that the orbits in the solar system are elliptical, not circular. Therefore, to make his system work, Copernicus had to postulate that there were loops in the orbits of the heavenly bodies that delayed them sufficiently so they did not complete their orbits too soon—it would not do for the earth to circle the sun in only three hundred days. However, these loops lacked any observational support—had they existed a heavenly body should have been observed looping. Consequently, *everything* in Copernicus's famous book *On the Revolutions of the Heavenly Spheres* is wrong, other than the placement of the sun in the center. It was nearly a century later that Johannes Kepler (1571–1639), a German Protestant, got things right by substituting ellipses for Copernicus's circles. Now each heavenly body was always where it was supposed to be, on time, and no loops were needed.

Of course, even with Kepler's additions, there still was not a scientific theory of the solar system in that there was no *explanation* of why it functioned as it did—of why, for example, bodies remained in their orbits rather than flying off into space. The achievement of such a theory awaited Isaac Newton (1642–1727). But over several prior centuries, many essential pieces of such a theory had been assembled: that the universe was a vacuum; that no pushers were needed because once in motion, the heavenly bodies would continue in motion; that the earth turned; that the sun was the center of the solar system; that the orbits were elliptical.

This record of systematic progress is why the distinguished historian of science I. Bernard Cohen (1914–2003) noted that "the idea that a Copernican revolution in science occurred goes counter to the evidence . . . and is the invention of later historians."[10] Most of Cohen's sophisticated colleagues agree.[11] Copernicus added a small step forward in a long process of normal science, albeit one having immense polemical and philosophical implications. It should be noted, too, that the scholars involved in this long process were not rebel secularists. Not only were they devout Christians; they were clergy—most of them were bishops and there even was a cardinal among them. And one more thing, they all were embedded in the great Scholastic universities.

Scholastic Universities

Christian Scholastics invented the university and gave it its modern shape. The first two universities appeared in Paris (where both Albertus Magnus and Thomas Aquinas taught) and Bologna, in the middle of the twelfth century. Then, Oxford and Cambridge were founded in about 1200, followed by a flood of new institutions during the remainder of the thirteenth century: Toulouse, Orleans, Naples, Salamanca, Seville, Lisbon, Grenoble, Padua, Rome, Perugia, Pisa, Modena, Florence, Prague, Cracow, Vienna, Heidelberg, Cologne, Ofen, Erfurt, Leipzig, and Rostock. There is a widespread misconception that these were not really universities, but consisted of only three or four teachers and a few dozen students. To the contrary, early in the thirteenth century Paris, Bologna, Oxford, and Toulouse probably enrolled a thousand to fifteen hundred students each—approximately five hundred new students enrolled in the University of Paris every year. Regardless of their enrollments, many "enlightened" recent historians mock these universities as intellectually "hopeless," being "corrupted by scholastic and ecclesiastical overlays."[12]

But it was in these "hopeless" early universities that science was born. Indeed, like modern universities, from earliest days the medieval universities were created and run by scholars and devoted not merely to educating, but to discovery. Marcia L. Colish described the Scholastic professors:

> They reviewed past authorities and current opinions, giving [their] analysis of them and [their] reasons for rejecting some and accepting others. Altogether, the methodology already in place by the early twelfth century shows the scholastics' willingness, and readiness, to criticise the foundation documents of their respective fields. More than simply receiving and expanding on the classical and Christian traditions, they set aside ideas from these traditions deemed to have outlived their usefulness. They also freely realigned the authorities they retained to defend positions that these authorities might well have thought strange and novel. [Commentaries] were now rarely summaries and explications of their author's views. Scholastic commentators were much more likely to take issue with their chosen author or to bring to bear on his work ideas from emerging schools of thought or the scholastic's own opinion.[13]

This intellectual style was facilitated by the governance of the Scholastic universities. Faculty controlled entry into their ranks and set their own standards of competence and achievement—and their autonomy was a function of "market" demand. In the words of Nathan Schachner (1895–1955): "The University was the darling, the spoiled child of the Papacy and Empire, of king and municipality alike. Privileges were showered on the proud Universities in a continuous golden stream . . . [as] municipalities competed violently for the honour of housing one within their walls; kings wrote siren letters to entice discontented groups of scholars from the domains of their rivals."[14]

The autonomy of universities was matched by the autonomy of individual faculty members. There was a great deal of movement from one university to another, facilitated by the fact that all instruction was in Latin so there were no language barriers. Hence even in those days of poor transportation and slow means of communication, all the leading scholars knew of one another and many had actually met. And the key to faculty movement was then as now *innovation*. Reputations were gained not by mastery of the old, but by advancing something new! And this was greatly facilitated by something truly unusual in intellectual life: an emphasis on *empiricism*.

Scholastic Empiricism

The early Scholastic scientists did not just sit in their studies and think about the world; they increasingly relied on careful observations of the matters involved, that is, on empiricism. For example, the Greeks, Romans, Muslims, and Chinese mostly based their "knowledge" of human physiology on philosophy and introspection, and some dissections of animals, but they rejected and condemned any thought of cutting up humans. Christian Scholastics were the first scholars to build their anatomical knowledge on human dissection! In 1315 Mondino de'Luzzi is known to have performed a human dissection in front of an audience of students and faculty at the University of Bologna. Soon human dissections were being conducted at all the Italian universities. By 1391 the first one was conducted in Spain, and the first in Vienna took place in 1404.[15] By midcentury, dissection was a customary part of anatomy classes all across Europe. In 1504, Copernicus took part in human dissections during his brief enrollment in medical courses at the University of Padua.[16]

According to Edward Grant, "the introduction [of human dissection] into the Latin west, made without serious objection from the Church, was a momentous occurrence."[17] Nevertheless, true to form, A. D. White went on and on about how the great anatomist Andreas Vesalius (1514–1564) "risked the most terrible dangers, and especially the charge of sacrilege, founded on the teachings of the Church" by conducting human dissections. White claimed that anyone who dissected a human body at this time risked "excommunication," but that the heroic Vesalius "broke without fear" from "this sacred conventionalism" and proceeded "despite ecclesiastic censure. . . . No peril daunted him."[18] White made these charges despite the well-known fact that the Holy Roman Emperor responded to Vesalius's "sacrilege" by ennobling him as a count and awarding him a lifetime pension!

The Scholastic commitment to empiricism was one of the vital keys to the rise of science. Although the aim of science is to formulate theories to explain natural phenomena, it requires that theories be put to and survive empirical tests. It was not science when Plato explained that the heavenly bodies must rotate in circles because on philosophical grounds that is the ideal shape. But it was science when Kepler corrected Copernicus by postulating elliptical orbits, with the empirical result that heavenly bodies always were observed to be where they were supposed to be.

Science did not suddenly burst forth in the sixteenth century. It began centuries before in the Scholastic commitment to empiricism, and it was nurtured in the early universities as scholars pursued systematic efforts to innovate. Moreover, the truly remarkable aspect of the rise of science is that it happened only once.[19] Many societies pursued alchemy, but only in Christian Europe did it lead to chemistry; many societies developed extensive systems of astrology, but only in Europe was astrology transformed into scientific astronomy. Why?

The God of Reason

SCIENCE AROSE ONLY IN Europe because only medieval Europeans believed that science was *possible* and *desirable*. And the basis of their belief was their image of God and his creation. This was dramatically asserted to a distinguished audience of scholars attending the 1925 Lowell Lectures at Harvard by the great philosopher and mathematician Alfred North Whitehead (1861–1947), who explained that science developed in Europe because of the widespread "faith in the possibility of science . . . derivative from medieval theology."[20] This claim shocked not only his audience, but Western intellectuals in general when his lectures were published. How could this world-famous thinker, coauthor with Bertrand Russell of the landmark *Principia Mathematica* (1910–1913), not know that religion is the unrelenting enemy of science? In fact, Whitehead knew better!

Whitehead had recognized that Christian theology was essential for the rise of science, just as non-Christian theologies had stifled the scientific enterprise everywhere else. He explained that "the greatest contribution of medievalism to the formation of the scientific movement [was] the inexpugnable belief . . . that there was a secret, a secret which can be unveiled. How has this conviction been so vividly implanted in the European mind? . . . It must come from the medieval insistence on the rationality of God, conceived as with the personal energy of Jehovah and with the rationality of a Greek philosopher. Every detail was supervised and ordered: the search into nature could only result in the vindication of faith in rationality."[21] Whitehead was, of course, merely summarizing what so many of the great early scientists had said—René Descartes justified his search for the "laws" of nature on ground that such laws must exist because God is perfect and therefore "acts in a manner as constant and immutable as possible."[22] That is, the universe functions according to rational rules or laws. As that great medieval Scholastic Nicole d'Oresme put it, God's creation "is much like that of a man making a clock and letting it run and continue its own motion by itself."[23] Furthermore, because God has given humans the power of reason it ought to be possible for us to discover the rules established by God.

Indeed, many of the early scientists felt morally obliged to pursue these secrets, just as Whitehead had noted. The great British philosopher concluded his remarks by noting that the images of God and creation found in the non-European faiths, especially those in Asia, are too impersonal or too irrational to have sustained science. Any particular natural "occurrence might be due to the fiat of an irrational despot" god, or might be produced by "some impersonal, inscrutable origin of things. There is not the same confidence as in the intelligible rationality of a personal being."[24] It should be noted that given their common roots, the Jewish conception of God is as suitable to sustaining science as is the Christian conception. But Jews were a small, scattered, and often repressed minority in Europe during this era and took no part in the rise of science—albeit Jews have excelled as scientists since their emancipation in the nineteenth century.

In contrast, most religions outside the Judeo-Christian tradition do not posit a creation at all. The universe is said to be eternal, without beginning or purpose, and never having been created, it has no creator. From this view, the universe is a supreme mystery, inconsistent, unpredictable, and (perhaps) arbitrary. For those holding this view, the only paths to wisdom are meditation or inspiration—there being nothing to reason about. But if the universe was created in accord with rational rules by a perfect, rational creator, then it ought to yield its secrets to reason and observation. Hence the scientific truism that nature is a *book* meant to be read.

Of course, the Chinese "would have scorned such an idea as being too naive for the subtlety and complexity of the universe as they intuited it,"[25] as explained by the esteemed Oxford historian of Chinese technology Joseph Needham (1900–1995). As for the Greeks, many of them also regarded the universe as eternal and uncreated; Aristotle condemned the idea "that the universe came into being at some point in time . . . as unthinkable."[26] Indeed, none of the traditional Greek gods would have been capable of such a creation. But, worst of all, the Greeks insisted on turning the cosmos, and inanimate objects more generally, into living things. Consequently, they attributed many natural phenomena to *motives*, not to inanimate forces. Thus, according to Aristotle, heavenly bodies move in circles because of their affection for doing so, and objects fall to the ground "because of their innate love for the centre of the world."[27] As for Islam, the orthodox conception of Allah is hostile to the scientific quest. There is no suggestion in the Qur'an that Allah set his creation in motion and then let it run. Rather, it is assumed that he often intrudes in the world and changes things as it pleases him. Thus through the centuries many of the most influential Muslim scholars have held that all efforts to formulate natural laws are blasphemy in that they would seem to deny Allah's freedom to act. Thus did the prevailing images of God and the universe deflect scientific efforts in China, ancient Greece, and Islam.[28]

It was only because Europeans believed in God as the Intelligent Designer of a rational universe that they pursued the secrets of creation. In the words of Johannes Kepler, "The chief aim of all investigations of the external world should be to discover the rational order and harmony imposed on it by God and which he revealed to us in the language of mathematics."[29] In similar fashion, in his last will and testament, the great chemist Robert Boyle (1627–1691) wrote to the members of the Royal Society of London, wishing them continuing success in "their laudable attempts to discover the true Nature of the Works of God."[30]

Perhaps the most remarkable aspect to the rise of science is that the early scientists not only searched for natural laws, confident that they existed, but *they found them*! It thus could be said that the proposition that the universe had an Intelligent Designer is the most fundamental of all scientific theories and that it has been successfully put to empirical tests again and again. For, as Albert Einstein (1879–1955) once remarked, the most incomprehensible thing about the universe is that it is comprehensible: "*a priori* one should expect a chaotic world which cannot be grasped by the mind in any way. . . . That is the 'miracle' which is constantly being reinforced as our knowledge expands."[31] And that is the "miracle" that testifies to a creation guided by intention and rationality.

That Christianity was essential to the rise of science was manifest not only in the philosophical sense, but is evident in the biographies of the men who achieved it—overwhelmingly they were very religious men. Elsewhere[32] I drew up a roster of the fifty-two major scientific stars during the era beginning with the publication of Copernicus's work in 1543 and stopping with persons born after 1680. Of these, thirty-two (or 62 percent) were very religious men. Newton, for example, devoted far more effort to theology than to physics, predicting the date of the Second Coming as 1948.[33] Of the remaining twenty, nineteen were quite religious and only one, Edmund Halley, could be called a skeptic. So much, then, for tales about the inherent conflict between religion and science.

Of course, the rise of science did engender some conflicts with the Catholic Church, as well as with the early Protestants. That in no way diminishes the essential role of the Christian conception of God in justifying and motivating science. It merely reflects that many Christian leaders failed to grasp the important differences between science and theology as to domain and evidence. That is, Christian theologians attempt to deduce God's nature and intentions from scripture; scientists attempt to discover the nature of God's creation by empirical means. In principle, the two efforts do not overlap, but in practice theologians have sometimes felt that a scientific position was an attack on faith (and some modern scientists have in fact attacked religion, albeit on spurious grounds). In early days, a major dispute took place because both Catholic and Protestant theologians were reluctant to accept that the earth was not the center of the universe, let alone not the center of solar system. Both Luther and the pope were opposed to the Copernican claim, and both attempted to defeat it, but their efforts had little impact and were never very vigorous. Unfortunately, this modest conflict has been blown into a monumental event by those determined to show that religion is the bitter enemy of science by turning Galileo Galilei (1564–1642) into a heroic martyr to blind faith. As Voltaire reported: "the great Galileo, at the age of fourscore, groaned away his days in the dungeons of the Inquisition, because he had demonstrated by irrefutable proofs the motion of the earth."[34] The Italian gadfly Giuseppe Baretti (1719–1789) added that Galileo was "put to the torture, for saying that *the earth moved*."[35]

What About Galileo?

IT IS TRUE THAT Galileo was called before the Roman Inquisition and charged with the heretical teaching that the earth moves—

around the sun or otherwise. And he was forced to recant. But he was neither imprisoned nor tortured; he was sentenced to a comfortable house arrest during which he died at age seventy-eight. More important, what got Galileo in trouble with the church were not his scientific convictions nearly as much as his arrogant duplicity. It happened this way.

Long before he became Pope Urban VIII (served 1623 to 1644), while still a cardinal, Matteo Barberini knew and liked Galileo. In 1623 when he published *Assayer*, Galileo dedicated the book to Barberini (the Barberini family crest appeared on the title page of the book), and the new pope was said to have been delighted by the many nasty insults it directed against various Jesuit scholars. *Assayer* was mainly an ill-conceived attack on Orazio Grassi, a Jesuit mathematician who had published a study that correctly identified comets as small heavenly bodies; Galileo ridiculed this claim, arguing wrongly that comets were but reflections on vapors arising from the earth.[36] In any event, *Assayer* prompted Pope Urban VIII to write an adulatory poem on the glory of astronomy. So, what went wrong?

It is important to put the Galileo affair in historical context. At this time, the Reformation stood defiant in northern Europe, the Thirty Years' War raged, and the Catholic Counter-Reformation was in full bloom. Partly in response to Protestant charges that the Catholic Church was not faithful to the Bible, the limits of acceptable theology were being narrowed. This led to increasing church interference in scholarly and scientific discussions. However, Urban VIII and other leading officials were not ready to clamp down on scientists, but proposed ways to avoid any conflicts between science and theology by separating their domains. Thus, Friar Marin Mersenne (1588–1648), the brilliant French mathematician, advised his network of leading scientific correspondents to defend their studies on grounds that God was free to place the earth anywhere he liked, and it was the duty of scientists to find out where he had put it.[37] More cautious early scientists adopted the tactic of identifying scientific conclusions as hypothetical or mathematical, hence being without direct theological implications. And that was what the pope asked Galileo to do, to acknowledge in his publications that "definitive conclusions could not be reached in the natural sciences. God in his omnipotence could produce a natural phenomenon in any number of ways and it therefore was presumptuous for any philosopher to claim that he had determined a unique solution."[38] That seemed an easy evasion. And, given Galileo's propensity to claim false credit for inventions made by others, such as the telescope, and his claim to have conducted empirical research he probably did not really perform, such as dropping weights from the Leaning Tower of Pisa, it would not seem to have stretched his ethical standards to have gone along with the pope. But to defy the pope in a rather offensive way was quite consistent with Galileo's ego.

In 1632 Galileo published his awaited *Dialogue Concerning the Two Chief World Systems*. Although the ostensible purpose of the book was to present an explanation of tidal phenomena, the two systems involved were Ptolemy's, in which the sun circles the earth, and Copernicus's wherein the earth circles the sun. The dialogue involves three speakers, two of them philosophers and the third a layman. It is the layman, Simplicio, who presents the traditional views in support of Ptolemy—the resemblance of the name to "simpleton" was obvious to all. This allowed Galileo to exploit the traditional "straw man" technique to ridicule his opponents. Although Galileo did include the disclaimer suggested by the pope, he put it in the mouth of Simplicio thereby disowning it.

The book caused an immense stir and, understandably, the pope felt betrayed—although Galileo never seemed to have grasped that fact and continued to blame the Jesuits and university professors for his troubles. Despite that, the pope used his power to protect Galileo from any serious punishment. Unfortunately, Galileo's defiant action stimulated a general crackdown by the Counter-Reformation church on intellectual freedom which otherwise may never have occurred. Ironically, much that Galileo presented in the book as correct science was not; his theory of the tides, for example, was nonsense, as Albert

Einstein pointed out in his foreword to a 1953 translation of Galileo's notorious book.[39] Equally ironic is the fact that the judgment against Galileo was partly motivated by efforts on the part of church leaders to suppress astrologers—some theologians mistakenly equating the claim that the earth moved with doctrines that fate was ruled by the motion of heavenly bodies.

So, what does the case of Galileo reveal? It surely demonstrates that powerful groups and organizations often will abuse their power to impose their beliefs, a shortcoming that certainly is not limited to religious organizations—the Communist regime in the Soviet Union outlawed Mendelian genetics on grounds that all variations within and across species are caused by the environment. But it also shows that Galileo was not some naive scholar who fell victim to a bunch of ignorant bigots—these same "bigots" ignored dozens of other prominent scientists, many of them resident in Italy! In any event, this celebrated case does nothing to alter the fact that the rise of science was rooted in Christian theology—indeed, for all his posturing, Galileo remained deeply religious. As William Shea noted, "Had Galileo been less devout, he could have refused to go to Rome [when summoned by the Inquisition]; Venice offered him asylum."[40] But he did not flee to Venice and often expressed his personal faith to his daughter and friends after his trial was over.

Of course, although Christianity was essential for the development of Western science, that dependency no longer exists. Once properly launched, science has been able to stand on its own, and the conviction that the secrets of nature will yield to prolonged inquiry is now as much a secular article of faith as it originally was Christian. The rise of an independent scientific establishment has given birth to new tensions between theology and science. If the church fathers were leery of the implications of science for theology, there now exists a militant group of atheists, only some of them actually scientists, who devote a great deal of effort to attacking religion as superstitious nonsense and to claiming that science refutes the existence of God and the possibility of miracles. They are greatly aided in these efforts by some religious leaders who attack scientific findings on the basis of their theological convictions.

Inerrancy and Divine Accommodation

IT IS WELL-KNOWN THAT some Christians believe that the Bible is to be understood literally and that it is without error, "including the historical and scientific parts."[41] It is much less well-known that this is a quite modern development, probably prompted mainly in response to scientific contradictions of the creation as it is presented in *Genesis*. Indeed, as Richard J. Coleman explained in 1975, "only in the last two centuries can we legitimately speak of a formal doctrine of inerrancy."[42] The commitment to literal inerrancy has created a field day for atheist attacks on the Bible. That God created the universe and everything in it during a six-day spurt of energy is ridiculed on the basis of massive evidence that the universe is billions of years old. And the story of Adam and Eve is lampooned in light of overwhelming evidence in favor of a long and complicated evolution of life on earth. And these "triumphs" of science over religion continue to mislead many, especially since "liberal" Christian clergy too often deal with the problem by admitting that, of course, the Bible is not to be taken too seriously.

Not only is all of this unnecessary; it is theologically illiterate. From early days, the great Christian theologians knew better than to commit to literal inerrancy! Rather, they assumed that scripture required interpretation and must not be taken literally since, as St. Augustine warned, "diverse things may be understood under these words."[43] An even more definitive theological objection to inerrancy is that all scripture was revealed within the confines of human comprehension *at the time*. Here we confront one of the most fundamental, yet remarkably neglected, of all Judeo-Christian premises, that of *Divine Accommodation*. This premise holds that God's revelations are always limited to the current capacity of humans to comprehend—that in order to communicate with humans God is forced to accommodate their incomprehension by resorting to the equivalent of "baby talk." This view is, of course, firmly rooted in the Bible. In Exodus 6:2 (in the Torah), when God tells Moses that he had made himself known to Abraham, Isaac, and Jacob not as Yahweh, but as El Shaddai,[44] presumably this was because the patriarchs were not ready to be told more.[45] Or, when asked by his disciples why he spoke to the multitudes in parables, Jesus replied that people differed greatly in what they could comprehend: "This is why I speak to them in parables, because seeing they do not see, and hearing they do not hear, nor do they understand."[46]

It was in this same spirit that Irenaeus (ca. 115–202) invoked the principle of divine accommodation to human limits in order to explain God's tolerance of human failings. A generation later Origen (ca. 185–251) wrote in *On First Principles* that "we teach about God both what is true and what the multitude can understand." Hence, "the written revelation in inspired scripture is a veil that must be penetrated. It is an accommodation to our present capacities . . . [that] will one day be superseded."[47]

Thomas Aquinas (1225–1274) agreed: "The things of God should be revealed to mankind only in proportion to their capacity; otherwise, they might despise what was beyond their grasp. . . . It was, therefore, better for the divine mysteries to be conveyed to an uncultured people as it were veiled."[48] So too, John Calvin (1509–1564) flatly asserted that God "reveals himself to us according to our rudeness and infirmity."[49] If scriptural comparisons between earlier and later portions of the Bible, for example, seem to suggest that God is changeable or inconsistent, that is merely because "he accommodated diverse forms to different ages, as he knew would be expedient for each. . . . [H]e has accommodated himself to men's capacity, which is varied and changeable."[50] The same constraints applied to those who conveyed God's words. Thus Calvin noted that in formulating *Genesis,* Moses "was ordained a teacher as well of the unlearned and rude as of the learned, he could not otherwise fulfill his office than by descending to this grosser method of instruction. . . . [Seeking to] be intelligible to all . . . Moses, therefore, adapts his discourse to common usage . . . such as the rude and unlearned may perceive."[51]

The principle of divine accommodation provides a truly remarkable key for completely reappraising the dispute over scripture and science. Calvin said straight out that *Genesis* is not a satisfactory account of the creation because it was directed to the unlearned and the primitive, even though, when they received it, the ancient Jews were far from being truly primitive. Consider that the ancient Jews would have been utterly mystified had God revealed creation in terms of Newtonian mechanics and an extensive discussion of genetics and mutation. Hence, John Calvin advised vis-à-vis Genesis: "he who would learn astronomy, and other recondite arts, let him go elsewhere."[52] As it stands, Genesis told the ancient Jews the important truth—that the universe was created by God. Indeed, that was enough to inspire Scholastic scholars to seek the rules according to which God's creation functions! Seen in this light, all scientific findings are fully compatible with theology, inspiring the learned response, "Aha! So that's how God did it!"

Finally, generations of attacks on religion in the name of science have fallen well short of their goal. The majority of American scientists still report themselves to be religious, and the more scientific their field, the higher the proportion who do so. That is, substantial majorities of mathematicians and physical scientists say they are religious, while only a minority of social scientists make that claim.[53]

Conclusion

THE ORIGINAL WARFARE BETWEEN religion and science never happened: Christianity not only did not impede the rise of science; it was essential to its having taken place. As for the contemporary conflict between religion and science, it is a battle limited to extremists. On the "science" side are militant atheists such as Richard Dawkins who claim science has proved there is no God. On the "religion" side are fundamentalists such as the late Henry M. Morris (1918–2006), who claim the Bible proves that much of modern science is nonsense. This is a debate that can best be described by quoting Shakespeare, as "full of sound and fury, signifying nothing."

PART V

Christianity Divided

CHAPTER SEVENTEEN

Two "Churches" and the Challenge of Heresy

PERHAPS THE GREATEST DIVISION IN the history of Christianity developed during the fourth century within the Roman Catholic Church. Conflicts inherent in this division eventually caused the eruption of heretical movements at the start of the second millennium—the suppression of which disfigured the Christian spirit.

One of the sad ironies of life is that sincere efforts to do good can so often have unfortunate results. Such was the case with one of Constantine's benevolent acts toward Christianity: When he showered privileges and status on the Christian clergy he inadvertently caused a "stampede into the priesthood."[1] Soon Christian offices, and especially the higher positions, were dominated by the sons of the aristocracy—some of them gaining bishoprics even before being baptized. As a result, many immoral, insincere, and indolent men were ordained, far too many of whom gained very important positions in the church. At the same time, of course, many who entered the religious life were not careerists or libertines, but were deeply committed Christians. Consequently, there arose what, in effect, became two parallel churches. These can usefully be identified as the *Church of Power* and the *Church of Piety*. In what follows, these two "Churches" are described and contrasted and their historical role in provoking and persecuting the great medieval heretical movements is examined.

The Church of Power

THE CHURCH OF POWER was the main body of the church as it evolved in response to the immense status and wealth bestowed on the clergy by Constantine. It included the great majority of priests, bishops, cardinals, and popes who ruled the church most of the time until the Counter-Reformation set in during the sixteenth century. Most clergy of the Church of Power were sensible and temperate men, but they tended to be worldly in both senses of that term—practical and morally lax.

This was reflected in the fact that their careers in the church were mainly determined by influence, commerce, and eventually heredity. Simony became the rule—an extensive and expensive traffic in religious offices, involving the sale not only of high offices such as bishoprics but even of lowly parish placements. There quickly arose great clerical families whose sons followed their fathers, uncles, and grandfathers into holy offices. Even the papacy soon ran in families. Pope Innocent (401–417) was the son of his predecessor Pope Anastasius (399–401). Pope Silverius (536–537) was the son of Pope Hermisdas (514–523). Many other popes were the sons, grandsons, nephews, and brothers of bishops and cardinals.

As early as the Council of Sardica in 341, church leaders promulgated rules against ordaining men into the priesthood following their appointment to a bishopric, requiring that bishops have previous service in a lower clerical office. These rules were frequently ignored: late in the fourth century Auxentius became bishop of Milan without even having been baptized. Or the rules were circumvented by a candidate's being rushed through ordination and a series of lower clerical ranks in a week or two prior to becoming a bishop.[2] This did not always result in the elevation of an impious opportunist—

St. Ambrose (340–397) went from baptism through ordination and the clerical ranks to his consecration as a bishop, all in eight days. But very often this allowed dissolute, corrupt, lax, and insincere persons to gain high positions in the church. St. Jerome (347–420) attacked many clerics of his era for having entered the church mainly in order "to have access to beautiful women."[3] And even Eusebius, in his laudatory biography of Constantine, complained that because of the "Emperor's forbearance . . . wicked rapacious men . . . [had] slipped into the Church."[4]

Power and Corruption

CONSEQUENTLY, BY THE START of the eleventh century, after centuries of rule by the Church of Power, European Christianity lay in political and moral ruin. Politically, the papacy was controlled by the aristocratic families of Rome in competition with the German Holy Roman Emperors. "Of the twenty-five popes between 955 and 1057, thirteen were appointed by the local aristocracy, while the other twelve were appointed (and no fewer than five dismissed) by the German emperors."[5] Note the rapid turnover rate: during this century papal reigns averaged only four years. Worse yet, during the "long" century between 872 and 1012, a third of all popes had died violent deaths,[6] many of them having been murdered as a result of the constant intrigues among the Roman ecclesiastical families.

Consider the making and unmaking of popes by Marozia (890–937), a promiscuous and domineering Roman noblewoman of the powerful Theophylact family.[7] When she was fifteen, Marozia became the mistress of Pope Sergius III (served 904–911), who had murdered Pope Leo V (served 903) to gain the papal throne and by whom Marozia had an illegitimate son. Marozia's mother was the mistress of Pope John X (served 914–928), whom Marozia conspired to have suffocated and replaced by Pope Leo VI (served 928), whom she quickly replaced with Stephen VII (served 928–931). At this point Marozia managed to get her illegitimate son—fathered by Pope Sergius—placed on the papal throne as Pope John XI (served 931–936). Subsequently, when her son Alberic became ruler of Rome, he so feared her conspiracies that he had her imprisoned. She eventually died in her cell.

Many popes in this era had no prior clerical experience—Pope John XII (served 955–964) was elected when he was only eighteen; Marozia's son John XI was only twenty-one when he became pope; John XIX (served 1024–1032) was elevated from layman to pope in a single day and his successor, Benedict IX (served 1032–1048), "was a layman and still in his twenties when elected"[8] and may never have been ordained a priest. That so many young men with no prior religious service became popes helps explain why the moral condition of the papacy in this era can best be described as "squalid."[9] Thus, John XII assembled a harem of young women—"some accused him of converting the Lateran Palace into a brothel."[10] He also consecrated a ten-year-old as bishop, had a cardinal castrated, and loudly invoked pagan gods when he gambled. At age twenty-eight he died in bed with a married woman, probably killed by her irate husband.[11] Benedict IX was an even more notorious pope. When he succeeded two of his uncles as pope, there followed the "spectacle of the Pope carousing and whoring his way around Rome," displaying himself as "unblushingly and arrogantly dissolute."[12] Eventually things got so bad that even the corrupt Roman aristocracy could not continue to look the other way, and so they paid him to leave office.

Keep in mind that dissolute living was not peculiar to popes or even to the hierarchy in Rome. At all levels of the church, everywhere, notorious clergy prospered. Many priests kept concubines, came to church drunk, or didn't show up at all, and otherwise discredited their offices. Not all, of course, but many.[13]

The Church of Piety

IN MANY WAYS THE Church of Piety was sustained as a reaction against the Church of Power. It pressed for virtue over worldliness, as would be expected given that most of its leaders as well as its rank-and-file were monks and nuns. Indeed, at the same time that there had begun a "stampede" into the priesthood by opportunistic sons of privilege, there was a rapid expansion of monasticism: by the middle of the fourth century there were tens of thousands of monks and nuns, nearly all of them living in organized communities. Naturally, those living an ascetic life felt themselves spiritually superior to others, as was in fact acknowledged by Catholic theology. However, their antagonism toward the regular clergy, and especially the church hierarchy, had a different basis; it was not merely that these men were not leading ascetic lives, but that so many were leading dissolute lives. This was an issue that would not subside. Again and again leaders of the Church of Piety attempted to reform the Church of Power, and during several notable periods they managed to gain control of the papacy and impose major changes. But most of the time, the "church" was the Church of Power. This may not have been entirely due to Constantine. Once it became the dominant religion, Christianity was bound to become more bureaucratic and worldly. But Constantine made this shift occur very rapidly and to a remarkable degree.

The Lazy Monopoly

ALTHOUGH THERE WAS CONSTANT competition between the two churches, when in control each faction conducted the affairs of the faith as a monopoly—with the exception of Jews, non-Christian faiths were not permitted. However, when in charge the Church of Piety pursued its affairs with far more vigor than did the Church of Power, which often neglected even to protect its best interests—unless these were seriously threatened. As Adam Smith (1723–1790) pointed out, all monopolies, even monopoly churches, are inclined to be complaisant and lazy. Smith noted that some religions depend on the voluntary support of members, while others are supported by the state. Clergy who must depend upon their members will usually exhibit far greater "zeal and industry" than those who are provided for by law. Smith also noted that history is full of examples wherein a kept clergy "reposing themselves upon their benefices, had neglected to keep up the fervour of faith and devotion in the great body of the people . . . having given themselves up to indolence."[14]

Constantine's favor transformed the church from an institution based entirely on member contributions and led by a clergy of but modest means into an institution based on immense state support and led by a rich and powerful clergy recruited from the upper ranks of society. He thereby created a lazy monopoly institution that behaved in precisely the way Smith described. Thus, subsequent to Constantine, church efforts to convert the rural areas (where nearly all Europeans lived) were feeble, and many pagans became "Christians" only to the extent of adding Jesus to their pantheon of gods. Missions to unconverted northern areas of Europe were slow to develop and then mostly settled for the baptism of kings and courts, leaving the populace relatively undisturbed. Even in the most Christian cities, mass attendance was very low and the religious instruction of the clergy, let alone the laity, was almost nonexistent, as was documented in chapter 16. Indeed, the lazy Church of Power tended even to ignore heresy until it was perceived as a very serious challenge to its rule.

A number of historians[15] of medieval religion have remarked the disappearance of heresy in Europe between about 500 and about 1100 CE—Malcolm Lambert claimed that until the eleventh century there had been no capital punishment for heresy since "the execution of Priscillian of Avila in 383."[16] But what really had disappeared was not heresy, but any serious concern about heresy by church authorities. Through the centuries there were many quite visible heretics, but they did not inspire mass movements sufficient to threaten the church monopoly and therefore were either ignored entirely or "treated mildly by the authorities."[17] Ironically, reform efforts by the Church of Piety eventually resulted in an unprecedented eruption of heretical mass movements beginning in the twelfth century, to which the Church of Power responded with brutal repression, as will be seen.

Piety and Reform

IN 1046, AFTER CENTURIES of dominance by the Church of Power, the Church of Piety suddenly was given control of the church by Holy Roman Emperor Henry III (1017–1056). Henry's determination to reform the church, beginning with the papacy, reflected the close connections that existed between monasticism and the nobility with the result that the nobility, as a group, may well have been more pious than most clergy of the Church of Power. It was very common for the sons and daughters of powerful families to enter the church,[18] and especially a religious order—three-fourths of ascetic medieval saints were from noble families, and 22 percent of them were the sons or daughters of kings.[19] Entering a religious order usually did not disrupt family ties; often the monastery or convent was nearby and frequent visits took place. Thus it was not unusual that of Henry's four[20] daughters, two became abbesses of convents. In addition, Henry's cousin Bruno was not only the bishop of Toul, but an ardent supporter of the Benedictine Abbey of Cluny, which was the hotbed of church reform. In 1049 Henry had Bruno seated as Pope Leo IX (served 1049–1054).

The new pope began an immediate cleansing of the church. First, he called a council at Rheims and demanded that all "the bishops and abbots present declare individually whether they had paid any money for their office."[21] In response, some fled and were excommunicated. Many confessed and were pardoned. Next up was celibacy. Leo vigorously attacked incontinent priests on all appropriate occasions and filled the high administrative offices of the church with monks. But perhaps the most radical step that Leo took was to become a traveling evangelist at a time when very few priests preached to the public at all and almost no one had ever laid eyes on a cardinal, let alone a pope. Throughout his five years in office Leo traveled constantly, and everywhere he went he preached "eloquently to huge crowds."[22] Always his theme was reform.

Leo's efforts were continued by Pope Victor II (served 1055–1057) and by Stephen IX (served 1057–1058), who were followed by the dynamic innovator Nicholas II (1059–1061). Having assembled a synod in Rome, Nicholas initiated a new and very dangerous policy. He ordered rank-and-file Christians to boycott masses and other sacraments if performed by priests who kept concubines or who had purchased their offices. Thus he opened the door for the laity to take an active role in church reform and acknowledged that the moral status of clergy influenced the validity of sacraments, a position that the church had rejected vis-à-vis the Donatists and would soon repudiate again when faced with "heretical" reformers.[23] Nicholas also reformed the process by which popes were selected. No longer would they be seated by powerful secular families or rulers—ever after popes were elected by the College of Cardinals.

Nicholas was followed by Alexander II (served 1061–1073), another eager reformer who also tried, with little success, to institute a crusade to drive the Muslims from Spain. After him came the famous Gregory VII (served 1073–1085), the first monk to become pope in centuries. Gregory too continued to attempt to end priestly misbehavior. Thus, he thundered that priests "persisting in fornication must not celebrate the mass, but are to be driven from the choir."[24] Following Gregory, the next three popes also were monks, including Urban II (served 1088–1099) who launched the First Crusade to recapture Jerusalem from Islam. And if Leo had initiated popular preaching, Urban not only preached far and wide on behalf of the crusade, but prompted hundreds, possibly thousands, of others to go out preaching to the public as well. The initial mission was to preach the Crusade, but soon the topic of church reform began to dominate. And all this agitation resulted in unprecedented levels of lay involvement in the affairs of the church. However, it was mainly the nobility and well-to-do urbanites who were aroused by the evangelists, while the "masses" remained little interested in the church even in this era. Even so, encouraging the laity to demand and help to sustain church reforms led to an outburst of protest movements when the Church of Power regained control. In response to these challenges, some reform movements were encapsulated and controlled within the structure of the church. The others were brutally attacked.

Encapsulation

FOR CENTURIES, THE CHURCH was able to deflect popular reformers from dangerous confrontations by channeling their energy into the formation of new monastic orders. Consider the careers of three men called by Pope Urban II from lives of ascetic seclusion to preach the First Crusade: Robert of Arbrissel (1045–1116), Vitalis of Mortain (1060–1122), and Bernard of Tiron (1046–1117). Each proved to be an extraordinarily effective evangelist able to draw and arouse large crowds. Each began by preaching the crusade, but once it was launched they continued their evangelism and turned most of their attention to denouncing the sins of the clergy in graphic fashion, never being reluctant to name dissolute local clergy. In response, many bishops attempted to stop their public preaching. One argued to the pope that "revelation of the sins of churchmen to the common people would be 'not to preach but to undermine.'"[25] Had the pope ordered them to stop, each may have been tempted to lead an opposition movement. But, of course, the pope was a former monk and strongly committed to reform. So, instead of becoming dissenters, each of the three ended up directing his energies to the formation of a new monastic organization. A few years later it became more dangerous to preach reform and more difficult to found an order.

It often has been remarked that St. Francis (1181–1226) was very lucky not to have been prosecuted for heresy. He was never ordained.

He engaged in public preaching on the virtues of poverty and humility, especially for the clergy. In 1209 Francis led his eleven followers to Rome, seeking papal permission to found a new religious order—it was a close-run thing. There was so much opposition to allowing any new religious orders that six years later, in 1215, the Fourth Lateran Council banned the creation of new orders entirely. Hence, Pope Innocent III (served 1198–1216) was reluctant to meet Francis, but finally was persuaded to do so and granted him the right to recruit more members, promising that if and when he had enough followers he could reapply for official recognition. In 1223 Pope Honorius III (served 1216–1227) approved the final Rule for the Order of Friars Minor (little friars) that came to be known as the *Franciscans*.

In similar fashion, St. Dominic (1170–1221) founded a mendicant order of friars in Toulouse in 1214, and (despite the council ban) it was approved by Pope Honorius III in 1216. They too were soon known by the name of their founder, becoming the *Dominicans*. Like the Franciscans, they also began with a mission of public preaching on behalf of church reform. However, their mission soon shifted to public preaching in support of the pope.

These examples display the remarkable capacity of the church to encapsulate potential dissident movements within its structure. A study of the writings of founders and leading members of various accepted religious orders reveals a remarkable level of theological variety—often involving greater differences than existed between the "mainstream" Catholic theology and that of groups denounced as heretics. The main difference between many sanctioned orders and others eventually denounced as heretical lay not in doctrinal differences but in whether the group was careful to fully acknowledge the authority of the Church of Power, especially in their public preaching. Thus, rather than continuing to press for church reforms, the Dominicans soon specialized in public preaching against all religious groups they judged to be insufficiently submissive.

Persecution

MEANWHILE, THE REFORMING IMPULSE was arousing substantial opposition to the Church of Power. A monk named Tanchelm (died 1115) preached reform in the Low Countries (he said that the church had become a brothel) and was murdered by a priest.[26] Several very popular reformers, including Henry the Monk (died 1148) and Arnold of Brescia (1090–1155), both of them ordained members of the clergy, were crushed by the church for persisting in their public preaching of reform. Henry was imprisoned and Arnold was hanged.[27] But it was too late. The reform spirit had become deeply embedded in the general public, and if the church could not be reformed from within, there were large numbers of people ready to turn elsewhere for genuine piety.

Keep in mind that religious monopolies are not the *normal* state of affairs in societies, although they have been the *usual* state. Monopolies are not normal because no one institution can adequately serve the great range of religious tastes that always exist in any society—from those wishing very intense religion to those wanting little or none. Monopolies can only exist by repressing the formation of other religious groups, especially the higher intensity groups known as sects. As Gordon Leff put it so well, heresy in medieval Europe "was the outlet of a society with no outlets. Their absence made tensions into explosions."[28]

It was a tribute to the administrative creativity of the church that it was able to divert and encapsulate so many sectarian initiatives through monasticism. But this solution was no longer sufficient when the papacy was fully recaptured by the Roman aristocracy in the person of Clement III (served 1187–1191). Once again ascending the papal throne became a family affair. Clement's nephew became Pope Innocent III (served 1198–1216). Innocent's nephew became, in turn, Pope Gregory IX (served 1227–1241), and Innocent's grandnephew was elected Pope Alexander IV (served 1254–1261). The return of the papacy to open worldliness so affronted the widespread demands for church reform that an eruption of new sect movements was inevitable. Sadly, so too was their vicious repression.

Cathars

The first great heresy to confront the Roman Church probably did not originate within the reform movement, but was greatly facilitated by the discontent the reformers aroused and reflected. The Cathars may have originated in the Bogomil movement that arose in Bulgaria in the tenth century. Whether or not that was where they began, the Cathars "offered a direct, headlong challenge to the Catholic Church, which [they] dismissed outright as the Church of Satan."[29] They quickly gained a following in the West because of the widespread discontent with the moral inadequacies of the church.[30]

Cathar theology closely resembled that of the early Gnostics. There are two gods, one good, the other evil. Human history proves that because the material world is so tragic, brutal, and wicked, the good god could not have had any involvement in it. Hence, the Cathars taught that the world was created by the evil god (a fallen angel), who is the god of the Old Testament. Christ was an angel sent by the good god with a message of salvation—that one must reject the evils of this world and form a personal relationship with the good god.[31]

Catharism offered two degrees of membership. The *perfecti* made extreme efforts to reject the world: no sex, no meat, eggs, or dairy products, no swearing of oaths, and an absolute prohibition on killing not only humans but animals. However, regular members "remained in the world, married, had children and ate meat," and were quite prepared to fight, kill, and die for their faith.[32] The Cathars had no priests, only bishops, all of whom were required to be *perfecti*.

Our earliest knowledge of the Cathars in the West comes from Cologne in 1143, and by then they already had a local bishop and a significant number of members.[33] Having been denounced as heretics, the Cathar bishop and his aide were brought before the local archbishop, and they frankly admitted teaching that theirs was the one true church. What the archbishop might have done in response to such a challenge is uncertain because at that point a mob rose from the audience, seized the two Cathars, and burned them. Several similar mob actions took place in England in 1156 and again in Cologne as well as in Metz in 1164.

However, the center of the Cathar movement was not in Germany or England, but in the Languedoc area of southern France, where they often were referred to as the Albigensians because their headquarters was in the city of Albi. Keep in mind that even in southern France the Cathars probably made up only about 1 percent of the population and probably no more than 10 percent in the cities such as Béziers that were most closely associated with them.[34] However, their influence was far greater than their numbers might suggest, since so many Cathars, including many *perfecti*, were members of the nobility and many others were recruited from the local Catholic clergy.[35] This is consistent with the point established in chapter 5, that religious movements usually are initiated by people of privilege.

Given the strength of the Cathars in southern France, when Pope Innocent III (a member of a Roman ecclesiastical family that produced nine popes) initiated a "crusade" against the Cathars in 1208, the persecuting forces consisted of knights from northern France, a leader of whom complained that "the lords of the Languedoc almost all protected and harboured the heretics, showing them excessive love and defending them against God and church."[36] In July 1209 the Cathar-controlled city of Béziers fell to the papal forces led by Arnaud, a Cistercian abbot, and all of its inhabitants were butchered, many having first been blinded, dragged behind horses, and used for target practice.[37] Arnaud wrote to Pope Innocent that "Today your Holiness, twenty thousand heretics were put to the sword, regardless of rank, age, or sex."[38]

Even so, the Cathars continued to resist and their persecution continued. More than two hundred *perfecti* were burned in 1244 and another group of *perfecti* were executed in 1321. Eventually groups of

Cathars found sanctuary in various mountain areas, where they may have survived into modern times.

Waldensians

Although the Cathars were outside the church by choice and from the beginning, the Waldensians began as an incipient monastic movement committed to church reform.[39] The group was originated by Peter Waldo (or Valdes), a very rich merchant in Lyon, France. In 1176, having commissioned translations of the New Testament into French so he could discover what the Gospels actually taught, Waldo gave away his wealth and began to preach a message of apostolic poverty. He rapidly attracted followers, most of them also possessed of wealth,[40] and they began to refer to themselves as the Poor Men of Lyon. In 1179 Waldensian representatives went to Rome to seek official recognition from the pope. Instead, they aroused considerable anxiety. As the Welsh chronicler and gossip Walter Map (1140–1210) observed: "They go about two by two, barefoot, clad in woolen garments, owning nothing, holding all things in common like the Apostles. . . . If we admit them, we shall be driven out."[41] The pope blessed their lifestyle, but forbade them to preach. Had they conformed they probably would have eventually been recognized as an order (their teachings were very close to those of St. Francis). But they continued to preach and hence in 1184 they were condemned as heretics by Pope Lucius III.

Initially, no serious efforts were made to suppress the Waldensians, probably because their area of greatest strength was not in southern France where they had begun, but along the Rhine in Germany. Here they benefitted from the local political disorganization and conflicts and from their substantial over-recruitment of upper-class followers.[42] But in 1211 the church was able to begin a campaign of persecution—more than eighty Waldensians were seized and burned in Strasbourg. Over the next several centuries a series of battles took place, but by slowly withdrawing into the Alps the Waldensians survived until 1532 when they became affiliated with the Swiss Calvinists. A Waldensian church still exists.

Conclusion

DESPITE PERSECUTION, THE DEMAND for reform would not die. New "heretical" groups continued to erupt: the Beghards and Beguines, the Fraticelli, the Humiliati, the Flagellants, and the Lollards. Soon came open rebellion in Prague as the queen and most of the nobility embraced Jan Hus (1372–1415) and his "Bohemian Reformation." Although Hus was given a safe conduct to defend his views at a church council in Constance, upon his arrival he was seized and marched to the stake. Then came Luther.

CHAPTER EIGHTEEN

Luther's Reformation

FAR TOO MANY HISTORIES OF the Reformation suppose that Martin Luther succeeded because he stood on the moral and theological high ground. In fact, for much of the twentieth century, accounting for the Reformation was regarded mainly as a theological, not an historical, enterprise.[1] However Luther had many predecessors, some of whom shared most of the his theological and moral positions, but that didn't save them. As Luther himself acknowledged,[2] Jan Hus had anticipated most of his reforms, for which Hus was burned alive, which is precisely what Pope Leo X had in mind for Luther too. Luther and his Reformation survived only because he attracted sufficient political and military support to thwart the forces sent to stifle him.

In the thousands of volumes written about the Reformation, many explanations have been offered as to why and how Luther and his movement succeeded in rallying so much support. Is it possible at this late date to say anything new? Yes. It turns out that some widely held claims about where and why Luther's Reformation succeeded are wrong; others have never been adequately tested; and some very important matters have been ignored. There were, of course, a number of somewhat independent Protestant Reformations that occurred in the sixteenth century, and I have written about each of them at length elsewhere.[3] Here I have chosen to focus on Luther's since his was the primary episode.

Creating a "Heretic"

MARTIN LUTHER[4] (1483–1546) WAS the son of a well-to-do German family. Although his father may have been of peasant origins, he soon owned copper mines and smelters and served for many years on the council of the city of Mansfeld in Saxony. After four years in prep schools, in 1501 the young Luther enrolled in the University of Erfurt, one of the oldest and best universities in Germany. His father hoped he would become a lawyer, but after a few months in law, he transferred to theology. Luther received his bachelor's degree in 1502 and his master's in 1505. He then entered an Augustinian monastery and in 1507 was ordained a priest. Meanwhile, in 1505 he was appointed to the faculty at the University of Wittenberg, where he also received his doctorate in 1512. Except for several short breaks caused by his conflict with the church, Luther remained at Wittenberg for the rest of his life.

In 1510 one of the pivotal events in Luther's life took place when he was selected as one of two German Augustinians to go to Rome to present an appeal concerning their order. Only ten years earlier, Ignatius Loyola (1491–1556), founder of the Jesuits, was advised not to go to Rome for there his faith might be shaken by the city's "stupendous depravity."[5] Luther received no such helpful warning and, although impressed by the history and grandeur of Rome, he was deeply shocked by the open blasphemy and impiety of the clergy, including priests who thought it amusing to recite parodies of the liturgy while celebrating mass. This was not some anti-Catholic tale Luther later told to justify his break with Rome. Such things were reported by many other devout visitors to Rome. For example, the celebrated Desiderius Erasmus (1466–1536) noted from his own visit to Rome only five years prior to Luther's that "with my own ears I heard the most loathsome blasphemies against Christ and His Apostles. Many acquaintances of mine have heard priests of the curia uttering disgusting words so loudly, even during mass, that all around them could hear."[6] And just as Erasmus remained within the church,

Luther had no thought of leaving even after seeing such dreadful excesses. Instead, like most other members of the Church of Piety had done through the centuries, he committed himself to reform. Even so, it was not until about seven years later that Luther did anything other than continue teaching.

It was the local sale of indulgences that finally prodded Luther to act. The basis for indulgences was the doctrine that all sins must be atoned by good works or penance before a soul can enter heaven. Since at death most people have many sins that have not been atoned, their souls must linger in purgatory—a kind of semi-hell—until they have done sufficient penance to atone for their sins. This doctrine stimulated many good works and the church assigned each of them a value as to the amount of time remitted from one's sentence to purgatory. For example, service in a crusade brought complete remission of time in purgatory. Soon it became accepted that gifts to the church allowed individuals to gain credits from purgatory, and this practice was formalized by the sale of signed and sealed certificates (known as indulgences), some of them specifying a period of remission, others providing dispensations to commit, or for having committed, various sins. Then in 1476 Pope Sixtus IV authorized the sale of indulgences to the living that would shorten the suffering of their dead loved ones in purgatory. As a popular sales slogan put it, "The moment the money tinkles in the collecting box, a soul flies out of purgatory."[7] The yield from indulgences was enormous, especially because trained, travelling "salesmen" led local sales efforts.

In 1517 Johannes Tetzel, a prominent Dominican indulgence salesman, organized a campaign in areas near Wittenberg—the proceeds to go to rebuilding St. Peter's basilica in Rome and to repay the archbishop of Metz the huge price he had paid to buy his office. Drafts of some of Tetzel's sermons survive and the following excerpt is typical: "Do you not hear the voices of your dead parents and other people, screaming and saying 'Have pity on me, have pity on me. . . . We are suffering severe punishments and pain, from which you could rescue me with a few alms, if you would.' "[8]

Luther was disgusted by the sale of indulgences. His critique of this practice became known as Luther's *Ninety-Five Theses on the Power and Efficacy of Indulgences*, which was a proposal to debate the issue and which he nailed to the door of the Castle Church. Contrary to myth, this was not an act of defiance—that church door was routinely used as a bulletin board by the Wittenberg faculty.[9] Luther nailed up his theses (written in Latin) on October 31, 1517. By December at least three different printers in three different cities had produced German translations. During the next several months translations were published in many other places including France, England, and Italy.[10] Probably because Luther's critique became so widely known outside the Latin-reading elite, the response of the church was angry and swift. Pope Leo X soon ordered Luther to Rome, and had he gone he probably would have become just another obscure martyr to reform. Fortunately for Luther, the German Elector Frederick objected to his summons (he too was opposed to the sale of Roman indulgences in Germany), and it was agreed that Luther would instead appear before Cardinal Cajetan in Augsburg.

Arriving in Augsburg on October 7, 1518, with a safe-conduct from Frederick, Luther discovered that the cardinal had no interest in anything but a retraction of his theses. When Luther refused, he was ordered into seclusion until he was ready to conform. Soon rumors reached Luther that the cardinal was planning to violate his safe-conduct and send him to Rome in chains. Friends helped Luther to escape and go back to Wittenberg where the faculty rallied to his cause and petitioned Frederick to protect him. Of course this amounted to an irreconcilable break with the church hierarchy, and Luther responded by publishing three famous, defiant tracts, now known as the *Reformation Treatises*. A primary emphasis was on how the Roman Church was bleeding Germany: "every year more than three hundred thousand gulden find their way from Germany to Rome, quite uselessly and fruitlessly; we get nothing but scorn and contempt. And yet we wonder that princes, nobles, cities, endowments, land and people are impoverished."[11] And he wrote of Rome and the pope in colorful, violent language: "Hearest thou this, O pope, not most holy, but most sinful? O that God from heaven would soon destroy thy throne and sink it in the abyss of hell! . . . O Christ, my Lord, look down, let the day of thy judgment break, and destroy the devil's nest at Rome."[12]

Of course, Luther did not merely issue criticisms of Rome. He proposed some radical changes in both practice and doctrine. He called for an end to the sale of indulgences, for no more masses to be said for the dead, for the elimination of all "holy days" except for Sundays, and for the whole congregation, not just the priest, to sip the communion wine. Luther also proposed that priests be allowed to marry and that no one be permitted to take binding monastic vows before the age of thirty—later he advised the dissolution of all religious orders and that there be no more vows of celibacy. As for doctrine, Luther asserted the absolute authority of Holy Scripture and that each human must discover the meaning of scripture and establish their own personal relationship with God. Most radical of all, Luther proposed that salvation is God's gift, freely given, and is gained entirely by faith in Jesus as the redeemer. That is, salvation cannot be earned or purchased by good works. Consequently, there is no purgatory since no atonement for sins is necessary or possible. One either has faith and is saved or lacks faith and is damned. As for good works, they are the result, or fruits, of faith.

Of course, the church attempted to stifle such "heresy." On June 15, 1520, Luther's writings were officially condemned and copies were burned in Rome. In response, the students at Wittenberg burned official pronouncements against Luther. Despite Luther's obvious, widespread popularity in Germany, the pope officially excommunicated him in January 1521. Next Luther was ordered to appear before the Imperial Diet meeting in Worms. Luther's friends urged him not to go, fearing for his life. But Luther refused to be deterred—it was the most important decision of his life and changed the course of Western history. Luther's journey to Worms was not that of an unimportant, excommunicated monk. Crowds of supporters thronged along the roads and "he was attended by a cavalcade of German knights."[13] During his hearing before the Diet, Luther refused to budge, closing with his immortal "Here I stand."

A rump session of the Diet organized by members loyal to Rome declared Luther an outlaw, but it was an empty gesture. A large number of German princes formed ranks in defense of Luther and in rebellion against the church (thus retaining the huge sums that had been extracted from their realms by Rome). Consequently, Luther could exult: "I declare, I have made a reformation which will make the pope's ears ring and hearts burst."[14]

The remainder of this chapter will attempt to explain why Lutheranism spread rapidly and soon replaced Catholicism as the monopoly state church in many parts of northern Europe. Let me emphasize that the focus is on Luther's Reformation. I ignore the "Peasants' War" and other "heretical" outbursts such as the Anabaptist rebellion at Münster.

Explaining the Reformation

IT HAS LONG BEEN fashionable for scholars, even non-Marxists, to trace all social movements to underlying "material" trends. In the instance at hand, the idea that doctrine played a role in generating the Lutheran Reformation has long been dismissed by social scientists, and the success of Lutheranism has been traced to "real causes"— to fundamental social changes such as the demise of feudalism, the growth of a money economy, the rise of credit, the expansion of trade, industrialization, urbanization, the expansion of the bourgeoisie, the declining military significance of heavy cavalry, increased taxes, and population growth, to name only a few.[15] All of these changes were in fact taking place at this time. But they can explain nothing about the success of the Reformation because these changes were as prevalent in areas that remained Catholic as they were in those that embraced Lutheranism.[16]

It is equally foolish to deny any role to doctrine in the success of

Luther's Reformation. It is hard to imagine a set of doctrines that could have presented such a profound and popular challenge to Catholic authority. Even so, most of the emphasis on doctrine is misplaced, stressing, as it does, theological intricacies that very few of those who embraced Lutheranism could possibly have understood or cared about. More serious is the fact that like the many social changes mistakenly cited above, doctrine too was a *constant*, while the success (or failure) of Lutheranism was a *variable*. That is, knowledge of Lutheran theology tells us nothing about why some places turned Lutheran and others did not. Thus, for all of their appeal, Lutheran doctrines must stand in the background.

Many Marxist historians have, of course, interpreted the Reformation as the remarkable success of a proletarian mass movement. For example, the Soviet historian M. M. Smirin (1895–1975) dismissed non-Marxist historians as "perverters of history," and revealed that "the true, scientific history" of the Reformation is the struggle of an oppressed people.[17] Although differing as to motivations, many non-Marxist historians have agreed that Lutheranism swept across Germany on a wave of enthusiasm among the masses. But it's not true.

The "masses"—the peasants and urban lower classes—were almost completely uninvolved in Luther's Reformation, both as it took place and afterward. As was documented in chapter 15, intensive efforts by Luther and his peers to reach out to the masses after Lutheranism had been established were resounding failures. Luther himself bitterly acknowledged this fact.[18]

Instead, Luther's Reformation was almost exclusively an urban phenomenon.[19] And within the urban context it is widely believed by historians that the Reformation spread rapidly because of its popularity among printers[20] and its appeal to students and professors,[21] to the urban bourgeoisie,[22] and to the nobility.[23] Each of these claims will be examined at some length and modified as necessary. But first it seems legitimate to sketch the grievances against the church that prompted many to embrace Lutheranism.

Reform and Discontent

As NOTED IN CHAPTER 17, strong forces for reform long existed both within and without the medieval church. But when the Church of Piety lost control of the papacy late in the twelfth century, many of the worst defects not only remained but prospered once again. The most obvious of these was widespread immorality and indolence among the clergy at all levels. Perhaps of greater political significance was the existence of excessive church wealth, privileges, and exactions.

The sins of the clergy, from popes through parish priests, have been sketched at length in several previous chapters. Here it seems sufficient to note the unsuitability of Pope Leo X (reigned 1513–1521), who drove Luther from the church. Born Giovanni de'Medici, the son of the famous patron of the arts and wastrel Lorenzo de'Medici,[24] he was the last nonpriest to be elected pope—he was not ordained until a week after his election, was consecrated a bishop two days later, and crowned pope two days after that. Leo fancied himself a humanist and intellectual, but he was most notably "indolent . . . a spendthrift who squandered more on pageants and gambling than on the needs of the Church."[25] His intense desire for money caused him to launch the aggressive campaigns to sell indulgences that affronted Luther and brought so many princes to Luther's defense.

For the princes, there need have been no theological objections to the sale of indulgences; it was fully sufficient that their sale caused the flow of large amounts of wealth from their subjects and off to Rome. In addition, the church was by far the richest and largest landowner in Europe. It is estimated that in 1522 the church owned half of the wealth in Germany, perhaps a fifth in France, and about a third in Italy. In Zurich in 1467, church groups held a third of all property, and similar proportions belonged to the church in many other cities.[26] The church usually paid no local taxes on any of its properties. In addition, the church enjoyed a huge cash flow by imposing tithes on everyone from peasants to kings in much of Europe. In contrast, the clergy and members of religious orders were exempted from all local taxes (including sales taxes on liquor) and could not be tried in local, secular courts, even for murder. Instead, they could only be tried in church courts which were notorious for imposing very lenient sentences.

Pamphlets and Printers

LUTHER'S REFORMATION WAS THE first social movement for which printed materials played an important role—the printing press was only just coming of age. Luther produced many pamphlets (often only four to six pages long) outlining his various disagreements with Rome, each written in vernacular German, and printers across Germany (as well as in other parts of Europe) pumped out copies because, although they were very cheap, they sold by the wagon load. Between 1517 and 1520, Luther turned out thirty pamphlets and short essays. These were published by more than twenty printing firms and it is estimated that altogether they sold more than three hundred thousand copies.[27] In 1522, Luther's translation of the New Testament into German appeared, and it "sold even more widely than any of Luther's other writings."[28]

Keep in mind that copyrights didn't exist in this era and that printers produced their own editions of anything they thought would sell—Luther protested when other printers rushed out his New Testament before the printer in Wittenberg had sold out his copies. However, it was the existence of aggressive local printers that spread Lutheran materials so widely and quickly. In most of the rest of Europe there were printers only in the largest cities, but in Germany there were printers even in many of the smaller towns. Hence, in Germany, books and pamphlets did not need to be transported long distances—most of Luther's writings were available locally as soon as the enterprising printer had obtained a copy elsewhere. In one famous incident, a copy of one of Luther's tracts was stolen from the printer's shop in Wittenberg and appeared in print in Nuremberg before the Wittenberg edition came out.[29] In addition, it is generally believed that printers were eager to produce Lutheran materials not only because they sold so well, but also because the great majority of printers supported Luther.[30]

Connections between printers, printing, and the Reformation have been well-tested in a remarkable new study by Hyojoung Kim and Steven Pfaff.[31] These young sociologists assembled data for each German town having a population of two thousand or more in 1520. Their goal was to test explanations of the success of the Reformation by seeing what factors determined which of these 461 towns turned Lutheran and which remained Catholic, using as their measure whether and when each town officially outlawed saying the Catholic mass. This measure overcomes all ambiguities and is well-documented. Notice too that there was no aspect of religious freedom involved in Luther's Reformation. What took place was a switch from one monopoly church to another.

Kim and Pfaff were able to study many key aspects of Luther's Reformation because they were able to assemble detailed information on each town, as will be seen. One of these facts was whether or not there was a local printer and whether this printer had produced an edition of Luther's Bible. Consistent with an immense historical literature, they hypothesized that towns with printers who had published Luther's Bible were more likely to turn Lutheran. And the results? Not so! During the early days of the Reformation, there was no correlation between printers of Lutheran Bibles and turning Lutheran; in later days the correlation is negative—towns where Luther's Bible was printed were significantly *less* likely to have turned Lutheran! This suggests that printers churned out Lutheran literature because it was so profitable, not necessarily because they agreed with it. In fact, that is precisely what Luther and many of his fellow Reformers believed. They often complained that the printers were merely profiteering from their work, and Luther denounced printers as "sordid mercenaries."[32]

Professors and Students

THE REFORMATION BEGAN AT the University of Wittenberg. As the distinguished Paul Grendler put it, "The activities of the first four or five years of the Lutheran Reformation resembled a young faculty uprising."[33] As word of Luther's activities spread, enrollment at Wittenberg nearly doubled by 1520 and soon it was the largest university in Germany. Most students attended Luther's theological lectures and nearly all of them heard Philipp Melanchthon[34] (1497–1560)—Luther's confidant and ally. Moreover, after completing their studies at Wittenberg, most students went home where they devoted themselves to spreading the Reformation. Nor was it only at Wittenberg that students were recruited as Reformation activists. Lutheranism attracted strong support in many other universities as well, especially at the University of Basel. In addition to taking the Reformation home with them, many students soon also became professors of theology and began to train more activists. A study of prominent leaders of the Reformation found that nearly all of them were, or had been, university professors.[35]

It turns out, however, that this is a very one-sided and misleading view of the connection between academia and the Reformation. Many other universities were hotbeds of anti-Lutheran, orthodox Catholicism—the University of Cologne came to be called the "German Rome," and the University of Louvain was equally anti-Lutheran. Students from these universities also went home and there they served as staunch defenders of the church.

Apparently universities, at least in Germany, keep their records forever. Not only do records remain for each student who enrolled in the sixteenth century, but the enrollment lists for specific classes, including those taught by Luther, can be reconstructed. In addition, student records include their home towns. For their set of 461 towns and cities, Kim and Pfaff were able to identify the number of residents who were enrolled in Wittenberg and in Basel during the years 1517 through 1522. They also identified the number who attended Cologne and Louvain. Finally, they created a measure of the total number of students from a town or city who enrolled in any university.

The results are compelling. The rate at which a town's young people went off to a university had no impact whatsoever on whether the town turned Lutheran or stayed Catholic. But if the larger proportion of students had gone off to Wittenberg or Basel, the city or town had a high probability of becoming Lutheran. Conversely, where enrollments in Cologne and Louvain predominated, the probability was that the town or city remained Catholic. Finally, university towns were more likely to remain Catholic than were towns and cities lacking a university. Despite the prominence of students and faculty in the Lutheran movement, universities tended to be conservative in the sense of upholding traditions. This also helps explain the negative correlation between printers and Lutheranism—university cities all had active presses.

Responsive City Governance

THE BACKBONE OF THE Lutheran Reformation was provided by the urban bourgeoisie: the merchants, bankers, lawyers, physicians, manufacturers, schoolmasters, shopkeepers, and bureaucrats, as well as members of the highly skilled guilds, such as printers and glass blowers, and many local priests. This does not mean, of course, that all or nearly all of the members of these groups favored Luther. It merely means that most of Luther's support came from these groups. That this was the base of Lutheran recruitment is well known,[36] and made obvious by the importance of the printed word for the spread of Lutheranism in an era of mass illiteracy—it is estimated that in 1500 only 3 to 4 percent of Germans could read.[37] What made these urban supporters so effective lay in the fact that in much of Germany, many towns and cities had sufficient autonomy so that they could opt to make Lutheranism the only lawful faith without suffering outside interference—at least not until the Wars of Religion began.

Towns and cities with substantial local political autonomy were known as "Free Imperial Cities," of which there were about sixty-five.[38] These cities owed no allegiance to local princes, but only to the Holy Roman Emperor, which is why they were called Imperial Cities. These cities paid their taxes directly to the emperor and remained in complete control of their own tax systems as well as their internal affairs. Some of these Imperial "Cities" can be ignored because they were tiny, having no more than a thousand residents.[39] A few had far less political freedom than the others because they were situated in a powerful duchy or principality and this imposed some degree of caution on the city fathers lest they provoke outside interference. But most of the Free Imperial Cities were located in the area along the Rhine known as the "Borderlands" where there were no large governmental units and thus very little threat of external interference. Fortunately for purposes of research, there were a number of other cities in this Borderland area that were similar in size and economy, but that were not Free Imperial Cities. Some of these cities were ruled by a prince bishop, others by a nearby prince, but in either case the local laity had very little authority.

To test the hypothesis that where the local bourgeoisie were in control, Lutheranism was far more likely to have been adopted, I collected information on all forty-three significant Free Imperial Cities and the twelve other cities that were located in the Borderlands. Of the Free Imperial Cities, nearly two-thirds (61 percent) became Protestant, while three-fourths (75 percent) of the non-Imperial Cities remained Catholic.[40] Using a slightly different set of cities, Kim and Pfaff found very similar results. Hence local political autonomy played an important role in the success of Luther's Reformation. But so did autocracy. Aside from the cities, many larger political units ruled by strong princes or kings turned Protestant too.

Royal Self-Interest

WE COME NOW TO an apparent contradiction about the spread of Luther's Reformation. In most of Europe, the decision to embrace Lutheranism or to remain steadfastly within the church was made by an autocratic ruler—a king or a prince. Nearly without exception the autocrats opted for Lutheranism in places where the Catholic Church had the *greatest* local power, and chose to remain Catholic in places where the church was extremely weak! To see why things turned out this way, it will be useful to contrast France and Spain, on the one hand, with Denmark and Sweden, on the other.

Beginning in 1296 when King Philip of France successfully imposed a tax on church income, papal authority steadily eroded in France. In 1516, the subordination of the church to the French monarchy was formalized in the Concordat of Bologna signed by Pope Leo X and King Francis I. The king was acknowledged to have the right to appoint all of the higher posts of the church in France: ten archbishops, eighty-two bishops, and every prior, abbot, and abbess of all of the many hundreds of monasteries, abbeys, and convents. This gave the king full control of all church property and income. As the esteemed Owen Chadwick noted, "When he [King Francis] wanted ecclesiastical money, his methods need not even be devious."[41] His appointees simply delivered.

If anything, the Spanish crown had even greater power over the church. It had long held the right to nominate archbishops and bishops, to fine the clergy, and to receive a substantial share of the tithes. Then in 1486, King Ferdinand and Queen Isabella gained the right to make all major ecclesiastical appointments, to prohibit appeals from Spanish courts to Rome, to impose taxes on the clergy, and to make it illegal to publish papal bulls and decrees in Spain or its possessions without prior royal consent.[42] Of course, as Spain became the center of the Holy Roman Empire, these policies were extended to many portions of Italy, to Portugal, the Netherlands, Austria, and southeastern Germany.

In contrast, in Denmark in 1500 from a third to half of all tillable land was owned by the church, and all lay people (including the nobility) were required to pay tithes. None of this income was shared with the crown and much of it went directly to Rome. The pope also had sole authority to make all ecclesiastical appointments in Denmark. Thus, in contrast to the king of France and the Spanish Holy Roman Emperor, when Christian III became king of Denmark in 1534, he faced an immense opportunity for gain by declaring for Lutheranism and confiscating all church properties and income in his realm. He did so and ushered in "an era of prosperity."[43]

Meanwhile Sweden had successfully rebelled against Danish rule and crowned King Gustavus I in 1528. Of course, the new king was desperate for funds while here too the church possessed unchallenged authority and immense wealth. So Gustavus also opted for Protestantism and confiscated all church "possessions and revenues."[44] To gain support among the nobility, Gustavus sold them appropriated church property at bargain prices—even so, the church possessions Gustavus kept increased the crown lands fourfold.[45]

The same principle of self-interest accounts for the decisions of the other rulers. German princes with much to gain from becoming Lutheran did so; others, such as prince bishops who already possessed control of church offices and income, remained Catholic. And did any king gain more from stripping the church of its wealth and power than did England's Henry VIII? Consider that from the shrine dedicated to St. Thomas à Becket alone, Henry's agents confiscated 4,994 ounces of gold, 4,425 ounces of silver gilt, 5,286 ounces of silver, and twenty-six cartloads of other treasure—and this was regarded as a trivial portion of the wealth confiscated from the church.[46]

It should be noted too that in many instances it was very much in the self-interest of the urban bourgeoisie that local church property be confiscated and church authority curtailed. The Free Imperial Cities were greatly burdened by the extensive and *untaxed* local holdings of the church and by the very substantial number of clergy and members of religious orders resident in their city and exempt from all taxes (including tithes to the church) and all duties of citizenship (such as taking their turn as sentries on the walls, as all able-bodied nonclerical males were required to do). In most of these cities, about a third of all property belonged to the church and as many as 10 percent of the residents were clergy, monks, or nuns. Here too there was much to be gained by expelling the church.

It is all well and good to note the widespread appeal of the doctrine that we are saved by faith alone, but it also must be recognized that Protestantism prevailed only where the local rulers or councils had not already imposed their rule over the church.

The Catholic Reformation

THERE IS AN IMMENSE irony about Luther's Reformation as well as the other Protestant Reformations that gained a secure footing in Europe at this time. Their "reforms" were not lasting as each soon exhibited many of the defects of a worldly religious monopoly, while the church against which they had rebelled was dramatically and lastingly reformed as the Protestant challenge enabled the Church of Piety to return to power, never again to be thwarted.

The Catholic Reformation (also known as the Counter-Reformation) was launched at the Council of Trent (1551–1552, 1562–1563). Simony—the sale of church offices—was ended. Priestly celibacy was enforced. Official, inexpensive Bibles in local languages (vulgates) were made available. But perhaps the most important decision taken at Trent was the establishment of a network of seminaries to train men for the local priesthood. No longer would there be priests who did not know the Seven Deadly Sins or were unable to indentify who preached the Sermon on the Mount. By the eighteenth century, in most places the church was staffed by literate men well versed in theology. Even more important, the seminaries produced priests whose vocations had been shaped and tested in a formal, institutional setting.[47]

But there also was a dark side to the Catholic Reformation. The new spirit of strictness shifted the economic and intellectual outlook of the church. A reemphasis on asceticism set the church against business and banking to such an extent that it could mistakenly be argued that Protestantism gave birth to capitalism, despite the fact that capitalism was fully developed in Europe many centuries before Luther was born.[48] The same sort of thing happened vis-à-vis science. As was seen in chapter 16, Western science is rooted in Christian theology and arose in the medieval universities. Unfortunately, the Catholic Reformation imposed increasingly severe intellectual restrictions so that Catholic Universities rapidly declined in scientific significance to such a degree that it came to be widely but mistakenly believed that, as with capitalism, the Reformation also gave birth to the Scientific Revolution.

Conclusion

IN THE OVERALL SENSE, the various Reformations reintroduced stable religious diversity within European Christianity, but few individuals actually had multiple options available to them. In most of northern Europe, not only was Roman Catholicism illegal, but so too were all varieties of Protestantism other than the one represented by the monopoly state church, to which everyone was required to belong. Thus Calvinists were prohibited from the Lutheran Scandinavian nations, and Lutherans were burned in Henry VIII's "Protestant" England. Meanwhile, Catholic monopolies persisted in Southern Europe (non-Catholics were not allowed to hold services in Spain until 1970). Consequently, the low level of Christian commitment among the general population was little improved by the rise of Protestantism. The Catholic Reformation may have resulted in some gains in popular piety among Southern Europeans, although the higher levels of participation that existed there may only have reflected that this area had originally been more vigorously Christianized in the days of the early church. In any event, when all was said and done, because the various Reformations also resulted in lazy and lax monopoly churches, Europe's splendid cathedrals and picturesque chapels continued to be rather empty on Sunday mornings.

Chapter Nineteen

The Shocking Truth About
the Spanish Inquisition

Lutherans were persecuted in many Catholic nations and even in "Protestant" England. In Spain, of course, they became targets of the Inquisition.

The term *Spanish Inquisition* brings to mind what is remembered as one of the most frightening and bloody chapters in Western history. According to the standard account, the Inquisition was created in 1478 by the Spanish monarchs Ferdinand and Isabella, and was charged with ridding Spain of heretics, especially Jews and Muslims who were pretending to be Christians. But the Inquisition also set its sights on all Protestants, witches, homosexuals, scientists, and other doctrinal and moral offenders.

For the first several years, the Inquisition was rather inactive, but after the fanatical Dominican monk Tomás de Torquemada was appointed grand inquisitor in 1483, this hideous Catholic institution tortured and murdered huge numbers of innocent people. Nearly every Saturday in every major Spanish city there was an *auto-de-fe* and the air was filled with ashes as screaming victims were burned at the stake, usually after having been mercilessly tortured. On many Saturdays, piles of offensive books, especially scientific treatises, also were burned during the *autos-de-fe*.

The Inquisition did not even pretend to observe any semblance of legal procedure, seizing people right and left on the flimsiest accusations as the inquisitors grew rich from confiscating the wealth of the accused. Writing in 1554, the English Protestant John Foxe reported on "the extreme dealing and cruel ravening of these Catholic Inquisitors of Spain, who, under the pretended visor of religion, do nothing but seek their private gain and spoiling of other men's goods."[1] Thirteen years later came the truly devastating exposé, written in Latin by Reginaldus Montanus: *A Discovery and Plaine Declaration of Sundry Subtill Practices of the Holy Inquisition of Spain*. Translated into English, French, Dutch, and German, it was widely circulated. Montanus's account "emphasize[d] the deviousness and trickery of the interrogation techniques, the variety of horrors in its torture chambers, and the appalling behavior of its familiars, prison keepers, and torturers."[2] The main part of the book follows an innocent victim through the entire ordeal, ending at the stake, and the book concludes with twelve case histories of Lutherans martyred for their faith.

Montanus's volume became the standard account. According to a recent edition of *The Columbia Encyclopedia*, "Torture of the accused . . . soon became customary and notorious. . . . Most trials resulted in a verdict of guilty."[3] On these grounds the popular historian Will Durant (1885–1981) informed several generations of readers that "we must rank the Inquisition . . . as among the darkest blots on the record of mankind, revealing a ferocity unknown in any beast."[4]

Not only historians, but novelists, painters, and screenwriters have repeatedly recreated scenes of brutal inquisitorial sadism— Edgar Allen Poe's story of "The Pit and the Pendulum" being a classic among them. Another is Dostoyevsky's passage in *The Brothers Karamazov* wherein the grand inquisitor encounters Christ as he raises a child from the dead, whereupon he has Jesus seized and informs him that: "Tomorrow I shall condemn thee and burn thee at the stake as the worst of heretics."

How many victims were there? Microsoft's *Encarta* says that Torquemada "executed thousands." Jonathan Kirsch placed the Inquisition's casualty list as "countless thousands."[5] The *Encyclopedia of Religious Freedom* puts Torquemada's total at ten thousand as does Edmond Paris,[6] who also claims that another 125,000 died of torture and privation in Torquemada's prisons. Many historians have accepted the "conservative" estimate that during the effective lifetime of the Inquisition more than thirty-five thousand people were burned at the stake,[7] but one very recent author claims that well over a hundred thousand died during Torquemada's tenure alone.[8] Another historian has proposed that the Inquisition burned "nearly two hundred thousand . . . in thirty-six years."[9] Yet another claims that overall the Inquisition condemned more than three million, "with about 300,000 burned at the stake."[10]

Despite these immense variations in estimated fatalities, everyone agrees that the Inquisition was a blood bath perpetrated by sadistic fanatics. In his recent exposé, *The Grand Inquisitor's Manual: A History of Terror in the Name of God* (2008), Jonathan Kirsch devoted the second paragraph of the book to invoking the image of "hooded men in dungeons lit only by torches . . . plying instruments of torture to the naked bodies of men and women whose only crime is to have entertained some thought that the Church regarded as heretical. . . . [T]he torturers are wholly without pity, and they work in the sure conviction that the odor of the charred flesh of humans is 'delectable to the Holy Trinity and the Virgin.'"

But the most shocking truth about the Spanish Inquisition is that everything above *is either an outright lie or a wild exaggeration*!

Creating the "Black Legend"

THE STANDARD ACCOUNT OF the Spanish Inquisition was invented and spread by English and Dutch propagandists in the sixteenth century during their wars with Spain and repeated ever after by malicious or misled historians eager to sustain "an image of Spain as a nation of fanatical bigots."[11] This image of Spain is now referred to by fair-minded historians as the "Black Legend," which the American historian Charles Gibson (1920–1985) defined as "the accumulated tradition of propaganda and Hispanophobia according to which [the Spanish are] . . . regarded as cruel, bigoted, exploitative, and self-righteous."[12] Although these tales of Spanish brutality originated in the days of Queen Elizabeth and the Spanish Armada, they refused to die, being sustained by generations of "respectable" British historians who also openly expressed their contempt and antagonism toward Roman Catholicism—attitudes reflected in the fact that Catholic students were denied admission to Oxford and Cambridge until 1871.

However, the wildest exaggerations about the Spanish Inquisition originated with and were repeatedly fueled by Spanish "defectors." Consider that "Montanus" (see above) was the pen name used by a renegade Spanish monk who became a Lutheran and fled to the Netherlands where he wrote his infamous book. As the distinguished Edward Peters noted, "Part of Montanus' appeal lay in the base of accuracy upon which he erected an otherwise extremely misleading description of the Inquisition to an audience prepared to believe the worst. . . . Montanus portrays every victim of the Inquisition as innocent, every Inquisition official as venal and deceitful, every step in the procedure as a violation of natural and rational law."[13] Again, early in the nineteenth century a sensational attack on the Inquisition was written by a Spanish émigré living in London, D. Antonio Puigblanch (1775–1840): *The Inquisition Unmasked: Being an Historical and Philosophical Account of the Tremendous Tribunal* (1816). This widely read two-volume work ran to nearly a thousand pages devoted to recounting the "enormous crimes . . . committed by this tribunal [that] . . . rendered its name so odious—crimes so much more revolting and abominable, because they have been committed under the sanction of religion."[14] Recently, Kessinger Publishing chose to include this work in its series of "rare reprints."

The Real Inquisition

THAT SUCH BIGOTRY FLOURISHED during Europe's era of religious wars is not surprising. Nor is it so surprising that this hateful nonsense was sustained during the era of intense anti-Catholicism that continued in England (and the United States) well into the twentieth century.[15] But there is no such excuse for those irresponsible contemporary "scholars" who continue to support such claims while ignoring or dismissing the remarkable research on the Inquisition that has been accomplished in the past generation.[16] Astonishing as it may seem, the new historians of the Inquisition have revealed that, in contrast with the secular courts all across Europe, the Spanish Inquisition was a consistent force for justice, restraint, due process, and enlightenment.[17]

These historians (many of them being neither Spanish nor Catholic) base their dissenting views on having gained full access to the complete archives of the Inquisitions of both Aragon and Castile, which together constituted the Spanish Inquisition. Subsequently, they have read the careful records made of each of the 44,701 cases heard by these two Inquisitions between 1540 and 1700. At the time they were written these records were secret so there is no reason for the clerks to have misrepresented the actual proceedings. Not only are these cases a goldmine of historical detail; each has been entered into a database in order to facilitate statistical analysis.[18] In addition, these historians have done an immense amount of more traditional research, pouring over diaries, letters, decrees, and other old documents. The results are solidly undeniable. The remainder of this chapter offers a summary of the major discoveries.

Deaths

THE TERM *AUTO-DE-FE* DOES not mean execution, let alone burning at the stake, but is best translated as "act of faith." The inquisitors were far more concerned with repentance than with punishment and therefore an *auto-de-fe* consisted of a public appearance by persons convicted of various offenses who offered public confessions of their guilt and were thereby reconciled to the church. Only very rarely did an *auto-de-fe* end with an offender being surrendered to the civil authorities for execution (the Inquisition did not ever conduct an actual execution). Even so, *autos-de-fe* were not frequent. In the city of Toledo, between 1575 and 1610, only twelve *autos-de-fe* were held, "at which 386 culprits appeared."[19] Obviously, then, the tales of weekly mass burnings all across Spain are malicious fantasies. So, how many did die?

The first decades of the Inquisition's operations were not as fully documented as they were after 1540, but historians now agree that these were its bloodiest days and that perhaps as many as fifteen hundred people may have been executed, or about thirty a year.[20] Turning to the fully recorded period, of the 44,701 cases tried, only 826 people were executed, which amounts to 1.8 percent of those brought to trial.[21] Together, this adds up to a total of about 2,300 deaths spread over more than two centuries, a total that is a far cry from the "conservative" estimates that more than thirty thousand were burned by the Inquisition. In fact, fewer people were executed by order of the Spanish Inquisition over more than two centuries than the three thousand French Calvinists who were killed in Paris alone during the St. Bartholomew's Day Massacre.[22] Or compare this with the thousands of English Lutherans, Lollards, and Catholics (in addition to two of his wives) that Henry VIII is credited with having boiled, burned, beheaded, or hanged.[23] The fact is that during the entire period 1480 through 1700, only about ten deaths *per year* were meted out by the Inquisition all across Spain—and usually to repeat offenders! By modern Western standards, of course, even ten executions a year for various acts of religious nonconformity seem a dreadful excess. But during the time in question there was no religious toleration anywhere in Europe and capital punishment was the norm for all offenses, religious or otherwise. In context, then, the Spanish Inquisition was remarkably restrained.

Torture

IN POPULAR CULTURE, THE term *Inquisition* is nearly a synonym for torture. As John Dowling (1808–1878) explained, "Of all the inventions of popish cruelty the Holy Inquisition is the masterpiece. . . . It was impossible for even Satan himself to conceive a more horrible contrivance of torture and blood."[24] Thus, as noted above, it has been taken for granted that many more poor souls died in the Inquisition's prisons and torture chambers than survived long enough to go to the stake.

This may be the biggest lie of all! Every court in Europe used torture, but the Inquisition did so *far less* than other courts. For one thing, church law limited torture to one session lasting no more than fifteen minutes, and there could be no danger to life or limb. Nor could blood be shed![25] There are, of course, very painful techniques that can be applied within these rules. But even so, torture was rarely used, perhaps because the "inquisitors themselves were sceptical of the efficacy and validity of torture as a method of conviction."[26] If torture was used, its progress was carefully recorded by a clerk and this material was included with the record of the case.[27] Based on these data, Thomas Madden has estimated that the inquisitors resorted to torture in only about 2 percent of all the cases that came before them.[28] Moreover, it is widely agreed that prisons operated by the Inquisition were by far the most comfortable and humane in Europe; instances have been reported of "criminals in Spain purposely blaspheming so as to be transferred to the Inquisition's prisons."[29]

So there it is. Contrary to the standard myth, the Inquisition made little use of the stake, seldom tortured anyone, and maintained unusually decent prisons. But what about its procedures? The remainder of the chapter examines the workings of the Inquisition, organized on the basis of the alleged offenses.

Witchcraft

PERHAPS NO HISTORICAL STATISTICS have been so outrageously inflated as the numbers of those executed as witches during the craze that took place in Europe from about 1450 to 1700. Many writers have placed the final death toll at nine million, drawing comparisons with the Holocaust.[30] And while it is acknowledged that Protestants burned a lot of witches too, historians have stressed the leading role played by the Inquisition; one prominent historian even claimed that the Inquisition began hunting witches because it had run out of heretics to burn.[31] Several others have blamed the whole thing on the dire effects of celibacy which inflamed priests to "a raging campaign of revenge and annihilation" against women.[32] Finally, it is widely claimed that the witch hunts ended only when the "Dark Ages" of religious extremism were overthrown by the "Enlightenment."[33]

Vicious nonsense, all of it.

Consider that the witch hunts reached their height *during* the so-called Enlightenment! Indeed, in his celebrated book *Leviathan*, Thomas Hobbes (1599–1679), the famous English philosopher and proponent of the "Enlightenment," wrote that "as for witches . . . they are justly punished."[34] Another leading figure of the "Enlightenment," Jean Bodin (ca. 1530–1596), served as a judge at several witchcraft trials and advocated burning witches in the slowest possible fires.[35] In fact, many of the distinguished scientists of the seventeenth century, including Robert Boyle, encouraged witch hunts.[36]

As for the death toll, in recent years competent scholars have carefully assembled the evidence nation-by-nation and found the "accepted" totals to be utterly fantastic. For example, it had long been assumed that in England from 1600 to 1680, "about forty-two thousand witches were burnt,"[37] but the most trustworthy figure turns out to be fewer than a thousand over a period of three centuries.[38] In similar fashion, the best estimate of the final death toll is not nine million, but about sixty thousand![39] Even that is a tragic total, but it needs to be recognized that a mere handful of these victims were sentenced to death by the Spanish Inquisition—so few that the distinguished historian William Monter entitled a chapter in his statistical study of the Inquisition as "Witchcraft: The Forgotten Offense."[40] This was in response to data showing that during the century 1540–1640, when the witch hunts were at their peak in most of Europe, the Inquisition of Aragon (one of the two Inquisitions functioning in Spain) executed only twelve people for "superstition and witchcraft."[41] This should have been acknowledged all along. Even the virulently anti-Catholic historian Henry C. Lea (1825–1909) agreed that witch hunting was "rendered comparatively harmless" in Spain and that this "was due to the wisdom and firmness of the Inquisition."[42] Let us examine this wisdom and firmness in some detail.

To begin, it is important to recognize what sustained the charge of witchcraft since it is not the case that the accusations were nothing but unfounded hysteria—many people actually were "doing something" that led them to be charged. What they were doing was practicing magic. As would be expected in an era that was extremely deficient in medical knowledge, medical magic abounded in Europe and so did magical attempts to influence weather, crops, love, wealth, and other human concerns. As was noted in chapter 15, the critical distinction was between church and nonchurch magic.

Church magic was plentiful: sacred wells, springs, groves, and shrines abounded where supplicants could seek all sorts of miracles and blessings. In addition, priests had an extensive array of incantations, prayers, and rites available for dealing with many human concerns and especially for treating illness—there were many priests who specialized in exorcism. Parallel to this elaborate system of church magic was an extensive culture of folk or traditional magic, a substantial portion of which also was devoted to treating medical problems. Some of this magic dated from pre-Christian times and much of it was a somewhat jumbled adaptation of church magic. This nonchurch magic was sustained by local practitioners, sometimes referred to as "Wise Ones." Often these practitioners performed nonmagical functions too, as in the case of midwives who combined their practical skills with magical spells to deliver babies. It should be mentioned that sometimes priests engaged in "corruptions" of church magic as in the case of a village priest who baptized coins in holy oil in hopes that they would be replaced as soon as they were spent,[43] and the many priests who baptized various objects such as magnets in hopes of creating love potions, although love potions were vigorously condemned by the church.[44] Even though performed by priests, such activities were regarded as nonchurch magic by the religious authorities.

All magic appears to work, some of the time. Thus some sufferers who turned to their local priest got well. But so did some who turned to their local "Wise One." This posed a serious theological issue, and the attempt to find a logical explanation resulted in tragedy. The question was posed: If church magic works because God invests it with the power to do so, why does nonchurch magic work too? Surely, these powers do not come from God. The conclusion seemed obvious: nonchurch magic works because Satan empowers it! Hence, to practice nonchurch magic constitutes invoking Satan and his demons. That is the definition of witchcraft.[45]

Efforts to expose and suppress evil in the form of nonchurch magic soon led to public panics in many parts of Europe. All sorts of lurid tales and fears spread rapidly and, especially in places where governance was weak, mobs and local authorities were swept up in the witchcraft craze. These same fears and impulses arose among people in Spain too, but there they were effectively squelched by the Inquisition.

One reason that the Inquisition prevented a witch craze in Spain is because during its very first cases involving the use of nonchurch magic, the inquisitors paid close attention to what the accused had to say. What they learned was that magical practitioners had no intention whatever of invoking Satanic forces. In fact, many thought they were using church magic! This was because the practices and procedures involved were very similar to those authorized for use by the clergy—recitation of fragments of liturgy, appeals to saints, sprinkling holy water taken from a local church on an afflicted area, and repeatedly making the sign of the cross. As a result, the accused seemed sincerely surprised to learn they had been doing anything wrong.

In fact, the main reason these efforts did not qualify as church magic was because the accused were not ordained and therefore they were not authorized to conduct such activities. Hence if their magic worked, it was not God's doing. That is, the Spanish inquisitors agreed with their colleagues elsewhere that nonchurch magic worked only because of Satanic intervention. However, because they had listened to the accused with a sympathetic ear, the Spanish inquisitors initiated a crucial distinction "between the implicit and explicit invocation of demons."[46] Thus they assumed that most accused of using nonchurch magic (including priests) were sincere Catholics who meant no harm and had been unaware of invoking demons. While it was wrong even to have implicitly invoked demons, it should be forgiven in the ordinary way, through confession and absolution. Consequently, nearly no witches were sent to the stake by the Spanish Inquisition and those who were usually had been convicted for the third or fourth time.

Even more important, the Inquisition used its power and influence to suppress witch hunting by local mobs or secular authorities. An example occurred in Barcelona in 1549, just as the most ferocious witch hunts broke out in other parts of Europe. Local officials accused seven women as witches and the official of the local branch of the Inquisition approved that they be burned. The members of the *Suprema* (the ruling body of the Inquisition) were appalled that such a thing could happen and sent the inquisitor Francisco Vaca to investigate. Upon arrival he sacked the local representative of the Inquisition and ordered the immediate release of two women still being held under sentence of death. After further investigation he dismissed all pending charges and required the return of all confiscated property to the families of the victims. In his report, Vaca dismissed the charges of witchcraft as "laughable" and wrote, "one of the most damning indictments of witch persecution ever recorded."[47] His colleagues on the *Suprema* agreed and thereafter turned their vengeance upon those who *conducted* unauthorized witch hunts, having several of them executed and sending others to serve long sentences in the galleys.[48]

Even so, in 1610 six persons were burned as witches by local officials in Logroño. When they heard of this, the *Suprema* dispatched Alonso de Salazar y Frias, who spent more than a year interviewing the local inhabitants and inviting them to repudiate their errors (mostly having to do with superstition and magic). At the end of his mission, Salazar reported that he had reconciled 1,802 persons to the church. He also reported the negative results of his investigation of witchcraft: "I have not found the slightest evidence that a single act of witchcraft has really occurred."[49] Salazar went on to suggest that efforts should be made to prevent public discussion and agitation concerning the topic; the preaching of sermons about witchcraft should especially be avoided, because he had discovered "that there were neither witches nor bewitched until they were talked and written about."[50]

Salazar's report soon circulated widely among clergy all across Europe. Many of them, including the Jesuit Friedrich von Spee, soon joined in denouncing witch hunts, and it was their influence, and especially their discrediting of evidence gained by torture, that brought witch burning to an end in Catholic areas—an effect that soon seeped into the Protestant areas as well. Some historians like to claim that witch hunting finally ended because it was attacked by participants in the "Enlightenment," such as Balthasar Bekker. But none of these "enlightened" attacks on witch hunts appeared until nearly a century after efforts by Catholic clergy had discredited the witch craze and made it entirely safe to say such things.[51]

Heresy

THE SPANISH INQUISITION WAS founded to deal with a social crisis concerning Jews and Muslims who had become Christians. The standard story misrepresents everyone involved. It portrays the Jewish and Muslim converts as overwhelmingly insincere, having only pretended to become Christians, while continuing to live as "crypto-Jews"

(*Marranos*) or "crypto-Muslims" (*Moriscos*). And it portrays the Inquisition as brutally determined to unmask all these pretenders and burn them for heresy. The truth is that nearly all of the Jewish and most of Muslim converts were sincere, and the Inquisition was founded to suppress and replace the chronic outbreaks of mob violence against them with due process, as well as to expose those whose conversions were insincere. Soon after the Inquisition began to operate, Luther's Reformation rocked the religious consciousness of Europe, soon joined by other Protestant movements. Although the Spanish crown was steadfastly Catholic, a small underground Lutheran movement arose in Spain (often involving priests and monks), and the Inquisition was directed to repress it.

Marranos

For more than a thousand years, more Jews lived in Spain than in "all the countries of medieval Europe combined."[52] It was in Spain that the renaissance of the Hebrew language was made possible by the creation of a Hebrew grammar—the Jews of the Diaspora had so completely lost the ability to read and write Hebrew that their scriptures had to be translated into Greek several centuries before the birth of Jesus. But in Spain, beginning in the tenth century there was a sudden flowering of Hebrew poetry and other writing.[53] Moreover, the center of this Hebrew renaissance was in the Christian areas of Spain and as Christian forces slowly drove the Muslims south, Jews continued to migrate north. When Jewish minorities have enjoyed amicable relations with their social environment, a substantial amount of conversion often has occurred,[54] and that is what happened in Spain. A wave of Jewish conversions to Christianity began in the fourteenth century, as tens of thousands accepted baptism, and came to be known as *conversos*.[55] This caused immense bitterness in the Spanish Jewish community—Maimonides proposed that *conversos* be stoned as idolaters. Worse yet, since Jewish leaders in Spain presumed that no Jew would willingly abandon the faith, they concluded that these conversions somehow must have been forced and insincere—a falsehood that has lived on to corrupt historical accounts ever after.[56] In fact, these conversions were so sincere that soon many of the leading Christians in Spain, including bishops and cardinals, were of *converso* family origins. Indeed, in 1391 the chief rabbi of Burgos had himself and his whole family baptized and eventually he became the bishop of Burgos.[57] The sheer number of Jewish converts as well as their prominence (King Ferdinand had a *converso* grandmother),[58] impeded assimilation and led to antagonisms between "old" and "new" Christians that eventually resulted in armed conflicts between the two. Not surprisingly, "old" Christians were inclined to accuse "new" ones of being insincere "crypto-Jews," and too often some Spanish Jews were eager to support such charges. That turned out to be misguided because antagonism toward the *conversos* soon was expanded to include attacks on the Jews by "old" Christians.

It was this mess that the Inquisition was commissioned to sort out. The inquisitors were able to stifle much of the mob action and disorder, but could not forge a lasting peace, with the tragic result being the edict of 1492 ordering that Spain's remaining Jews either convert or leave. However, the Inquisition eventually dissipated the conflicts over "crypto-Jews." It did so largely by failing to discover many offenders. Although many cases were tried, the actual total was far below what would have been expected given the huge and angry literature on the topic, which often seems to suggest that most *conversos* were dragged before the inquisitors. The data for the Inquisition in Aragon (1540–1640)—one of the two divisions of the Spanish Inquisition, and the one for which executions are broken down by offense—show that only 942 or 3.6 percent of all the cases tried involved charges of being a Marrano, far below the numbers tried for being Moriscos or Luteranos (Protestants). Some of these alleged Marranos were exonerated. Not only that, but only 16 of the 942 defendants (1.7 percent) were executed.[59] So much then for claims such as that by Cecil Roth (1899–1970), who wrote that Marranos "furnished a disproportionately large number . . . of those condemned to death,"[60] of Netanyahu's fraudulent charge that the Inquisition "burned them by the thousands."[61]

Moriscos

Morisco refers to a Muslim who falsely converted rather than leave Spain subsequent to the Christian Reconquest. Moriscos posed a far more serious threat than did Jews or converts from Judaism. They were far more numerous, they had a distinctive geography wherein they often constituted the majority of residents, they spoke their own language, and their conversions often had been compelled. Indeed, the Moriscos mounted several bloody insurrections.[62] Even so, many Jewish historians have claimed that Moriscos were treated far more leniently than Marranos by the Inquisition: "far fewer Moriscos than conversos [crypto-Jews] were sentenced."[63] Wrong! The Inquisition in Aragon tried 7,472 cases based on accusations of being a Morisco, or 29 percent of all the cases it heard. Of these, 181 were executed, or 2.4 percent, which was slightly more than the rate for Marranos.

Luteranos

The various Protestant Reformations made little headway in Spain. In large part this was because earlier attempts at church reform had been extremely successful in Spain. As Yale's celebrated Roland Bainton (1894–1984) put it: "Spain originated the Catholic reformation before ever the Protestant had begun."[64] The result was a remarkable increase in popular support for the church and the lack of the substantial discontent that elsewhere favored Lutheranism and Calvinism. In fact, most who embraced or even dabbled in Protestantism (referred to in Spain as *Luteranos*) seem to have been clergy. In any event, 2,284 people were brought before the Inquisition in Aragon charged with being Luteranos, or 8.8 percent of all the cases heard. These cases resulted in 122 executions, or 5.3 percent of those charged—more than twice the rate as for those charged as Moriscos.

During the life of the Spanish Inquisition all European nations persecuted religious minorities and dissenters.[65] In addition to hunting for Lollards and Lutherans, the English searched high and low for undercover Catholic priests and executed those they found. The French martyred thousands of Huguenots and the Dutch Calvinists also hanged priests. Anabaptists were harassed in both the Lutheran and the Catholic parts of Germany, while in Geneva Calvin persecuted both Anabaptists and Catholics. But somehow, these activities have been treated as "different" from the Spanish Inquisition's persecution of Luteranos.

Sexuality

THE INQUISITORS ALSO CONCERNED themselves with sexual misbehavior, dividing the offenses into four main categories.

Solicitation involved a priest using the confessional and his powers of granting or withholding absolution to have sexual activities with a woman. Of the 44,701 cases in the main database, there are 1,131 cases of solicitation, or 2.5 percent of all cases. A priest convicted of this offense could at the very least expect a severe flogging, followed by lifelong shame. Those discovered to have had an extensive career of solicitations were sentenced to long terms of penal servitude, and several notorious cases resulted in executions.

Bigamy probably was quite widespread in this era when divorce was nearly unavailable, but only rarely did it become such a public scandal as to attract the attention of the Inquisition (on grounds that it was sacrilegious). Even so, the major database includes 2,645 cases of bigamy (or 5.9 percent of the total). In addition to cancellation of the second marriage, the usual penalty involved only public disgrace and a period of banishment from the community of residence.

Women made up 20 percent of those convicted of bigamy.[66]

Sodomy primarily consisted of male homosexuality, but some cases of female homosexuality also were tried, as were some cases involving heterosexual anal intercourse (usually based on accusations by a wife). Sodomy is not broken out in the statistics based on the 44,701 cases because in 1509 the *Suprema* ordered that "no action be taken against homosexuals except when heresy was involved."[67] That is, action was to be taken only when claims were made that sodomy was not a sin. Consequently, the Inquisition of Castile "never again exercised jurisdiction over sodomy,"[68] although the Inquisition of Aragon continued to do so. However, the published data are based only on the cities of Barcelona, Valencia, and Saragossa (1560–1700). Of the 1,829 cases of sexual offences in these three cities, sodomy prosecutions made up 38 percent.[69] In the execution data, also based only on the Aragon Inquisition (1540–1640), 167 were executed for "Sodomy," as compared with 12 for "Superstition and Witchcraft" and 122 for being "Protestants."[70]

Even so, the Inquisition was more lenient toward sodomy (and most sexual offenses) than were the secular courts. Most of those convicted of sodomy by the Inquisition were whipped or given short terms in the galleys, and even many of the death sentences were commuted. By contrast, in this era the secular courts in most of Europe treated homosexuality as a capital offense.[71] For example, from the twelfth century on, civil courts in France and Italy sent "sodomites" to the stake. Henry VIII requested that parliament pass an "anti-buggery" law and in 1533 a statute was passed making sodomy punishable by hanging. In 1730 Holland also made sodomy a capital crime. In practice, however, the general public was reluctant to accuse people of sodomy, and the courts, both secular and religious, were not eager to bring them to trial.

Bestiality accounted for 27 percent of the cases of sexual offences in the three cities, although sometimes bestiality was included in the sodomy category rather than being separated. This offense usually involved young, single men, often those employed as herders, although several women also were convicted of sex with pet dogs. Bestiality was "almost invariably punished ruthlessly"[72] by the Inquisition. But even here, as in all other cases involving sexual offences, "penalties to women remained far milder than those punishing male sexuality."[73]

Book Burning

IT IS TRUE THAT the Inquisition did burn some books. Many of these contained theological heresies such as Lutheran doctrines, but very few, if any, scientific books were burned—the Spanish never even put Galileo's works on their list of forbidden books.[74] It seems of particular interest that of the books that the Inquisition did burn, most were condemned as pornographic![75] It seems that although the first printed books were Bibles and prayer books, quite soon printers discovered an eager, if underground, market for smut.[76]

Conclusion

GREAT HISTORICAL MYTHS DIE hard even when there is no vested resistance to new evidence. But in this case, many recent writers continue to spread the traditional myths about this "holy terror" even though they are fully aware of the new findings.[77] They do so because they are determined to show that religion, and especially Christianity, is a dreadful curse upon humanity. So these writers casually dismiss the new studies as written by "apologists"[78] and go on as before about the sadistic monsters in black robes.

PART VI

New Worlds and Christian Growth

CHAPTER TWENTY

Pluralism and American Piety

CHRISTIANITY WAS TRANSFORMED AND RENEWED by crossing the Atlantic. Not in Latin America, which until recently was a replica of the superficial piety of Europe (see chapter 22). But in North America, Christianity encountered invigorating new conditions.

Even in early times, Europeans marveled at the high level of religious commitment in America, despite the fact that it was very low by today's standards. In 1776, on the eve of the Revolutionary War, only about 17 percent of those living in one of the thirteen colonies actually belonged to a religious congregation[1]; hence more people probably were drinking in the taverns on Saturday night than turned up in church on Sunday morning. As for this being an "era of Puritanism," from 1761 through 1800, a third (33.7 percent) of all first births in New England occurred after less than nine months of marriage, and therefore single women in Colonial New England were more likely to engage in premarital sex than to attend church.[2]

Nevertheless, in 1818 the radical English journalist William Cobbett (1763–1835) was astonished by the number and size of the churches in American villages: "and, these, mind, not poor shabby Churches, but each of them larger and better built and far handsomer than Botley Church [the lone church in his English village], with the church-yards kept in the neatest order, with a headstone to almost every grave. As to the Quaker Meeting-house, it would take Botley Church into its belly, if you were first to knock off the steeple."[3] A few years later the famous French visitor Alexis de Tocqueville (1805–1859) noted that "there is not a country in the world where the Christian religion retains a greater influence over the souls of men than in America."[4] At midcentury, a Swiss theologian observed that attendance at Lutheran churches was far higher in New York City than in Berlin.[5]

If European visitors were amazed at American religiousness, Americans who travelled in Europe were equally amazed at the lack of religious participation they observed there. For example, Robert Baird (1798–1863), the first major historian of American religion, reported in 1844, after spending eight years on the continent, that nowhere in Europe did church attendance come close to the level taken for granted by Americans.[6]

But why? Why did America become so well churched? What are the effects of the extraordinary religious pluralism that exists in the United States, and how do these many faiths manage to coexist peacefully? These questions are the focus of this chapter.

Colonial Pluralism

THE VERY LOW LEVEL of religious participation that existed in the thirteen colonies merely reflected that the settlers brought with them the low level that prevailed in Europe. Keep in mind that few of the colonists were members of intense sects who had come to establish Zion in America—Puritans did not even make up the majority of persons aboard the *Mayflower*. That the Puritans ruled Massachusetts, imposing their morality into law, has tended to mask the fact that, even in Massachusetts most colonists did not belong to a church congregation—only 22 percent did belong.

In addition, some of the larger denominations, such as the Anglicans and Lutherans, were overseas branches of state churches and not only displayed the lack of effort typical of such establishments, but were remarkable for sending disreputable clergy to minister to the colonies. As the celebrated Edwin S. Gaustad (1923–2011) noted, there was constant grumbling by Anglican vestrymen "about clergy that left England to escape debts or wives or onerous duties, seeing [America] as a place of retirement or refuge."[7] The great evangelist George Whitefield (1714–1770) noted in his journal that it would be better "that people had no minister than such as are generally sent over . . . who, for the most part, lead very bad examples."[8]

Finally, most colonies suffered from having a legally established denomination, supported by taxes. The Anglicans were the established church in New York, Virginia, Maryland, North and South Carolina, and Georgia. The Congregationalists (Puritans) were established in New England. There was no established church in New Jersey and Pennsylvania and, not surprisingly, these two colonies had higher membership rates than did any other colony.[9] Therein lies a clue as to the rise of the amazing levels of American piety. Recall from chapter 17 that Adam Smith explained that established religions, being monopolies, inevitably are lax and lazy and that ever since Constantine embraced the faith, European Christianity has suffered from a lack of effort to arouse popular commitment. But these lazy monopolies did not survive in the United States.

Following the Revolutionary War, state religious establishments were discontinued (although the Congregationalists held on as the established church of Massachusetts until 1833), and even in 1776 there was substantial pluralism building up everywhere (see table 20.1). This increased rapidly with the appearance of many new Protestant sects—most of them being of local origins. With all of these denominations placed on an equal footing, there being no government favoritism, there arose intense competition among the churches for member support. That was the "miracle" that mobilized Americans on behalf of faith with the result that by 1850 a third of Americans belonged to a local congregation. By the start of the twentieth century, half of Americans belonged, and today about 70 percent belong.[10]

Table 20.1: Number of Congregations in the Thirteen Colonies by Denomination, 1776

Denomination	Number of Congregations
Congregational	668
Presbyterian (all divisions)	588
Baptist (all divisions)	497
Anglican (Church of England)	495
Quakers	310
German Reformed	159
Lutheran (all synods)	150
Dutch Reformed	120
Methodist	65
Roman Catholic	56
Moravian	31
Separatist and Independent	27
Dunker	24
Mennonite	16
Huguenot	7
Sandemanian	6
Jewish	5
TOTAL	3,228

Sources: Paullin, Atlas of the Geography of the United States *(1932), and Finke and Stark*, The Churching of America, 1776–1990 *(1992; 2005).*

Throughout the nineteenth century, there was widespread awareness that it was competitive pluralism that accounted for the increasingly great differences in the piety of Americans and Europeans. The German nobleman Francis Grund (1798–1863), who arrived in Boston in 1827, noted that establishment makes the clergy "indolent and Lazy," because

a person provided for cannot, by the rules of common sense, be supposed to work as hard as once who has to exert himself for a living. . . . Not only have Americans a greater number of clergymen than, in proportion to the population, can be found on the Continent or in England; but they have not one idler amongst them; all of them being obliged to exert themselves for the spiritual welfare of their respective congregations. The Americans, therefore, enjoy a three-fold advantage: they have more preachers; they have more active preachers, and they have cheaper preachers than can be found in any part of Europe.[11]

Another German, the militant atheist Karl T. Griesinger, complained in 1852 that the separation of church and state in America fueled religious efforts: "Clergymen in America [are] like other businessmen; they must meet competition and build up a trade. . . . Now it is clear . . . why attendance is more common here than anywhere else in the world."[12]

Pluralism Misconceived

ODDLY, THE RECOGNITION THAT competition among religious groups was the dynamic behind the ever-rising levels of American religious participation withered away in the twentieth century as social scientists began to reassert the charges long leveled against pluralism by monopoly religions: that disputes among religious groups undercut the credibility of all, and hence religion is strongest where it enjoys an unchallenged monopoly. Thus Steve Bruce claimed that "pluralism threatens the plausibility of religious belief systems by exposing their human origins. By forcing people to do religion as a matter of personal choice rather than as fate, pluralism universalizes 'heresy.' A chosen religion is weaker than a religion of fate because we are aware that we chose the gods rather than the gods choosing us."[13] Long before Bruce ventured these lines, this view had been formulated into elegant sociology by the prominent Peter Berger, who repeatedly argued that pluralism inevitably destroys the plausibility of all religions because only where a single faith prevails can there exist a "sacred canopy" that spreads a common outlook over an entire society, inspiring universal confidence and assent. For, as Berger explained, "the classical task of religion" is to construct "a common world within which all of social life receives ultimate meaning binding on every-body."[14] Thus, by ignoring the stunning evidence of American history, Bruce, Berger, and their many supporters concluded that religion was doomed by pluralism and that to survive, therefore, modern societies would need to develop new, secular canopies.

But Berger was quite wrong, as even he eventually admitted quite gracefully (see chapter 21). It seems to be the case that people don't need all-embracing sacred canopies, but are sufficiently served by "sacred umbrellas," to use Christian Smith's wonderful image.[15] Smith explained that people don't need to agree with all their neighbors in order to sustain their religious convictions; they only need a set of like-minded friends—pluralism does not challenge the credibility of religions because groups can be entirely committed to their faith despite the presence of others committed to another. Thus, in a study of Catholic charismatics, Mary Jo Neitz found their full awareness of religious choices "did not undermine their own beliefs. Rather they felt they had 'tested' the belief system and been convinced of its superiority."[16] And in her study of secular Jewish women who convert to Orthodoxy, Lynn Davidman stressed how the "pluralization and multiplicity of choices available in the contemporary United States can actually strengthen Jewish communities."[17]

But if they have been forced to retreat from the charge that pluralism is incompatible with faith, critics of pluralism now advance spurious notions about the consequences of competition for religious authenticity. The new claim is that competition must "cheapen" religion—that in an effort to attract supporters, churches will be forced to vie with one another to offer less demanding faiths, to ask for less in the way of member sacrifices and levels of commitment. Here too it was Peter Berger who made the point first, and most effectively. Competition among American faiths, he wrote, has placed all churches at the mercy of "consumer preference."[18] Consumers will prefer "religious products that can be made consonant with secularized consciousness." For "religious contents to be modified in a secularizing direction . . . may lead to a deliberate excision of all or nearly all 'supernatural' elements from the religious tradition . . . [or] it may just mean that the 'supernatural' elements are de-emphasized or pushed into the background, while the institution is 'sold' under the label of values congenial to secularized consciousness."[19] If so, then the successful churches will be those that require no leap of faith vis-à-vis the supernatural, impose few moral requirements, and are content with minimal levels of participation and support. In this way, pluralism leads to the ruination of religion. Thus did Oxford's Bryan Wilson (1926–2005) dismiss the vigor of American religion on grounds of "the generally accepted superficiality of much religion in American society,"[20] smugly presuming that somehow greater depth was being achieved in the empty churches of Britain and the Continent. In similar fashion, John Burdick proposed that competition among religions reduces their offerings to "purely opportunistic efforts."[21]

Successful Religious "Firms"

THE CONCLUSION THAT COMPETITION among faiths will favor "low cost" religious organizations mistakes price for value. As is evident in most consumer markets, people do not usually rush to purchase the cheapest model or variety, but attempt to maximize by selecting the item that offers the most for their money—that offers the best value. In the case of religion, people do not flock to faiths that ask the least of them, but to those that credibly offer the most religious rewards for the sacrifices required to qualify. This has been demonstrated again and again. For a variety of reasons, various Christian churches have greatly reduced what they ask of their members, both in terms of beliefs and morality, and this always has been followed by a rapid decline in their membership and a lack of commitment on the part of those who stay. Thus were the dominant American denominations of

1776 overwhelmed by the arrival on the scene of far stricter denominations such as the Methodists who had, by 1850, become by far the largest denomination in America. Then, by the dawn of the twentieth century, the Methodists had greatly reduced the moral requirements to be a member in good standing and their decline already had begun. Meanwhile, the Southern Baptists continued to be an unflinchingly "expensive" religion and soon replaced the Methodists as the nation's largest Protestant body—and so they remain.[22]

This pattern of differential success shows up overwhelmingly in table 20.2, which reports changes in the membership of various American denominations from 1960 through 2006 or 2007 (depending on the most recent statistics reported by a denomination). To take account of population growth, membership is calculated as per one thousand U.S. population that year. Another way to interpret the statistics is as reflecting changes in each group's "market share." The denominations at the top of the table are the very liberal Protestant bodies that the media often identify as the "mainline," albeit that they might more accurately be identified now as the "sideline." Each of these bodies is notable for discarding traditional Christian teachings and for asking little of its clergy and members—the Episcopalians long tolerated John Shelby Spong, an extremely vocal atheist, as a bishop. Since 1960, each of these denominations has suffered a catastrophic loss of members. Thus, in 1960 there were 12.4 members of the United Church of Christ (formerly the Congregationalists) per one thousand Americans; in 2007 they had only 3.8 members per thousand. The Episcopalians fell from 18.1 to 7.0 and the Methodists from 54.7 down to 26.6. It also is significant that the "cheapest" American religious body, the Unitarian-Universalists, has never been able to attract a significant following and is declining nonetheless.

Midway down the table is the Roman Catholic Church. For all of its travails during this era, it has declined by only 4 percent. Meanwhile, the huge Southern Baptist Convention managed to grow by 2 percent.

From there on down the table are denominations that embrace traditional beliefs and impose high standards of morality and com-

Table 20.2: Some Growing and Declining American Denominations
American Members per 1,000 U.S. Population

Denomination	1960	2006–2007	% Change
United Church of Christ	12.4	3.8	–69
Episcopal Church	18.1	7.0	–61
Presbyterian Church (USA)	23.0	9.8	–57
United Methodist Church	54.7	26.6	–55
Evangelical Lutheran Church in America	29.3	15.6	–47
Unitarian-Universalist	1.0	0.7	–30
Quakers (all meetings)	0.7	0.5	–29
Roman Catholic	233.0	229.9	–4
Southern Baptist Convention	53.8	55.0	+2
Foursquare Gospel	0.5	0.9	+80
Seventh-day Adventist	1.8	3.4	+89
Latter-day Saints (Mormons)	8.2	19.4	+138
Jehovah's Witnesses	1.3	3.6	+177
Assemblies of God	2.8	9.6	+242
Church of God (Cleveland, TN)	0.9	3.2	+260
Church of God in Christ	2.2	18.6	+743

Sources: Yearbook of American Churches, 1962, and Yearbook of American and Canadian Churches, 2008, 2009; Yearbook of Jehovah's Witnesses, 1961.

mitment on both clergy and members. Each of these groups has grown at a prodigious rate. Perhaps no Christian denomination asks as much of members as does the Jehovah's Witnesses, and the Witnesses continue to grow rapidly. Similarly, the Assemblies of God grew by almost two-and-a-half times during this period (and grew even faster worldwide). Having increased at a rate in excess of 700 percent, the very conservative, African-American Church of God in Christ is now much larger than any of the liberal denominations except the Methodists and likely will pass them within another decade or two. Even so, some of the most rapidly growing Christian groups are not included in the table. For example, the Association of Vineyard Churches didn't exist in 1960, having been founded in 1978, and today has more than fifteen hundred churches worldwide. Indeed, the most robust set of American congregations are omitted from the table for lack of trend statistics—the large and very rapidly growing body of evangelical, nondenominational churches, very few of which even existed in 1960. These churches now enroll about 34 Americans per thousand population,[23] making them more than half the size of the Southern Baptists. Claims that these nondenominational churches, especially the megachurches among them, thrive by going "light on doctrine and sin,"[24] are utterly false. These are demanding churches.[25]

Conclusion: competition does not reward "cheap" religion.

This is further demonstrated by the results of decisions made at the Second Vatican Council meetings of the Roman Catholic Church during the early 1960s. Among the many actions taken by the bishops were some that greatly reduced the sacrifices required of nuns and monks. For example, many orders of nuns were allowed to abandon their elaborate garb and wear clothing that does not identify them as members of a religious order. Other council actions revoked rules requiring many hours of daily prayer and meditation in convents and monasteries. These and many similar "reforms" were widely hailed as inaugurating a worldwide renewal of the religious orders. Within a year, a rapid decline ensued. Many nuns and monks withdrew from their orders. Entry rates plummeted. The orders shrank. Thus, the number of nuns in the United States fell from 176,671 in 1966 when the council adjourned, to 71,487 in 2004, and the number of monks fell by half. Similar declines took place around the world. These declines have nearly always been explained (usually by ex-nuns who now are professors of sociology)[26] as the result of placing too severe demands upon members of the orders—demands incompatible with modern life. But what is truly revealing is that the process has turned out to be reversible. Some religious orders reinstated the old requirements and some new orders were founded that again ask for high levels of sacrifice. These orders have been growing![27] So much for the claims that the levels of sacrifice were too high.

But it is not merely that more demanding religious groups *attract* and hold more members than do the less demanding faiths. They *recruit* them! That is, their members are sufficiently committed so that they seek to bring others into the fold, something members of the less demanding faiths seem reluctant to do. Nearly half of all members of the various evangelical Protestant denominations report that they have personally witnessed to a stranger within the past month and two-thirds have witnessed to friends.[28]

Finally, critics of pluralism like to cite Islam as proof that monopoly faiths are the strongest, pointing out the high levels of religious belief and participation present in most Muslim societies. All this reflects is that, just as most Muslims think Christianity is monolithic, most Christians have the equally erroneous notion that Islam is monolithic. In fact, there is an immense amount of variation within Islam—not just major divisions such as that between Sunnis and Shiites, but even at the level of local mosques.[29] That is, within towns having, say, four mosques there will be as much variation among them as there is within American towns having four Protestant churches. The reason for this degree of pluralism in Islam arises from the fact that "individual clergy (*ulama*) must raise their own revenues via active recruitment of members; their career livelihood depends upon vigorous participation of the faithful."[30] Hence, competition among the local mosques helps to generate high levels of religiousness in Islam just as it does within American Christianity. In addition, of course, most Muslim nations labor under very repressive governments that exert considerable pressure on citizens to display public piety.

Mystical America

IT IS WELL-KNOWN THAT Americans have unusually high rates of religious participation and that the majority embrace traditional Christian beliefs. For example, more than half contributed $500 or more to their church during 2006 and 18 percent gave $2,000 or more. Excluding grace said before meals or prayers recited in church, a third of Americans pray several times a day and half pray at least once a day. As for beliefs, 82 percent believe in heaven; 75 percent believe that Hell exists; 70 percent believe in demons; 53 percent expect the Rapture, and only 4 percent say they do not believe in God.[31]

But there is a very neglected aspect of American religion that only recently has begun to be examined: mystical or religious experiences. Efforts to examine such experiences back in the 1960s in the first major surveys of religion in America were thwarted when several prominent theological consultants objected on grounds that mysticism is so rare and constitutes such bizarre behavior that it was pointless to devote questions to it and, worse yet, to ask about it would offend most respondents.[32] The theologians were utterly wrong! The 2007 the Baylor National Survey of American Religion, conducted by the Gallup Organization, asked:

Please indicate whether or not you have ever had any of the following experiences:

I heard the voice of God speaking to me. Yes: 20 percent.

I felt called by God to do something. Yes: 44 percent.

I was protected from harm by a guardian angel. Yes: 55 percent.

Many will try to dismiss the guardian angel finding as a mere figure of speech, a way in which people acknowledge a lucky break. Subsequent follow-ups involving conversations with pastors and many congregants strongly suggest otherwise—that people meant their answer literally. Consider too that 61 percent of Americans say they believe "absolutely" in the existence of angels and another 21 percent think they "probably" exist. No wonder television series such as *Touched by an Angel* have been so popular. In any event, future Baylor surveys will pursue American mystical experiences in considerable detail.

Pluralism and Religious Civility

IF FOR A LONG time it was widely, if erroneously, believed that pluralism weakens all religions, it also was taken for granted that pluralism must result in religious conflicts, even to the point of warfare and persecution. The English philosopher Thomas Hobbes (1588–1679) argued that to maintain public peace and order, the state must thwart all outbursts of religious dissent—at least until such time as humans outgrew their "credulity" and "ignorance" and finally rejected all gods as "creatures of their own fancy."[33] Meanwhile, there must be a single, authoritative church under control of the sovereign. A century later David Hume (1711–1776) agreed. Only where there is a monopoly religion can there be religious tranquility. For where there are many sects, the leaders of each will express "the most violent abhorrence of all other sects," causing no end of trouble. Therefore, wise politicians will support and sustain a single religious organization and repress all challengers.[34] These views seemed consistent with the religious history of Europe and its legacy of hatred, massacres, and war. But, on closer inspection, it can be seen that it was the effort to repress challengers that produced all this bloodshed.

As usual, Adam Smith (1723–1790) got it right by standing the conventional argument on its head: religious conflicts stem not from too many religious groups competing in a society, but from too few! Indeed, Smith argued that his friend Hume had mistakenly supported the most "dangerous and troublesome" situation: a one church monopoly. What was desirable was a:

> society divided into two or three hundred, or perhaps as many [as a] thousand small sects, of which no one could be considerable enough to disturb the publick tranquility. The teachers of each sect, seeing themselves surrounded in all sides with more adversaries than friends, would be obliged to learn the candour and moderation which is so seldom to be found among the teachers of great sects. . . . The teachers of each little sect, finding themselves almost alone, would be obliged to respect those of almost every other sect, and the concessions which they would mutually find it both convenient and agreeable to make to one another . . . [would result] in publick tranquility.[35]

To put Smith's insights more formally: Where there exist competing religions, norms of *religious civility* will develop to the extent that there exists a *pluralistic equilibrium*. Norms of religious civility exist when public expressions and behavior are governed by mutual respect. A pluralistic equilibrium exists when power is sufficiently diffused among a set of competitors so that conflict is not in anyone's interest.

Keep in mind too that civility refers to public settings—each religious group remains free to express its exclusive grasp of truth and merit in private, and many will do so. Thus, for example, traditional Jewish groups continue to teach that Jesus was not the promised messiah and most Christian groups continue to teach that the Jews erred in rejecting Jesus, but in the United States both Christians and Jews affirm the legitimacy of one another and in public each is careful to give no offense. In fact, it has become very common for Christian and Jewish clergy to participate together in public ceremonies during which all religious utterances are limited to those acceptable to both. So, Smith was right. Of course, the rise of religious civility in America took several centuries, during which there was a great deal of "publick disorder" and suffering.

Conclusion

PLURALISM HOLDS THE KEY to the vitality of American religiousness as well as to the development of religious civility. One might think that economists long ago would have pointed this out to their colleagues in sociology who were so enamored of the strength of monopolies, since Adam Smith had laid out the whole analysis with such clarity long ago. Trouble is that until very recently, economists were so little interested in religion that the entire chapter on these matters in Smith's classic *The Wealth of Nations* was (and is) omitted from most editions.[36] It was not until I began working out the stimulating effects of pluralism on my own that someone suggested I read Smith—and I found this puzzling because initially I could find nothing on the topic in the readily available editions. Today, colleagues in economics find my emphasis on pluralism and competition fairly obvious, while many sociologists of religion continue to believe that I am obviously wrong—that competition harms religion and that I have been misled by inappropriate analogies with capitalism. Of course, the great majority of social scientists pay no attention to such peripheral matters, being secure in their knowledge that religion is doomed and soon must vanish.

CHAPTER TWENTY-ONE

Secularization

FACTS AND FANTASIES

IN 1710, THE ENGLISH FREETHINKER Thomas Woolston (1670–1731) expressed his confidence that religion would vanish by 1900.[1] Voltaire (1695–1778) thought this much too pessimistic and predicted that religion would be gone from the Western world within the next fifty years—by about 1810.[2]

Similar predictions of the end of religion have continued ever since, eventually coming to be known as the *secularization thesis*: that in response to modernization, and especially to modern science, religion must lose its plausibility and wither away. The term *secularization* was coined by the German sociologist Max Weber (1864–1920), who defined it as the "disenchantment of the world"—the "emancipation" of the modern mind from supernaturalism. For, as the distinguished anthropologist Anthony F. C. Wallace informed thousands of undergraduates in 1966, the "future of religion is extinction . . . belief in supernatural powers is doomed to die out all over the world as a result of the increasing adequacy and diffusion of scientific knowledge. . . . [T]he process is inevitable."[3]

In full agreement, sociologist Peter Berger informed readers of the *New York Times* in 1968 that the end was near, that by "the 21st century, religious believers are likely to be found only in small sects, huddled together to resist a worldwide secular culture. . . . [T]he predicament of the believer is increasingly like that of a Tibetan astrologer on a prolonged visit to an American university."[4]

In support of the secularization thesis, social scientists cited the extremely low levels of church attendance in much of Europe—as low as 4 percent a week in the Scandinavian nations. It was taken for granted that these figures represented a massive decline from premodern times when medieval Europeans had flocked to church on every occasion. Of course, that "evidence" vanishes in light of the fact that European church attendance was always very low. But, what has most vexed proponents of the modernization-causes-secularization thesis is that the most industrialized and scientific nation of earth remains so very religious: the great majority of Americans continue to be active church members. Not only that, Americans show no signs of losing their belief in supernatural beings.

This is hardly a new discovery. The perceptive French visitor Alexis de Tocqueville noted during the 1830s, vis-à-vis the secularization theorists: "Unfortunately, the facts by no means accord with their theory. There are certain populations in Europe whose unbelief is only equaled by their ignorance and debasement; while in America, one of the freest and most enlightened nations in the world, the people fulfill with fervor all the outward duties of religion."[5] Thus it has been imperative for believers in secularization to dismiss or discredit the American "exception."

The American "Exception"

THE FIRST LINE OF attack has been to dismiss American piety as an illusion. After his three-month tour of America in 1905, Max Weber claimed to have discovered the real situation behind the American religious facade: "Closer scrutiny revealed the steady progress of the characteristic process of secularization, to which in modern times all phenomena that originated in religious conceptions succumb." Fifty years later Weber's views were strongly reiterated by the British sociologist Bryan Wilson: "Appearances to the contrary the quality of religious life may be no higher in America than in Britain. . . . [T]he secular meaning of such [religious] affiliation in America together with the long recognized lack of depth in many religious manifestations in the United States suggest that religion is in decline in both countries."[6] A few years later, Wilson claimed that "few observers doubt that the actual contents of what goes on in the major churches in Britain is very much more 'religious' than what occurs in American churches."[7] But Wilson failed to identify or cite any such "observers."

Unlike Weber and Wilson, many committed to the secularization thesis were fully aware that Americans really are more religious than Europeans and recognized the need to explain this away. A favorite tactic has been to dismiss the United States as intellectually backward. The celebrated British scholar David Martin (who rejects this claim) summed up the snobbery of many of his colleagues thus: "the United States is a case of arrested development, whose evolution has been delayed. . . . [T]he American system of education is . . . superficial . . . [and] one may confidently anticipate that once education has made sufficient progress in America or once dormant class consciousness has been awakened, then the anodyne of bogus religion will cease to exercise any influence."[8] Martin suggested that these views are "confused." They also are nonsense.

Another frequent line is that what appears to be religiousness in America is really ethnicity.[9] People remain loyal Lutherans in order to associate with fellow Scandinavians or Germans; Presbyterians are clinging to their Scottish heritage; and Southern Baptists are unrepentant Scots-Irish, confederate racists. This "explanation" ignores that as the importance of ethnicity has faded among Americans, their religious participation has not declined and that the most successful and rapidly growing faiths have no ethnic ties at all. Indeed, one of the most vigorous sectors of American religion even lacks denominational ties—the independent evangelical churches.

Most recently, the claim has been widely trumpeted in the media that, finally, American religion is ebbing away and America is soon to become secularized. In a press release issued early in March 2009, the director of the American Religious Identification Survey (ARIS) reported that 15 percent of Americans responding to a brief telephone interview selected the "no religion" response when asked their religious preference. This was almost double the 8 percent who gave that response to a similar poll in 1990. The press release revealing these results also stressed that the "mainline" Christian denominations had suffered substantial declines over the same period.

This announcement produced ecstatic reactions on the atheist websites as well as a huge response in the national media. *USA Today* headlined "Most Religious Groups in USA Have Lost Ground, Survey Finds."[10] Jon Meacham, then-editor of *Newsweek*, wrote a lead story entitled "The End of Christian America."[11] (No, there was no question mark.) But anyone without an axe to grind and with minimal knowledge of poll data on American religion knew that these conclusions were absurd; that the real meaning of the "no religion" response had been carefully omitted from the press release; and that the decline of the "mainline" denominations has been going on for generations (see chapter 20).

The ARIS is conducted by Barry Kosmin, a British sociologist who now directs the Institute for the Study of Secularism in Society and Culture at Trinity College, a small liberal arts school in Hartford, Connecticut. Kosmin is a dedicated proponent of the secularization thesis, as is reflected in the name of his institute. Although he is not well informed about American religion, Kosmin cannot help but be aware of the extensive research literature showing that the great majority of Americans who respond that they have "no religion" are not atheists (as his press release implied) but are quite religious! It is true that "no religion" is the answer that the 3 or 4 percent of Americans who profess atheism give to pollsters, but most people who give this response seem to mean only that they do not belong to a church. Thus, recent studies[12] have found that more than 90 percent of them pray and 39 percent pray weekly or more often. Only 14 percent do not believe in God and half of them believe in angels. As might be expected of people who seldom attend any church, some of their beliefs are not very orthodox—18 percent define their God as some sort of higher power or cosmic force. Forty-five percent believe astrology is true and another 8 percent think it could be true. Half of those who said "no religion" frequent New Age bookstores, and they are especially prone to believe in ghosts, Bigfoot, and Atlantis.[13] There may be some basis for disputing whether or not such people are Christians, but it is beyond question that they are religious. Keep in mind that the secularization thesis is about the end of religion, not about the end of any specific faith. Were Canada to turn Muslim overnight, that would be an immense religious change, but it would not be an instance of secularization.

The ARIS press release also failed to note that the percentage of Americans who actually belong to a local church congregation has continued to rise over this same period, from 64 percent in 1990 to about 70 percent in 2007.[14] Finally, although the press release suggested otherwise, the percentage of Americans who are atheists hasn't changed in the past sixty years—4 percent told the Gallup Poll in 1944 that they did not believe in God, exactly the same percentage as in the Baylor National Survey of Religion in 2007.

Thus have years of efforts to dismiss the American "exception" ended in failure. More recently it has been recognized that when the perspective is expanded to the world at large, America is not an exception at all.

World Religiousness

IN 1997 PETER BERGER was interviewed by *Christian Century*.[15] Among the questions he was asked was: "What is your sense of whether and how secularization is taking place?" Keep in mind that Berger had long been a militant, if eloquent, proponent of the secularization theory. He answered: "I think that what I and most other sociologists of religion wrote in the 1960s about secularization was a mistake. Our underlying argument was that secularization and modernity go hand in hand. With more modernization comes more secularization. It wasn't a crazy theory. There was some evidence for it. But I think it's basically wrong. Most of the world today is certainly not secular. It's very religious." And so it is.

The Gallup World Poll is based on national opinion surveys conducted in 160 nations, including 97 percent of the world's population. Thus far Gallup has not been permitted to ask any questions about religion in China, but respondents in all the other nations were asked whether they had "attended a religious place of worship or religious service within the last seven days?" Worldwide, 53 percent replied that they had. And, except in China, everyone was asked, "Is religion an important part of your daily life?" Around the globe, 76 percent said yes.

Moreover, few of those who did not regard religion as important in their lives were atheists. Although no belief questions have been included yet in the Gallup World Poll, an item on belief in God was included in the World Values Surveys conducted in many nations in 2001–2002. In very few nations were there more atheists than the 4 percent found in the United States: Canada and India also have 4 percent, but atheists make up only 1 percent of Poles and 2 percent of Mexicans. France has the most atheists, but even there they amount to only 14 percent.[16] Perhaps the most striking finding is that the percentage of atheists in Russia has fallen to 4 percent.

The massive survival of religion in Russia has stunned many sociologists. It would be unnecessarily vindictive now to quote the litany of claims by my colleagues in times past about how the "enlightened" soviet educators were freeing the masses from the grip of "superstition" and launching a new era of completed secularization. But it seems fair to quote from a paper I presented at a conference in 1979 while the rulers of the Kremlin still seemed fully in control: "Secular states cannot root out religion. . . . Lenin's body may be displayed under glass, but no one supposes that he has ascended to sit on the right hand, or even the left hand, of Marx. . . . [D]ams along the Volga do not light up the meaning of the universe. . . . In making faith more costly, [repressive states] also make it more necessary and valuable. Perhaps religion is never so robust as when it is an underground church."[17] And so it seems. There may or may not be any atheists in fox holes, but there are precious few in Russia today despite generations of antireligious education.[18] A similar pattern seems to be emerging in China. After decades of brutal repression of religion, suddenly there are millions of Chinese Christians, there has been a huge revival of Buddhism, and the percentage of Chinese who say they have no religion has rapidly been falling.[19]

Understanding the European "Exception"

IN THE SAME INTERVIEW in which he retracted his support for secularization theory, and having noted that most of the world is very religious, Peter Berger made this additional point: "The one exception to this is Western Europe. One of the most interesting questions in the sociology of religion today is not, How do you explain fundamentalism is Iran? but, Why is Western Europe different?" Why, indeed?

Christianization?

Characteristically coming directly to the point, Andrew Greeley once wrote: "There could be no de-Christianization of Europe . . . because there never was any Christianization in the first place. Christian Europe never existed."[20] What Greeley had in mind was the slow and careless effort of the church following the conversion of Constantine to spread north into most of Europe. That is, the Christianity that triumphed over Rome was a dedicated, energetic social movement in a very competitive environment. Subsequent to the conversion of

Constantine, Christianity left most of the rest of Europe only nominally converted, at best, being a lazy monopoly church that sought to extend itself not by missionizing the masses, but by baptizing kings. Hence, what slowly arose in Europe was, long before the Reformation, a patchwork of state churches that settled for the allegiance of the elite, with little or no regard for the populace. Thus, for example, the "Christianization" of a Scandinavian kingdom often involved little more than the baptism of the nobility and legal recognition of the ecclesiastical sovereignty of the church. This left the task of missionizing the people to a "kept" clergy whose welfare was almost entirely independent of mass assent or support, with a predictable lack of results.[21] This is the legacy that accounted for the remarkable lack of religious participation and Christian piety in medieval times—a lack that has continued to this day.

To demonstrate the connection between the lack of effective missionizing centuries ago and the lack of religious participation in Europe today, for each of sixteen nations of Western Europe I calculated the number of centuries since their supposed Christianization (twenty-one minus the century), with values ranging from seventeen for Italy down to eight for Finland.[22] I then coded the current church attendance rate for each country, based on the World Values Surveys. As suspected, the duration of Christianity is extremely highly correlated with contemporary rates of church attendance, $r = 0.72$.[23] It's not that Scandinavians, for example, have stopped going to church; they never did go. In contrast, attendance remains quite high in Southern Europe, in the areas that were Christianized before Constantine. So, the historic lack of effective missionizing partly explains Europe's "exceptionalism."

Lazy, Obstructionist State Churches

In most European nations there is nothing resembling a religious "free" market. In many there are still established state churches supported by taxes. In most of the rest, a particular religion is the object of considerable government "favoritism." And in nearly all European nations, the government bureaucracy engages in overt and covert interference with all religious "outsiders" and "newcomers" that challenge the established religious order.

There are Lutheran state churches in Denmark, Finland, Iceland, and Norway, while in Sweden, the established position of the Church of Sweden (Lutheran) was ended in 2006, although the government continues to collect a religious tax on its behalf. There are two state churches in Germany, the Evangelical Church (Protestant) and the Roman Catholic Church, both supported by taxes, and their clergy are classified as civil servants. Some cantons in Switzerland recognize Roman Catholicism as the state church; other cantons support an Evangelical Reformed state church. The Roman Catholic Church receives tax support in Austria and payments of more than six billion Euros a year in Spain. In Italy, people choose the group to receive their church tax from a short list of Christian denominations and in Belgium there is no church tax, but the government provides very substantial support to Catholicism, Protestantism, Anglicanism, Judaism, Islam, and a category called "nondenominational." There is no church tax in the Netherlands, but the two primary Protestant churches and the Roman Catholics receive many large subsidies. No religious group receives direct government support in France, but the Catholic schools receive huge subsidies, and immense favoritism is shown to the Roman Catholic Church by the bureaucracy. Finally, the Church of England remains the established faith, but is not supported by taxes or government funds, being able to sustain itself from huge endowments built up during prior centuries of mandatory tithing.

These close links between church and state have many consequences. First of all, they create lazy churches. The money continues to come whether or not people attend, so there is no need for clergy to exert themselves. Second, these links encourage people to view religion "as a type of public utility."[24] Individuals need do nothing to preserve the church; the government will see to it. This attitude makes it difficult for nonsubsidized faiths to compete—people will be reluctant to contribute to a church. Thus, when some German evangelists attempted television ministries, they drew viewers, but not contributions,[25] since religion is supposed to come free.

The existence of favored churches also encourages government hindrance and harassment of other churches. The French government has officially designated 173 religious groups (most of them evangelical Protestants, including Baptists) as dangerous cults, imposing heavy tax burdens upon them and subjecting their members to official discrimination in such things as employment. Subsequently, Belgium has outdone the French, identifying 189 dangerous cults, including the Quakers, the YWCA (but not the YMCA), Hasidic Jews, Assemblies of God, the Amish, Buddhists, and Seventh-day Adventists.

But even groups not condemned by parliamentary action are targets of government interference. As the distinguished British sociologist James Beckford noted, all across Europe government bureaucrats impose "administrative sanctions . . . behind a curtain of official detachment."[26] Many Protestant groups report waiting for years to obtain a building permit for a church, or even for a permit to allow an existing building to be used as a church. This is especially common in Scandinavian nations where it is often ruled that there is "no need" for an additional church in some area, and hence no permit is granted.[27] In Germany, many Pentecostal groups have been denied tax-free status unless they register with the government as secular groups such as sports clubs rather than as churches. Subsequently, the government sometimes revokes their tax-exempt status and imposes unpayable fines and back tax demands on congregations.[28]

Nevertheless, many European scholars are adamant that their nations enjoy full religious liberty. To challenge that claim, it no longer is necessary to recite examples of state intrusions because Brian Grim and Roger Finke[29] have created quantitative measures of government interference in religious life. They based their coding on the highly respected annual *International Religious Freedom Report* produced by the U.S. Department of State. One of Grim and Finke's measures is the Government Regulation Index, which reflects "the restrictions placed on the practice, profession, or selection of religion by the official laws, policies, or administrative actions of the state," scored from 0.0 (no restrictions) to 10.0 (only one religion allowed). On this measure, most European nations appear to offer a fair amount of religious freedom, although far less than the United States, France having the highest level of restrictions (3.9). But Grim and Finke's second measure, the Government Favoritism Index, tells a very different story.

The favoritism index is based on "subsidies, privileges, support, or favorable sanctions provided by the state to a select religion or a small group of religions." This index also varies from 0.0 (no favoritism) to 10.0 (extreme favoritism). Taiwan scores 0.0 and Saudi Arabia and Iran each score 9.3. And while Afghanistan and the United Arab Emirates score 7.8, so do Iceland, Spain, and Greece, while Belgium scores 7.5, slightly higher than Bangladesh's 7.3 and India's 7.0. Morocco scores 6.3, while Denmark scores 6.7, Finland 6.5, Austria 6.2, Switzerland 5.8, France 5.5, Italy 5.3, and Norway 5.2. Europe has a religious "market" highly distorted by government policies of favoritism.

"Enlightened" Churches

Not content to make little or no effort to arouse public religious participation, in much of Europe the dominant churches, especially the Protestant state churches, have modeled themselves on those American denominations that have been declining so precipitously. In the name of theological "enlightenment" they offer extremely inexpensive religion, stripped of moral demands and of all but the vaguest sort of supernaturalism. In this regard, the recent case of a parish priest in the Church of Denmark is instructive.

Thorkild Grosbøll served for many years as the priest of the Danish Church in Tarbaek, a town about ten miles north of Copenhagen. In 2003 he published a book in which he explained that he did not believe in God. This attracted some attention and led to an interview with a national newspaper in which Grosbøll said, "God belongs in the past. He actually is so old fashioned that I am baffled by modern people believing in his existence. I am thoroughly fed up with empty words about miracles and eternal life."[30] Subsequently, he told the *New York Times*, "I do not believe in a physical God, in the afterlife, in the resurrection, in the Virgin Mary. . . . And I believe Jesus was [only] a nice guy."[31] Nevertheless, Grosbøll planned to continue as a priest, obviously assuming that his beliefs were within the acceptable limits of the Danish Church. And that appears to be the case. It was not until a year after these outbursts that Grosbøll's bishop relieved him of his duties. Later, the case was transferred to an ecclesiastical court. Then in 2006 Grosbøll resumed serving as a parish priest after reconfirming his priestly vows, but without recanting any of his views, albeit he was instructed not to talk to the press. The Ministry of Ecclesiastical Affairs had decided that no further action was needed since Grosbøll was eligible for retirement in February 2008.

This was not a freak event. The Scandinavian state churches have been flirting with irreligion for at least a century. Consider that in Sweden the church has been largely controlled locally by elected boards, the candidates being nominated by the national political parties. That has meant that for several generations the favored candidates were socialists, which often has resulted in placing avowed atheists in charge of the church. "Members of parish boards and the church council are elected more for their political positions and conviction than for their religious faith. No religious qualifications are required of the candidates—indeed, they need not even be baptized or confirmed. The state church is governed by a majority of nonbelievers—citizens who seldom or never attend church services."[32] As with other Scandinavian state churches, until disestablishment was adopted in 2006, the Church of Sweden was controlled by the Ministry of Ecclesiastical Affairs, and for many years the Minister of Ecclesiastical Affairs was Alva Myrdahl, a well-known leftist economist and nonbeliever. She was inspired to appoint a commission to compose a new Swedish translation of the New Testament, on grounds that "the timeworn Holy Bible [is] becoming increasingly marginalized in the modern, rational, world view."[33] Even its ardent supporters acknowledge that this translation (published in 1981) contains "sweeping transformation[s] of accepted interpretations. . . . In important ways, it must of necessity run against the grain of Bible traditions."[34] This demystified translation is now the official Church of Sweden version. Is it really any wonder that by far the majority of the Swedes who are in church of a Sunday attend small Protestant denominations that oppose the state church?

It is instructive too that the Roman Catholic Church has nowhere in Europe been at the mercy of the state vis-à-vis its teachings and scriptures. And religion remains far stronger in the Catholic nations of Europe than in the Protestant regions.

Clearly, the lack of meaningful religious messages did not cause the decline of Europe's churches, but, given the fate of similar American denominations, it seems likely that this lack *keeps them empty*.

Believing Nonbelongers

So far the discussion has been focused on lazy and empty churches in Europe. But just as the nonattending medieval Europeans had religion (if a rather unorthodox mixture), so do most Europeans today. So much so that the British sociologist Grace Davie coined the term "believing non-belongers."[35]

It is close to the truth to say that almost no one goes to church in the Scandinavian nations—about one person out of twenty or even fewer attends weekly. But it is equally true to say no one admits to being an atheist—again about one person in twenty. In all but Sweden, the majority of Scandinavians identify themselves as a "religious person," and even in Sweden, 62 percent pray.[36] The majority of Norwegians believe in life after death and that the Bible "is inspired by God."[37] New Age beliefs in such things as reincarnation, "healing" crystals, and ghosts are widespread all across Scandinavia[38] (echoing the magical religion of their medieval ancestors). Similar patterns exist in all of the European societies that have been held as exemplars of secularization. It is absurd to call these secularized societies when what they really are is unchurched.

Leftist Politics

During the French Revolution, the French Encyclopedist Denis Diderot (1713–1784) proposed that freedom required that "the last king be strangled with the guts of the last priest." What this reflected, in addition to Diderot's liking for excessive rhetoric, is that in Europe the link between church and state tended to result in church support for the aristocracy in opposition to rebels and revolutionaries. As a result, in 1911 the British Socialist Party officially declared that "it is a profound truth that Socialism is the natural enemy of religion." Indeed, the entire European Left took this position, often expressing angry and strident atheism. Thus, in data collected in 1957 by the British Gallup Organization, supporters of the Conservative Party were almost twice as likely to attend church at least "now and again" (62 percent) than were supporters of the Labour Party (36 percent).[39] An even stronger effect of Leftism on church attendance existed in France at this same time: 7 percent of Communist voters and 16 percent of Socialists said they currently were practicing their faith (Catholicism), compared with 67 percent of the Gaulists and 68 percent of the Peasant and Independent Party voters. In the Netherlands, based on data from 1956, 79 percent of voters supporting the Anti-Revolutionary Party had attended church in the past seven days, compared with 10 percent of the Labor Party.[40]

Consequently, it has often been argued that the popularity of Leftist parties in Europe prompted substantial defections from religion, at least from participation in the churches. But given that participation has always been low, it probably is more the case that the success of the Left in Europe had much to do with the churches having been weak in the first place. An exception may be France, both because of the out-of-control intensity of the revolution and its militant anticlericalism, legacies which long lived on in the post–World War II popularity of the French Communist Party and in the fact that France far surpasses other European nations in terms of the prevalence of militant atheism. Another exception may be Spain where bitterness going back to the Franco era still animates leftist antagonisms toward the church.

But it seems suggestive that while support for the extreme Left has greatly declined in Europe, the dominant churches—especially the state churches—have become progressively leftist. This has not brought them any resurgence in attendance.

Statistical Moonshine

Peter Berger is remarkable for having the flexibility of mind and the openness to evidence to renounce his long commitment to the secularization thesis. Many other social scientists have done nothing of the sort. Lacking the grasp of plausibility that Berger possesses, these folks proceed as if everything continues to support their belief that modernization and religion are utterly incompatible. Recently, Pippa Norris and Ronald Inglehart[41] brought joy to those holding this perspective by offering statistical evidence that, indeed, worldwide there is a powerful negative correlation between various measures of religiousness such as church attendance and frequency of prayer and various measures of economic development such as per capita Gross Domestic Product. The more modern the nation, the less religious! Of course, all they had demonstrated is that Europe is less religious than the rest of the world and that European nations dominate the high end of economic development. But we already knew that. Norris and Inglehart shed no light on why Europe is different, other than to reiterate the tired refrain that it is the inevitable result of modernization.

Worse yet, this is statistical moonshine. There is considerable variation in religiousness among European nations as there is in their levels of economic development. But, if one examines the relationships between measures of development and religiousness *only among* the thirty-seven nations of Europe, one finds no significant correlations at all! That is, Italy is as modern as Sweden which tells us nothing about why Italians flock to church and Swedes do not. The same is true if one examines these correlations among Muslim nations. The more developed Muslim nations should be less religious, but it isn't so. There is no correlation between religiousness measured by mosque attendance and GNP per capita. The same finding holds for the nations of Sub-Saharan Africa. If modernization truly causes secularization, these effects must show up when other dominant cultural variations are held constant. They do not.

Conclusion

BEHIND THE SECULARIZATION THESIS has always lain an enormous conceit that recently has been brazenly displayed by the militant atheist and biologist Daniel Dennett when he identified himself and his antireligious confederates as "brights," in contrast to those dullards whose minds are still infected with religious delusions.[42] But there also is a barely concealed desperation behind Dennett's arrogant pronouncements and those of the writers of the other recent aggressively atheist books. For the truth is, religion is not passing away; instead it is very obviously making a great deal of headway around the world. As will be seen in the next chapter, never before has there been such widespread and intense piety in Latin America. Not only are there now few atheists in Russia; there now are millions of Christians in China. There even are signs that religion may be making gains in Europe. In most of Europe the fertility rates have dropped far below replacement levels with the impending consequence of rapidly declining "native" populations, foretelling a Sweden without Swedes and a France without French. What has gone little noticed is that the Europeans who go to church are continuing to have children to such an extent that this factor alone could result in a far more religious Europe.[43] In addition, the impact of tens of thousands of American missionaries, many of them self-financed volunteers, is beginning to result in some aggressive and competitive churches in Europe despite the regulatory barriers placed in their way.[44] Indeed, the development of only a modest amount of religious competition in Italy seems to have played a role in producing a quite significant Italian religious revival.[45] And so it goes.

Chapter Twenty-Two

Globalization

The Age of Exploration also was a new beginning of Christian world missions. In 1492 when Columbus sailed, there were few Christians outside of Europe, and even after Christianity had come to dominate the rapidly developing Western Hemisphere, most people on earth still had never heard of Jesus. During the 1850s, it was the consensus among European scholars that Buddhism was the largest of the great world religions,[1] but at that very moment things began to change as serious efforts at Christian missionizing got under way.

By 1900 there were 5,278 American Protestant missionaries serving abroad as well as 5,656 from Britain and about 2,200 from Continental nations—in addition to several thousand Roman Catholic missionaries.[2] Since World War II, most Christian missionaries abroad have been Evangelical American Protestants, and today hundreds of thousands of missionaries from the United States are spread all around the globe, including large numbers at work in Europe.[3] This total does not include about 1.6 million Americans who go abroad on short-term missions every year at their own expense.[4] Nor does it include about five thousand missionaries sent abroad from Latin American nations. In addition, there are large numbers of Christian missionaries, perhaps more than seventy thousand, at work from non-Western nations.[5] As a result of all this effort, Christianity has become by far the largest religion on earth.

Faiths on Earth

STATISTICS ON WORLDWIDE RELIGIOUS affiliation are only rough estimates and necessarily include very nominal "members" of all the major faiths.[6] Thus, for example, nearly everyone in Europe is included in the Christian total, even though many European "Christians" have never been inside a church and many others have only been there once, when they were baptized as infants. The many shortcomings in world religion statistics are not the fault of those who assembled them, but are due to a lack of more accurate information. There have been no reliable, nation-by-nation statistics to add up.

This gap now can be filled by data from the Gallup Organization's World Poll. Beginning in 2007, Gallup has conducted annual surveys in each of 160 nations having about 97 percent of the world's population. Except in China, all respondents were asked: "Could you tell me what your religion is?" In addition, Gallup asked: "Have you attended a place of worship or religious service within the past seven days?" Of course, these questions were carefully translated into all of the local languages. Hence, in principle, the data from these surveys can provide an accurate and far more informative portrait of the world's religions.

However there are several unavoidable shortcomings to the revised statistics. In many nations, respondents were given the choice of affirming that they were Roman Catholics, Protestants, or Orthodox Christians. But in many places, although people know the name of their local Christian church, they are unfamiliar with terms such as Protestant or Catholic. Consequently, in many countries, it was necessary to settle for the response "Christian," without further specification. Hence, to create worldwide statistics, even those who reported being Protestant, Catholic, or Orthodox must be placed in the undifferentiated category "Christian." The same applies to Muslim respondents. For many nations there is no breakdown even for Sunnis and Shiites, and hence everyone is simply identified as a "Muslim."

A second deficiency is that even though by now there are a total of nearly four hundred thousand respondents to the World Polls, there still are too few cases to allow reliable statistics to be computed for many smaller religions, including Shinto, Zoroastrianism, Taoism, and Confucianism (a statistic for Jews is possible because Israel is included in the World Polls). This made it necessary to combine these, and all other small religions, into a hodge-podge category called "Other." In the next several years, as the size of the world sample increases it will be possible to break down the "Other" category. In addition, there are those people who said they had no religion, responded they were secular, or atheists, or agnostics. All of these respondents were collapsed into the category "Secular." However, some of these "secular" people said they attended religious services!

A final difficulty concerns China. Unfortunately, no foreign polling firm, including Gallup, is permitted to ask questions about religion in China. Worse yet, even the results of polling about religion by Chinese firms are probably quite unreliable as there is substantial evidence that many people feel it is too risky to admit to an interviewer that they are religious. To further complicate matters, the Chinese have such a peculiar definition of religion that they grossly understate their own religiousness. For example, the Chinese Communist Party has been adamant for some years that Confucianism is merely a philosophy and definitely not a religion. However, when Anna Xiao Dong Sun[7] visited a number of temples in China, she observed many visitors earnestly praying to statues of Confucius for a variety of blessings and benefits—and most of these worshippers would no doubt say they have no religion. Nor would most Chinese agree that they had a religion even while they make requests and offer gifts of food to statues of the several hundred other gods found in the folk temples. In similar fashion, many Chinese do not apply the term *religion* to the devotions they conduct at their ancestral shrines. Of course, if China were an average-size nation none of this would matter much. But when one contemplates adding more than a billion people to the statistics, immense distortions enter the picture. For example, the percentage of religious people in the world would artificially be very substantially reduced, and the secular category would falsely be very inflated. Consequently, China will be treated separately later in this chapter; here the world religious statistics presented below omit China.

Nominal Members

TABLE 22.1 SHOWS THE membership of the great world religions outside of China. Around the world, a total of 2.2 billion people (41 percent) give their religion as Christian, far outnumbering Muslims, who total 1.4 billion (27 percent). Hindus are the third largest religious group, with 1 billion affiliates (19 percent), followed by Buddhists with 289 million (5 percent). Jews make up only 12 million (less than 0.1 percent) and the other faiths number 119 million (2 percent). Secularists make up 240 million (5 percent).

Table 22.1: Worldwide Nominal Religious Affiliations (China Excluded)

Religion	Number	Percent
Christians	2,195,674,000	41%
Muslims	1,429,772,000	27%
Hindus	1,011,709,000	19%
Buddhists	289,856,000	5%
Jews	12,849,000	*
Others	119,195,000	2%
Secular	240,650,000	5%
TOTAL	5,299,705,000	100%

Less than 0.1 percent.

The major difference between these statistics and those most commonly cited has to do with the secular category. This group usually is estimated at about 16 percent of the world population, a percentage that probably is obtained only by including most Chinese as unreligious. Inflating the secular category causes a corresponding decrease in all the others, hence the proportion Christian usually is set at about 33 percent and Islam at 21. That emphasizes why it is prudent not to include China. Be that as it may, these findings are very unsatisfactory in other ways.

Active Membership

WHAT DOES IT MEAN to be a Christian or a Muslim or a member of any faith? Surely it implies some degree of involvement and participation. The available measure of active membership is very stringent— "Have you attended a place of worship or religious service within the past seven days?" Table 22.2 is limited to those who attended in the past week.

Table 22.2: Worldwide Active Religious Affiliations (China Excluded)

Religion	Number	Percent	Percent Reduction
Christians	1,281,042,000	44%	42%
Muslims	857,620,000	29%	40%
Hindus	579,192,000	20%	43%
Buddhists	130,512,000	4%	55%
Jews	4,604,000	*	64%
Other	59,724,000	2%	50%
Secular	23,570,000	1%	90%
TOTAL	2,936,277,000	100%	45%

Less than 0.1 percent.

Contrary to stereotypes that all Muslims are ardent worshippers, their numbers have been reduced almost as greatly as those for

Christians when the data are limited to weekly attendees. The table also reveals that more than 23 million of those classified as Secular had attended a religious service in the past seven days! The overall finding is that nothing much has changed when only active members are examined. Christianity is still by far the largest of the religions (44 percent), followed by Islam (29 percent).

Regional Variations

CHRISTIANITY IS NOT ONLY the largest religion in the world, it also is the least regionalized. There are only trivial numbers of Muslims in the Western Hemisphere and in Eastern Asia, but there is no region without significant numbers of Christians—even in the Arab region of North Africa and the Middle East, 4 percent of the population are Christians. However there is a more interesting way to examine Christian regionalism, as can be seen in table 22.3.

Table 22.3: The Regional Distribution of Christians (China Excluded)

Region	Nominal Affiliations	Weekly Attendees Only
North America	13%	24%
Latin America	25%	22%
Europe	28%	13%
Middle East and North Africa	1%	1%
Sub-Saharan Africa	23%	30%
South Central Asia	5%	6%
South Eastern Asia	2%	3%
Eastern Asia	2%	1%
Oceania	1%	*
TOTAL	100%	100%

Less than 0.5 percent.

There are some interesting surprises here. Christians are more likely to live in Europe than elsewhere (28 percent), when only nominal affiliation is considered, with Latin America second (25 percent) and North America a distant fourth (13 percent). But when the statistics are based on weekly church attendees, Europe (13 percent) falls to a distant fourth, North America (24 percent) rises to second, and Sub-Saharan Africa rises to the top (30 percent). Despite the prominence of African bishops in the squabbles going on within the Anglican Communion, few know how highly Christianized is the entire subcontinent. This is further disguised by the common tendency to treat Africa as a whole rather than to divide it into the overwhelmingly Arab North and the Black South. When treated as a united "continent," Africa has a Muslim majority. But that is very misleading since Christians make up 66 percent of Sub-Saharan Africans, compared with 29 percent who are Muslims. Philip Jenkins has, of course, called attention to the strength of Christianity in Africa and in the entire "global south."[8]

Christian Africa

THE PRESENCE OF SO many Christians in Africa is not easily explained. Yes, Christianity reached these African communities as a result of European Colonialism—where the colonizers went, the missionaries followed. But it was taken for granted, both by Europeans and by African nationalists, that the collapse of European empires would quickly be followed by a return to precolonial, "authentically" African cultural forms. But nothing of the sort took place, at least not in the realm of religion. Instead, African Christianity has continued to thrive to such an extent that when only Christians who attend church weekly are counted, as already noted there are more Christians in this part of Africa than anywhere else on earth.

An immense amount has been written about how this came about, with about equal stress placed on the immense number of Protestant missionaries stationed there and on the remarkable proliferation of thousands of African-born Protestant denominations. But these explanations have ignored the fact that at least 150 million of these African Christians are Roman Catholics. Thus, while there are more Protestants than Catholics in Sub-Saharan Africa, as shown in table 22.4, in many nations Catholics substantially outnumber Protestants.

Table 22.4: Catholics and Protestants in Sub-Saharan Africa

Nation	Catholics	Protestants
Burundi	74%	20%
Rwanda	64%	29%
Angola	55%	33%
Mozambique	53%	34%
Cameroon	44%	35%
Central African Republic	44%	41%
Congo Republic	44%	46%
Togo	44%	17%
Uganda	39%	42%
Madagascar	38%	55%
Democratic Republic of Congo	36%	58%
Zambia	35%	59%
Burkina Faso	32%	7%
South Africa	29%	53%
Kenya	28%	57%
Benin	27%	13%
Zimbabwe	27%	60%
Tanzania	26%	20%
Chad	26%	18%
Namibia	25%	73%
Malawi	25%	63%

Nation	Catholics	Protestants
Ghana	25%	38%
Botswana	24%	20%
Nigeria	22%	33%
Liberia	14%	48%
Sierra Leone	11%	12%
Guinea	8%	1%
Senegal	5%	0%
Mali	3%	1%
Ethiopia	1%	16%
Djibouti	0%	0%
Mauritania	0%	0%
Niger	0%	1%
TOTAL	25%	32%

To write about the Christianization of Africa only in Protestant terms omits a major part of the story. Indeed, Catholic periodicals abound in reports of rapid growth in Africa, of substantial upward trends in the number of African priests and seminarians. In the twenty-year period 1989–2009, according to official statistics the number of priests in these Sub-Saharan nations rose from 16,580 to 30,339, and the number of seminarians surged from 10,305 to 25,162. This is a stunning achievement.

But there is a profound mystery here. The official Catholic statistics as to the numbers of priests and seminarians are extremely accurate since they are produced by counting individuals fully documented in church records. But there are no master lists of individual members, and it is up to every parish to calculate and report its membership. These reports may be inaccurate and in the case of Sub-Saharan Africa, the official church statistics claim *far fewer* members than the Gallup interviewers have found! *The Statistical Yearbook of the Church* reported that in 2006 there were 158 million Catholics in the whole of Africa. The Gallup World Polls (2007–2008) found 194 million Catholics in Sub-Saharan Africa. The official statistic is at least 22 percent too low. This underestimate is the result of the fact that in 21 of the 34 nations, the official statistic is too low, often very much too low. How could this happen? What could cause the bishops in Mozambique, for example, to report that only 23 percent of the population is Catholic, when Catholics actually are a majority (53 percent)? Obviously, the bishops simply had no idea how large their flock had become. But why?

After failing to find any statistical evidence as to why this undercounting has occurred, and having taken up the matter with African experts in the Vatican, the only plausible explanation I can offer is that much of the rapid growth has been poorly documented because it is taking place in outlying areas where local priests are too overworked by rapid growth to keep their membership statistics up-to-date. Needless to say, church officials found this to be a quite gratifying error.

Latin American Pluralism

LATIN AMERICA WAS LONG regarded as the Roman Catholic continent, fully Christianized by missionary monks and Spanish swords by the end of the seventeenth century. Throughout the twentieth century, official church statistics reported that well over 90 percent of Latin Americans were Roman Catholics. But it wasn't so.

Although for several centuries the Roman Catholic Church was the only legal religion in Latin America, its popular support was neither wide nor deep. Many huge rural areas were without churches or priests, a vacuum in which indigenous faiths persisted.[9] Even in the large cities with their splendid cathedrals, mass attendance was very low: as recently as the 1950s perhaps only 10 to 20 percent of Latin Americans were active participants in the faith.[10] Reflective of the superficiality of Latin Catholicism, so few men entered the priesthood that all across the continent most of the priests have always been imported from abroad.[11]

Meanwhile, the recent eruption of Protestantism (mostly of the Pentecostal variety) all across Latin America has enrolled millions of dedicated converts.[12] This challenge has so upset the Catholic hierarchy that even Pope John Paul II, often a voice for religious tolerance, bitterly attacked the "evangelical sects" as "voracious wolves."[13] But has the conversion of millions of Latin Americans to Protestantism really damaged the Catholic Church? The effects of competition could, of course, overwhelm a lazy monopoly faith. But it also could stimulate an energetic response, transforming the erstwhile monopoly into an effective and far stronger religious institution—which is what has happened in Latin America.

Protestants in Latin America

The first Protestants permitted to live in Latin America were small enclaves of foreign merchants, most of them British and Americans who settled in the nineteenth century, but no Protestant churches or missionaries were permitted. Until well into the twentieth century there even were legal bans on the sale of Bibles in most nations of Latin America, which led to the widespread belief that only Protestants accepted the Bible.[14]

The Catholic legal hegemony began to break down late in the nineteenth century and early in the twentieth as "liberal" revolutions strained the relations between the governments and the Catholic Church—the toleration of Protestantism being a form of political payback for the Church having supported the conservative regimes.

Initially, nothing much happened. Indeed, many prominent American denominations that were involved in substantial overseas mission efforts rejected Latin American ventures on grounds that these already were Christian nations. But the evangelical denominations rejected this "gentlemen's agreement" on grounds that "the Catholic Church had failed to connect with the majority of the population."[15] The result was a permanent split in American mission efforts, although little trace of the split now exists since the denominations that thought it improper to send missionaries to Latin America have pretty much abandoned all their missionary activities everywhere.[16] So it was that Latin America was missionized intensively, but only by conservative groups—with Pentecostal bodies soon surging ahead.

By 1900 there were 610 American Protestant missionaries deployed in continental Latin America, and by 1923 the total had risen to 1,627.[17] In 1996 there were nearly twelve thousand.[18] To put that total in perspective, in 1996 there were substantially more full-time American missionaries in many Latin American nations than there were Roman Catholic diocesan priests! In Honduras there were five missionaries per priest, and missionaries outnumbered priests two to one in Panama and Guatemala. Even so, these statistics did not include thousands of American missionaries on shorter tours. But even more important, the number of American missionaries in Latin America has *fallen* dramatically in the past decade. In 2004 there were only 5,116.[19] Why? Because they have been replaced by Latin Americans! In many Latin American nations today, native-born evangelical Protestant clergy far outnumber both foreign missionaries and local Catholic priests.[20]

The rapid increase in native-born Protestant clergy spurred the rapid growth of Protestant denominations in Latin America. But although it is well known that this is taking place, statistics on actual Protestant membership have been scarce, scattered, and of suspect validity. That is no longer the case. The Gallup Organization's World Polls provide the first accurate data on the number of self-identified Protestants and Catholics in Latin American nations. No surveys were conducted in Cuba, Jamaica, and Puerto Rico. Four tiny nations included in the Gallup World Polls were omitted on grounds that they are not an historic part of "Latin" America. Three of them are former British colonies: Guyana, Belize, and Trinidad and Tobago. Haiti is a French-speaking, cultural outlier. That leaves eighteen nations that are culturally and historically identified with Latin America.

Combining the surveys conducted in 2007 and 2008 maximizes the accuracy of the statistics. Every survey asked respondents their religious affiliation. The results are shown in table 22.5.

Table 22.5: Percent Protestant and Catholic, 2007–2008
(Gallup World Polls)

Nation	Protestant	Rom. Catholic	Other	Secular
El Salvador	38%	61%	1%	0%
Nicaragua	37%	61%	1%	1%
Guatemala	36%	61%	1%	2%
Honduras	36%	62%	1%	1%
Brazil	24%	71%	4%	1%
Costa Rica	24%	74%	2%	0%
Chile	20%	74%	3%	3%
Dominican Republic	20%	69%	0%	11%
Panama	18%	80%	2%	0%
Bolivia	17%	81%	1%	1%
Peru	16%	82%	1%	1%
Uruguay	12%	64%	6%	18%
Colombia	11%	88%	1%	0%
Ecuador	11%	87%	1%	1%
Paraguay	9%	89%	2%	0%
Argentina	9%	85%	2%	4%
Mexico	9%	86%	3%	1%
Venezuela	5%	91%	2%	2%

These statistics reveal that Protestantism has become a major religious presence in most of Latin America. Protestants make up 20 percent or more of the population in eight of these eighteen nations, and more than a third in four of them. Only in Venezuela (5 percent) has

Protestant growth been minimized. The "Other" category includes indigenous Indian and African faiths. The "Secular" category consists of those who said they had no religion. The high total for the secular category in Uruguay (18 percent) probably reflects the fact that more than 80 percent of Uruguayans are of direct European descent.[21]

Unfortunately, it is not possible to separate the "Protestants" into their constituent denominations. The major American evangelical groups such as the Assemblies of God, United Brethren, Churches of Christ, and various Baptist bodies are well represented. But there are many purely local Protestant groups as well, most of them having Pentecostal roots. For example, in Brazil, an autonomous Pentecostal body known as *Brasil Para o Christo* (Brazil for Christ) has attracted more than a million members.[22] In addition to large Latin-born Protestant groups, there are hundreds of small independent groups. Hence the growth of Protestantism in Latin America has been the growth of meaningful pluralism.

The Catholic Response

Faced with serious competition, the Latin church has responded very energetically. This has been ignored in nearly every published study of Protestant growth in Latin America. Thus Harvey Cox enthusiastically repeated David Stoll's prediction, made in 1990, that five or six Latin nations would have Protestant majorities by 2010 and that Protestants would be on the verge of becoming majorities in several more nations.[23] But it didn't happen. Only in four Latin countries do Protestants constitute even a third of the population. Of course, had the bishops continued to embrace their illusions and done nothing to compete with their Protestant challengers, Stoll's predictions may well have come to pass. And if observers failed initially to see that the church would vigorously respond to the challenge, probably it was because the initial tactic endorsed by the bishops was primarily political rather than religious, and proved to be utterly ineffective.

Known as Liberation Theology, this response to Protestant inroads mixed Marxism and Catholicism and aimed at "mobilizing the poor to struggle for their own liberation,"[24] thereby planning to enlist the masses in support of the Christian Socialism. The term *Liberation Theology* was coined by the Peruvian Dominican priest Gustavo Gutiérrez in 1968 and popularized by his book *A Theology of Liberation* (1971). In it he redefined salvation, discarding the emphasis on the individual and arguing instead that salvation is collective, taking the form of freeing the masses from bondage. Although they made no mention of Gutiérrez's claims about salvation, the notion that the church must liberate the masses was officially sanctioned at a conference of the Latin American Catholic bishops at Medellín, Columbia, in 1968.

The primary tactical means proposed to achieve liberation was the "Base Community" (*communidades de base*), wherein a liberationist leader would gather a small group to live and work together in a socialist commune where their political and moral awareness would be raised, meanwhile providing a model of self-improvement for others living in surrounding areas. The long-range plan was to rebuild societies from below, from a new "base." Appropriately, Base Communities were explicitly linked to the long tradition of experimental utopian communities.[25] And although it was intended that the Base Communities be formed by gathering the poor, it turned out that, as with so many other utopian communities, they mainly attracted the relatively privileged.[26] In any event, even many highly committed liberationists admit that their moment has passed.[27]

Liberation Theology failed as a social movement, if for no other reason than that it was an ideological misfit. It lacked credibility to the political Left because of its religious rhetoric and connections to the church. Its emphasis on political goals and tactics made it a nonstarter in competition with religious movements. What remains noteworthy is that, as Anthony Gill demonstrates, Liberation Theology was not initiated primarily in response to the poverty of the masses, but in response to the Protestant threat. National church leaders sanctioned

Liberation Theologians and their programs to the extent that Protestant groups were making headway in their nations.[28]

In remarkable contrast, the second Catholic response to Protestant competition has proved to be immensely popular and effective: the Catholic Charismatic Renewal movement (CCR). Often described as Catholic Pentecostalism, CCR involves intense prayer meetings that often include "speaking in tongues." And just as Protestant evangelists often fill Latin American soccer stadia for revival meetings, CCR also fills these same stadia. In 1999, an album of samba-inspired religious music by CCR television star Father Marcelo Rossi outsold all other CDs in Brazil.[29] Perhaps the most remarkable thing about the CCR is that, although many priests participate in it, "it is generally a lay movement."[30] In fact, were it not for the centrality of the Virgin Mary, it would be difficult to distinguish the CCR from Protestant Pentecostal groups. Both groups experience baptism in the Holy Spirit, both engage in glossolalia, both are deeply committed to faith healing, and both groups originated in the United States—Protestant Pentecostalism in Los Angeles in 1906, and the Catholic Charismatic Renewal at Duquesne University in Pittsburgh in 1967. CCR was taken south by American priests in the early 1970s.

The fundamental organizational unit of CCR is the weekly prayer group, having lay leaders and an average of about thirty members. These groups gather during the week to pray, engage in spontaneous glossolalia, sing, and contemplate; on Sundays, the CCR members flock to mass. There are tens of thousands of these prayer groups in Latin America, and the CCR has become a very capable competitor in the relatively free-market Latin American religious economy.

Salvatore Martinez, coordinator of CCR in the Vatican, informed me that there probably are more than sixty million official members worldwide and perhaps another forty million belong to independent charismatic Catholic groups. Martinez added that much of the membership as well as current growth is in Latin America. Unfortunately, there are no reliable statistics on membership broken down by nations.[31] However, there are statistics that indirectly reflect the energizing effect of the CCR. Table 22.6 shows the percentage of Catholics in each Latin American nation who said "yes," when asked, *Have you attended a place of worship or religious service in the past seven days?*

Table 22.6: Percent of Catholics Who Attended Church in Past Seven Days (Gallup World Polls)

Nation	Attended in Past Seven Days
Guatemala	72%
El Salvador	66%
Honduras	66%
Colombia	63%
Ecuador	63%
Costa Rica	61%
Mexico	60%
Panama	60%
Bolivia	59%
Nicaragua	58%
Paraguay	56%
Peru	53%
Dominican Republic	49%
Brazil	45%
Venezuela	41%
Argentina	31%
Chile	31%
Uruguay	16%

In most of Latin America today, Catholics are attending church at a truly remarkable level. In eight of these nations the weekly attendance rate is 60 percent or higher—72 percent in Guatemala. Four more nations have mass attendance rates above 52 percent. Compare this with Spain where only 33 percent say they attend mass weekly. Argentina and Chile have attendance rates about the same as Spain, and only in Uruguay (16 percent) is attendance at the low level thought to have been typical of Latin nations several decades ago—and Uruguay is a deviant case in many other ways as well.

Entirely in keeping with the expected effects of pluralism, Catholic attendance rates are highly correlated with the Protestant challenge: the larger the percentage Protestant, the higher the rate of Catholic attendance.[32]

Obviously, the Catholic Church has undergone a stunning renewal in Latin America. Where once the bishops were content with bogus claims about a Catholic continent and a reality of low levels of commitment, the Catholic churches in Latin America are now filled on Sundays with devoted members, many of them also active in charismatic groups that meet during the week. And the source of this remarkable change has been the rapid growth of intense Protestant faiths, thus creating a highly competitive pluralist environment.

This is not the first time such a thing has happened. Toward the middle of the nineteenth century, when a massive influx of Catholic immigrants began in America, they brought with them the low levels of participation and concern that prevailed in their European nations of origin. Initially, many of these Catholic immigrants defected to Protestant groups that aggressively missionized among them. But the American Catholic clergy quickly adjusted by adopting Protestant recruitment techniques (including revival meetings) and soon the American Catholic Church was far stronger and more effective than any in Europe.[33]

In Latin America, the Catholic Church has reached these amazing heights of member commitment by adopting the major elements of their Protestant Pentecostal competitors with the result that the illusory Catholic continent is truly becoming a Charismatic Christian continent. Thus, the churching of Latin America.

Christians in China

THROUGH MUCH OF THE twentieth century, the prevailing view among Western intellectuals was that the Chinese were immune to religion—an immunity that long preceded the Communist rise to power. When in 1934 Edgar Snow quipped that "in China, opium is the religion of the people," the media "experts" chuckled in agreement and dismissed the million Chinese claimed as converts by Christian missionaries as nothing but "rice Christians"—cynical souls who had frequented the missions for the benefits they provided. Then in 1949 Mao Zedong came to power and it was widely agreed that China soon would be a model of the fully secularized, postreligious society.

But, it wasn't to be. Instead, faith in a coming postreligious China proved to be the opium of Western intellectuals as well as of Marxist ideologists. It turns out that the Chinese Christians in 1949—those ridiculed in the West as rice Christians—were so "insincere" that they endured decades of bloody repression during which their numbers grew! And as official repression has slacked off, Christianity emerged (partly) from underground and has been growing at an astonishing rate in China.

Unfortunately, there is a great deal of disagreement over just how astonishing the growth has been: Are there now sixteen million or two hundred million Christians in China? Both numbers have been asserted with great confidence and with claims of being "official," but perhaps the most widely accepted claim is that there are one hundred thirty million Chinese Christians. That total is often attributed to a survey conducted by the Chinese government.[34] But no Chinese scholars or polling agencies know of such a survey and that total is not supported by any of the known surveys. Some of the confusion may arise from the fact that the Chinese government does keep track of how many people belong to Christian groups officially registered under the terms of the Three Self Patriotic Movement (TSPM). These groups now enroll about sixteen million members. But, as the government frankly admits, there may easily be several times that number of Christians since there are tens of thousands of Christian house churches in China that are not registered with TSPM. How many members do they have?

Unfortunately, thus far the Chinese government will not allow "foreign" survey companies to ask questions about religion. Hence although the Gallup Organization's branch in Beijing conducts many surveys, these include no questions about religion or other "sensitive" issues. However, this limit does not apply to Chinese firms. So, if treated with caution, some useful conclusions can be drawn from a national survey of Han China, based on 7,021 interviews conducted in 2007 by Horizon, Ltd., China's largest and most respected polling firm. The data have been made available to Baylor's Program of Research on China, especially for use by scholars from China who participate in Baylor's Chinese Postdoctoral Fellowship Program.

The survey found that 3.1 percent of Chinese admit to being Christians (2.9 percent Protestants and 0.2 percent Catholics). This suggests that there are about 35.3 million Christians in China. However, this should be regarded as the *lowest* plausible number since there is every reason to assume that surveys greatly undercount Chinese Christians. Many Chinese refuse to participate in survey studies, and it is assumed that Christians are unusually likely to do so (it remains somewhat risky for Chinese to be identified as Christians). In addition, some Christians who do agree to be interviewed are likely to think it unwise to admit being a Christian when asked that question by a stranger. To get an accurate estimate of the number of Chinese Christians requires a correction factor for both of these suppressors.

To address these concerns my colleagues at Baylor and I launched a follow-up study in cooperation with colleagues at Peking University in Beijing (where I am an honorary professor of sociology). Based on contacts in the Chinese Christian community, we were able to obtain samples of members of Chinese house churches from many of the same areas used in the original survey sample. Survey interviewers were sent to seek interviews with these people, all of whom were active Christians (but this was unknown to the interviewers). Of these known Christians, 62 percent refused to be interviewed compared with an overall refusal rate of 38 percent for the original survey. Adjusting for this difference in response rates yields an estimate of 58.9 million Christians sixteen and over.

In addition, of those known Christians who did agree to be interviewed, 9 percent did not admit to being Christians when asked. Correcting for that suppressor, brings the number of Christians sixteen and older to 64.3 million Chinese. Of course, this total is for 2007. Obviously the total is higher now. It seems entirely credible to estimate that there are about 70 million Chinese Christians in 2011.

Moreover, Christian growth is not limited to a few segments of the Chinese population. Based on an analysis of the Horizon, Ltd., survey,[35] there are no significant age effects. Christians are equally likely to have grown up in rural and urban areas. Christians are quite evenly spread across all levels of education. And with Communist Party members removed (since they must, at the very least, keep their Christianity a secret), middle and upper income Chinese are significantly more apt to be Christians than are those with lower incomes. Of course, as is true of all religious groups around the world,[36] Chinese women (3.8 percent) are more apt to be Christians than are men (1.6 percent). Even so, there would seem to be no demographic barriers to continued Christian expansion in China.

One reason that so many Western academic observers may have so greatly overestimated the number of Christians in China is that there is such a pronounced Christian climate on the campuses of the leading universities—far more so than even on most sectarian American campuses. Moreover, it has become a common conviction even among non-Christian Chinese intellectuals that Christianity played the essential role in the rise of Western civilization, and hence it might be vital to the economic and scientific development of China as well. As a result, the Chinese exhibit a strong interest in Christian history, to such an extent that large numbers of books on that topic have been translated and published in China, including three of mine, with more to come soon (probably including this one).

Why Christianity Grows

MARK 16:15 QUOTES THE risen Jesus: "And he said to them, 'Go into all the world and preach the gospel to the whole creation.'" That is the "secret" to Christian growth: Christianity is able to motivate so many of its followers to proselytize on behalf of their faith that it currently is growing rapidly by way of conversions in what historically have been non-Christian regions.

That brings us to a fundamental issue: Why does Christianity have such appeal? Four major aspects will be assessed: message, scripture, pluralism, and the link to modernity.

Message

As Augustine pointed out in his *Confessions*, the basic Christian message is so simple that it can easily be grasped by children, while its theological ramifications are sufficient to challenge the most powerful intellects. This is fully apparent in the Christian conception of divinity. Like Judaism and Islam, Christianity conceives of God as a transcendent, omnipotent, merciful "being," who is also somewhat mysterious, remote, and awesome. But unlike Judaism and Islam, Christianity also embraces the Son, a very human and approachable figure. Consequently, while God dominates the Christian worldview, the Son dominates the affective dimension—adults speak of Jesus having come into their lives, children sing "Jesus loves me," and Christ and his cross dominate Christian art. When Christians seek to convert others, their emphasis usually is on Jesus, which is facilitated by the fact that the Gospels are the story of Jesus.

And the fundamental message of the Gospels is that Christ died for our sins, and hence all who accept Jesus as their Savior will enjoy everlasting life after death. This is the doctrine that forms the core of the Christian appeal and gives meaning, purpose, and duration to human life. Nor must one pursue a painfully ascetic existence in order to gain these blessings. Good Christians are free to pursue an abundant life enhanced by an enlightened morality. Put another way, Christianity not only offers the immense reward of eternal life, but many profound blessings here and now—as was demonstrated in chapter 6.

However, it would be misleading to represent the typical Christian as engaged in an ongoing existential calculus to weigh the benefits of faith, while overlooking the potent and widespread mystical and emotional aspects of the Christian experience. Through the centuries countless Christians have reported direct encounters with Jesus, Mary, and other sacred beings.[37] This is but one form of the many experiential confirmations of faith that abound in Christianity, from a quiet sense of the closeness of God to ecstatic episodes and speaking in tongues.[38] Other world religions seem unable to produce these mystical manifestations in a general population, or do so only among a cloistered few. This is not to minimize Christianity's intellectual side. Every year thousands of serious books on Christian history and theology are published, read, and discussed.

Scripture

However, unlike most religious "texts" associated with other world religions, neither the Old nor New Testament is a compendium of veiled meanings, mysteries, and conundrums—there is nothing about the sound of one hand clapping. For the most part, the Bible consists of clearly expressed narratives about people and events. Although there are many theologically challenging passages (in Paul's letters, for example) and some deeply mystical sections, most of the stories are suitable for people of *all ages and cultural backgrounds*, in addition to which they are interesting! Consider the Christmas story or the confrontations between Moses and the pharaoh.

Unfortunately, for many centuries popular Christianity had only an oral existence. This was not merely because of the general lack of literacy, but also because the only written scriptures were in Latin or Greek, and hence readable only by a small elite. The church was militantly opposed to translations into "vulgar" languages, in part because it wanted to avoid disputed interpretations which were bound to arise to the extent that more people had access to scripture. Today, when the Bible has been translated into nearly two thousand languages, this unwillingness may seem peculiar. But, of course, to some extent the church's reluctance was well founded in that increased access to scripture did indeed lead to conflicts and thence to the almost endless proliferation of separate Christian bodies. On the other hand, this proliferation so energizes the faithful that it has played a major role in the spread of Christianity—missionizing is remarkably competitive.

Pluralism

Chapter 17 examined how the lazy monopoly church of medieval times was very slow to convert northern Europe and long neglected the rural populations. And chapter 20 showed the vigorous religious situation that arises with pluralism—when religious bodies compete for members and support. That chapter also demonstrated how churches that no longer believe that they possess a unique truth rapidly lose out.

The same principles apply to mission efforts. Thus, late in the nineteenth century, following his world tour of American missions in Asia and Africa, the prominent American Baptist William Folwell Bainbridge[39] noted that where a mission had an exclusive territory it did not display nearly the level of activity and effectiveness he observed in places where two or more Christian missions were in competition.[40] He counted it as a blessing that there were so many different mission efforts and strongly advised against dividing up the mission territories to avoid duplications of effort.

In those days, a great majority of American missionaries abroad were trained and supported by what are today defined as "liberal" denominations: Congregationalists (now the United Church of Christ), Presbyterians, Methodists, and Episcopalians. But early in the twentieth century leaders of these denominations began to suffer from a loss of conviction: Was there any theological or moral basis for attempting to convert non-Christians? In January 1930 a group of leading liberal theologians was assembled to "rethink" missions, and in the report they issued in 1932, these liberal leaders charged that "it is a humiliating mistake" for Christians to think their faith is superior, for anything in Christianity that "is true belongs, in its nature to the human mind everywhere." Thus, "phrases like 'evangelization of the world' . . . [are] downright embarrassing."[41] Therefore, these leaders proposed that if missionaries were to be sent out at all, it should not be to evangelize but to perform social services—to teach sanitation, not salvation.

Of course, few found this a sufficient motivation to undertake a life of sacrifice in strange lands. Consequently, the liberal denominations no longer play a significant role in what has since become an enormous mission effort. But had there still been only one Christian organization, foreign missions probably never would have begun in the first place, and certainly they would have disappeared in the 1930s. Instead, it was only the liberal Protestant mission effort that ended, as scores of conservative and evangelical Protestant denominations continue to send out huge numbers of missionaries. Faced with these Protestant challenges, the Roman Catholic Church also currently sustains a very large and effective mission force, especially in Africa.

Of course, in many parts of the world foreign missionaries have become superfluous as local Christians have taken over the work of spreading the faith. Here too, pluralism plays a major role, for Christianity sustains a tradition of innovation and adaptation. Hence locals not only take over missionizing; they often form new denominations especially suited to their particular situation and culture—there are thousands of new Christian groups in Africa, for example. The formation of new Christian organizations ensures local pluralism and, of course, the competition among them energizes each. In the end, Christianity grows, partly because so many Christians work so hard to make it grow.

Modernity

The liberal proposal that missionaries devote themselves to teaching about such things as sanitation touches upon a final and very significant aspect of the spread of Christianity. Inevitably, as the religion of the West, Christianity is associated with Western modernity. Thus, for many in the less-developed world, it is nearly impossible to separate their embrace of Christianity from their acceptance of modern culture in general. The West's demonstrable wisdom in such things as medicine and technology seems to certify Western wisdom concerning God as well. Indeed, many conclude that the West's knowledge of God forms the basis for its progress in other respects. As one of China's leading economists put it, "in the past twenty years, we have realized that the heart of your culture is your religion: Christianity. That is why the West is so powerful. The Christian moral foundation of social and cultural life was what made possible the emergence of capitalism and then the successful transition to democratic politics. We don't have any doubt about this."[42] Neither do I.[43]

Conclusion

PERHAPS THE MOST ESSENTIAL aspect of Christianity that has facilitated its globalization is its remarkable cultural flexibility. Wherever it goes, the faith is adapted to the local culture—made possible by its universal message. Hence, worldwide Christianity is an enormous tent within which thousands of distinct churches sustain a common faith in Christ.

CONCLUSION

IN LITTLE MORE THAN TWENTY years will come the two-thousandth
anniversary of the Crucifixion. During these two millennia Christianity has passed through many decisive moments, both tragic and triumphant. Excluding the Christ story from the list, three events stand
out as being far more crucial than all the rest to the historical trajectory of the faith—two of them were exceedingly beneficial, and one
of them was a great misfortune. Of course, each of the three has been
given attention in previous chapters, but to conclude my reexamina-
tion of the Christian story, it seems appropriate to meditate a bit further on why these developments made such a difference.

Council of Jerusalem

BY FAR THE MOST important event in the entire rise of Christianity
was the meeting in Jerusalem in around the year 50, when Paul was
granted the authority to convert Gentiles without them also becoming observant Jews. This meeting is reported both in Paul's letter to
the Galatians 2:1–10, and in Acts 15.

Having returned to Jerusalem accompanied by his loyal assistants
Barnabas and Titus (who was of Gentile origins), Paul stated the case
for Gentile converts on grounds that "we believe that we shall be saved
through the grace of the Lord Jesus, just as they will" (Acts 15:11). Not

surprisingly Paul's position was hotly disputed, since few Jewish Christians in Jerusalem had any contact with Gentiles other than Roman
officials and soldiers, so their contempt for Gentiles had not been tem-
pered by familiarity. What seems truly surprising is that James, the
brother of Jesus and head of the church, did not side with Paul's opponents. James was known as "the righteous," partly because he led an
extremely ascetic life, and he could well have been expected to demand
that all converts fully observe the Law. Instead, he blessed Paul's proposal and required only that Gentile converts observe the Ten Commandments and not eat meat that has been strangled (Acts 15:20).

Until this decision was made, Christianity was just another Jewish
sect. Although Judaism had made a substantial number of converts,
it seems unlikely that any religion unalterably linked to an ethnicity could have become a world religion—not even with the added
Christian aspect. Having worked to spread the faith outside Palestine,
Paul was fully aware of this ethnic barrier—he had encountered many
Gentile "God fearers" who attended and even helped to finance synagogues, but who remained marginal since they refused to fully accept
the Law. He also had recognized how many marginal Jews might convert if they could have a form of Judaism that freed them from fully
observing the Law. Indeed, as noted in chapter 4, once enabled to
bring in converts not required to observe the Law, Paul seems to have
devoted most of his efforts to these two groups—probably perceiving
them as "low hanging fruit." But the true importance of the Jerusalem Council's ruling was not its effect on Paul, but on rank-and-file
Christians who now were able to reach out far more effectively to
their Gentile friends, relatives, and neighbors—a process that eventually assembled the world's largest religion.

The Conversion of Constantine

CONSTANTINE'S INVOLVEMENT IN CHRISTIAN doctrinal disputes
established the basis for an intolerant monopoly church responsible

for centuries of negligence, followed by centuries of brutal heresy hunting and conflict.

It is true that Constantine never made Christianity the official faith of the empire and was surprisingly tolerant of paganism. But he was incapable of permitting diversity within Christianity and quite willing to use the powers of the state to suppress all challenges to the prevailing orthodoxy. This set a precedent for future emperors who did invest the church with official status, as well as for popes who freely called upon the state to defend their monopoly against all significant dissenters.

Religious dissent is inevitable because no single religious body can serve the entire spectrum of human religious preferences. In any society, some people prefer a very lax and permissive religion (or none at all); others want a somewhat more vigorous religion; while still others seek an intense and strict religious life. Consequently, wherever religious freedom prevails there will exist a multitude of religious bodies based on these different "market sectors" of religious demand. But where there is no freedom to dissent—where a monopoly attempts to dominate all demand—conflict is inevitable. Moreover, since a monopoly religion will always drift toward permissiveness, the challenges will come from those with the most intense religious preferences—precisely those most willing to take risks and make sacrifices for their faith. Hence, the medieval centuries of heresy-hunting and religious wars trace directly back to Constantine, as does a Europe wherein the people have long been so neglected by lazy monopoly churches that only small bands of worshippers huddle in the continent's magnificent churches.

Had Constantine not made himself the arbiter and enforcer of Christian orthodoxy, but confined himself to policies of state neutrality, all this might have been spared, and Europe may have prospered from effective and sincere religious competition—as came to pass in America much more than a millennium later.

The Reformations

THE THIRD GREAT SHIFT in the trajectory of Christian history was in response to the Reformations of the sixteenth century. In the long run, these Reformations undid much of Constantine's harm to Christianity. In the shorter run, the Reformations merely replaced the lazy and intolerant Catholic monopoly with a number of equally lazy and intolerant Protestant monopolies. Hence, the Protestant Henry the VIII burned Lollards and Lutherans, and his successors hunted high and low for Catholic priests. Luther persecuted Anabaptists as well as Catholics, and Calvin excluded nearly everyone. Meanwhile, the nations of Western Europe became involved in long and bloody wars over which religion should prevail, and in the end a barely tolerated diversity remained. However, the survival of dissenting Protestants, whether as unpopular minorities or as monopoly state churches, encouraged other dissenters, and some of them succeeded in adding to the existing diversity.

Perhaps the most often overlooked benefit of the Reformation was the transformation of the Catholic Church into a vigorous assembly of highly educated and devoted nuns and priests whose efforts have strengthened the faith both in Europe and abroad. Thus the end result of the Reformations was to reenergize Christianity, enabling it to grow once more: the faith is now thriving in Africa, Latin America, and China because so many separate Christian denominations are working so hard to "preach the gospel to every creature."

Summing Up

FINALLY, I HAVE TRIED to bring some of the pivotal moments in the Christian journey to life and to expose many falsifications and errors in the traditional tellings. In closing, here are a few of the points I hope readers will consider and remember:

• The first generation of the Jesus Movement consisted of a tiny and fearful minority existing amid a Palestinian environment abundant in zealots willing to assassinate even high priests for not being sufficiently orthodox and pious—let alone willing to tolerate Jews who claimed the messiah had come.

• The mission to the Jews probably was quite successful: large numbers of Jews in the Diasporan communities outside Palestine probably did convert to Christianity.

• Christianity was not a religion based on the slaves and lowest classes of Romans, but was particularly attractive to the privileged. Jesus himself may have been from a wealthy background.

• Christian mercy had such profound worldly consequences that Christians even outlived their pagan neighbors.

• In a Roman world quite short of women, women greatly outnumbered men among the early Christians. This occurred in part because Christians did not "discard" female infants and Christian women did not have a substantial mortality rate from abortions done in a world without antibiotics or even knowledge of germs. It also occurred because women were more likely than men to convert.

• Paganism was not quickly stamped out by a triumphant and intolerant Christianity, but disappeared very slowly and lingers still in various New Age and esoteric circles.

• For centuries, there probably were more Christians in the Middle East and North Africa than in Europe. Christianity was eventually destroyed in these areas by Islamic persecution and repression.

• The crusaders were not greedy colonialists, but marched east for religious motives and at great risk and personal expense. Many knowingly went bankrupt and few of them lived to return.

- The so-called Dark Ages not only weren't dim, but were one of the most inventive times in Western history.

- Despite medieval Europe's great cathedrals, most Europeans of that era were, at best, barely Christian. Few ever attended church.

- Science arose only in the West because efforts to formulate and discover laws of nature only made sense if one believed in a rational creator.

- The Spanish Inquisition was a quite temperate body that was responsible for very few deaths and saved a great many lives by opposing the witch hunts that swept through the rest of Europe.

- Religious competition increases the level of religiousness prevailing in a society. In the long run it also results in norms of religious civility.

- The claim that religion must soon disappear as the world becomes more modern is nothing but wishful thinking on the part of academic atheists.

- Despite the low levels of religious participation prevalent in Europe, religion is thriving, perhaps as never before, all around the globe; excluding China, but including Europe, 76 percent of the earth's inhabitants say religion is important in their daily lives.

- More than 40 percent of the people on earth today are Christians and their number is growing more rapidly than that of any other major faith.

Palm Sunday, 2011
Corrales, New Mexico

BIBLIOGRAPHY

Abbott, Frank Frost. 1911. *The Common People of Ancient Rome*. New York: Chautauqua.

Abun-Nasr, Jamil. 1971. *A History of the Maghrib*. Cambridge: Cambridge Univ. Press.

Africa, Thomas W. 1969. *The Ancient World*. Boston: Houghton Mifflin.

———. 1971. "Urban Violence in Imperial Rome." *Journal of Interdisciplinary History* 2:3–21.

Aikman, David. 2003. *Jesus in Beijing: How Christianity Is Transforming China and Changing the Global Balance of Power*. Washington, DC: Regnery.

Albright, William Foxwell. 1957. *From the Stone Age to Christianity: Monotheism and the Historical Process*. New York: Doubleday Anchor Books.

———. 1961. *Samuel and the Beginnings of the Prophetic Movement*. Cincinnati: Hebrew Union College Press.

Alföldi, Andrew. 1948. *The Conversion of Constantine and Pagan Rome*. Oxford: Clarendon.

Allen, Charlotte. 1998. *The Human Christ: The Search for the Historical Jesus*. New York: Free Press.

———. 1996. "The Search for the No-Frills Jesus: Q." *Atlantic Monthly* (December): 51–68.

Alter, Robert. 2004. *The Five Books of Moses*. New York: W. W. Norton.

Alvarez, Lizette. 2003. "Tarbaek Journal: Fury, God and the Pastor's Disbelief." *New York Times*, World section. July 8.

Andrea, A. J. 2003. "The Crusades in Perspective: The Crusades in Modern Islamic Perspective." *History Compass* 1:1–4.

Armitage, Angus. 1951. *The World of Copernicus*. New York: Mentor Books.

Armstrong, Karen. [1991] 2001. *Holy War: The Crusades and Their Impact on Today's World*. 2nd ed. New York: Random House.

———. 1992. *Muhammad: A Biography of the Prophet*. New York: HarperCollins.

Asberg, Christer. 1990. "The Swedish Bible Commission and Project NT 81." In *Bible Reading in Sweden*, edited by Gunnar Hanson, 15–22. Uppsala: Univ. of Uppsala.

Athanassiadi, Polymnia. 1993. "Persecution and Response in Late Paganism: The Evidence of Damascius." *Journal of Hellenic Studies* 113:1–29.

Atiya, Aziz S. 1968. *History of Eastern Christianity*. Notre Dame: Univ. of Notre Dame Press.

Audisio, Gabriel. 1990. "How to Detect a Clandestine Minority: The Example of the Waldenses." *Sixteenth Century Journal* 21:205–16.

Ayer, Joseph Cullen, Jr. [1913] 1941. *A Source Book for Ancient Church History*. New York: Scribner.

Ayerst, David, and A. S. T. Fisher. 1971. *Records of Christianity*. Vol. 1. Oxford: Basil Blackwell.

Bagnall, Roger S. 1982. "Religious Conversion and Onomastic Change in Early Byzantine Egypt." *Bulletin of the American Society of Papyrologists* 19:105–24.

———. 1987. "Conversion and Onomastics: A Reply." *Zeitschrift für Papyrologies und Epigraphik* 69:243–50.

———. 1993. *Egypt in Late Antiquity*. Princeton: Univ. of Princeton Press.

Bailey, Cyril. 1932. *Phases in the Religion of Ancient Rome*. Berkeley: Univ. of California Press.

Baillie, John. 1951. *The Belief in Progress*. New York: Scribner.

Bainbridge, William F. 1882. *Around the World Tour of Christian Missions: A Universal Survey*. New York: C. R. Blackall.

Bainbridge, William Sims. 1997. *The Sociology of Religious Movements*. New York: Routledge.

Bainton, Roland. [1952] 1985. *The Reformation of the Sixteenth Century*. Boston: Beacon.

———. 1995. *Here I Stand: A Life of Martin Luther*. New York: Penguin.

Baird, Robert. 1844. *Religion in America*. New York: Harper & Bros.

Baldet, Jacques. 2003. *Jesus the Rabbi Prophet*. Rochester, VT: Inner Traditions.

Balsdon, J. P. V. D. 1963. *Roman Women: Their History and Habits*. New York: John Day.

Baly, Denis. 1957. *The Geography of the Bible*. New York: Harper & Bros.

Bamberger, Bernard J. 1939. *Proselytism in the Talmudic Period*. New York: Hebrew Union College Press.

Bammel, Ernst. 1995. "Jewish Activity Against Christians in Palestine According to Acts." In *The Book of Acts in Its Palestinian Setting*, edited by Richard Bauckham, 357–64. Grand Rapids: Eerdmans.

Barber, Malcom. 2000. *The Cathars of Languedoc*. New York: Addison Wesley Longman.

Barclay, Brig, Cycil Nelson, and Brian Betham Schofield. 1981. "Gunnery." In *Encyclopaedia Britannica*. Chicago: Univ. of Chicago Press.

Barnes, Timothy D. 1968. "Legislation Against the Christians." *Journal of Roman Studies* 58:32–50.

———. 1981. *Constantine and Eusebius*. Cambridge: Harvard Univ. Press.

———. 1995. "Statistics and the Conversion of the Roman Aristocracy." *Journal of Roman Studies* 85:135–47.

Barnett, Paul. 2005. *The Birth of Christianity: The First Twenty Years*. Grand Rapids: Eerdmans.

———. 2008. *Paul: Missionary of Jesus*. Grand Rapids: Eerdmans.

Baron, Salo Wittmayer. 1952. *A Social and Religious History of the Jews*. Vols. 1 and 2. New York: Columbia Univ. Press.

Barrett, David B. 1982. *World Christian Encyclopedia*. Oxford: Oxford Univ. Press.

Barrett, David B., George T. Kurian, and Todd M. Johnson. 2001. *World Christian Encyclopedia*. 2nd ed. Oxford: Oxford Univ. Press.

Barrow, Logie. 1980. "Socialism in Eternity." *History Workshop* 9:37–69.

Batey, Richard A. 1991. *Jesus and the Forgotten City*. Grand Rapids: Baker Book House.

Bauckham, Richard. 1990. *Jude and the Relatives of Jesus in the Early Church*. Edinburgh: T&T Clark.

———. 2002. *Gospel Women: Studies of the Named Women in the Gospels*. Grand Rapids: Eerdmans.

———. 2006. *Jesus and the Eyewitnesses: The Gospels as Eyewitness Testimony*. Grand Rapids: Eerdmans.

———. 2007a. *The Testimony of the Beloved Disciple*. Grand Rapids: Baker Academic.

———. 2007b. "James and the Jerusalem Community." In *Jewish Believers in Jesus: The Early Centuries*, edited by Oskar Skarsaune and Reidar Hvalik, 55–95. Peabody, MA: Hendrickson.

Baumgarten, Albert I. 1997. *The Flourishing of Jewish Sects in the Maccabean Era*. Leiden: Brill.

Beach, Harlan P. 1903. *A Geography and Atlas of Protestant Missions, vol.2. Statistics and Atlas*. New York: Student Volunteer Movement for Foreign Missions.

Beard, Mary. 1990. "Priesthood in the Roman Republic." In *Pagan Priests*, edited by Mary Beard and John North, 19–48. London: Duckworth.

Beard, Mary, and John North. 1990. "Introduction." In *Pagan Priests*, edited by Mary Beard and John North, 1–14. London: Duckworth.

Beard, Mary, John North, and Simon Price. 1998. *Religions of Rome*. 2 vols. Cambridge: Cambridge Univ. Press.

Becker, Carl Heinrich. 1926. "The Expansion of the Saracens—Africa and Europe." In *The Cambridge Medieval History*, ed. J. B. Bury, H. M. Gwatkin, and J. P. Whitney, 2:366–90. Cambridge: Cambridge Univ. Press.

Becker, George. 2000. "Educational 'Preference' of German Protestants and Catholics: The Politics Behind Educational Specialization." *Review of Religious Research* 41:311–27.

Beckford, James A. 1985. *Cult Controversies: The Societal Response to New Religions*. London: Tavistock.

Bede. [730] 1955. *Ecclesiastical History of the English People*. London: Penguin Classics.

Bell, Susan Groag. 1973. *Women: From the Greeks to the French Revolution*. Palo Alto, CA: Stanford Univ. Press.

Benin, Stephen D. 1993. *The Footprints of God: Divine Accommodation in Jewish and Christian Thought*. Albany: State Univ. of New York Press.

Benko, Stephen. 1984. *Pagan Rome and the Early Christians*. Bloomington: Univ. of Indiana Press.

Berger, Peter L. 1968. "A Bleak Outlook Is Seen for Religion." *New York Times*, April 25, 3.

———. 1969. *The Sacred Canopy*. New York: Doubleday Anchor Books.

———. 1979. *The Heretical Imperative: Contemporary Possibilities of Religious Affiliation*. New York: Doubleday.

———. 1997. "Epistemological Modesty: An Interview with Peter Berger." *Christian Century* 114 (October 29):972–75, 978.

Berger, Peter, Grace Davie, and Effie Fokas. 2008. *Religious America, Secular Europe?* Burlington, VT: Ashgate.

Beskow, Per. 1983. *Strange Tales About Jesus*. Philadelphia: Fortress.

Betz, Hans Dieter. 1992. "Paul." In *The Anchor Bible Dictionary*, edited by David Noel Freedman. New York: Doubleday.

Beugnot, Arthur Auguste. 1835. *Histoire de la destruction du paganisme en Occident*. 2 vols. Paris: Firmin Didot Freres.

Biagent, Michael. 2006. *The Jesus Papers*. San Francisco: Harper San Francisco.

Biagent, Michael, Richard Leigh, and Henry Lincoln. 1983. *Holy Blood, Holy Grail*. New York: Dell.

Bickerman, Elias. 1979. *The God of the Maccabees*. Leiden: Brill.

Bloch, Herbert. 1963. "The Pagan Revival in the West at the End of the Fourth Century." In *The Conflict Between Paganism and Christianity in the Fourth Century*, edited by Arnaldo Momigliano, 193–218. Oxford: Clarendon.

Bloch, Marc. [1940] 1961. *Feudal Society*. 2 vols. Chicago: Univ. of Chicago Press.

———. 1975. *Slavery and Serfdom in the Middle Ages*. Berkeley: Univ. of California Press.

Bloomberg, Craig. 1987. *The Historical Reliability of the Gospels*. Downers Grove, IL: IVP Academic.

Boak, Arthur E. R. 1955. *Manpower Shortage and the Fall of the Roman Empire in the West*. Ann Arbor: Univ. of Michigan Press.

Boak, Arthur E. R., and William G. Sinnigen. 1965. *A History of Rome to A.D. 565*. 5th ed. New York: Macmillan.

Bock, Darrell L. 2006. *The Missing Gospels: Unearthing the Truth Behind Alternative Christianities*. Nashville: Thomas Nelson.

Boff, Leonardo. 1986. *Ecclesiogenesis*. Maryknoll, New York: Orbis Books.

Bolce, Louis, and Gerald De Maio. 1999. "Religious Outlook, Culture War Politics, and Antipathy Roward Christian Fundamentalists." *Public Opinion Quarterly* 63:29–61.

Bolton, Brenda. 1983. *The Medieval Reformation*. London: Edward Arnold.

Bonnassie, Pierre. 1991. *From Slavery to Feudalism in South-Western Europe*. Cambridge: Cambridge Univ. Press.

Boorstin, Daniel J. 1983. *The Discoverers*. New York: Random House.

Bossy, John. 1970. "The Counter-Reformation and the People of Catholic Europe." *Past and Present* 47:51–70.

———. 1985. *Christianity in the West 1400–1700*. Oxford: Oxford Univ. Press.

Bostom, Andrew G. 2005. "Jihad Conquests and the Imposition of *Dhimmitude*—A Survey." In *The Legacy of Jihad*, edited by Andrew G. Bostom, 24–124. Amherst, NY: Prometheus Books.

Botticini, Maristella, and Zvi Eckstein. 2006. "From Farmers to Merchants, Voluntary Conversions and the Diaspora: A Human Capital Interpretation of Jewish History." *Carlo Alberto Notebooks* 2:1–36.

Bouwsma, William J. 1979. "The Renaissance and the Drama of Western History." *American Historical Review* 84:1–15.

Bowersock, Glen W. 1978. *Julian the Apostate*. Cambridge: Harvard Univ. Press.

———. 1990. *Hellenism in Late Antiquity*. Ann Arbor: Univ. of Michigan Press.

Bradbury, Scott. 1994. "Constantine and the Problem of Anti-Pagan Legislation in the Fourth Century." *Classical Philology* 89:120–39.

Bradley, Walter L. 2001. "The 'Just So' Universe: The Fine-Tuning of Constants and Conditions in the Cosmos." In *Signs of Intelligence: Understanding Intelligent Design*, edited by William A. Dembski and James M. Kushiner, 157–70. Grand Rapids: Brazos Press.

Brady, Thomas A., Jr. 1978. *Ruling Class, Regime and Reformation at Strasbourg, 1520–1555*. Leiden: Brill.

———. 1985. *Turning Swiss: Cities and Empire, 1450–1550*. Cambridge: Cambridge Univ. Press.

Brandon, S. G. F. 1951. *The Fall of Jerusalem and the Christian Church*. London: SPCK.

Braudel, Fernand. 1977. *Afterthoughts on Material Civilization and Capitalism*. Baltimore: Johns Hopkins Univ. Press.

Brent, Michael, and Elizabeth Fentress. 1996. *The Berbers*. Oxford: Blackwells.

Bridbury, A. R. 1969. "The Dark Ages." *The Economic History Review*. 22:526–37.

Briggs, C. W. 1913. "The Apostle Paul in Arabia." *Biblical World* 41: 255–59.

Briggs, Robin. 1989. *Communities of Belief: Cultural and Social Tensions in Early Modern France*. Oxford: Clarendon.

———. 1998. *Witches and Neighbors: The Social and Cultural Context of European Witchcraft*. New York: Penguin Books.

Brolis, Maria Teresa. 2002. "A Thousand and One Women: The Register for the Confraternity of Misericordia Maggiore in Bergamo." *Catholic Historical Review* 88:230–46.

Brøndsted, Johannes. 1965. *The Vikings*. Baltimore: Penguin Books.

Brooke, Christopher. 1971. *Medieval Church and Society*. London: Sidgwick & Jackson.

Brooke, John, and Geoffrey Cantor. 1998. *Reconstructing Nature*. Oxford: Oxford Univ. Press.

Brooke, Rosalind, and Christopher Brooke. 1984. *Popular Religion in the Middle Ages*. London: Thames and Hudson.

Brooten, Bernadette. 1982. *Women Leaders in the Ancient Synagogue*. Chico, CA: Scholars.

Broshi, Magen. 2001. *Bread, Wine, Walls and Scrolls*. Sheffield, UK: Sheffield Academic Press.

Brown, Peter. 1978. *The Making of Late Antiquity*. Cambridge: Harvard Univ. Press.

———. 1981. *The Cult of the Saints*. Chicago: Univ. of Chicago Press.

———. 1988. *The Body and Society*. New York: Columbia Univ. Press.

———. 1992. *Power and Persuasion in Late Antiquity: Towards a Christian Empire*. Madison, WI: Univ. of Wisconsin Press.

———. 1995. *Authority and the Sacred: Aspects of the Christianization of the Roman World*. Cambridge: Cambridge Univ. Press.

———. 1998. "Christianization and Religious Conflict." *Cambridge Ancient History* 13:632–64.

———. 2002. *Poverty and Leadership in the Later Roman Empire*. Hanover, NH: Univ. Press of New England.

Browne, Laurence E. [1933] 1967. *The Eclipse of Christianity in Asia*. New York: Howard Fertig.

Bruce, Frederick Fyvie. 1981. *The New Testament Documents: Are They Reliable?* 6th ed. Grand Rapids: Eerdmans.

———. 1982. *The Epistle of Paul to the Romans*. Grand Rapids: Eerdmans.

Bruce, Steve. 1992. *Religion and Modernization*. Oxford: Clarendon Press.

Brunt, P. A. 1971. *Italian Manpower, 225 B.C.–A.D. 14*. Oxford: Oxford Univ. Press.

Buchanan, George Wesley. 1964. "Jesus and the Upper Class." *Novum Testamentum* 7:195–209.

Bulliet, Richard W. 1979a. *Conversion to Islam in the Medieval Period: An Essay in Quantitative History*. Cambridge: Harvard Univ. Press.

———. 1979b. "Conversion to Islam and the Emergence of Muslim Society in Iran." In Nehemia Levtzion, ed. *Conversion to Islam*, 30–51. New York: Holmes & Meier.

Bundy, David. 2007. "Early Asian and East African Christianities." Vol. 2 of *The Cambridge History of Christianity*, edited by Augustine Casiday and Frederick W. Norris, 118–48. Cambridge: Cambridge Univ. Press.

Burckhardt, Jacob. [1880] 1949. *The Age of Constantine the Great*. New York: Pantheon Books.

———. [1885] 1990. *The Civilization of the Renaissance in Italy*. New York: Penguin Books.

Burdick, John. 1993. *Looking for God in Brazil*. Berkeley: Univ. of California Press.

Burkert, Walter. 1985. *Greek Religion*. Cambridge: Harvard Univ. Press.

———. 1987. *Ancient Mystery Cults*. Cambridge: Harvard Univ. Press.

———. 2004. *Babylon, Memphis, Persepolis: Eastern Contexts of Greek Culture*. Cambridge: Harvard Univ. Press.

Burn, A. R. 1953. "Hic breve vivitur." *Past and Present* 4:2–31.

Burr, George Lincoln. 1897. *Translations and Reprints from the Original Sources of European History*. Philadelphia: Univ. of Pennsylvania Press.

Burridge, Richard A., and Graham Stanton. 2004. *What Are the Gospels? A Comparison with Graeco-Roman Biography*. 2nd ed. Grand Rapids: Eerdmans.

Bush, M. L. 1967. *Renaissance, Reformation, and the Outer World, 1450–1660*. London: Blandford.

Bütz, Jeffrey J. 2005. *The Brother of Jesus and the Lost Teachings of Christianity*. Rochester, VT: Inner Traditions.

Cadbury, Henry J. 1955. *The Book of Acts in History*. London: Adam & Charles Black.

Cahill, Jane, Karl Reinhard, David Tarler, and Peter Warnock. 1991. "Scientists Examine Remains of Ancient Bathroom." *Biblical Archaeology Review* 17 (May–June):64–69.

Calvin, John. [ca. 1555] 1980. *Sermons on the Ten Commandments*. Grand Rapids: Baker Book House.

Carcopino, Jerome. 1940. *Daily Life in Ancient Rome*. New Haven: Yale Univ. Press.

Carlson, Stephen C. 2005. *The Gospel Hoax: Morton Smith's Invention of Secret Mark*. Waco: Baylor Univ. Press.

Carmignac, Jean. 1987. *The Birth of the Synoptics*. Chicago: Franciscan Herald.

Carroll, James. 2001. *Constantine's Sword: The Church and the Jews*. Boston: Houghton Mifflin.

Cartwright, Frederick F. 1972. *Disease and History*. New York: Dorset.

Case, Shirley Jackson. 1911. "Is Jesus a Historical Character? Evidence for an Affirmative Opinion." *American Journal of Theology* 15:205–27.

———. 1912. *The Historicity of Jesus*. Chicago: Univ. of Chicago Press.

———. 1932. *Jesus Through the Centuries*. Chicago: Univ. of Chicago Press.

Casey, Maurice. 1991. *From Jewish Prophet to Gentile God: The Origins and Development of New Testament Christology*. Louisville: Westminster John Knox.

Chadwick, Henry. 1966. *Early Christian Thought in the Classical Tradition.* Oxford: Oxford Univ. Press.

———. 1967. *The Early Church.* Harmondsworth, Middlesex: Penguin Books.

Chadwick, Henry, and G. R. Evans. 1987. *Atlas of the Christian Church.* New York: Facts on File.

Chadwick, Owen. 1972. *The Reformation.* Rev. ed. London: Penguin.

Chandler, Tertius. 1987. *Four Thousand Years of Urban Growth: An Historical Census.* Lewiston, NY: Edward Mellon.

Cheetham, Nicholas. 1983. *Keeper of the Keys: A History of Popes from St. Peter to John Paul II.* New York: Scribner.

Chejne, Anwar G. 1983. *Islam and the West: The Moriscos.* Albany: State Univ. of New York Press.

Chesnut, R. Andrew. 1997. *Born Again in Brazil.* New Brunswick, NJ: Rutgers Univ. Press.

———. 2003a. *Competitive Spirits: Latin America's New Religious Economy.* Oxford: Oxford Univ. Press.

———. 2003b. "A Preferential Option for the Spirit: The Catholic Charismatic Renewal in Latin America's New Religious Economy." *Latin American Politics and Society* 45:55–85.

Christian, William A., Jr. 1981. *Apparitions in Late Medieval and Renaissance Spain.* Princeton: Princeton Univ. Press.

Chuvin, Pierre. 1990. *A Chronicle of the Last Pagans.* Cambridge: Harvard Univ. Press.

Clark, Gillian. 1981. "Roman Women." *Greece & Rome,* second series, 28:193–212.

Clark, Gordon H. 1989. *Thales to Dewey.* Jefferson, MD: Trinity Foundation.

Clarke, G. W. 1973. "Double-Trials in the Persecution of Decius." *Historia* 22:650–63.

Clauss, Manfred. 2000. *The Roman Cult of Mithras.* New York: Routledge.

Cloke, Gillian. 2000. "Women, Worship and Mission." In Philip F. Esler, *The Early Christian World,* 1:422–51. London: Routledge.

Cobbett, William. 1818. *Journal of a Year's Residence in the United States of America* (as excerpted in Powell, 1967:43–48).

Cochrane, Charles Norris. [1940] 1957. *Christianity and Classical Culture.* Oxford: Oxford Univ. Press.

Cohen, Abraham. 1975. *Everyman's Talmud.* New York: Schocken.

Cohen, I. Bernard. 1985. *Revolution in Science.* Cambridge: Belknap.

Cohen, Jere. 1980. "Rational Capitalism in Renaissance Italy." *American Journal of Sociology* 85:1340–55.

———. 1987. *From the Maccabees to the Mishna.* Philadelphia: Westminster.

Cohen, Shaye J. D. 1992. "Was Judaism in Antiquity a Missionary Religion?" In *Jewish Assimilation, Acculturation and Accommodation,* edited by Menachem Mor, 14–23. Lanham, MD: Univ. Press of America.

Cohn, Norman. 1975. *Europe's Inner Demons.* New York: Basic Books.

Cole, Richard G. 1984. "Reformation Printers: Unsung Heroes." *Sixteenth Century Journal* 15:327–39.

Coleman, Richard J. 1975. "Biblical Inerrancy: Are We Going Anywhere?" *Theology Today* 31:295–303.

Colish, Marica L. 1997. *Medieval Foundations of the Western Intellectual Tradition, 400–1400*. New Haven: Yale Univ. Press.

Collingwood, R. G. and J. A. L. Myres. 1937. *Roman Britain and the English Settlements*. 2nd ed. London: Macmillan.

Collins, John J. 2007. "Pre-Christian Jewish Messianism: An Overview." In *The Messiah in Early Judaism and Christianity*, edited by Magnus Zetterholm, 1–20. Minneapolis: Fortress.

Collins, Randall. 1986. *Weberian Sociological Theory*. Cambridge: Cambridge Univ. Press.

Contreras, Jaime, and Gustave Henningsen. 1986. "Forty-four Thousand Cases of the Spanish Inquisition (1540–1700): Analysis of a Historical Data Bank." In Gustav Henningsen and John Tedeschi, *The Inquisition in Early Modern Europe: Studies on Sources and Methods*, 100–129. Dekalb: Northern Illinois Univ. Press.

Conzelmann, Hans. 1987. *Acts of the Apostles: A Commentary on the Acts of the Apostles*. Minneapolis: Augsburg Fortress.

Cooper, D. Jason. 1996. *Mithras: Mysteries and Initiation Rediscovered*. York Beach, ME: Weiser Books.

Corrigan, John A., Carlos M. N. Eire, Frederick M. Denny, and Martin S. Jaffee. 1998. *Readings in Judaism, Christianity, and Islam*. Upper Saddle, NJ: Prentice-Hall.

Costen, Michael. 1997. *The Cathars and the Albigensian Crusade*. Manchester, UK: Manchester Univ. Press.

Coulton, C. G. [1923–1950] 1979. *Five Centuries of Religion*. 4 vols. Cambridge: Cambridge Univ. Press.

———. 1925. *The Medieval Village*. Cambridge: Cambridge Univ. Press.

———. 1938. *Medieval Panorama*. New York: Macmillan.

———. [1938] 1959. *Inquisition and Liberty*. Boston: Beacon Hill.

Countryman, L. William. 1980. *The Rich Christian in the Church of the Early Empire: Contradictions and Accommodations*. New York: Edwin Mellen.

Cox, Harvey. 1995. *Fire from Heaven: The Rise of Pentecostal Spirituality and the Reshaping of Religion in the Twenty-First Century*. Cambridge, MA: Da Capo Press.

Craffert, Pieter F., and Pieter J. J. Botha. 2005. "Why Jesus Could Walk on the Sea but He Could Not Read and Write." *Neotestamentica* 39: 5–35.

Croft, Pauline. 1972. "Englishmen and the Spanish Inquisition 1558–1625." *English Historical Review* 87:249–68.

Crosby, Alfred W. 1997. *The Measure of Reality*. Cambridge: Cambridge Univ. Press.

Crossan, John Dominic. 1991. *The Historical Jesus: The Life of a Mediterranean Jewish Peasant*. San Francisco: HarperCollins.

———. 1994. *Jesus: A Revolutionary Biography*. San Francisco: Harper San Francisco.

———. 1998. *The Birth of Christianity: Discovering What Happened in the Years Immediately After the Execution of Jesus*. San Francisco: Harper San Francisco.

Cumont, Franz. [1906] 1956. *Oriental Religions in Roman Paganism*. New York: Dover.

Curry, Andrew. 2002. "The Crusades, the First Holy War." *U.S. News & World Report* (April 8):36.

Daly, Mary. 1978. *Gyn/Ecology: The Metaethics of Feminism*. Boston: Beacon.

Daniel, Ralph Thomas. 1981. "Music, Western." In *Encyclopaedia Britannica*, 12:704–15. Chicago: Univ. of Chicago Press.

Daniel-Rops, Henri. 1962. *Daily Life in Palestine at the Time of Christ*. London: Phoenix.

Danielson, Dennis Richard. 2000. *The Book of the Cosmos*. Cambridge, MA: Perseus Publishing.

Danzger, M. Herbert. 1989. *Returning to Tradition: The Contemporary Revival of Orthodox Judaism*. New Haven: Yale Univ. Press.

Darwin, Francis, and A. C. Sewards, eds. 1903. *More Letters of Charles Darwin*. 2 vols. New York: Appleton and Company.

Davidman, Lynn. 1991. *Tradition in a Rootless World: Women Turn to Orthodox Judaism*. Berkeley: Univ. of California Press.

Davie, Grace. 1994. *Religion in Britain Since 1945: Believing Without Belonging*. Oxford: Blackwell.

Davies, Norman. 1996. *Europe: A History*. Oxford: Oxford Univ. Press.

DeConick, April D. 2002. "The Original 'Gospel of Thomas.'" *Vigiliae Christianae* 56:167–99.

———. 2005. *Recovering the Original Gospel of Thomas*. New York: Continuum.

———. 2007. *The Thirteenth Apostle: What the Gospel of Judas Really Says*. New York: Continuum.

Decter, Jonathan P. 2007. *Iberian Jewish Literature: Between al-Andalus and Christian Europe*. Bloomington: Univ. of Indiana Press.

de Flaix, M. Fournier, and Alice R. Jackson. 1892. "Development of Statistics of Religion." *Publications of the American Statistical Association* 3 (17):18–37.

Deismann, Adolf. 1927. *Light from the Ancient East*. London: Hodder and Stoughton.

De la Croix, Horst, and Richard G. Tansey. 1975. *Gardiner's Art Through the Ages*. 6th ed. New York: Harcourt Brace Jovanovich.

Delacroix, Jaques, and Ranccois Nielson. 2001. "The Beloved Myth: Protestantism and the Rise of Industrial Capitalism in Nineteenth-Century Europe." *Social Forces* 80:509–53.

Delumeau, Jean. 1977. *Catholicism Between Luther and Voltaire*. London: Burns & Oats.

Dennett, Daniel C. 2006. *Breaking the Spell: Religion as as Natural Phenomenon.* New York: Viking.

de Roover, Raymond. 1958. "The Concept of the Just Price: Theory and Economic Policy." *The Journal of Economic History.* 18:418–34.

de Ste. Croix, G. E. M. 1954. "Aspects of the 'Great' Persecutions." *Harvard Theological Review* 47:75–113.

———. 1963a. "Why Were the Early Christians Persecuted?" *Past and Present* 26:6–38.

———. 1963b. "Why Were the Early Christians Persecuted? A Rejoinder." *Past and Present* 27:28–33.

de Tocqueville, Alexis. [1835–1939] 1956. *Democracy in America.* 2 vols. New York: Vintage Books.

Devine, A. M. 1985. "The Low Birth-Rate of Ancient Rome: A Possible Contributing Factor." *Rheinisches Museum* 128:3–4, 313–17.

Dibelius, Martin. 1934. *From Tradition to Gospel.* London: Nicholson and Watson.

Dickens, A. G. 1974. *The German Nation and Martin Luther.* New York: Harper & Row.

———. 1991. *The English Reformation.* 2nd ed. University Park: Pennsylvania State Univ. Press.

Dodd, C. H. 1970. *The Founder of Christianity.* New York: Macmillan.

Dodds, E. R. 1965. *Pagan and Christian in an Age of Anxiety.* New York: W. W. Norton.

Dolan, Jay P. 1975. *The Immigrant Church: New York's Irish and German Catholics, 1815–1865.* Baltimore: Johns Hopkins Univ. Press.

———. 1978. *Catholic Revivalism: The American Experience, 1830–1900.* Notre Dame: Univ. of Notre Dame Press.

Donalson, Malcolm Drew. 2003. *The Cult of Isis in the Roman Empire.* Lewiston, ME: Edwin Mellen.

Dowling, John. [1845] 2002. *The History of Romanism.* Lincolnshire, IL: Vance.

Drake, H. A. 1996. "Lambs into Lions: Explaining Early Christian Intolerance." *Past and Present* 153:3–36.

———. 2000. *Constantine and the Bishops: The Politics of Intolerance.* Baltimore: Johns Hopkins.

Drake, Stillman, and C. D. O'Malley. 1960. *The Controversy of the Comets of 1618.* Philadelphia: Univ. of Pennsylvania Press.

Drogus, Carol Ann. 1995. "Review: The Rise and Decline of Liberation Theology: Churches, Faith, and Political Change in Latin America." *Comparative Politics* 27:465–77.

Duby, Georges. 1994. *The Knight, the Lady, and the Priest.* Chicago: Univ. of Chicago Press.

Duffy, Eamon. 1987. "The Late Middle Ages: Vitality or Decline?" In *Atlas of the Christian Church,* edited by Henry Chadwick and G. R. Evans, 86–95. New York: Facts on File.

———. 1992. *Stripping the Altars*. New Haven: Yale Univ. Press.

———. 1997. *Saints and Sinners: A History of Popes*. New Haven: Yale Univ. Press.

Duke, Sean. 1998. "Irish Bridge Sheds Light on Dark Ages." *Science* 279:480.

Dunn, J. D. G. 1985. *The Evidence for Jesus*. Philadelphia: Westminster.

Durant, Will. 1950. *The Age of Faith*. Vol. 4 of *The Story of Civilization*. New York: Simon and Schuster.

———. 1957. *The Reformation*. New York: Simon and Schuster.

Dworkin, Andrea. 1974. *Woman Hating: A Radical Look at Sexuality*. New York: Dutton.

Ebaugh, Helen Rose. 1993. *Women in the Vanishing Cloister: Organizational Decline of Catholic Religious Orders*. New Brunswick, NJ: Rutgers Univ. Press.

Edbury, Peter. 1999. "Warfare in the Latin East." In *Medieval Warfare: A History*, edited by Maurice Keen, 89–112. Oxford: Oxford Univ. Press.

Edwards, James R. 2005. *Is Jesus the Only Savior?* Grand Rapids: Eerdmans.

Edwards, Lyford P. 1919. *The Transformation of Early Christianity from an Eschatological to a Social Movement*. Menasha, WI: George Banta.

Edwards, Mark U. 1994. *Printing, Propaganda, and Martin Luther*. Berkeley: Univ. of California Press.

Ehrman, Bart D. 2003. *Lost Christianities: The Battles for Scripture and the Faiths We Never Knew*. Oxford: Oxford Univ. Press.

———. 2005. *Misquoting Jesus: The Story Behind Who Changed the Bible and Why*. San Francisco: Harper San Francisco.

———. 2006. *The Lost Gospel of Judas Iscariot: A New Look at Betrayer and Betrayed*. Oxford: Oxford Univ. Press.

Einstein, Albert. 1987. *Letters to Solovine*. New York: Philosphical Library.

Eisenstein, Elizabeth L. 1979. *The Printing Press as an Agent of Change*. Cambridge: Cambridge Univ. Press.

Ekelund, Robert B., Robert F. Hèbert, Robert Tollison, Gary M. Anderson, and Audrey B. Davidson. 1996. *Sacred Trust: The Medieval Church as an Economic Firm*. New York: Oxford Univ. Press.

Eliade, Mircea. [1958] 1974. *Patterns in Comparative Religion*. New York: New American Library.

Ellerbe, Helen. 1995. *The Dark Side of Christian History*. Windermere, FL: Morningstar and Lark.

Elliott, T. G. 1996. *The Christianity of Constantine the Great*. Scranton: Univ. of Scranton Press.

Engels, Friedrich. [1873] 1964. "Dialectics of Nature." Reprinted in Karl Marx and Friedrich Engels, *On Religion*, 152–93. Atlanta: Scholars Press.

———. [1894] 1964. "On the History of Early Christianity." Reprinted in Karl Marx and Friedrich Engels, *On Religion*, 316–59. Atlanta: Scholars Press.

Erdmann, Carl. 1977. *The Origin of the Idea of Crusade*. Princeton: Princeton Univ. Press.

Erdoes, Richard. 1988. *AD 1000: Living on the Brink of the Apocalypse*. New York: Harper & Row.

Eusebius [ca. 325] 1927. *The Ecclesiastical History and the Martyrs of Palestine*. London: Society for Promoting Christian Knowledge.

Evans, Craig A. 2001. "Context, Family and Formation." In *The Cambridge Companion to Jesus*, edited by Markus Bockmuel, 11–24. Cambridge: Cambridge Univ. Press.

———. 2002a. "Introduction: Finding a Context for Jesus." In *The Missing Jesus: Rabbinic Judaism and the New Testament*, edited by Bruce Chilton, Craig A. Evans, and Jacob Neusner, 1–9. Leiden: Brill.

———. 2002b. "The Misplaced Jesus: Interpreting Jesus in a Judaic Context." In *The Missing Jesus: Rabbinic Judaism and the New Testament*, edited by Bruce Chilton, Craig A. Evans, and Jacob Neusner, 11–39. Leiden: Brill.

———. 2006. *Fabricating Jesus: How Modern Scholars Distort the Gospels*. Downers Grove, IL: InterVarsity.

Ewen, C. L'Estrange. 1929. *Witch Hunting and Witch Trials*. London: Kegan, Paul, Trench, Trübner.

Farmer, David L. 1991. "Marketing the Produce of the Countryside, 1200–1500." In *The Agrarian History of England and Wales*, vol. 3, *1348–1500*, edited by Edward Miller, 324–58. Cambridge: Cambridge Univ. Press.

Fears, J. Rufus. 1987. "Sol Invictus." In *The Encyclopedia of Religion*, edited by Mircea Eliade. New York: Macmillan.

Feldman, Louis H. 1981. "Judaism, History of, III, Hellenic Judaism." In *Encyclopaedia Britannica*. Chicago: Univ. of Chicago Press.

———. 1992. "Was Judaism a Missionary Religion in Ancient Times?" In *Jewish Assimilation, Acculturation and Accommodation*, edited by Menachem Mor, 23–37. Lanham, MD: Univ. Press of America.

———. 1993. *Jew and Gentile in the Ancient World*. Princeton: Princeton Univ. Press.

Ferguson, Everette. 1990. "Deaconess." In *The Encyclopedia of Early Christianity*, edited by Everette Ferguson, New York: Garland.

Ferguson, John. 1970. *The Religions of the Roman Empire*. Ithaca, NY: Cornell Univ. Press.

Ferguson, Wallace K. 1939. "Humanist Views of the Renaissance." *American Historical Review* 45:1–28.

Fernandez, André. 1997. "The Repression of Sexual Behavior by the Aragonese Inquisition between 1560 and 1700." *Journal of the History of Sexuality* 7:469–501.

Ferngren, Gary B. 2009. *Medicine and Health Care in Early Christianity*. Baltimore: Johns Hopkins Univ. Press.

Ferrill, Arthur. 1986. *The Fall of the Roman Empire: The Military Explanation*. London: Thames and Hudson.

Filotas, Bernadette. 2005. *Pagan Survivals, Superstitions and Popular Cultures in Early Medieval Pastoral Literature*. Toronto: Pontifical Institute of Medieval Studies.

Findlen, Paul. 1993. "Humanism, Politics and Pornography in Renaissance Italy." In *The Invention of Pornography*, edited by Lynn Hunt, 49–108. Cambridge, MA: M.I.T. Press.

Finegan, Jack. 1992. *The Archeology of the New Testament*. Rev. ed. Princeton: Princeton Univ. Press.

Finke, Roger, and Rodney Stark. 1992. *The Churching of America, 1776–1990: Winners and Losers in Our Religious Economy*. New Brunswick, NJ: Rutgers Univ. Press.

———. 2005. *The Churching of America, 1776–1990: Winners and Losers in Our Religious Economy*, 2nd ed. New Brunswick, NJ: Rutgers Univ. Press.

Finley, M. I. 1973. *The Ancient Economy*. Berkeley: Univ. of California Press.

———. 1977. *Atlas of Classical Archaeology*. New York: McGraw-Hill.

Finocchiaro, Maurice A. 2009. "Myth 8: That Galileo Was Imprisoned and Tortured for Advocating Copernicanism." In *Galileo Goes to Jail: And Other Myths About Science and Religion*, edited by Ronald L. Numbers, 68–78. Cambridge: Harvard Univ. Press.

Fischoff, Ephraim. 1968. "The Protestant Ethic and the Spirit of Capitalism: The History of a Controversy." In *The Protestant Ethic and Modernization: A Comparative View*, edited by S. H. Eisenstadt, 67–86. New York: Basic Books.

Fletcher, Richard. 1997. *The Barbarian Conversion: From Paganism to Christianity*. New York: Henry Holt.

Flint, Valerie I. J. 1991. *The Rise of Magic in Early Medieval Europe*. Princeton: Princeton Univ. Press

Fogel, Robert William. 2000. *The Fourth Great Awakening and the Future of Egalitarianism*. Chicago: Univ. of Chicago Press.

Foltz, Richard. 2000. *Religions of the Silk Road*. New York: St. Martin's.

Fox, Robin Lane. 1987. *Pagans and Christians*. New York: Knopf.

France, John. 1997. *Victory in the East*. Cambridge: Cambridge Univ. Press.

Franits, Wayne E. 2004. *Dutch Seventeenth Century Genre Painting*. New Haven: Yale Univ. Press.

Freeman, Charles. 1999. *The Greek Achievement: The Foundation of the Western World*. New York: Penguin Books.

Fremantle, Anne. 1954. *The Age of Belief*. New York: Mentor.

Frend, W. H. C. 1959. "The Failure of the Persecutions in the Roman Empire." *Past and Present* 16:10–30.

———. 1965. *Martyrdom and Persecution in the Early Church*. Oxford: Basil Blackwell.

———. 1984. *The Rise of Christianity*. Philadelphia: Fortress.

Frier, Bruce W. 1994. "Natural Fertility and Family Limitation in Roman Marriage." *Classical Philology* 89:318–33.

Fuller, Russell. 2003. "The Rabbis and the Claims of the Openness Advocates." In *Beyond the Bounds*, edited by John Piper, Justine Taylor, and Paul Kjoss Helseth, 23–41. Wheaton, IL: Crossway Books.

Funk, Robert. 1996. *Honest to Jesus*. San Francisco: Harper San Francisco.

Funk, Robert W., Roy W. Hoover, and the Jesus Seminar. 1993. *The Five Gospels: The Search for the Authentic Words of Jesus*. New York: Macmillan.

Furseth, Inger, and Pal Repstad. 2006. *An Introduction to the Sociology of Religion*. Aldershot, UK: Ashgate.

Gager, John G. 1975. *Kingdom and Community: The Social World of Early Christianity*. Englewood Cliffs, NJ: Prentice-Hall.

———. 1983. *The Origins of Anti-Semitism: Attitudes Towards Judaism in Pagan and Christian Antiquity*. New York: Oxford Univ. Press.

Galvao-Sobrinho, Carlos R. 1995. "Funerary Epigraphy and the Spread of Christianity in the West." *Athenaeum* 83:431–66.

Gambero, Luigi. 1991. *Mary and the Fathers of the Church*. San Francisco: Ignatius.

Gamble, Harry Y. 1995. *Books and Readers in the Early Church: A History of Early Christian Texts*. New Haven: Yale Univ. Press.

Gardner, Helen, and Sumner McK. Crosby. 1959. *Helen Gardner's Art Through the Ages*. New York: Harcourt, Brace, & World.

Gasque, W. Ward. 2000. *A History of the Interpretation of the Acts of the Apostles*. Eugene, OR: Wipf and Stock.

Gatrell, V. A. C. 1994. *The Hanging Tree: Execution and the English People, 1770–1868*. Oxford: Oxford University Press.

Gaustad, Edwin S. 1987. *Faith of Our Fathers*. San Francisco: Harper & Row.

Gawthrop, Richard, and Gerald Strauss. 1984. "Protestantism and Literacy in Early Modern Germany." *Past and Present* 104:31–55.

Gay, Peter. 1966. *The Enlightenment: An Interpretation*. New York: Norton.

Geffcken, Johannes. [1920] 1978. *The Last Days of Greco-Roman Paganism*. Amsterdam: North-Holland.

Geisler, Norman, and William Nix. 1986. *A General Introduction to the Bible*. Chicago: Moody Publishers.

Geller, M. J. 1994. "Early Christianity and the Dead Sea Scrolls." *Bulletin of the School of Oriental and African Studies, University of London* 57:82–86.

Georgi, Dieter. 1995. "The Early Church: Internal Migration of New Religion." *Harvard Theological Review* 88:35–68.

Gerber, Jane S. 1994. *The Jews of Spain*. New York: The Free Press.

Gerhardsson, Birger. 2001. *The Reliability of the Gospel Tradition*. Peabody. MA: Hendrickson.

Gershevitch, Ilya. 1964. "Zoroaster's Own Contribution." *Journal of Near Eastern Studies* 23:12–28.

Getty-Sullivan, Mary Ann. 2001. *Women in the New Testament*. Collegeville, MN: Liturgical Press.

Gibbon, Edward. [1776–1788] 1994. *The History of the Decline and Fall of the Roman Empire*. 3 vols. London: Allen Lane: Penguin.

Gierke, Otto. [1873] 1977. *Associations and Law: The Classical and Early Christian Stages*. Toronto: Univ. of Toronto Press.

Gies, Frances and Joseph Gies. 1994. *Cathedral, Forge, and Waterwheel: Technology and Invention in the Middle Ages*. New York: HarperCollins.

Gil, Moshe. 1992. *A History of Palestine, 634–1099*. Cambridge: Cambridge Unive. Press.

Gilchrist, John. 1969. *The Church and Economic Activity in the Middle Ages*. New York: St. Martin's Press.

Gill, Anthony. 1998. *Rendering Unto Caesar: The Catholic Church and the State in Latin America*. Chicago: Univ. of Chicago Press.

———. 2005. "The Political Origins of Religious Liberty." *Interdisciplinary Journal of Research on Religion* 1 (1):1–35.

Gilliam, J. F. 1961. "The Plague Under Marcus Aurelius." *American Journal of Philology* 82:225–51.

Gillingham, John. 1999. "An Age of Expansion: c. 1020–1204." In *Medieval Warfare: A History*, edited by Maurice Keen, 59–88. Oxford: Oxford Univ. Press.

Gilmont, Jean-Francois. 1998. *The Reformation and the Book*. Aldershot, UK: Ashgate.

Gimpel, Jean. 1961. *The Cathedral Builders*. New York: Grove.

———. 1976. *The Medieval Machine: The Industrial Revolution of the Middle Ages*. New York: Penguin Books.

Gingerich, Owen. 1975. "'Crisis' Versus Aesthetic in the Copernican Revolution." *Vistas in Astronomy* 17:85–93.

Given, James B. 1997. *Inquisition and Medieval Society: Power, Discipline, and Resistance in Languedoc*. Ithaca, NY: Cornell Univ. Press.

Glock, Charles Y. 1964. "The Role of Deprivation in the Origin and Evolution of Religious Groups." In *Religion and Social Conflict*, edited by Robert Lee and Martin E. Marty, 24–26. New York: Oxford Univ. Press.

Glubb, Lieutenant-General Sir John Bagot. [1963] 1995. *The Great Arab Conquests*. New York: Barnes and Noble.

Gnoli, Gherardo. 1987. "Magi." In *The Encyclopedia of Religion*, edited by Mircea Eliade. New York: Macmillan.

———. 2000. *Zoroaster in History*. New York: Bibliotheca Persica.

Goldstein, Jonathan A. 1987. "How the Authors of 1 and 2 Maccabees Treated the 'Messianic' Promises." In *Judaisms and Their Messiahs at the Turn of the Christian Era*, edited by Jacob Neusner, William Scott Green, and Ernest S. Fredrichs, 139–68. Cambridge: Cambridge Univ. Press.

Goodenough, Erwin R. [1931] 1970. *The Church in the Roman Empire*. New York: Cooper Square.

———. 1962. *An Introduction to Philo Judaeus*. 2nd ed. Oxford: Blackwell.

Goodish, Michael. 1976. "Sodomy in Medieval Secular Law." *Journal of Homosexuality* 1:295–302.

Goodman, Martin. 1994. *Mission and Conversion: Proselytizing in the Religious History of the Roman Empire*. Oxford: Clarendon.

Goodspeed, Edgar. 1931. *Strange New Gospels*. Chicago: Univ. of Chicago Press.

Gorman, Michael J. 1982. *Abortion and the Early Church*. Downers Grove, IL: InterVarsity.

Grant, Edward. 1971. *Physical Science in the Middle Ages*. New York: Wiley.

———. 1994. *Planets, Stars, and Orbs: The Medieval Cosmos, 1200–1687*. Cambridge: Cambridge Univ. Press.

———. 1996. *The Foundations of Modern Science in the Middle Ages: Their Religious, Institutional, and Intellectual Contexts*. Cambridge: Cambridge Univ. Press.

Grant, Michael. 1978. *The History of Rome*. New York: Faber and Faber.

Grant, Robert M. [1970] 1990. *Augustus to Constantine: The Rise and Triumph of Christianity in the Roman World*. San Francisco: Harper San Francisco.

———. 1973. *The Jews in the Roman World*. New York: Scribner.

———. 1977. *Early Christianity and Society: Seven Studies*. London: Collins.

———. 1986. *Gods and the One God*. Philadelphia: Westminster.

Greeley, Andrew J. 1970. "Religious Intermarriage in a Denominational Society." *American Sociological Review* 75:949–52.

Greely, Andrew M. 1995. *Religion as Poetry*. New Brunswick, NJ: Transaction Publishers.

Green, Joel B. 1997. *The Gospel of Luke*. Grand Rapids: Eerdmans.

Grendler, Paul F. 2004. "The Universities of the Renaissance and Reformation." *Renaissance Quarterly* 57:1–42.

Grim, Brian J., and Roger Finke. 2010. *The Price of Freedom Denied*. New York: Cambridge Univ. Press.

Grimm, Harold J. 1962. "Social Forces in the German Reformation." *Church History* 31:3–13.

———. 1969. "The Reformation and the Urban Social Classes in Germany." In *Luther, Erasmus and the Reformation*, edited by John C. Olin, James D. Smart, and Robert E. McNally, SJ, 75–86. New York: Fordham Univ. Press.

Gryson, Roger. 1976. *The Ministry of Women in the Early Church*. Collegeville, MN: The Liturgical Press.

Haas, Christopher J. 1983. "Imperial Policy and Valarian's Persecution of the Church, A.D. 257–260." *Church History* 52:133–44.

Hagner, Donald A. 2007. "Paul as a Jewish Believer—According to His Letters." In *Jewish Believers in Jesus: The Early Centuries*, edited by Oskar Skarsaune and Reidar Hvalik, 96–120. Peabody, MA: Hendrickson.

Hale, J. R. 1977. *Florence and the Medici*. London: Thames & Hudson.

Haliczer, Stephen. 1990. *Inquisition and Society in the Kingdom of Valencia, 1487–1834*. Berkeley: Univ. of California Press.

Halsberghe, Gaston H. 1972. *The Cult of Sol Invictus*. Leiden: Brill.

Hamilton, Bernard. 2000. *The Leper King and His Heirs: Baldwin IV and the Crusader Kingdom of Jerusalem*. Cambridge: Cambridge Univ. Press.

Hamilton, Richard F. 1996. *The Social Misconstruction of Reality: Validity and Verification in the Scholarly Community*. New Haven: Yale Univ. Press.

Handlin, Oscar. ed. 1949. *This Was America*. Cambridge: Harvard Univ. Press.

Hannemann, Manfred. 1975. *The Diffusion of the Reformation in Southwestern Germany, 1518–1534*. Chicago: Univ. of Chicago Department of Geography, Research Paper No. 167.

Hanson, R. P. C. 1968. *The Acts*. Oxford: Clarendon.

Hare, Douglas. 1967. *The Theme of Jewish Persecution of Christians in the Gospel According to Matthew*. Cambridge: Cambridge Univ. Press.

Harl, K. W. 1990. "Sacrifice and Pagan Belief in Fifth- and Sixth-Century Byzantium." *Past and Present* 128:7–27.

Harnack, Adolf von. 1904. *The Expansion of Christianity in the First Three Centuries*. Vol. 1. New York: Putnam's Sons.

———. 1905. *The Expansion of Christianity in the First Three Centuries*. Vol. 2. New York: Putnam's Sons, 1905.

———. [1924] 1990. *Marcion: The Gospel of the Alien God*. Durham, NC: Labyrinth.

Harris, Marvin. [1977] 1991. *Cannibals and Kings*. New York: Vantage.

Harris, William V. 1982. "The Theoretical Possibility of Extensive Infanticide in the Graeco-Roman World." *Classical Quarterly*, new series, 32:114–16.

———. 1989. *Ancient Literacy*. Cambridge: Harvard Univ. Press.

———. 1994. "Child Exposure in the Roman Empire." *Journal of Roman Studies* 84:1–22.

Hay, Denys. 1977. *The Church in Italy in the Fifteenth Century*. Cambridge: Cambridge Univ. Press.

Hayes, Carlton, J. H. 1917. *Political and Social History of Modern Europe*. 2 vols. New York: Macmillan.

Heaton, Tim B. 1990. "Religious Group Characteristics, Endogamy, and Interfaith Marriages." *Sociological Analysis* 51:363–76.

Heine, Susanne. 1988. *Women and Early Christianity*. Minneapolis: Augsburg.

Hemer, Colin J. 1990. *The Book of Acts in the Setting of Hellenistic History*. Winona Lake, IN: Eisenbrauns.

Hengel, Martin. 1974. *Judaism and Hellenism: Studies in their Encounter in Palestine During the Early Hellenistic Period*. 2 vols. Philadelphia: Fortress.

———. 1989. *The "Hellenization" of Judea in the First Century After Christ*. London: SCM.

Henningsen, Gustav. 1980. *The Witches Advocate: Basque Witchcraft and the Spanish Inquisition (1609–1614)*. Reno: Univ. of Nevada Press.

Henningsen, Gustav, and John Tedeschi. 1986. *The Inquisition in Early Modern Europe: Studies on Sources and Methods*. Dekalb: Northern Illinois Univ. Press.

Heyob, Sharon Kelly. 1975. *The Cult of Isis among Women in the Greco-Roman World*. Leiden: Brill.

Hibbert, Christopher. [1974] 2003. *The House of Medici: Its Rise and Fall*. New York: HarperCollins.

Hill, Christopher. 1967. *Reformation to the Industrial Revolution, 1530–1780*. London: Penguin Books.

Hill, Craig C. 2007. "The Jerusalem Church." In *Jewish Christianity Reconsidered*, edited by Matt Jackson-McCabe, 39–56. Minneapolis: Fortress.

Hillenbrand, Carole. 1999. *The Crusades: Islamic Perspectives*. Edinburgh: Edinburgh Univ. Press.

Hirschfeld, Nicolle. 1990. "The Ship of Saint Paul: Historical Background." *Biblical Archaeologist* 53 (March):25–30.

Hobbes, Thomas. [1651] 1956. *Leviathan*. Vol. 1. Chicago: Henrey Regnery.

Hodgson, Marshall G. S. 1974. *The Venture of Islam: Conscience and History in a World Civilization*. 3 vols. Chicago: Univ. of Chicago Press.

Holborn, Louise W. 1942. "Printing and the Growth of a Protestant Movement in Germany from 1517 to 1524." *Church History* 11:123–37.

Holinshed, Raphael. [1587] 1965. *Holinshed's Chronicles*. New York: AMS.

Hollister, C. Warren. 1992. "The Phases of European History and the Nonexistence of the Middle Ages." *Pacific Historical Review* 61:1–22.

Hookham, Hilda. 1981. "Timur." In *Encyclopaedia Britannica*. Chicago: Univ. of Chicago Press.

Hopkins, Keith. 1965. "The Age of Roman Girls at Marriage." *Population Studies* 18:309–27.

———. 1966. "On the Probable Age Structure of the Roman Population." *Population Studies* 20:245–64.

———. 1998. "Christian Number and its Implications." *Journal of Early Christian Studies*. 6:185–226.

———. 2004. "Controlling Religion: Rome." In *Religions of the Ancient World: A Guide*, edited by Sarah Iles Johnston, 572–75. Cambridge: Belknap.

Horsley, Richard A., and John S. Hanson. 1985. *Bandits, Prophets, and Messiahs: Popular Movements in the Time of Jesus*. Minneapolis: Winston.

Hout, Michael, and Claude Fischer. 2002. "Americans with 'No Religion': Why Their Numbers Are Growing." *American Sociological Review* 67:165–90.

Hughes, Pennethorne. 1952. *Witchcraft*. London: Longmans, Green.

Hultgren, Arland J. 1976. "Paul's Pre-Christian Persecutions of the Church: Their Purpose, Locale, and Nature." *Journal of Biblical Literature* 95:97–111.

Hume, David. 1754. *The History of England*. 6 vols. London: A. Millar.

Hunt, Dave. 1994. *A Woman Rides the Beast: The Roman Catholic Church and the Last Days*. Eugene, OR: Harvest House.

Hunt, Edwin S., and James M. Murray. 1999. *A History of Business in Medieval Europe, 1200–1550*. Cambridge: Cambridge Univ. Press.

Hurtado, Larry W. 1999. "Pre–70 Jewish Opposition to Christ-Devotion." *Journal of Theological Studies* 50:35–58.

———. 2003. *Lord Jesus Christ: Devotion to Jesus in Earliest Christianity*. Grand Rapids: Eerdmans.

———. 2006. *The Earliest Christian Artifacts: Manuscripts and Christian Origins*. Grand Rapids: Eerdmans.

Hutchison, William R. 1987. *Errand to the World: American Protestant Thought and Foreign Missions*. Chicago: Univ. of Chicago Press.

Hvalvik, Reidar. 2007. "Jewish Believers and Jewish Influence in the Roman Church Until the Early Second Century." In *Jewish Believers in Jesus: The Early Centuries*, edited by Oskar Skarsaune and Reidar Hvalik, 179–216. Peabody, MA: Hendrickson.

Hyde, H. Montgomery. 1964. *A History of Pornography*. New York: Dell.

Hyslop, Theo B. 1925. *The Great Abnormals*. New York: Doran.

Iannaccone, Laurence R. 1982. "Let the Women Be Silent." *Sunstone* 7 (May–June):38–45.

Introvigne, Massimo. 2005. "Niches in the Islamic Religious Market and Fundamentalism: Examples from Turkey and Other Countries." *Interdisciplinary Journal of Research on Religion* 1: article 3. Available at www.religjournal.com.

Introvigne, Massimo, and Rodney Stark. 2005. "Religious Competition and Revival in Italy: Exploring European Exceptionalism." *Interdisciplinary Journal of Research on Religion* 1: article 5. Available at www.religjournal.com.

Irwin, Robert. 1986. *The Middle East in the Middle Ages: The Early Mamluk Sultanate 1250–1382*. Carnondale, IL: Southern Illinois Univ. Press.

———. 2006. *Dangerous Knowledge: Orientalism and Its Discontents*. Woodstock and New York: The Overlook Press.

Isaac, Jules. 1964. *The Teaching of Contempt: Christian Roots of Anti-Semitism*. New York: Holt, Rinehart, and Winston.

———. 1971. *Jesus and Israel*. New York: Holt, Rinehart, and Winston.

Issawi, Charles. 1957. "Crusades and Current Crisis in the Near East: A Historical Parallel." *International Affairs* 33:269–79.

Jaki, Stanley L. 1986. *Science and Creation*. Edinburgh: Scottish Academic Press.

———. 2000. *The Savior of Science*. Grand Rapids: Eerdmans.

James, William. [1902] 1958. *The Varieties of Religious Experience*. New York: A Mentor Book.

Jamison, Alan G. 2006. *Faith and Sword: A Short History of Christian-Muslim Conflict*. London: Reaktion Books.

Jeffrey, Peter. 2007. *The Secret Gospel of Mark Unveiled*. New Haven: Yale Univ. Press.

Jenkins, Philip. 2001. *Hidden Gospels: How the Search for Jesus Lost Its Way*. Oxford: Oxford Univ. Press.

———. 2002. *The Next Christendom: The Coming of Global Christianity*. Oxford: Oxford Univ. Press.

———. 2003. *The New Anti-Catholicism: The Last Acceptable Prejudice*. Oxford: Oxford Univ. Press.

———. 2008. *The Lost History of Christianity*. San Francisco: HarperOne.

Johnson, Luke Timothy. 1996. *The Real Jesus: The Misguided Quest for the Historical Jesus and the Truth of the Traditional Gospels*. San Francisco: Harper San Francisco.

Johnson, Paul. 1976. *A History of Christianity*. New York: Atheneum.

———. 1987. *A History of the Jews*. New York: Harper & Row.

———. 2003. *Art: A New History*. New York: HarperCollins.

Jonas, Hans. 1967. "Delimitation of the Gnostic Phenomenon—Typological and Historical." In *Le Origini Dello Gnosticismo*, edited by U. Bianchi, 90–108. Leiden: Brill.

———. 2001. *The Gnostic Religion*. 3rd ed. Boston: Beacon.

Jones, A. H. M. 1948. *Constantine and the Conversion of Europe*. London: Hodder & Stoughton.

Jones, E. L. 1987. *The European Miracle*. 2nd ed. Cambridge: Cambridge Univ. Press.

Jones, Paul. 2006. "From Intra-Jewish Polemics to Persecution: The Christian Formation of the Jew as Religious Other." *Encounter* (Spring).

Jones, W. T. 1969. *The Medieval Mind*. New York: Harcourt, Brace and World.

Judge, E. A. 1960a. *The Social Pattern of Christian Groups in the First Century*. London: Tyndale.

———. 1960b. "The Early Christians as a Scholastic Community." *Journal of Religious History* 1:125–41.

———. 1986. "The Quest for Mercy in Late Antiquity." In *God Who Is Rich in Mercy: Essays Presented to D. B. Knox*, edited by P. T. O'Brien and D. G. Peterson, 107–21. Sydney: Macquarie Univ. Press.

———. 2008. *Social Distinctives of the Christians of the First Century*. Peabody, MA: Hendrickson.

Justin Martyr. [ca. 150] 1948. "First Apology." *Writings of Saint Justin Martyr*. New York: Christian Heritage.

Kadushin, Max. 1965. *The Rabbinic Mind*. 2nd ed. New York: Blaisdell.

Kaelber, Lutz. 1997. "Weavers into Heretics? The Social Organization of Early-Thirteenth-Century Catharism in Comparative Perspective." *Social Science History* 21:111–37.

Kamen, Henry. 1993. *The Phoenix and the Flame: Catalonia and the Counter Reformation*. New Haven: Yale Univ. Press.

———. 1997. *The Spanish Inquisition: An Historical Revision*. London: Weidenfeld & Nicholson.

Karsh, Efraim. 2007. *Islamic Imperialism: A History*. New Haven: Yale Univ. Press.

Katz, Steven T. 1994. *The Holocaust in Historical Context*. Vol. 1. New York: Oxford Univ. Press.

Kaufmann, Eric. 2010. *Shall the Religious Inherit the Earth?* London: Profile Books.

Kaufmann, Yehazkel. 1970. *The Babylonian Captivity and Deutero-Isaiah*. New York: Union of American Hebrew Congregations.

Kautsky, Karl. [1908] 1953. *Foundations of Christianity*. New York: Russell & Russell.

Kedar, Benjamin Z. 1974. "The General Tax of 1183 in the Crusading Kingdom of Jerusalem: Innovation or Adaptation?" *English Historical Review* 89:339–45.

———. 1984. *Crusade and Mission: European Approaches Toward the Muslims*. Princeton: Princeton Univ. Press.

———. [1990] 2002. "The Subjected Muslims of the Frankish Levant." In *The Crusades: The Essential Readings*, edited by Thomas F. Madden, 235–64. Oxford: Blackwell.

Kee, Howard Clark. 1970. *Jesus in History*. New York: Harcourt, Brace & World.

———. 1987. "Christology in Mark's Gospel." In *Judaisms and Their Messiahs at the Turn of the Christian Era*, edited by Jacob Neusner, William Scott Green, and Ernest S. Fredrichs, 187–208. Cambridge: Cambridge Univ. Press.

———. 1990. *What Can We Know About Jesus?* Cambridge: Cambridge Univ. Press.

Keen, Benjamin. 1969. "The Black Legend Revisited: Assumptions and Realities." *Hispanic American Historical Review* 49:703–19.

Kent, Stephen A. 2001. *From Slogans to Mantras: Social Protest and Religious Conversion in the Late Viet Nam War Era*. Syracuse, NY: Syracuse Univ. Press.

Kenyon, Sir Frederic George. 1949. *The Bible and Archeology*. New York: Harper.

Keresztes, Paul. 1968. "Marcus Aurelius a Persecutor?" *Harvard Theological Review* 61:321–41.

———. 1970a. "The Constitutio Antoniana and the Persecutions Under Caracalla." *American Journal of Philology* 91:446–59.

———. 1970b. "The Emperor Septimius Severus: A Precursor of Decius." *Histoira* 19:565–78.

———. 1973. "The Jews, the Christians, and Emperor Domitan." *Vigiliae Christianae* 27:1–28.

———. 1983. "From the Great Persecution to the Peace of Galerius." *Vigiliae Christianae* 37:379–99.

Khalidi, Tarif. 1981. "The Idea of Progress in Classical Islam." *Journal of Near Eastern Studies* 40:277–89.

Kieckhefer, Richard. 1976. *European Witch Trials: Their Foundations in Popular and Learned Culture*. Berkeley: Univ. of California Press.

———. 1989. *Magic in the Middle Ages*. Cambridge: Cambridge Univ. Press.

Kim, Hyojoung, and Steven Pfaff. Forthcoming. "Structure and Dynamics of a Religious Insurgency: The Early Reformation in 16th Century Central Europe."

King, Karen L. 2003a. *What Is Gnosticism?* Cambridge: Belknap.

———. 2003b. *The Gospel of Mary of Magdala: Jesus and the First Woman Apostle*. Santa Rose, CA: Polebridge.

Kirsch, Jonathan. 2004. *God Against the Gods*. New York: Viking.

———. 2008. *The Grand Inquisitor's Manuel: A History of Terror in the Name of God*. San Francisco: HarperOne.

Kister, M. J. 1986. "The Massacre of the Banū Qurayza: A Re-examination of a Tradition." *Jerusalem Studies of Arabic and Islam* 8:61–96.

Kitchen, K. A. 2003. *On the Reliability of the Old Testament*. Grand Rapids: Eerdmans.

Kittleson, James. 1986. *Luther the Reformer*. Minneapolis: Augsburg Fortress.

Klaiber, Jeffrey L. 1970. "Pentecostal Breakthrough." *America* 122 (4):99–102.

Klauck, Hans-Joseph. 2003. *The Religious Context of Early Christianity*. Minneapolis: Fortress Press.

Klinghoffer, David. 2005. *Why the Jews Rejected Jesus*. New York: Doubleday.

Knight, Margaret. 1974. *Honest to Man: Christian Ethics Re-examined*. Buffalo, NY: Prometheus Books.

Knobler, Adam. 2006. "Holy Wars, Empires, and the Portability of the Past: The Modern Uses of the Medieval Crusade." *Comparative Studies in Society and History* 48:293–325.

Knohl, Israel. 2000. *The Messiah Before Jesus*. Berkeley: Univ. of California Press.

———. 2008. "The Messiah Son of Joseph." *Biblical Archaeology Review* 34 (September/October):58–62, 78.

Koenig, Harold G. 1998. *Handbook of Religion and Mental Health*. New York: Academic Press.

Koester, Helmut. 1982a. *Introduction to the New Testament*, vol. 1, *History, Culture, and Religion in the Hellenistic Age*. Philadelphia: Fortress.

———. 1982b. *Introduction to the New Testament*, vol. 2, *History and Literature of Early Christianity*. Philadelphia: Fortress.

Komoszewski, J. Ed, M. James Sawyer, and Daniel B. Wallace. 2006. *Reinventing Jesus*. Grand Rapids: Kregel.

Kox, Willem, Wim Meeus, and Harm t'Hart. 1991. "Religious Conversion of Adolescents: Testing the Lofland and Stark Model of Religious Conversion." *Sociological Analysis* 52:227–40.

Kraemer, Ross Sherpard. 1992. *Her Share of the Blessings: Women's Religions among Pagans, Jews, and Christians in the Greco-Roman World*. Oxford: Oxford Univ. Press.

Kripal, Jeffery J. 2007. *Esalen: America and the Religion of No Religion*. Chicago: Univ. of Chicago Press.

Ladurie, Emmanuel LeRoy. 1974. *The Peasants of Languedoc*. Urbana: Univ. of Illinois Press.

Lambert, Malcolm. 1992. *Medieval Heresy: Popular Movements from the Gregorian Reform to the Reformation*. 2nd ed. Oxford: Basil Blackwell.

———. 1998. *The Cathars*. Oxford: Blackwell.

LaMonte, John L. 1932. *Feudal Monarchy in the Latin Kingdom of Jerusalem, 1100–1291*. Cambridge: Harvard Univ. Press.

Landes, David S. 1998. *The Wealth and Poverty of Nations*. New York: W. W. Norton.

Lane, Frederic Chapin. [1934] 1992. *Venetian Ships and Shipbuilders of the Renaissance*. Baltimore: Johns Hopkins Univ. Press.

Lang, Bernard. 1983. *Monotheism and the Prophetic Majority*. Sheffield, UK: Almond.

Latourette, Kenneth Scott. 1937. *A History of the Expansion of Christianity*. Vol. 1. New York: Harper & Bros.

———. 1975. *A History of Christianity*. Vol. 2. Rev. ed. San Francisco: Harper San Francisco.

Layton, Bentley. 1987. *The Gnostic Scriptures*. Garden City, NY: Doubleday.

Lea, Henry C. 1902. "The Eve of the Reformation." In *The Cambridge Modern History*, 1:653–692. Cambridge: Cambridge Univ. Press.

———. 1906–1907. *A History of the Inquisition in Spain*. 4 vols. New York: Macmillan.

Leadbetter, Bill. 2000. "Constantine." In *The Early Christian World*, vol. 2, edited by Philip E. Esler, 1069–87. London: Routledge.

Leatham, Miguel C. 1997. "Rethinking Religious Decision-Making in Peasant Millenarianism: The Case of Nueva Jerusalem." *Journal of Contemporary Religion* 12:295–309.

Le Blant, Edmond. 1880. "La Richesse et la Christianisme à l'âge des Persécutions." *Revue Archéologique* 39:220–30.

Lecky, W. E. H. [1865] 1903. *History of the Rise and Influence of the Spirit of Rationalism in Europe*. New York: D. Appleton.

Leff, Gordon. [1967] 1999. *Heresy in the Later Middle Ages*. Manchester: Manchester Univ. Press.

Lefkowitz, Mary R., and Maureen B. Fant. 2005. *Women's Life in Greece and Rome: A Source Book in Translation*. 3rd ed. Baltimore: Johns Hopkins Univ. Press.

Leloup, Jean-Yves. 2002. *The Gospel of Mary Magdalene*. Rochester, VT: Inner Traditions.

Leon, Harry J. [1960] 1995. *The Jews of Ancient Rome*. Peabody, MA: Hendrickson Publishers.

Lester, Robert C. 1993. "Buddhism: The Path to Nirvana." In *Religious Traditions of the World*, edited by H. Byron Earhart, 849–971. San Francisco: Harper San Francisco.

Levack, Brian P. 1995. *The Witch-Hunt in Early Modern Europe*. 2nd ed. London: Longman.

Levenson, David. B. 1990. "Julian." In *Encyclopedia of Early Christianity*, edited by Everett Ferguson, 510–11. New York: Garland.

Levine, Lee I. 1998. *Judaism and Hellenism in Antiquity*. Seattle: Univ. of Washington Press.

Levy-Rubin, Milka. 2000. "New Evidence Relating to the Process of Islamization in Palestine in the Early Muslim Period: The Case of Samaria." *Journal of the Economic and Social History of the Orient* 43:257–76.

Lewis, Bernard. 2002. *What Went Wrong? Western Impact and Middle East Response*. Oxford: Oxford Univ. Press.

Lichter, S. Robert, Stanley Rothman, and Linda Lichter. 1986. *The Media Elite*. Bethesda, MD: Adler & Adler.

Lieberman, Saul. 1945. *Greek in Jewish Palestine*. New York: Jewish Theological Seminary of America.

———. 1962. *Hellenism in Jewish Palestine*. 2nd ed. New York: Jewish Theological Seminary of America.

Liebeschuetz, J. H. W. G. 1979. *Continuity and Change in Roman Religion*. Oxford: Clarendon.

Lindberg, David C. 1978. *Science in the Middle Ages*. Chicago: Univ. of Chicago Press.

———. 1986. "Science and the Early Church." In *God and Nature: Historical Essays on the Encounter Between Christianity and Science*, edited by David C. Lindberg and Ronald L. Numbers, 19–48. Berkeley: Univ. of California Press.

———. 1992. *The Beginnings of Western Science*. Chicago: Univ. of Chicago Press.

Lindberg, David C., and Ronald L. Numbers, eds. 1986. *God and Nature: Historical Essays on the Encounter Between Christianity and Science*. Berkeley: Univ. of California Press.

Lindsay, Jack. 1968. *The Ancient World: Manners and Morals*. New York: Putnam's Sons.

Lindsey, Robert L. 1989. *Jesus Rabbi and Lord: The Hebrew Story of Jesus Behind the Gospels*. Oak Creek, WI: Cornerstone.

Lintott, Andrew W. 1968. *Violence in Republican Rome*. Oxford: Oxford Univ. Press.

Little, Donald P. 1976. "Coptic Conversion to Islam Under the Mahri Mamlūks, 692–755/1293–1354." *Bulletin of the School of Oriental and African Studies, University of London* 39:552–69.

Little, Lester K. 1978. *Religious Poverty and the Profit Economy in Medieval Europe*. Ithaca, NY: Cornell Univ. Press.

Littman, R. J., and M. L. Littman. 1973. "Galen and the Antonine Plague." *American Journal of Philology* 94:243–55.

Liu, Eric. Forthcoming. "Risk Preference and Religiosity in the Chinese Context."

Llorente, Juan Antonio. [1823] 1967. *A Critical History of the Inquisition of Spain*. Williamstown, MA: John Lilburne.

Lodberg, Peter. 1989. "The Churches in Denmark." In *Danish Christian Handbook*, edited by Peter Briierly, 6–9. London: MARC Europe.

Lofland, John, and Rodney Stark. 1965. "Becoming a World-Saver: A Theory of Conversion to a Deviant Perspective." *American Sociological Review* 30:862–75.

Löhr, Winrich. 2007. "Western Christianities." In Augustine Casiday and Frederick W. Norris, *The Cambridge History of Christianity*, Vol. 2, 9–51. Cambridge: Cambridge Univ. Press.

Lopez, Robert S. 1967. *The Birth of Europe*. New York: M. Evans.

———. 1976. *The Commercial Revolution of the Middle Ages, 950–1350*. Cambridge: Cambridge Univ. Press.

———. 1977. "The Practical Transmission of Medieval Culture." In *By Things Seen: Reference and Recognition in Medieval Thought*, edited by David Lyle Jeffrey, 125–42. Ottawa: Univ. of Ottawa Press.

Luther, Martin. [1520] 1915. *Works*. Vol. 2. Philadelphia: Muhlenberg Press.

Luttwak, Edward N. 1976. *The Grand Strategy of the Roman Empire*. Baltimore: Johns Hopkins Univ. Press.

MacCulloch, Diarmaid. 2010. "Evil Is Just." *London Review of Books* 32 (May 13):23–24.

Mack, Burton. 1988. *A Myth of Innocence: Mark and Christian Origins*. Philadelphia: Fortress.

———. 1993. *The Lost Gospel: The Book of Q and Christian Origins*. New York: HarperCollins.

MacKenzie, Norman, and Jeanne MacKenzie. 1977. *The Fabians*. New York: Simon & Schuster.

MacMullen, Ramsay. 1963. *Soldier and Civilian in the Later Roman Empire*. Cambridge: Harvard Univ. Press.

———. 1981. *Paganism in the Roman Empire*. New Haven: Yale Univ. Press.

———. 1984. *Christianizing the Roman Empire*. New Haven: Yale Univ. Press.

———. 1997. *Christianity & Paganism in the Fourth to Eighth Centuries*. New Haven: Yale Univ. Press.

Macmurray, John. 1938. *The Clue to History*. London: Student Christian Movement.

Madden, Thomas F. 1999. *A Concise History of the Crusades*. Lanham, MD: Rowman & Littlefield.

———. 2002a. "The Real History of the Crusades." *Crisis Magazine*, online edition, April 1.

———. 2002b. "The Crusades in the Checkout Aisle." *Crisis Magazine* e-letter, April 12.

———. 2003. "The Truth About the Spanish Inquisition." *Crisis Magazine* (October):24–30.

Malherbe, Abraham J. 2003. *Social Aspects of Early Christianity*. 2nd ed. Eugene, OR: Wipf and Stock.

Maltby, William S. 1971. *The Black Legend in England: The Development of Anti-Spanish Sentiment, 1558–1660*. Durham, NC: Duke Univ. Press.

Manchester, William. 1993. *World Lit Only by Fire: The Medieval Mind and the Renaissance*. New York: Little, Brown.

Marozzi, Justin. 2004. *Tamerlane: Sword of Islam, Conqueror of the World*. Cambridge, MA: Da Capo Books.

Marshall, Paul, Lela Gilbert, Roberta Green Ahmanson, eds. 2010. *Blind Spot: When Journalists Don't Get Religion*. Oxford: Oxford Univ. Press.

Martin, David. 1969. *The Religious and the Secular*. New York: Schocken Books.

——. 1990. *Tongues of Fire: The Explosion of Protestantism in Latin America*. Oxford: Basil Blackwell.

Marty, Martin. 2004. *Martin Luther*. New York: Viking Penguin.

Marx, Karl. [1844] 1964. "Contribution to the Critique of Hegel's Philosophy of Right." In Karl Marx and Friedrich Engels, *On Religion*, 41–58. New York: Schocken Books.

Maslow, Abraham. 1971. *The Farther Reaches of Human Nature*. New York: Penguin Compass.

Mason, Stephen E. 1962. *A History of the Sciences*. Rev. ed. New York: Macmillan.

Matter, E. Ann. 2008. "Orthodoxy and Deviance." In vol. 3 of *The Cambridge History of Christianity*, 510–30. Cambridge: Cambridge Univ. Press.

Mattingly, Harold. 1967. *Christianity in the Roman Empire*. New York: Norton.

Mayer, Hans Eberhard. 1972. *The Crusades*. Oxford: Oxford Univ. Press.

McAdam, Doug. 1988. *Freedom Summer*. New York: Oxford Univ. Press.

McBrien, Richard P. 2000. *Lives of the Popes*. San Francisco: Harper San Francisco.

McBroom, Patricia. 1966. "Martyrs May Not Feel Pain." *Science News* 89: 505–6.

McKechnie, Paul. 2001. *The First Christian Centuries: Perspectives on the Early Church*. Downers Grove, IL: InterVarsity.

——. 2009. "Christian City Councillors in the Roman Empire Before Constantine." *Interdisciplinary Journal of Research on Religion* 5: article 1. Available at www.religjournal.com.

——. Forthcoming. "Christian City Councillors in Third Century Phyrgia."

McLendon, Hiram J. 1959. "Plato Without God." *Journal of Religion* 39:88–102.

McNally, Robert E., SJ. 1969. "The Reformation: A Catholic Reappraisal." In *Luther, Erasmus and the Reformation*, edited by John C. Olin, James D. Smart, and Robert E. McNally, SJ, 26–47. New York: Fordham Univ. Press.

McNamara, Jo Ann. 1976. "Sexual Equality and the Cult of Virginity in Early Christian Thought." *Feminist Studies* 3:145–58.

McNeill, William H. 1976. *Plagues and Peoples*. Garden City, NY: Doubleday.

Meeks, Wayne. 1983. *The First Urban Christians*. New Haven: Yale Univ. Press.

Meeks, Wayne, and Robert L. Wilken. 1978. *Jews and Christians in Antioch in the First Four Centuries of the Common Era*. Missoula, MT: Scholars Press.

Meggitt, Justin J. 1998. *Paul, Poverty and Survival*. Edinburgh: T&T Clark.

Meier, John P. 1994. *A Marginal Jew: Rethinking the Historical Jesus*. 3 vols. Garden City, NY: Doubleday.

Merkelbach, R. 1992. "Mithra, Mithraism." In, *The Anchor Bible Dictionary*, edited by David Noel Freedman. New York: Doubleday.

Merton, Robert K. 1938. "Science, Technology and Society in Seventeenth-Century England." *Osiris* 4 (pt. 2):360–632.

Metzger, Bruce M., and Bart D. Ehrman. 2005. *The Text of the New Testament: Its Transmission, Corruption, and Restoration*. 4th ed. New York: Oxford Univ. Press.

Meyer, Ben F. 1992. "Jesus Christ." In *The Anchor Bible Dictionary*, edited by David Noel Freedman. New York: Doubleday.

Meyer, Marvin. 2005. *The Gnostic Discoveries: The Impact of the Nag Hammadi Library*. San Francisco: Harper San Francisco.

Meyers, Eric M. 1988. "Early Judaism and Christianity in the Light of Archaeology." *Biblical Arachaeologist* 51:69–79.

Michaud, Joseph. 1999. *The History of the Crusades*. Vol. 3. Cambridge: Cambridge Univ. Press.

Midelfort, H. C. Eric. 1981. "Heartland of the Witchcraze: Central and Northern Europe." *History Today* 31:27–31.

Millard, Alan. 2000. *Reading and Writing in the Time of Jesus*. New York: New York Univ. Press.

Miller, Alan S. 2000. "Going to Hell in Asia: The Relationship Between Risk and Religion in a Cross-cultural Setting." *Review of Religious Research* 42:5–18.

Miller, Alan S., and Rodney Stark. 2002. "Gender and Religiousness: Can the Socialization Explanation Be Saved?" *American Journal of Sociology* 107:1399–1423.

Moehring, Hannes. 1959. "The Persecution of the Jews and Adherents of the Isis Cult at Rome A.D. 19." *Novum Testamentum* 3:293–304.

Moeller, Bernd. 1972. *Imperial Cities and the Reformation*. Philadelphia: Fortress.

Moffett, Samuel Hugh. 1992. *A History of Christianity in Asia: Beginnings to 1500*. San Francisco: Harper San Francisco.

Momigliano, Arnaldo, ed. 1963. *The Conflict Between Paganism and Christianity in the Fourth Century*. Oxford: Clarendon Press.

Mommsen, Theodore E. 1942. "Petrarch's Conception of the 'Dark Ages.'" *Speculum* 17:226–42.

Monroe, Arthur Eli. 1975. *Early Economic Thought: Selections from Economic Literature Prior to Adam Smith*. New York: Gordon Press.

Monter, E. William. 1990. *Frontiers of Heresy: The Spanish Inquisition from the Basque Lands to Sicily*. Cambridge: Cambridge Univ. Press.

Monter, E. William, and John Tedeschi. 1986. "Towards a Statistical Profile of Italian Inquisitions, Sixteenth to Eighteenth Centuries." In Henningsen and Tedeschi, *The Inquisition in Early Modern Europe*, 130–57.

Montgomery, Field-Marshall Viscount (Bernard). 1968. *A History of Warfare*. New York: World.

Montgomery, Robert L. 2002. *The Lopsided Spread of Christianity*. Westport, CT: Praeger.

Montgomery, T. S. 1979. "Latin American Evangelicals: Oaxtepec and Beyond," In *Churches and Politics in Latin America*, edited by Daniel H. Levine, 87–107. Beverley Hills, CA: Sage.

Moore, George Foot. 1927. *Judaism in the First Centuries of the Christian Era*. Vol. 1. Cambridge: Harvard Univ. Press.

Moore, R. I. 1976. *The Birth of Popular Heresy*. New York: St. Martin's Press.

———. 1985. *The Origins of European Dissent*. Oxford: Basil Blackwell.

Morris, Colin M. 1991. *The Papal Monarchy*. Oxford: Oxford Univ. Press.

———. 1993. "Christian Civilization (1050–1400)." In *The Oxford History of Christianity*, edited by John McManners, 205–42. Oxford: Oxford Univ. Press.

Mullett, Michael A. 1999. *The Catholic Reformation*. London: Routledge.

Murray, Alexander. 1972. "Piety and Impiety in Thirteenth-Century Italy." *Studies in Church History* 8:83–106.

Musurillo, Herbert. 1972. *The Acts of the Christian Martyrs*. Oxford: Oxford Univ. Press.

Nash, Ronald H. 1992. *The Gospel and the Greeks*. Richardson, TX: Probe Books.

Needham, Joseph. 1954–1984. *Science and Civilization in China*. 6 vols. Cambridge: Cambridge Univ. Press.

———. 1980. "The Guns of Khaifengfu." *Times Literary Supplement*, January 11.

Neitz, Mary Jo. 1987. *Charisma and Community: A Study of Religious Commitment Within the Charismatic Renewal*. New Brunswick, NJ: Transaction.

Nelson, Geoffrey K. 1969. *Spiritualism and Society*. New York: Schocken.

Netanyahu, B. 2001. *The Origins of the Inquisition in Fifteenth Century Spain*. 2nd ed. New York: New York Review Books.

Neusner, Jacob. 1975. *First Century Judaism in Crisis*. Nashville: Abingdon.

———. 1984. *Messiah in Context: Israel's History and Destiny in Formative Judaism*. Philadelphia: Fortress.

Nicolle, David. 2005. *Historical Atlas of the Islamic World*. London: Mercury Books.

Niebuhr, H. Richard. 1929. *The Social Sources of Denominationalism*. New York: Henry Holt.

Nisbet, Robert. 1980. *History of the Idea of Progress*. New York: Basic Books.

Noble, Thomas F. X. 2008. "The Christian Church as an Institution." In *The Cambridge History of Christianity*, vol. 3, 249–74. Cambridge: Cambridge Univ. Press.

Nock, Arthur Darby. 1933a. *Conversion: The Old and New in Religion from Alexander to the Great Augustine of Hippo*. Oxford: Clarendon.

———. 1933b. "The Vocabulary of the New Testament." *Journal of Biblical Literature* 52:131–39.

———. 1938. *St. Paul*. New York: Harper & Bros.

———. 1949. "The Problem of Zoroaster." *American Journal of Archaeology* 53:272–85.

Nolan, Patrick, and Gerhard Lenski. 2006. *Human Societies*. 10th ed. Boulder: Paradigm.

Norris, Pippa, and Ronald Inglehart. 2004. *Sacred and Secular: Religion and Politics Worldwide*. Cambridge: Cambridge Univ. Press.

North, John. 1974. "Conservatism and Change in Roman Religion." *Papers of the British School in Rome* 44:1–12.

———. 1979. "Religious Toleration in Republican Rome." *Proceedings of the Cambridge Philological Society* 25:85–103.

———.1980. "Novelty and Choice in Roman Religion." *Journal of Roman Studies* 70:186–91.

———. 2004. "Rome." In *Religions of the Ancient World: A Guide*, edited by Sarah Iles Johnston, 225–32. Cambridge: Belknap.

Obelkevich, James. 1976. *Religion and Rural Society*. Oxford: Oxford Univ. Press.

Oberman, Heiko A. 1992. *Luther: Man Between God and the Devil*. New York: Doubleday.

Oborn, George Thomas. 1933. "Why Did Decius and Volarian Proscribe Christianity?" *Church History* 2:67–77.

Odahl, Charles M. 2004. *Constantine and the Christian Empire*. London: Routledge.

O'Neil, Mary R. 1981. "Discerning Superstition: Trials of Clerics and Exorcists in Sixteenth Century Italy." Paper presented at the International Congress on Medieval Studies, Kalamazoo, Michigan.

———. 1987. "Magical Healing, Love Magic and the Inquisition in Late Sixteenth Century Modena." In *Inquisition and Society in Early Modern Europe*, edited by Stephen Haliczer, 88–114. London: Croom Helm.

Oost, Stewart Irvin. 1961. "The Alexandrian Seditions Under Philip and Gallienus." *Classical Philology* 56:1–20.

Osiek, Carolyn, and David L. Balch. 1997. *Families in the New Testament World: Households and House Churches*. Louisville: Westminster John Knox.

Osiek, Carolyn, and Margaret Y. MacDonald. 2006. *A Woman's Place: House Churches in Earliest Christianity*. Minneapolis: Fortress.

Ozment, Steven. 1975. *The Reformation in the Cities*. New Haven: Yale Univ. Press.

———. 1980. *The Age of Reform 1250–1550*. New Haven: Yale Univ. Press.

Packer, James E. 1967. "Housing and Population in Imperial Ostia and Rome." *Journal of Roman Studies* 57:80–95.

Pagels, Elaine. 1979. *The Gnostic Gospels*. New York: Random House.

———. 2003. *Beyond Belief: The Secret Gospel of Thomas*. New York: Random House.

Pagels, Elaine, and Karen L. King. 2007. *Reading Judas: The Gospel of Judas and the Shaping of Christianity*. New York: Viking.

Paris, Edmond. 1961. *Genocide in Satellite Croatia, 1941–1954*. Chicago: American Institute for Balkan Affairs.

Parker, Geoffrey. 1992. "Success and Failure During the First Century of the Reformation." *Past and Present* 136:43–82.

Parkes, James. [1934] 1969. *The Conflict of the Church and the Synagogue*. New York: Atheneum.

Parkin, Tim G. 1992. *Demography and Roman Society*. Baltimore: Johns Hopkins Univ. Press.

Pastor, Ludwig. 1898. *The History of the Popes*. 14 vols. St. Louis: B. Herder.

Paullin, Charles O. 1932. *Atlas of the Geography of the United States*. Washington, DC: Carnegie Institution and New York Geographical Society.

Payne, Robert. [1959] 1995. *The History of Islam*. New York: Barnes & Noble.

———. 1984. *The Dream and the Tomb: A History of the Crusades*. New York: Stein & Day.

Peachey, Paul. 1970. "Marxist Historiography of the Radical Reformation: Causality or Covariation?" *Sixteenth Century Essays and Studies* 1:1–16.

Pearson, Birger A. 2008a. "The Secret Gospel of Mark: A Twentieth Century Forgery." *Interdisciplinary Journal of Research on Religion* 3. Available at www.religjournal.com.

———. 2008b. "Judas Iscariot Among the Gnostics: What the Gospel of Judas *Really* Says." *Biblical Archaeology Review* (May/June):52–57.

Pelikan, Jaroslav. 2005. *Whose Bible Is It?* New York: Viking.

Perez, Joseph. 2005. *The Spanish Inquisition: A History*. New Haven: Yale Univ. Press.

Perkins, Pheme. 1980. *The Gnostic Dialogue*. New York: Paulist Press.

———. 1990. "Gnosticism." In *Encyclopedia of Early Christianity*, edited by Everett Ferhuson, 371–76. New York: Garland.

Perlmann, M. 1942. "Notes on Anti-Christian Propaganda in the Mamlūk Empire." *Bulletin of the School of Oriental and African Studies, University of London* 10:843–61.

Pernoud, Régine. 2000. *Those Terrible Middle Ages: Debunking the Myths*. San Francisco: Ignatius.

Peters, Edward. 1989. *Inquisition*. Berkeley: Univ. of California Press.

———. 2004. "The *Firanj* are Coming—Again." *Orbis* (Winter):3–17.

Peters, F. E. 1993. *The Distant Shrine: The Islamic Centuries in Jerusalem*. New York: AMS Press.

Pettazzoni, Raffaele. 1954. *Essays on the History of Religions*. Leiden: Brill.

Pettersson, Thorlief. 1990. "The Holy Bible in Secularized Sweden." In *Bible Reading in Sweden*, edited by Gunnar Hanson, 23–45. Uppsala: Univ. of Uppsala.

Phillips, Jonathan. 1995. "The Latin East 1098–1291." In Jonathan Riley-Smith, editor, *The Oxford Illustrated History of the Crusades*, 112–40. Oxford: Oxford Univ. Press.

Pliny. 1969. *The Letters of Pliny the Younger*. London: Penguin Classics.

Pohlsander, Hans A. 1996. *The Emperor Constantine*. 2nd ed. London: Routledge.

Pomeroy, Sarah B. 1975. *Goddesses, Whores, Wives, and Slaves: Women in Classical Antiquity*. New York: Schocken Books.

Porter, Roy. 1998. *The Greatest Benefit to Mankind*. New York: W. W. Norton.

Powell, Milton B., ed. 1967. *The Voluntary Church*. New York: Macmillan Co.

Prawer, Joshua. 1972. *The Crusaders' Kingdom: European Colonialism in the Middle Ages*. New York: Praeger.

Pritz, Ray A. 1988. *Nazarene Jewish Christianity*. Jerusalem: Magnes.

Puigblanch, D. Antonio. 1816. *The Inquisition Unmasked: Being an Historical and Philosophical Account of the Tremendous Tribunal*. 2 vols. London: Baldwin, Cradock, and Joy.

Purkiss, Diane. 1996. *The Witch in History*. London: Routledge.

Raftus, J. A. 1958. "The Concept of Just Price: Theory and Economic Policy: Discussion." *The Journal of Economic History*. 18:435–37.

Ramsay, W. M. 1893. *The Church in the Roman Empire Before A.D. 170*. New York: Putnam's Sons.

Rawlings, Helen. 2006. *The Spanish Inquisition*. Oxford: Blackwell.

Rawson, Beryl, ed. 1986. *The Family in Ancient Rome*. Ithaca, NY: Cornell Univ. Press.

Read, Piers Paul. 1999. *The Templars*. New York: St. Martin's Press.

Redman, Ben Ray. 1949. *The Portable Voltaire*. New York: Penguin Books.

Reynolds, Joyce, and Robert Tannenbaum. 1987. *Jews and God-Fearers at Aphrodisias*. Cambridge: Cambridge Univ. Press.

Richard, Jean. 1999. *The Crusades, c. 1071–c. 1291*. Cambridge: Cambridge Univ. Press.

Riddle, Donald W. 1931. *The Martyrs: A Study in Social Control*. Chicago: Univ. of Chicago Press.

Riddle, John M. 1994. *Contraception and Abortion from the Ancient World to the Renaissance*. Cambridge: Harvard Univ. Press.

Riley, Gregory J. 1997. *One Jesus, Many Christs*. San Francisco: Harper San Francisco.

Riley-Smith, Jonathan. 1973. *The Feudal Nobility and the Kingdom of Jerusalem, 1174–1277*. New York: Macmillan.

———. 1978. "Peace Never Established: The Case of the Kingdom of Jerusalem." *Transactions of the Royal Historical Society*, 5th series, 28:87–112.

———. 1983. "The Motives of the Earliest Crusaders and the Settlement of Latin Palestine, 1095–1100." *English Historical Review* 98:721–36.

———. 1986. *The First Crusade and the Idea of Crusading*. Philadelphia: Univ. of Pennsylvania Press.

———, ed. 1991. *The Atlas of the Crusades*. New York: Facts on File.

———, ed. 1995. *The Oxford Illustrated History of the Crusades*. Oxford: Oxford Univ. Press.

———. 1997. *The First Crusaders, 1095–1131*. Cambridge: Cambridge Univ. Press.

———. 1999. *Hospitallers: The History of the Order of Saint John*. London: Hambledon.

———. 2002a. "Casualties and the Number of Knights on the First Crusade." *Crusades* 1:13–28.

———. 2002b. "Early Crusaders to the East and the Costs of Crusading, 1095–1130." In *The Crusades: The Essential Readings*, edited by Thomas F. Madden, 156–71. Oxford: Blackwell.

———. 2003. "Islam and the Crusades in History and Imagination, 8 November 1898–11 September 2001." *Crusades* 2:151–67.

———. 2005. *The Crusades: A History*. 2nd ed. London: Continuum.

Rives, J. B. 1995. *Religion and Authority in Roman Carthage from Augustus to Constantine*. New York: Oxford Univ. Press.

———. 1999. "The Decree of Decius and the Religion of Rome." *Journal of Roman Studies* 89:135–54.

Rivkin, Ellis. 1987a. "Sadducees." In *The Encyclopedia of Religion*, edited by Mircea Eliade. New York: Macmillan.

———. 1987b. "Essenes." In *The Encyclopedia of Religion*, edited by Mircea Eliade. New York: Macmillan.

Robbins, Rossell Hope. 1959. *The Encyclopedia of Witchcraft and Demonology*. New York: Crown.

Roberts, Michael. 1968. *The Early Vasas: A History of Sweden, 1523–1611*. Cambridge: Cambridge Univ. Press.

Robertson, John M. 1902. *A Short History of Christianity*. London: Watts.

Robinson, Charles Henry. 1923. *History of Christian Missions*. New York: Charles Scribner's Sons.

Robinson, Dwight Nelson. 1913. "A Study of the Social Position of the Devotees of the Oriental Cults in the Western World, Based on the Inscriptions." *Transactions and Proceedings of the American Philological Association* 44:151–61.

Robinson, John A. T. 1976. *Redating the New Testament*. Philadelphia: Westminster.

———. 1985. *The Priority of John*. Oak Park, IL: Meyer-Stone Books.

Rodinson, Maxime. 1980. *Muhammad*. New York: Random House.

Roetzel, Calvin J. 1985. *The World Shaped by the New Testament*. Atlanta: John Knox.

Roller, Lynn. 1999. *In Search of God the Mother: The Cult of Anatolian Cybele*. Berkeley: Univ. of California Press.

Rörig, Fritz. 1969. *The Medieval Town*. Berkeley: Univ. of California Press.

Rosen, Edward. 1971. *Three Copernican Treatises* (3rd edition). New York: Octagon Books.

Rostovtzeff, Michael. 1926. *The Social and Economic History of the Roman Empire*. Oxford: Clarendon Press.

Roth, Cecil. [1964] 1996. *The Spanish Inquisition*. New York: Norton.

Roth, Louise M., and Jeffrey C. Kroll. 2007. "Risky Business: Assessing Risk Preference Explanations for Gender Differences in Religiosity." *American Sociological Review* 72:205–20.

Roth, Norman. 2002. *Conversos, Inquisition, and the Expulsion of the Jews from Spain*. Madison: Univ. of Wisconsin Press.

Rudolph, Kurt. 1987. *Gnosis: The Nature and History of Gnosticism*. San Francisco: Harper San Francisco.

Ruether, Rosemary. 1974. *Faith and Fratricide: The Theological Roots of Anti-Semitism*. New York: Seabury.

Rummel, R. J. 2008. *Death by Government*. New Brunswick, NJ: Transaction.

Runciman, Sir Steven. 1951. *A History of the Crusades*. 3 vols. Cambridge: Cambridge Univ. Press.

Rupp, Ernest Gordon. 1981. "Luther, Martin." *Encyclopaedia Britannica*. 15th ed. Chicago: Univ. of Chicago Press.

Russell, Bertrand. 1959. *Wisdom of the West*. New York: Doubleday.

Russell, Jeffrey Burton. 1965. *Dissent and Reform in the Early Middle Ages*. Berkeley: Univ. of California Press.

———, ed. 1971. *Religious Dissent in the Middle Ages*. New York: John Wiley & Sons.

———. 1997. *Inventing the Flat Earth: Columbus and Modern Historians*. Westport, Conn: Praeger.

Russell, Josiah Cox. 1958. *Late Ancient and Medieval Population*. Philadelphia: American Philosophical Society.

———. 1972. *Medieval Regions and Their Cities*. Bloomington: Indiana Univ. Press.

Rutgers, Leonard Victor. 1992. "Archaeological Evidence for the Interaction of Jews and Non-Jews in Late Antiquity." *American Journal of Archaeology* 96:101–18.

Rydenfelt, Sven. 1985. "Sweden and Its Bishops." *Wall Street Journal*, August 21, A25.

Saldarini, Anthony J. 1988. *Pharisees, Scribes, and Sadducees in Palestinian Society: A Sociological Approach*. Wilmington, DE: M. Glazier.

Salih, Abu, and B. T. A. Evetts. 1895. *The Churches and Monasteries of Egypt and Some Neighbouring Countries*. Oxford, Clarendon.

Salzman, Michele Renee. 1990. *On Roman Time: The Codex-Calendar of 354*. Berkeley: Univ. of California Press.

———. 2002. *The Making of a Christian Aristocracy: Social and Religious Change in the Western Roman Empire*. Cambridge: Harvard Univ. Press.

Samuelsson, Kurt. [1957] 1993. *Religion and Economic Action*. Toronto: Univ. of Toronto Press.

Sanders, E. P. 1995. *The Historical Figure of Jesus*. London: Penguin Books.

Sandison, A. T. 1967. "Sexual Behavior in Ancient Societies." In *Diseases in Antiquity*, edited by Don Brothwell and A. T. Sandison, 734–55. Springfield, IL: Charles C. Thomas.

Sawyer, P. H. 1982. *Kings and Vikings: Scandinavia and Europe, AD 700–1100*. London: Methuen.

Schachner, Nathan. 1938. *The Medieval Universities*. New York: Frederick A. Stokes.

Schäfer, Peter. 1997. *Judeophobia: Attitudes Towards the Jews in the Ancient World*. Cambridge: Harvard Univ. Press.

Schaff, Philip. [1855] 1961. *America: A Sketch of Its Political, Social, and Religious Character*. Cambridge: Harvard Univ., Belknap Press.

———. 1910. *History of the Christian Church*. Vol. 1. New York: Scribner.

Schiffman, Lawrence H. 1987. "Essenes." In *The Encyclopedia of Religion*, edited by Mircea Eliade. New York: Macmillan.

Schmied, Gerhard. 1996. "US-Televangelism on German TV." *Journal of Contemporary Religion* 11:95–96.

Schnabel, Eckhard J. 2004. *Early Christian Mission*. 2 vols. Downers Grove, IL: InterVarsity.

Schoedel, William R. 1985. *Ignatius of Antioch*. Philadelphia: Fortress.

———. 1991. "Ignatius and the Reception of the Gospel of Matthew in Antioch." In *Social History of the Matthean Community: Cross Disciplinary Approaches*, edited by David L. Balch, 129–77. Minneapolis: Fortress.

Schonfield, Hugh J. 1965. *The Passover Plot: New Light on the History of Jesus*. New York: Bernard Geiss Associates.

Schwiebert, Ernest. 1950. *Luther and His Times*. St. Louis: Concordia.

———. 1996. *The Reformation*, vol. 2, *The Reformation as a University Movement*. Minneapolis: Fortress.

Scribner, Bob. 1977. "Is There a Social History of the Reformation?" *Social History* 2:483–505.

———. 1982. "Religion, Society and Culture: Reorientating [sic] the Reformation." *History Workshop* 14:2–22.

Scroggs, Robin. 1972. "Paul and the Eschatological Woman." *Journal of the American Academy of Religion* 40:283–303.

———. 1974. "Paul and the Eschatological Woman: Revisited." *Journal of the American Academy of Religion* 42:532–37.

Seaver, James Everett. 1952. *Persecution of the Jews in the Roman Empire (300–428)*. Lawrence: Univ. of Kansas Press.

Selthoffer, Steve. 1997. "The German Government Harasses Charismatic Christians." *Charisma*, June: 22–24.

Setzer, Claudia. 1994. *Jewish Responses to Early Christians: History and Polemics, 30–150 CE*. Minneapolis: Fortress.

Seznec, Jean. 1972. *The Survival of the Pagan Gods*. Princeton: Princeton Univ. Press.

Shaw, Brent D. 1991. "The Cultural Meaning of Death: Age and Gender in the Roman Family." In *The Family in Italy from Antiquity to the Present*, edited by D. I. Kertzer and R. P. Sallers, 66–90. New Haven: Yale Univ. Press.

———. 1996. "Seasons of Death: Aspects of Mortality in Imperial Rome." *Journal of Roman Studies* 86:100–138.

Shea, William R. 1986. "Galileo and the Church." In *Lindberg and Numbers*, 1986:114–35.

Shelton, Jo-Ann. 1988. *As the Romans Did*. Oxford: Oxford Univ. Press.

Sherkat, Darren E., and T. Jean Blocker. 1994. "The Political Development of Sixties Activists." *Social Forces* 72:821–42.

Siberry, Elizabeth. 1995. "Images of the Crusades in the Nineteenth and Twentieth Centuries." In *The Oxford Illustrated History of the Crusades*, edited by Jonathan Riley-Smith, 365–85. Oxford: Oxford Univ. Press.

Sibly, W. A. and M. D. Sibly. 2003. *The Chronicle of William of Puylaurens: The Albigensian Crusade and Its Aftermath*. Woodbridge, UK: Boydell.

Siewert, John A., and Edna G. Valdez. 1997. *Mission Handbook: USA and Canadian Christian Ministries Overseas*. 17th ed. Grand Rapids, MI: Zondervan.

Sinnigen, William G. 1961. "The Roman Secret Service." *Classical Journal* 57:65–72.

Sisci, Francesco. 2009. "China's Catholic Moment." *First Things* (June–July) No. 194:27–30.

Sivan, Emmanuel. 1973. *Modern Arab Historiography of the Crusades*. Tel Aviv: Tel Aviv Univ., Shiloah Center for Middle Eastern and African Studies.

Smallwood, E. Mary. 1981. *The Jews Under Roman Rule: From Pompey to Diocletian*. Reprint with corrections. Leiden: Brill.

———. 1999. "The Diaspora in the Roman Period Before CE 70." In *The Cambridge History of Judaism*, vol. 3, edited by William Horbury, W. D. Davies, and John Sturdy, 168–91. Cambridge: Cambridge Univ. Press.

Smilde, David. 2005. "A Qualitative Comparative Analysis of Conversion to Venezuelan Evangelicalism: How Networks Matter." *American Journal of Sociology* 111:757–96.

Smith, Adam. [1759] 1982. *The Theory of Moral Sentiments*. Indianapolis: Liberty Classics.

———. [1776] 1981. *An Inquiry into the Nature and Causes of the Wealth of Nations*. 2 vols. Indianapolis: Liberty Fund.

Smith, Christian. 1998. *American Evangelicalism*. Chicago: Univ. of Chicago Press.

Smith, Daniel Scott. 1985. "The Dating of the American Sexual Revolution: Evidence and Interpretation." In John F. Crosby, ed., *Reply to Myth: Perspectives on Intimacy*. New York: Wiley.

Smith, Morton. 1971. "Zealots and Sicarii: Their Origins and Relation." *Harvard Theological Review* 64:1–19.

———. 1973. *The Secret Gospel: The Discovery and Interpretation of the Secret Gospel According to Mark*. New York: Harper & Row.

———. 1978. *Jesus the Magician*. San Francisco: Harper San Francisco.

———. 1987. *Palestinian Parties and Politics That Shaped the Old Testament*. 2nd ed. London: SCM.

Sordi, Marta. 1986. *The Christians and the Roman Empire*. Norman, OK: Univ. of Oklahoma Press.

Southern, R. W. 1970a. *Medieval Humanism and Other Studies*. New York: Harper Torchbooks.

———. 1970b. *Western Society and the Church in the Middle Ages*. London: Penguin Books.

Spielvogel, Jackson J. 2000. *Western Civilization*. 4th ed. Belmont, CA: Wadsworth.

Spong, John Shelby. 1994. *Born of a Woman: A Bishop Rethinks the Birth of Jesus*. San Francisco: HarperCollins.

Stambaugh, John E. 1988. *The Ancient Roman City*. Baltimore: Johns Hopkins Press.

Stanton, Graham N. 2004. *Jesus and the Gospel*. Cambridge: Cambridge Univ. Press.

Stark, Rodney. 1964. "Class, Radicalism, and Religious Involvement." *American Sociological Review* 29:698–706.

———. 1965a. "Religion and Radical Politics: A Comparative Study." In Charles Y. Glock and Rodney Stark, *Religion and Society in Tension*, 201–26. Chicago: Rand McNally.

———. 1965b. "A Taxonomy of Religious Experience." *Journal for the Scientific Study of Religion* 5:97–116.

———. 1981. "Must All Religions Be Supernatural?" In Bryan Wilson, ed., *The Social Impact of New Religious Movements*, 159–77. New York: Rose of Sharon Press.

———. 1987. "How New Religions Succeed: A Theoretical Model." In David Bromley and Phillip E. Hammond, eds., *The Future of New Religious Movements*, 11–29. Macon: Mercer Univ. Press.

———. 1996a. "So Far, So Good: A Brief Assessment of Mormon Membership Projections." *Review of Religious Research* 38:175–78.

———. 1996b. "Why Religious Movements Succeed or Fail: A Revised General Model." *Journal of Contemporary Religion*, 11:133–46.

———. 1999. "Secularization, R.I.P." *Sociology of Religion* 60:249–73.

———. 2001. *One True God: Historical Consequences of Monotheism*. Princeton: Princeton Univ. Press.

———. 2002. "Physiology and Faith: Addressing the 'Universal' Gender Difference in Religiousness." *Journal for the Scientific Study of Religion* 41:495–507.

———. 2003. *For the Glory of God: How Monotheism Led to Reformations, Science, Witch-Hunts, and the End of Slavery*. Princeton: Princeton Univ. Press.

———. 2004. *Exploring the Religious Life*. Baltimore: The Johns Hopkins Univ. Press.

———. 2005. *The Victory of Reason: How Christianity Led to Freedom, Capitalism, and Western Success*. New York: Random House.

———. 2006. *Cities of God*. San Francisco: Harper San Francisco.

———. 2007a. *Discovering God: A New Look at the Origins of the Great Religions*. San Francisco: HarperOne.

———. 2007b. *Sociology*. 10th ed. Belmont, CA: Wadsworth.

———. 2008. *What Americans Really Believe*. Waco: Baylor Univ. Press.

———. 2009. *God's Battalions: The Case for the Crusades*. San Francisco: HarperOne.

Stark, Rodney, and William Sims Bainbridge. 1985. *The Future of Religion*. Berkeley: Univ. of California Press.

———. 1987. *A Theory of Religion*. Bern: Peter Lang.

———. 1996. *Religion, Deviance, and Social Control*. New York: Routledge.

Stark, Rodney, and Roger Finke. 2000. *Acts of Faith: Explaining the Human Side of Religion*. Berkeley: Univ. of California Press.

Stark, Rodney, Eva Hamberg, and Alan S. Miller. 2005. "Exploring Spirituality and Unchurched Religions in America, Sweden, and Japan." *Journal of Contemporary Religion* 20:1–21.

Stark, Rodney, and Laurence R. Iannaccone. 1994. "A Supply-Side Reinterpretation of the 'Secularization' of Europe." *Journal for the Scientific Study of Religion* 33:230–52.

———. 1997. "Why the Jehovah's Witnesses Grow So Rapidly: A Theoretical Application." *Journal of Contemporary Religion* 12:133–57.

Stark, Rodney, and Eric Y. Liu. 2011. "The Religious Awakening in China." *Review of Religious Research* 52:282–89.

Stegemann, Ekkhard W., and Wolfgang Stegemann. 1999. *The Jesus Movement*. Minneapolis: Fortress.

Stern, Menahem. 1976. "The Period of the Second Temple." In *A History of the Jewish People*, edited by Haim Hillel Ben-Sasson, 185–303. Cambridge: Harvard Univ. Press.

Stevens, Marty E. 2006. *Temples, Tithes, and Taxes: The Temple and Economic Life of Ancient Israel*. Peabody, MA: Hendrickson.

Stoll, David. 1990. *Is Latin America Turning Protestant?* Berkeley: Univ. of California Press.

Stow, Kenneth R. 1992. *Alienated Minority: The Jews of Medieval Latin Europe*. Cambridge: Harvard Univ. Press.

Strauss, Gerald. 1975. "Success and Failure in the German Reformation." *Past and Present* 67:30–63.

———. 1978. *Luther's House of Learning: Indoctrination of the Young in the German Reformation*. Baltimore: Johns Hopkins Press.

———. 1988. "The Reformation and Its Public in an Age of Orthodoxy." In *The German People and the Reformation*, edited by R. Po-Chia Hsia, 194–214. Ithaca, NY: Cornell Univ. Press.

Strobel, Lee. 2007. *The Case for the Real Jesus*. Grand Rapids: Zondervan.

Sullins, Paul D. 2006. "Gender and Religion: Deconstructing Universality, Constructing Complexity." *American Journal of Sociology* 112:838–80.

Sun, Anna Xiao Dong. 2005. "The Fate of Confucianism as a Religion in

Socialist China: Controversies and Paradoxes." In *State, Market, and Religions in Chinese Societies*, edited by Fengang Yang and Joseph B. Tamney, 229–53. Leiden: Brill.

Swanson, Guy E. 1967. *Religion and Regime: A Sociological Account of the Reformation*. Ann Arbor: Univ. of Michigan Press.

Swanson, R. N. 1995. *Religion and Devotion in Europe, c. 1215–c.1515*. Cambridge: Cambridge Univ. Press.

Tadmor, Hayim. 1976. "The Period of the First Temple." In *A History of the Jewish People*, edited by Haim Hillel Ben-Sasson, 91–182. Cambridge: Harvard Univ. Press.

Tcherikover, Victor. 1958. "The Ideology of the Letter of Aristeas." *Harvard Theological Review* 51:59–85.

——. [1959] 1999. *Hellenistic Civilization and the Jews*. Peabody, MA: Hendrickson.

Theissen. Gerd. 1978. *Sociology of Early Palestinian Christianity*. Philadelphia: Fortress.

——. 1982. *The Social Setting of Pauline Christianity*. Philadelphia: Fortress.

——. 1987. *The Shadow of the Galilean: The Quest for the Historical Jesus in Narrative Form*. Philadelphia: Fortress.

——. 1991. *The Gospels in Context*. Minneapolis: Fortress.

Theissen, Gerd, and Annette Merz. 1998: *The Historical Jesus: A Comprehensive Guide*. Minneapolis: Fortress.

Thiering, Barbara. 1992. *Jesus and the Riddle of the Dead Sea Scrolls*. San Francisco: HarperCollins.

Thomas, Keith. 1971. *Religion and the Decline of Magic*. New York: Scribner.

Thorley, John. 1981. "When Was Jesus Born?" *Greece & Rome*, second series, 28:81–89.

Thumma, Scott, and Dave Travis. 2007. *Beyond Megachurch Myths*. San Francisco: Jossey-Bass.

Thurston, Bonnie Bowman. 1989. *The Widows: A Women's Ministry in the Early Church*. Minneapolis: Fortress.

Tobin, Gary A., and Aryeh K. Weinberg. 2007. *Profiles of the American University*, vol. 2, *Religious Beliefs and Behavior of College Faculty*. San Francisco: Institute for Jewish and Community Studies.

Tracy, James D. 1999. *Europe's Reformations, 1450–1650*. Lanham, MD: Rowman & Littlefield.

Trebilco, Paul. 2004. *The Early Christians in Ephesus from Paul to Ignatius*. Grand Rapids: Eerdmans.

Tresmontant, Claude. 1989. *The Hebrew Christ: Language in the Age of the Gospels*. Chicago: Franciscan Herald.

Trethowan, W. H. 1963. "The Demonopathology of Impotence." *British Journal of Psychiatry* 109:341–47.

Trevor-Roper, H. R. [1969] 2001. *The Crisis of the Seventeenth Century: Religion, the Reformation, and Social Change*. Indianapolis: Liberty Fund.

Troeltsch, Ernst. [1912] 1931. *The Social Teachings of the Christian Churches*. 2 vols. New York: Macmillan.

Trombley, Frank R. 1985. "Paganism in the Greek World at the End of Antiquity: The Case of Rural Anatolia and Greece." *Harvard Theological Review* 78:327–52.

Turcan, Robert. 1996. *The Cults of the Roman Empire*. Oxford: Blackwell.

Turner, Ralph H., and Lewis M. Killian, 1987. *Collective Behavior*. 3rd. ed. Englewood Cliffs, NJ: Prentice-Hall.

Tyerman, Christopher. 1998. *The Invention of the Crusades*. Toronto: Univ. of Toronto Press.

———. 2006. *God's War: A New History of the Crusades*. Cambridge: Belknap.

Underhill, Evelyn. 1911. *Mysticism*. London: Methuen.

Urbach, Efraim. 1975. *The Sages: Their Concepts and Beliefs*. Jerusalem: Magnes.

Vermes, Geza. 1981. *Jesus the Jew: A Historian's Reading of the Gospel*. Philadelphia: Fortress.

———. 1983. *Jesus the Jew: A Historian's Reading of the Gospel*. 2nd ed. New York: Macmillan.

———. 1984. *Jesus and the World of Judaism*. Philadelphia: Fortress.

Veyne, Paul. 1990. *Bread and Circuses: Historical Sociology and Political Pluralism*. New York: Viking.

Vogt, Joseph. 1974. *Ancient Slavery and the Ideal of Man*. Oxford: Oxford Univ. Press.

Walker, P. C. Gordon. 1937. "Capitalism and the Reformation." *Economic History Review* 8:1–19.

Wallace, Anthony F. C. 1966. *Religion: An Anthropological View*. New York: Random House.

Wallis, Roy. 1986. "The Caplow–de Tocqueville Account of Contrasts in European and American Religion: Confounding Considerations." *Sociological Analysis* 47:50–52.

Walsh, John Evangelist. 1982. *The Bones of Saint Peter*. London: Victor Gollancz.

Walsh, Michael. 1986. *The Triumph of the Meek: Why Early Christianity Succeeded*. San Francisco: Harper and Row.

Walzer, Michael. 1965. *The Revolution of the Saints*. Cambridge: Harvard Univ. Press.

Warrior, Valerie M. 2002. *Roman Religion: A Sourcebook*. Newburyport, MA: Focus Publishing.

Watson, Andrew. 1974. "The Arab Agricultural Revolution and Its Diffusion." *Journal of Economic History* 34:8–35.

Weber, Max. [1904–1905] 1958. *The Protestant Ethic and the Spirit of Capitalism*. New York: Scribner.

———. [1922] 1993: *The Sociology of Religion*. Boston: Beacon.

Weiner, Eugene, and Anita Weiner. 1990. *The Martyr's Conviction: A Sociological Analysis*. Atlanta: Scholars' Press.

Weiss, Johannes. [1937] 1959. *Earliest Christianity: A History of the Period A.D. 30–150.* 2 vols. New York: Harper Torchbooks.

Welliver, Dotsey, and Minnette Northcut. 2005. *Mission Handbook, 2005–2006.* Wheaton, IL: EMIS.

Wells, Peter S. 2008. *Barbarians to Angels: The Dark Ages Reconsidered.* New York: Norton.

West, Martin. 1988. "Early Greek Philosophy." In *The Oxford History of Greece and the Hellenistic World,* edited by John Boardman, Jasper Griggin, and Oswyn Murray, 126–41. Oxford: Oxford Univ. Press.

White, Andrew Dickson. 1986. *A History of the Warfare of Science with Theology in Christendom.* New York: D. Appleton.

White, Jefferson. 2001. *Evidence and Paul's Journeys.* Hilliard, OH: Parsagard.

White, K. D. 1984. *Greek and Roman Technology.* London: Thames and Hudson.

White, L. Michael. 1990. "Mithraism." In *Encyclopedia of Early Christianity,* edited by Everett Ferguson, 609–10. New York: Garland.

White, Lynn, Jr. 1940. "Technology and Invention in the Middle Ages." *Speculum* 15:141–56.

———. 1962. *Medieval Technology and Social Change.* Oxford: Oxford Univ. Press.

White, Michael. 1997. *Isaac Newton: The Last Sorcerer.* Reading, MA: Addison-Wesley.

Whitechapel, Simon. 2002. *Flesh Inferno: Atrocities of Torquemada and the Spanish Inquisition.* New York: Creation Books.

Whitefield, George. [1756] 1969. *George Whitefield's Journals.* Gainesville, FL.: Scholars' Facsimiles and Reprints.

Whitehead, Alfred North. [1925] 1967. *Science and the Modern World.* New York: Free Press.

Wild, John. 1949. "Plato and Christianity: A Philosophical Comparison." *Journal of Bible and Religion* 17:3–16.

Wilken, Robert L. 1984. *The Christians as the Romans Saw Them.* New Haven: Yale Univ. Press.

Williams, Arthur L. 1935. *Adversus Judaeos.* Cambridge: Cambridge Univ. Press.

Williams, Michael Allen. 1996. *Rethinking "Gnosticism": An Argument for Dismantling a Dubious Category.* Princeton: Princeton Univ. Press.

Williams, Stephen. 1985. *Diocletian and the Roman Recovery.* New York: Methuen.

Wilson, Bryan. 1966. *Religion in Secular Society.* London: C. A. Watts.

———. 1982. *Religion in Sociological Perspective.* Oxford: Oxford Univ. Press.

Witherington, Ben, III. 1997. *The Jesus Quest: The Third Search for the Jew of Nazareth.* Downers Grove, IL: InterVarsity.

———. 1998. *The Paul Quest: The Renewed Search for the Jew of Tarsus.* Downers Grove, IL: InterVarsity.

———. 2006. *What Have They Done With Jesus?* San Francisco: Harper San Francisco.

Witt, R. E. 1997. *Isis in the Ancient World*. Baltimore: Johns Hopkins Univ. Press.

Wolfson, Harry Austryn. 1947. "The Knowability and Describability of God in Plato and Aristotle." *Harvard Studies in Classical Philology* 56:233–49.

Wood, Ian N. 2008. "The Northern Frontier: Christianity Face to Face With Paganism." *The Cambridge History of Christianity*, vol. 3, 230–46. Cambridge: Cambridge Univ. Press.

Woolston, Thomas. 1735. *Works of Thomas Woolston*. London: J. Roberts.

Wright, N. T. 1992. *Christian Origins and the Question of God*, vol. 1, *The New Testament and the People of God*. London: SPCK.

———. 2003. *The Resurrection of the Son of God*. Minneapolis: Fortress.

———. 2006. *Judas and the Gospel of Jesus*. Grand Rapids: Baker Books.

Wrigley, E. A. 1969. *Population and History*. New York: McGraw-Hill.

Wuthnow, Robert. 1988. *The Restructuring of American Religion: Society and Faith Since World War II*. Princeton, NJ: Princeton Univ. Press.

———. 1989. *Communities of Discourse*. Cambridge: Harvard Univ. Press.

———. 2009. *Boundless Faith: The Global Outreach of American Churches*. Berkeley: Univ. of California Press.

Yardini, Ada. 2008. "A New Dead Sea Scroll in Stone." *Biblical Archaeology Review* 34 (January/February):60–61.

Ye'or, Bat. 1996. *The Decline of Eastern Christianity Under Islam*. Rutherford, NJ: Fairleigh Dickinson Univ. Press.

Zeitlin, Solomon. 1964. "The Dates of the Birth and the Crucifixion of Jesus." *Jewish Quarterly Review* 55:1–22.

Zeman, J. K. 1976. "Restitution and Dissent in the Late Medieval Renewal Movements: The Waldensians, the Hussites and the Bohemian Brethren." *Journal of the American Academy of Religion* 44:7–27.

Zetterholm, Magnus. 2003. "The Covenant for Gentiles? Covenantal Nomism and the Incident at Antioch." In *The Ancient Synagogue from Its Origins until 200 CE*, edited by Birger Olsson and Magnus Zetterholm, 168–88. Stockholm: Amlqvist & Wiksell.

Zinsser, Hans. [1934] 1960. *Rats, Lice and History*. New York: Bantam.

NOTES

For complete information, please see the entry for the work's author and date in the bibliography.

Chapter 1: The Religious Context

1. Albright 1957, 265.
2. Baly 1957; Eliade [1958] 1974.
3. For an extended discussion: Stark 2007a.
4. Gnoli 2000.
5. Gershevitch 1964, 14.
6. Gershevitch 1964.
7. Nock 1949
8. Gnoli 1987.
9. Liebeschuetz 1979, 1.
10. Liebeschuetz 1979, 3.
11. Liebeschuetz 1979, 8.
12. MacMullen 1981, 109.
13. Beard 1990, 27.
14. Stark 2007a, 98.
15. Beard, North, and Price 1998, 1:87.
16. Stark 2007a.
17. Ferguson 1970, 27.
18. Bailey 1932, 258.
19. Beard, North, and Price 1998, 1:280.
20. Clauss 2000, 26–27.
21. Cumont [1906] 1956, 20–45.
22. Burkert 1985, 109.
23. Cumont [1906] 1956, 30.

24. Pettazzoni 1954, 208.
25. Liebeschuetz 1979, 40.
26. Cumont, [1906] 1956, 39.
27. Pettazzoni 1954, 62.
28. Beard, North, and Price 1998, 1:284.
29. Cumont [1906] 1956, 44.
30. Beard, North, and Price 1998, 1:286.
31. Cumont [1906] 1956, 43–44.
32. Beard, North, and Price 1998, 1:297.
33. Beard, North, and Price 1998, 1:42.
34. Beard, North, and Price 1998, 1:287.
35. North 1979.
36. North 2004, 231.
37. Stark and Finke 2000, chap. 6.
38. Beard, North, and Price 1998, 2:275.
39. Gierke 1977.
40. Pliny, 1969, 271–72.
41. Beard, North, and Price 1998, 1:92.
42. Beard, North, and Price 1998, vol. 1; Klauck 2003.
43. For the relevant extracts see Beard, North, and Price 1998, 2:288–90; Warrior 2002, 99–105.
44. Hopkins 2004, 573; also Warrior 2002.
45. Beard, North, and Price 1998, 2:290–91.
46. North 1979, 87.
47. North 1979; Beard, North, and Price 1998, 1:92–96; Burkert 2004.
48. North 1979, 86.
49. Burkert 2004, chap. 4.
50. Burkert 2004, 77.
51. Burkert 2004, 80.
52. North 1979.
53. Beard, North, and Price 1998, 1:95.
54. Bailey 1932, 186.
55. Grant 1986, 34.
56. Bailey 1932, 186.
57. Josephus, *Jewish Antiquities* 3.18.
58. Bailey 1932, 186.
59. Cumont [1906] 1956, 81.
60. Cumont [1906] 1956, 82.
61. Turcan 1996, 86–87.
62. Cumont [1906] 1956, 52.
63. Cumont [1906] 1956, 53.
64. Beard, North, and Price 1998, 1:97.
65. Quoted in Augustine, *City of God* 6.11.
66. Tacitus, *The Histories* 5.1–13 (The Jews).

67. Moehring 1959, 296.
68. Smallwood 1981, 129.
69. Tacitus, *Annals* 2.85.
70. Suetonius, *Tiberius* 36.
71. Cassisu Dio, *Historia Romana* 67.14.
72. Leon [1960] 1995, 23–27.
73. Bailey 1932, 258.
74. Grant 1986, 103.
75. Witt 1997, 129.
76. Bailey 1932, 271.
77. Stark 2006.

Chapter 2: Many Judaisms

1. If we accept that Herod still ruled when Jesus was born, it could have been no later than 4 BCE. For well-founded discussions of the year Jesus was born see Thorley 1981 and Zeitlin 1964.
2. Grant 1973, 64.
3. Grant 1973, 69.
4. Grant 1973, 80–81.
5. Evans 2002b, 2.
6. Batey 1991
7. Feldman 1981, 310.
8. Stern 1976, 204.
9. Feldman 1981, 310.
10. Feldman 1981, 310.
11. Stark 2007b.
12. Stark and Bainbridge 1985, chap. 7.
13. For a recent statement of the theory see Stark and Finke 2000.
14. Stevens 2006, 93–96.
15. Stern 1976, 194.
16. Feldman 1981, 310.
17. Stern 1976, 192.
18. Stern 1976, 194.
19. Cohen 1987; Georgi 1995.
20. Baumgarten 1997.
21. Josephus, *Jewish Antiquities.*
22. Baumgarten 1997, 42–43.
23. Baumgarten 1997, 47–48.
24. Rivkin 1987a, 563.
25. Rivkin 1987a, 564.
26. Rivkin 1987a, 563.

27. Rivkin 1987b, 269.
28. *Antiquities of the Jews* 13.10.7.
29. Both quotes from Rivkin 1987b, 271.
30. Cohen 1987, 210.
31. Josephus, *Jewish War* 2.8.2–5.
32. Rivkin 1987b, 163.
33. Schiffman 1987, 164.
34. Baumgarten 1997.
35. Baumgarten 1997; Smith 1971.
36. Josephus, *Jewish Antiquities* 17.10.10.
37. Horsley and Hanson 1985, 205.
38. Quoted in Horsley and Hanson 1985, 200.
39. Horsley and Hanson 1985, 202.
40. Bauckham 2007b, 62.
41. *The Life of Falvius Josephus* 2.
42. Daniel-Rops 1962, 397.
43. Daniel-Rops 1962, 424.
44. Daniel-Rops 1962, 425.
45. Neusner 1984, ix.
46. Kee 1987, 190.
47. Daniel-Rops 1962, 425.
48. Goldstein 1987, 69.
49. Collins 2007, 12.
50. Daniel-Rops 1962, 427–28.
51. Quoted in Collins 2007, 19.
52. For an excellent modern summary, see Klinghoffer 2005.
53. Knohl 2000; 2008.
54. Yardini 2008. It is written in the first person and line 77 reads "I Gabriel."
55. Yardini 2008.

Chapter 3: Jesus and the Jesus Movement

1. Josephus, *Jewish Antiquities* 20.9.1.
2. Josephus, *Jewish Antiquities* 18.3.3.
3. Tacitus, *Annals* 15.44.3
4. Evans 2006.
5. Craffert and Botha 2005; Crossan 1994; Funk 1996.
6. Gamble 1995.
7. For extreme variation in conclusions see: Vermes 1983; 1984; Casey 1991.
8. Burridge and Stanton 2004.

9.   Witherington 1997, 92.
10. Edwards 2005, 29.
11. Nock 1938, 21.
12. Vermes 1981, 21.
13. For a summary see Baldet 2003.
14. Bütz 2005, 53–54; Crossan 1994, 135.
15. Evans 2001, 19.
16. Evans 2001, 19.
17. Tresmontant 1989.
18. Witherington 1997, 26–27.
19. Batey 1991.
20. Evans 2002b, 23.
21. Crossan 1991.
22. Sanders 1995, 12.
23. Frend 1984, 57.
24. Sanders 1995, 102.
25. Witherington 1997, 90–91.
26. Sanders 1995, 98.
27. Sanders 1995, 98.
28. Hill 2007, 45.
29. Conzelmann 1987.
30. Gasque 2000, 249; Hanson 1968.
31. Hanson 1968; Hirschfeld 1990; White 2001.
32. White 2001.
33. Baly 1957.
34. Baly 1957; Bruce 1981.
35. Bruce 1981, 82.
36. Cadbury 1955, 41.
37. Edwards 2005, 40–43.
38. Bruce 1982; Cadbury 1955; Hemer 1990; White 2001.
39. Meggitt 1998.
40. Edwards 2005, 42.
41. Cadbury 1955, 3.
42. Eusebius, *Ecclesiastical History* 8.2–4.
43. Lieberman 1962, 203.
44. Barnett 2005, 114.
45. Tresmontant 1989, 4.
46. Hurtado 2003.
47. Stegemann and Stegemann 1999.
48. Acts 9:31.
49. Barnett 2005, 31.
50. Crossan 1998, ix.
51. Crossan 1998, 470.

52. Nock 1938, 90.
53. Hvalvik 2007, 182–83.
54. Hvalvik 2007, 191.
55. Stark 2004.
56. Bauckham 2002.
57. Bauckham 2006, 130.
58. For a superb summary see Bauckham 1990.
59. Quoted in Eusebius, *The Ecclesiastical History* 2.1.
60. Bauckham 2007b, 68.
61. Tertullian, *Against Marcion* 4.19.
62. Origen, *Commentary on Matthew* 10.18.
63. Gambero 1991.
64. Bauckham 2007b, 58.
65. Schaff 1910, 247.
66. Bauckham 2007b, 61.
67. Bauckham 2007b, 65.
68. Hurtado 1999.
69. Parkes [1934] 1969; Seaver 1952; Williams 1935.
70. Seaver 1952, 7.
71. Jones 2006; Musurillo 1972.
72. Jones 2006; Setzer 1994.
73. Hultgren 1976.
74. Bammel 1995; McKechnie 2001, 49.
75. Josephus, *Jewish Antiquities* 20.9.1.
76. Eusebius, *The Ecclesiastical History* 3.5.2.
77. Eusebius, *The Ecclesiastical History* 3.5.3.
78. Brandon's (1951) claims that the retreat to Pella is mythical are unconvicing. See Pritz 1988.
79. Bauckham 2007b, 79.
80. Atiya 1968; Jenkins 2008; Moffett 1992.
81. Luke refers to him as "the most excellent Theophilus," which strongly suggests he was a high Roman official. Some suppose the dedication indicates that he supported Luke during his writing.
82. Malherbe 2003, 47. Also Judge 1960a; 1960b.
83. Judge 1960a; 1960b, 134; Malherbe 2003, 47.
84. MacMullen 1997, 5.
85. Koester 1982b, 110.
86. Koester 1982b, 110.
87. Lofland and Stark 1965.
88. Kox, Meeus, and t'Hart 1991; Smilde 2005; Stark and Finke 2000.
89. Meeks 1983, 75.

Chapter 4: Missions to the Jews and the Gentiles

1. Kaufmann 1970, 7.
2. Kaufmann 1970, 9.
3. Tadmor 1976, 163–64.
4. Kaufmann 1970, 14.
5. This group made up the local Jewish community that eventually produced the remarkable Babylonian Talmud.
6. Tadmor 1976, 168.
7. Tcherikover [1959] 1999, 353.
8. Finegan 1992, 325–26.
9. Tcherikover [1959] 1999, 346.
10. Roetzel 1985, 52.
11. Grant 1986, 45, 104.
12. Corrigan et al. 1998, 88.
13. Frend 1984, 35.
14. Tcherikover 1958, 81.
15. Stark 2001, chap. 4.
16. Tcherikover 1958, 81.
17. Stark 1987; 1996a; Stark and Finke 2000.
18. Leatham 1997; Stark 1996b; Stark and Finke 2000.
19. For an excellent discussion see Hagner 2007.
20. 2 Cor. 11:24–25.
21. Nock 1938, 121.
22. Frend 1984, 100.
23. Meeks and Wilken 1978, 31.
24. Leadbetter 2000, 1077.
25. Rutgers 1992, 115.
26. Baron 1952; Stow 1992.
27. Botticini and Eckstein 2006.
28. Meyers 1988, 73–74.
29. Meyers 1988, 76.
30. Weiss [1937] 1959, 2:670.
31. Rutgers 1992, 118.
32. Harnack 1904, 1:10–11.
33. Josephus, *Jewish War* 7.44
34. Reynolds and Tannenbaum 1987; Zetterholm 2003.
35. Stark 2006, table 4.7.
36. Stark 2006, chap. 5.
37. For an extended account of these matters see Stark 2001.
38. Riley 1997, 39.
39. Riley 1997.
40. Tertullian, *Apology* 21.15.

41. In Benin 1993, 52.
42. Bailey 1932, 270–71.
43. Pelikan 2005.
44. Stark 2006, table 5.8.

Chapter 5: Christianity and Privilege

1. Engels [1894] 1964.
2. Kautsky [1908] 1953.
3. Goodenough [1931] 1970, 37.
4. Troeltsch [1912] 1931, 1:331.
5. Niebuhr 1929, 19.
6. Glock 1964; Stark and Bainbridge 1987.
7. Stark 2007a.
8. Stark 2008.
9. Judge 1960a; 1960b.
10. Harnack 1905, 227.
11. Ramsay 1893, 57.
12. For a summary see Buchanan 1964.
13. Frend 1984, 57.
14. Bütz 2005, 53.
15. Buchanan 1964, 203.
16. Theissen and Merz 1998, 166.
17. Buchanan 1964, 205.
18. Trebilco 2004, 406.
19. Buchanan 1964, 209.
20. Meggitt 1998, 75–97.
21. Nock 1938, 21.
22. Nock 1938, 21.
23. Quoted in Nock 1938, 21–22.
24. Frend 1984, 93.
25. Cloke 2000, 427.
26. Judge 1960b, 8
27. Malherbe 2003; Judge 1960a; 1960b.
28. Judge 1960a, 130.
29. Meeks 1983, 57.
30. Green 1997, 44.
31. Judge 2008, 142–43.
32. Harnack 1905, 195–97.
33. Theissen 1982.
34. St. Ignatius, *To the Romans.*
35. Sordi 1986, 28.
36. *The Letters of the Younger Pliny* 10.96.

37. Tertullian, *Apology* 37.4.

38. Tertullian, *To Scapula* 4.1–4; 5.1–3.

39. Le Blant 1880.

40. Harnack 1905, 180.

41. Salzman 2002, table 4.3.

42. McKechnie, forthcoming.

43. Deismann 1927, 466.

44. Deismann 1927, 62.

45. Deismann 1927, 247.

46. Dibelius 1934, 1,9.

47. See, for example, Latourette 1937, 75.

48. Nock 1933b, 138.

49. Gamble 1995, 33.

50. Gamble 1995, 34.

51. Malherbe 2003.

52. Harris 1989.

53. Bauckham 2006; Gamble 1995; Gerhardsson 2001; Millard 2000; Stanton 2004.

54. Gamble 1995, 23.

55. Gamble 1995, 25.

56. Gamble 1995, 27.

57. Millard 2000, 223–24.

58. Stanton 2004, 189.

59. Bauckham 2006, 288.

60. Evans 2001.

61. Evans 2001.

62. Gager 1975; Meeks 1983; Theissen 1978; 1982.

63. Lester 1993, 867

64. Quoted in Burkert 1985, 297.

65. Costen 1997; Lambert 1992; 1998; Russell 1965; Stark 2003.

66. Costen 1997, 70.

67. Lambert 1992.

68. Tracy 1999.

69. Ladurie 1974.

70. Stark 2004.

71. Niebuhr 1929.

72. Lang 1983.

73. Baumgarten 1997.

74. Kripal 2007.

75. Maslow 1971.

76. Fogel 2000, 2.

77. McAdam 1988; Sherkat and Blocker 1994.

78. Kent 2001.

79. Barrow 1980; MacKenzie and MacKenzie 1977; Nelson 1969.

80. Stark and Bainbridge 1996, chap. 9.
81. Stark 2003; 2004, chap. 3; Stark and Finke 2000.
82. Dickens 1991, 128.
83. Stark 2007a; 2003.
84. Marx [1844] 1964, 42.

Chapter 6: Misery and Mercy

1. The phrase was coined by the Swedish-American Industrial Workers of the World (IWW) organizer Joe Hill (Joel Hägglund) in his song "The Preacher and the Slave," 1911.
2. Burn 1953.
3. Meeks 1983.
4. Harnack 1905; Stark 2006.
5. Our enormous debt to Tertius Chandler, Gerald Fox, and Josiah Cox Russell for reconstructing historical population data is acknowledged far too seldom.
6. Stark 2009.
7. Josephus, *Jewish War* 3:2; Broshi 2001, 110; Schnabel 2004, 182.
8. Broshi 2001, 110.
9. Chandler 1987, 463.
10. See Africa 1971, 4n9.
11. Stambaugh 1988.
12. Stark 1996, 150.
13. Carcopino 1940, 45–46.
14. Finley 1977.
15. Carcopino 1940, 33.
16. Carcopino 1940, 31–32.
17. Africa 1971, 4.
18. Stambaugh 1988, 178.
19. Carcopino 1940, 23.
20. Carcopino 1940, 36.
21. Packer 1967, 87.
22. White 1984, 168.
23. Quoted in White 1984, 168.
24. Stambaugh 1988.
25. Carcopino 1940, 42.
26. Stambaugh 1988.
27. Wrigley 1969.
28. Carcopino 1940, 47.
29. Africa 1971, 5.
30. Lintott 1968.
31. Cassisu Dio, *The Roman History* 67.11.

32. Africa 1971.
33. Sinnigen 1961, 68.
34. Shaw 1996, 114.
35. Cahill et al. 1991, 69.
36. Stambaugh 1988, 137.
37. Bagnall 1993, 187.
38. Bagnall 1993, 185.
39. Judge 1986, 107.
40. Quoted in Harnack 1904, 172–73.
41. Eusebius, *The History of the Church* 6:43.
42. Schoedel 1991, 148.
43. Johnson 1976, 75.
44. Tertullian, *Apology*, chap. 39.
45. Harnack 1904, 161.
46. Zinsser [1934] 1960.
47. Gilliam 1961; McNeill 1976; Russell 1958.
48. Zinsser [1934] 1960, 135.
49. Eusebius, *History of the Church* 7.22.
50. Thucydides, *Peloponnesian War* 2.47, 2.51, 2.52.
51. Cochrane [1940] 1957, 155.
52. Cyprian, *Mortality* 15–20.
53. Dionysius, *Festival Letters*, in Eusebius, *The History of the Church* 7.22.
54. McNeill 1976, 108.
55. Quoted in Ayer [1913] 1941, 332–33.

Chapter 7: Appeals to Women

1. Harnack 1905, 220.
2. Frend 1984, 99.
3. Chadwick 1967, 56.
4. Harnack 1905, 227.
5. Salzman 2002. This finding prompted the author to offer a lengthy, but quite implausible, argument that women had not been more apt than men to embrace Christianity.
6. Stark 2004.
7. Liu, forthcoming; Miller 2000; Miller and Stark 2002; Roth and Kroll 2007; Stark 2002; 2004; Sullins 2006.
8. Lefkowitz and Fant 2005; Osiek and MacDonald 2006; Pomeroy 1975; Shelton 1988.
9. Quoted in Scroggs 1972, 290.
10. Frend 1984, 67.
11. Quoted in Bell 1973, 72.

12. Witherington 1990, 5.
13. Witherington 1990, 7.
14. Brooten 1982; Kraemer 1992.
15. Frend 1984, 67.
16. For an excellent summary see Heine 1988. For a fine feminist analysis of greater sexual equality among Christians in contrast with pagans, see McNamara 1976.
17. Shaw 1996, 107; also Shaw 1991.
18. Shaw 1996, 110.
19. Scroggs 1972, 283.
20. Scroggs 1972; 1974.
21. Iannaccone 1982.
22. *The Letters of the Younger Pliny* 10.96.
23. Quoted in Gryson 1976, 134.
24. Ferguson 1990.
25. Brown 1988, 144–45.
26. Meeks 1983, 71.
27. Harris 1994, 1.
28. Quoted in Lefkowitz and Fant 1992, 187.
29. Lindsay 1968, 168.
30. Lindsay 1968.
31. Gorman 1982.
32. *First Apology.*
33. Quoted in Hopkins 1965, 314.
34. *The Roman History.*
35. Hopkins 1965.
36. Clark 1981, 200.
37. Quoted in Hopkins 1965, 314.
38. Geller 1994, 83.
39. Geller 1994, 83.
40. This was often gotten around by ruling that a marriage had been invalid and hence no divorce was required.
41. Chadwick 1967, 59.
42. Brunt 1971, 137–38; also Harris 1982.
43. Clark 1981, 195.
44. Balsdon 1963, 173.
45. Clark 1981, 195.
46. Balsdon 1963, 173.
47. Russell 1958.
48. Brunt 1971; Boak 1955.
49. Pomeroy 1975.
50. Sandison 1967, 744.
51. Riddle 1994.
52. Harris 1994.

53. Gorman 1982; Riddle 1994.
54. Aulas Cornelius Celsus, *De medicina* 7.29.
55. Plato, *Republic* 5.9.
56. Aristotle, *Politics* 7.14.10.
57. Rawson 1986.
58. Boak 1955; Devine 1985; Parkin 1992.
59. Collingwood and Myres 1937.
60. Frier 1994.
61. Martin 1990.
62. Harnack 1905, 234.
63. Walsh 1986, 216.
64. Sordi 1986, 27.
65. Heaton 1990.
66. Greeley 1970.

Chapter 8: Persecution and Commitment

1. Tacitus, *Annals* 15.44.
2. According to Clement of Alexandia, *Stromata* 7.11.
3. Mattingly 1967, 31–36.
4. Frend 1984, 109.
5. Sordi 1986, 31.
6. de Ste. Croix 1963a, 7.
7. *The Letters of the Younger Pliny* 10.96.
8. *The Letters of the Younger Pliny* 10.97 (Trajan to Pliny).
9. Mattingly 1967, 39.
10. de Ste. Croix 1963a.
11. Noted in Keresztes 1968.
12. Keresztes 1968.
13. Keresztes 1968.
14. Eusebius, *The Ecclesiastical History* 5.1.41–56.
15. Frend 1984, 318.
16. Oost 1961, 4.
17. Oborn 1933.
18. Ferrill 1986; Jones 1948; Luttwak 1976; MacMullen 1963.
19. Jones 1948, 23–24.
20. Rostovtzeff 1926.
21. Abbott 1911.
22. Rives 1999, 137.
23. Boak and Sinnigen 1965, 415.
24. Rives 1999, 142.
25. Quoted in Frend 1965, 405.
26. Rives 1999, 141.

27. Eusebius, *The Ecclesiastical History* 6.41.7.
28. Eusebius, *The Ecclesiastical History* 7.12.
29. Mattingly 1967, 54: coins minted at the time make this certain.
30. Eusebius, *The Ecclesiastical History* 8.1.
31. Mattingly 1967, 56.
32. Barnes 1981, 19; Mattingly 1967, 56.
33. Barnes 1981, 19.
34. Rostovtzeff 1926, 453–54.
35. Frend [1965] 1981, 491.
36. Mattingly 1967, 57.
37. Barnes 1981, 24.
38. Barnes 1981, 24.
39. Grant 1978, 308.
40. Barnes 1981, 31.
41. Frend 1965, 413.
42. Barnes 1981, 201.
43. de Ste. Croix 1963a; Frend 1984; Mattingly 1967.
44. Eusebius, *The Martyrs of Palestine* 1.
45. Mattingly 1967, 45.
46. de Ste. Croix 1963a, 22.
47. Edwards 1919, 21.
48. Riddle 1931, 64.
49. McBroom 1966.
50. Schoedel 1991, 135.
51. Ignatius, *Epistle to the Romans.*
52. Fremantle 1954, 191.
53. Weiner and Weiner 1990, 80–81.
54. Quoted in Benko 1984, 141.
55. Eusebius [ca. 325] 1927.

Chapter 9: Assessing Christian Growth

1. Harnack 1905, 466n.
2. Josephus, *Jewish War* 6.9.3.
3. Josephus, *Jewish War* 7.9.1.
4. Grant 1977, 9.
5. Barrett 1982, 23.
6. Turner and Killian 1987.
7. Kee 1990, 6.
8. Grant 1977, 146.
9. Schnabel 2004, 815.
10. Fox 1987, 269.

11. Wilken 1984, 31.
12. Fox 1987, 317.
13. Goodenough [1931] 1970; Grant 1978; MacMullen 1984. Gibbon [1776–1788] 1994 supposed the number of Christians at that time to be only three million (1: chap. 15).
14. Stark and Iannaccone 1997; Stark 1996.
15. McKechnie 2001, 57.
16. (r = .86) Bagnall,1982; 1987.
17. I am grateful to Professor Galvao-Sobrinho for graciously providing me with his raw data.
18. Galvao-Sobrinho 1995.
19. Details on each are provided in Stark 2006.
20. Nolan and Lenski 2006, 155.
21. Stark 2006.
22. Countryman 1980, 169.
23. Grant 1977, 7.
24. Tertullian, *Apology* 37.8.

Chapter 10: Constantine's Very Mixed Blessings

1. Burckhardt [1880] 1949, 281.
2. Burckhardt [1880] 1949, 292.
3. Drake 2000; Pohlsander 1996.
4. Elliott 1996.
5. Eusebius, *Life of Constantine*.
6. Pohlsander 1996, 19–20.
7. Pohlsander 1996, 21.
8. Pohlsander 1996.
9. Barnes 1981, 44.
10. Barnes 1981, 275.
11. Eusebius, *Life of Constantine* 4.60.
12. Odahl 2004.
13. Leadbetter 2000, 1077.
14. Although often called St. Peter's Cathedral, technically it is a basilica, not a cathedral, as it is not the seat of a bishop.
15. Walsh 1982.
16. Eusebius, *Life of Constantine* 3.26–28.
17. Grant [1970] 1990, 246.
18. Leadbetter 2000, 1078.
19. Duffy 1997, 18.
20. Frend 1984, 487.
21. Frend 1984, 487.
22. Fletcher 1997, 19.

23. Duffy 1997, 27.
24. Eusebius, *Life of Constantine* 1.44.1–3.
25. Grant [1970] 1990, 236.
26. Geffcken [1920] 1978, 120.
27. Both quotes from Bradbury 1994, 123.
28. Drake 2000, 247.
29. Drake 1996, 29.
30. Brown 1995; Drake 2000.
31. Drake 2000, 244.
32. Quoted in Drake 2000, 244–87.
33. Drake 2000, 247.
34. Moffett 1992, 140.
35. Montgomery 2002, 44.
36. Moffett 1992, 140.
37. Bundy 2007, 132.
38. Moffett 1992, 145.

Chapter 11: The Demise of Paganism

1. Kirsch 2004, 18.
2. Bowersock 1990, 6.
3. MacMullen 1997, 2.
4. Gibbon [1776–1788] 1994, 1: 15.447.
5. Gibbon [1776–1788] 1994, 1: 2.57.
6. In *Toleration and Other Essays*.
7. Gibbon [1776–1788] 1994 1: 16.539.
8. Gibbon [1776–1788] 1994, 1: 20.750.
9. Brown 1998, 633.
10. Brown 1998, 641.
11. Among them Peter Brown, Jean Delumeau, H. A. Drake, and Ramsay MacMullen.
12. Quoted in Brown 1998, 641.
13. Brown 1998; MacMullen 1997.
14. Harl 1990, 14.
15. MacMullen 1997, 28.
16. Trombley 1985.
17. Stark 2006, chap. 3.
18. Even one of the strongest current proponents of the traditional view that Constantine quickly destroyed paganism has admitted that there is no evidence of pagan protests: "The opposition to Christianity can [only] be guessed rather than demonstrated" (Momigliano 1963, 94).
19. Winkelman, quoted in Drake 2000, 246.

20. Drake 2000, 249.
21. Salzman 1990.
22. Both quotations from Brown 1995, 12.
23. Brown 1995, 15.
24. Brown 1995, 18.
25. For a summary see Stark 2004, chap. 3.
26. Bowersock 1978, 18.
27. Gibbon [1776–1788] 1994, 2: 23.864
28. Levenson 1990, 510.
29. Bowersock 1978, 79–93.
30. Bowersock 1978, 16.
31. Geffcken [1920] 1978, 139.
32. Levenson 1990, 510.
33. Bowersock 1978, 18.
34. Gibbon [1776–1788] 1994, 2: 23.866–67.
35. Chuvin 1990. 44.
36. Geffcken [1920] 1978. 144.
37. Athanassiadi 1993, 13.
38. Drake 2000, 434.
39. Drake 2000, 435.
40. Drake 2000, 434.
41. Drake 2000, 436.
42. *Oratio xviii*, quoted in Drake 1996, 34.
43. Wilken 1984, 128.
44. Bloch 1963, 195.
45. Harl 1990, 7.
46. Harl 1990.
47. Lactantius, *Divine Institutes* 5.23.
48. Harl 1990, 27.
49. Harl 1990, 14.
50. MacMullen 1997; Trombley 1985.
51. Quoted in Bradbury 1994, 133.
52. Brown 1992, 23.
53. Bradbury 1994, 133.
54. Quoted in Brown 1995, 42.
55. Brown 1995, 42.
56. Bradbury 1994, 135–36.
57. Brown 1998, 632.
58. Brown 1998, 642.
59. Gibbon [1776–1788] 1994, 3: 28.71, 77.
60. Beugnot 1835; Bloch 1963.
61. Stark 1996.
62. Brown 1992, 136.
63. For a summary see Brown 1992.

64. MacMullen 1997, 159.
65. Fletcher 1997, 236.
66. Brøndsted 1965, 306.
67. *Ecclesiastical History* 1.30.
68. Thomas 1971, 48.
69. MacMullen 1997, 123–24.
70. MacMullen 1997, 108.
71. Quoted in MacMullen 1997, 115.
72. Thomas 1971, 48.
73. Wood 2008, 231.
74. Delumeau 1977, 176.
75. Seznec 1972, 3.
76. Wood 2008, 230.
77. Quoted in Strauss 1975, 63.
78. Stark 2008; 2004.
79. Quoted in Brown 1998, 634.
80. Dodds 1965, 132.
81. Brown 1998, 633.

Chapter 12: Islam and the Destruction of Eastern and North African Christianity

1. Paul "used 'the East' and 'Arabia' as interchangeable terms" (Briggs 1913, 257).
2. Atiya 1968; Jenkins 2008; Moffett 1992; Stark 2009.
3. Löhr 2007, 40.
4. Jenkins 2002, 17.
5. My calculation based on Barrett 1982, 796.
6. Jenkins 2002, 17.
7. Jenkins 2008, 3.
8. Noble 2008, 251.
9. My calculation based on Barrett 1982, 796.
10. Nicolle 2004, 25.
11. Kister 1986; Rodinson 1980.
12. Quoted in Karsh 2007, 4.
13. Glubb [1963] 1995, 284.
14. Abun-Nasr 1971.
15. Brent and Fentress 1996.
16. Brent and Fentress 1996.
17. Ye'or 1996, 48.
18. Becker 1926, 370.
19. Hodgson 1974, 1:308

20. Little 1976, 554.
21. Lofland and Stark 1965; Stark and Finke 2000.
22. Bulliet 1979a.
23. Hodgson 1974, vol. 1.
24. Hodgson 1974, 1:268.
25. Payne [1959] 1995, 105.
26. Hodgson 1974; Payne [1959] 1995.
27. Quoted in Peters 1993, 90.
28. Gil 1992, 470.
29. Quoted in Gil 1992, 470.
30. Little 1976.
31. Little 1976, 563.
32. Little 1976, 567.
33. Quoted in Little 1976, 568.
34. Browne [1933] 1967, 163.
35. Quoted in Foltz 2000, 129.
36. Browne [1933] 1967, 167.
37. Browne [1933] 1967, 169.
38. Browne [1933] 1967, 170.
39. Browne [1933] 1967, 171.
40. Jenkins 2008.
41. Marozzi 2004, 264.
42. Moffett 1992, 485.
43. Jenkins 2008, 138.
44. Jenkins 2008, 3.

Chapter 13: Europe Responds

1. For full treatment of this topic see Stark 2009.
2. Prawer 1972. Nowhere in the book does Prawer define colonialism and even he admits that the flow of wealth was from Europe into the kingdom of Jerusalem.
3. Ekelund et al. 1996.
4. Quotes from Madden 2002a.
5. Curry 2002, 36.
6. *New York Times*, June 20, 1999, 4.15.
7. Ontario Consultants on Religious Tolerance, www.religioustolerance.org/chr_cru1.htm.
8. Quoted in Richard 1999, 475.
9. Quoted in Riley-Smith 2005, 298.
10. Quoted in Richard 1999, 475.
11. Riley-Smith 2003, 154.

12. *The Decline and Fall,* 6.58.
13. France 1997; Mayer 1972.
14. Mayer 1972, 22–25.
15. Ekelund et al. 1996. This is one of the most inept and uninformed efforts at trying to apply economic principles by analogy that I have ever encountered.
16. Quoted in Riley-Smith 2003, 159.
17. Spielvogel 2000, 259.
18. Armstrong [1991] 2001, xii.
19. Including Alfred J. Andrea, Peter Edbury, Benjamin Z. Kedar, Thomas F. Madden, Edward M. Peters, Jean Richard, Jonathan Riley-Smith, and Christopher Tyerman.
20. Runciman 1951, 1:49.
21. Runciman 1951, 1:47.
22. Runciman 1951, 1:79.
23. Payne 1984, 18–19.
24. Payne 1984, 28–29.
25. Five major versions of the speech exist, each being incomplete, and there are several translations of each into English. I have selected excerpts from several versions.
26. Carroll 2001, 241.
27. Edbury 1999, 95.
28. Edbury 1999; Read 1999.
29. Edbury 1999, 95.
30. Gillingham 1999, 59.
31. Madden 1999, 12.
32. Riley-Smith 1997.
33. Riley-Smith 1997.
34. Riley-Smith 1997, 49.
35. Riley-Smith 1997, 29–30.
36. Riley-Smith 1997, 28.
37. Erdoes 1988, 26.
38. Riley-Smith 1997, 28.
39. Quoted in Riley-Smith 1997, 72.
40. Hillenbrand 1999, 54.
41. Hamilton 2000; LaMonte 1932; Prawer 1972; Riley-Smith 1973; Runciman 1951; Tyerman 2006.
42. Quoted in Hillenbrand 1999, 77.
43. Tyerman 2006, 178.
44. Madden 1999, 49.
45. Tyerman 2006, 179.
46. Riley-Smith 1997, 17.
47. Issawi 1957, 272.
48. Phillips 1995, 112.

49. Madden 2002a, 3.
50. Kedar 1984.
51. Kedar 1984.
52. Runciman 1951, 3:480.
53. Madden 2002b; Tyerman 2006, xv.
54. Irwin 2006, 213.
55. Tyerman 2006, 351.
56. Siberry 1995, 368.
57. Siberry 1995, 115.
58. Quoted in Madden 1999, 78.
59. Madden 1999, 181.
60. Madden 1999, 181.
61. Michaud 1999, 18.
62. Madden 1999, 181–82.
63. Armstrong [1991] 2001, 448.
64. Quoted in Hillenbrand 1999, 230.
65. Armstrong [1991] 2001, xiv.
66. Riley-Smith 2003, 160–61.
67. Peters 2004, 6.
68. Hillenbrand 1999, 4–5.
69. Quoted in Hillenbrand 1999, 45.
70. There was no Arabic term for "Crusades."
71. Knobler 2006, 310.
72. Knobler 2006, 310.
73. Knobler 2006, 310.
74. Lewis 2002, 3.
75. Peters 2004; Riley-Smith 2003.
76. Andrea 2003, 2.
77. Quoted in Sivan 1973, 12.
78. Knobler 2006, 320.
79. Various Muslims quoted by Riley-Smith 2003, 162.

Chapter 14: The "Dark Ages" and Other Mythical Eras

1. Fremantle 1954, ix.
2. Mommsen 1942, 237.
3. *Works* 12.
4. Quoted in Gay 1966.
5. Gibbon [1776–1788] 1994, vol. 6, 71.
6. Russell 1959, 142.
7. Burckhardt [1860] 1990, 19; Stark 2005.
8. Russell 1959, 232.
9. Bouwsma 1979, 4.

10. Hollister 1992, 7.
11. *Wall Street Journal*, Dec. 28, 2009, A15.
12. Harris [1977] 1991, 235.
13. Jones 1987, xxiii–xxiv.
14. Bridbury 1969, 533.
15. Vogt 1974, 25. Despite his concern for the "masses," Friedrich Engels took the same position; see Finley 1980, 12.
16. Jones 1987, 106.
17. Gimpel 1976, viii, 1.
18. White 1940, 151.
19. Stark 2006.
20. Chandler 1987.
21. Stark 2003; 2005.
22. Lopez 1976, 43.
23. Gimpel 1976, 16.
24. Gies and Gies 1994, 113.
25. Stark 2005, chap. 5.
26. Gies and Gies 1994, 117.
27. Duke 1998, 480.
28. Gimpel 1976, 25–27.
29. Stark 2005, chap. 5.
30. Landes 1998, 46.
31. Montgomery 1968; White 1962.
32. Lane [1934] 1992, 35–53.
33. Barclay, Nelson, and Schofield 1981, 488.
34. Needham 1980.
35. In *The Communist Manifesto*, 1848.
36. Collins 1986; Stark 2005.
37. Stark 2005.
38. In his *Commentary on the Sentences of Peter Lombard*, quoted in de Roover 1958, 422.
39. I have relied on the translations of Aquinas's *Summa Theologica* provided by Monroe 1975.
40. Little 1978, 181.
41. Gilchrist 1969; Little 1978; Raftus 1958.
42. Gilchrist 1969, 67.
43. Hunt and Murray 1999, 73.
44. Little 1978, 181.
45. Southern 1970b, 40.
46. Stark 2003, chap. 4.
47. Stark 2003, chap. 4.
48. Bonnassie 1991, 30.
49. Bloch 1975, 14.
50. In Bonnassie 1991, 54.

51. Bloch 1975, 11.
52. Bloch 1975, 30.
53. Daniel 1981, 705.
54. Gardner and Crosby 1959, 236.
55. De la Croix and Tansey 1975, 353.
56. Johnson 2003, 190.
57. Lopez 1967, 198.
58. Colish 1997, 266.
59. Cohen 1985; Gingerich 1975; Jaki 2000; Rosen 1971.
60. Hollister 1992, 8.
61. Grant 1996, 23.
62. Pernoud 2000, 24.
63. Ferguson 1939, 8.
64. Stark 2003, chap. 2.
65. Stark 2007a, chap. 1.
66. Stark 2005.

Chapter 15: The People's Religion

1. Durant 1950.
2. Freemantle 1954.
3. Murray 1972, 83.
4. Manchester 1993, 20.
5. Walzer 1965, 4.
6. Murray 1972, 92.
7. Murray 1972, 92.
8. Murray 1972, 93–94.
9. Quoted in Coulton 1938, 193.
10. Quoted in Coulton 1938, 188.
11. *Dives and Pauper* 1976, 189.
12. Coulton 1938, 194.
13. Strauss 1975, 49.
14. Strauss 1975, 49.
15. Strauss 1975, 49.
16. Strauss 1978, 278.
17. Strauss 1978, 278–79.
18. Strauss 1978, 283.
19. Thomas 1971, 161–62.
20. Strauss 1978, 284.
21. Strauss 1975, 56–57.
22. Strauss 1978, 284.
23. Strauss 1975, 59.

24. Strauss 1978, 273.
25. Coulton 1938, 189–90.
26. Farmer 1991, 336; Hay 1977, 64.
27. Morris 1993, 232.
28. Christian 1981, 154.
29. Strauss 1975, 50.
30. Strauss 1975, 51.
31. Strauss 1978, 270.
32. Strauss 1978, 278.
33. Strauss 1975, 58.
34. Strauss 1978, 291.
35. Strauss 1978, 270.
36. Quoted in Thomas 1971, 165.
37. Quoted in Thomas 1971, 164.
38. Quoted in Thomas 1971, 164.
39. Quoted in Strauss 1978, 298.
40. Franits 2004, 35.
41. Bede [730] 1955, 340.
42. Coulton 1938, 157.
43. Quoted in Coulton 1938, 157.
44. Thomas 1971, 164.
45. Coulton 1938, 158.
46. Thomas 1971, 165.
47. Hay 1977, 56.
48. Duffy 1987, 88.
49. Delumeau 1977.
50. Strauss 1975, 52.
51. Strauss 1975, 55.
52. Duffy 1987, 88.
53. Duffy 1987, 88.
54. Duffy 1997, 146.
55. Lea 1902, 672.
56. Pastor 1898, 5:475.
57. Duffy 1987, 88.
58. Quoted in Murray 1972, 93.
59. Swanson 1995. If that seems like a very large number of priests for a single diocese, in this era as many as 10 percent of the population in some cities were priests (Ozment 1980, 211).
60. *Epistle* 94.
61. Hay 1977, 63.
62. Coulton 1938, 174.
63. Duffy 1997.
64. Brooke and Brooke 1984, 116.
65. Fletcher 1997, 16.

66. Duffy 1987, 88.
67. Coulton 1938, 156.
68. Hay 1977, 56.
69. Ozment 1980, 219.
70. Ozment 1980, 219.
71. Bossy 1985, 37; Ozment 1980, 218–19.
72. Thomas 1971, 161.
73. Thomas 1971, 163.
74. Quoted in Thomas 1971, 163.
75. Quoted in Thomas 1971, 163.
76. Obelkevich 1976, 279.
77. Strauss 1988, 211.
78. Kieckhefer 1989, 10.
79. Quoted in Flint 1991, 240.
80. Kieckhefer 1989, 62.
81. Quoted in Kieckhefer 1989, 19.
82. Kieckhefer 1989, 82.
83. Flint 1991; Thomas 1971.
84. Quoted in Kieckhefer 1989, 3.
85. Quoted in Kieckhefer 1989, 4.
86. Flint 1991, 189.
87. Flint 1991, 189.
88. O'Neil 1981, 11.
89. Strauss 1978, 304.
90. Strauss 1978, 304.
91. Katz 1994, 417; Kieckhefer 1976, 79–80; Stark 2003, chap. 3.
92. Cohn 1975, 169.
93. Kieckhefer 1976, 79.
94. Katz 1994; Midelfort 1981.
95. Stark 2003, chap. 3.
96. Quoted in Parker 1992, 45.

Chapter 16: Faith and the Scientific "Revolution"

1. White 1896, 2:108–9.
2. Grant 1971; 1994; Hamilton 1996; Russell 1997.
3. Russell 1997.
4. Bloch [1940] 1961, 83.
5. Darwin and Seward 1903, 1:195.
6. *Essay concerning Human Understanding* 3.9.
7. I have written at length on this in Stark 2003, chap. 2.
8. Danielson 2000, 98; Mason 1962, 120–21.
9. Crosby 1997, 104.

10. Cohen 1985, 107.
11. Jaki 2000; Rosen 1971.
12. Manchester 1993, 103–4.
13. Colish 1997, 266.
14. Schachner 1938, 3.
15. Porter 1998.
16. Armitage 1951.
17. Grant 1996, 205.
18. White 1896, 2:50.
19. Grant 1996.
20. Whitehead [1925] 1967, 13.
21. Whitehead [1925] 1967, 12.
22. Descartes, *Oeuvres* 8.61.
23. Quoted in Crosby 1997, 83.
24. Whitehead [1925] 1967, 13.
25. Needham 1954–1984, vol. 1, 581.
26. Lindberg 1992, 54.
27. Jaki 1986, 105.
28. I have written extensively on this in Stark 2003, chap. 2.
29. Quoted in Bradley 2001, 160.
30. Quoted in Merton 1938, 447.
31. Einstein, *Letters to Solovine*, 131.
32. Stark 2003, 160–63.
33. White 1997, 158–62.
34. Quoted in Finocchiaro 2009, 68.
35. Quoted in Finocchiaro 2009, 68.
36. Drake and O'Malley 1960.
37. Brooke and Cantor 1998, 20.
38. Brooke and Cantor 1998, 110.
39. *Dialogue Concerning the Two Chief World Systems*. Published by University of California Press.
40. Shea 1986, 132.
41. Geisler and Nix 1986, 5.
42. Coleman 1975, 296.
43. *Confessions* 12.
44. Some have claimed that *Shaddai* means mountain, but most scholars regard the meaning of the word as unknown.
45. This is the traditional Torah version. Also see Alter 2004, 339.
46. Matt. 13:13; also Mark 4:11–12 and Luke 8:10.
47. Quoted in Benin 1993, 11.
48. Quoted in Benin 1993, 183.
49. Calvin [ca. 1555] 1980, 52–53.
50. Quoted in Benin 1993, 173–74.
51. Quoted in Benin 1993, 195.

52. Quoted in Benin 1993, 195.
53. Stark 2003, 194.

Chapter 17: Two "Churches" and the Challenge of Heresy

1. Fletcher 1997, 38.
2. Johnson 1976.
3. Cheetham 1983, 23.
4. Eusebius, *Life of Constantine* 4.54.2.
5. Duffy 1997, 87.
6. Cheetham 1983; Duffy 1997.
7. Cheetham 1983; Duffy 1997.
8. Duffy 1997, 87.
9. Duffy 1997, 87.
10. McBrien 2000, 157.
11. Cheetham 1983; McBrien 2000.
12. Cheetham 1983, 84.
13. Pastor 1898.
14. Smith [1759] 1982, 788–89.
15. Lambert 1992; Matter 2008; Moore 1976; 1985; Russell 1965; 1971.
16. Lambert 1992, 12.
17. Lambert 1992, 25.
18. Most of the religious orders had such high entry fees that only the rich could afford to join—the poor were admitted only to servile positions.
19. Stark 2004, 56.
20. A fifth daughter died at age six.
21. Cheetham 1983, 90.
22. Cheetham 1983, 87.
23. Costen 1997; Duffy 1997; McBrien 2000; Morris 1991.
24. Moore 1994, 54.
25. Moore 1985, 85.
26. Lambert 1992, 50.
27. Brooke 1971; Cheetham 1983; Costen 1997; Lambert 1998; 1992; Moore 1985; 1976; Russell 1965.
28. Leff [1967] 1999, 47.
29. Lambert 1998, 21.
30. Barber 2000; Brooke 1971; Costen 1997; Lambert 1998; 1992; Moore 1985; Russell 1965.
31. Costen 1997, 65.
32. Lambert 1998, 21.
33. Lambert 1992.

34. Kaelber 1997, 113.
35. Costen 1997, 70.
36. Quoted in Costen 1997, 70.
37. Johnson 1976, 252.
38. Quoted in Sibly and Sibly 2003, 128.
39. Brooke 1971; Costen 1997; Lambert 1998; 1992; Moore 1985; Russell 1965.
40. Lambert 1992, 69.
41. Quoted in Johnson 1976, 251.
42. Lambert 1992, 69.

Chapter 18: Luther's Reformation

1. Moeller 1972.
2. Luther [1520] 1915, 141.
3. Stark 2003.
4. Bainton 1995; Kittleson 1986; Marty 2004; McNally 1969; Oberman 1992; Schweibert 1950.
5. Oberman 1992, 149.
6. Oberman 1992, 149.
7. Chadwick 1972, 42.
8. Quoted in Oberman 1992, 188.
9. Schwiebert 1950, 314.
10. Eisenstein 1979.
11. Luther [1520] 1915, 84.
12. Luther [1520] 1915, 139.
13. Rupp 1981, 192.
14. Quoted in Strauss 1975, 32.
15. Brady 1978; Durant 1957; Engels [1873] 1964; Grimm 1969; 1962; Ozment 1980; Swanson 1967; Tracy 1999; Weber [1904–1905] 1958; Wuthnow 1989.
16. Becker 2000; Braudel 1977; Cohen 1980; Delacroix and Nielson 2001; Fischoff 1968; Hamilton 1996; Samuelsson [1957] 1993.
17. Quoted in Grimm 1962, 5.
18. Strauss 1975.
19. Dickens 1974; Ozment 1975; Moeller 1972.
20. Edwards 1994; Eisenstein 1979; Gilmont 1998.
21. Grendler 2004; Schwiebert 1996.
22. Grimm 1969; 1962; Ozment 1975; Moeller 1972.
23. Hanneman 1975.
24. Hale 1977; Hibbert [1974] 2003.
25. Bainton [1952] 1985, 18.

26. Durant 1957; Hayes 1917; Ozment 1975.
27. Holborn 1942, 129.
28. Holborn 1942, 130.
29. Holborn 1942, 131.
30. Cole 1984; Edwards 1994; Gilmont 1998; Holborn 1942.
31. Kim and Pfaff, forthcoming.
32. Holborn 1942, 134.
33. Grendler 2004, 18.
34. Schwiebert 1996, 471.
35. Grendler 2004, 19.
36. Brady 1985; Grimm 1962; Strauss 1988; 1978.
37. Ozment 1980, 201.
38. Moeller 1972.
39. Rörig 1969.
40. Stark 2003, 111.
41. Chadwick 1972, 26.
42. Bush 1967; Hill 1967; Latourette 1975.
43. Latourette 1975, 735.
44. Latourette 1975, 737.
45. Roberts 1968.
46. Johnson 1976, 267.
47. Mullett 1999.
48. Stark 2005.

Chapter 19: The Shocking Truth About the Spanish Inquisition

1. Maltby 1971, 35.
2. Peters 1989, 133–34.
3. "Inquisition." In *The Columbia Encyclopedia*, 6th ed. (New York: Columbia Univ. Press, 2001).
4. Durant 1950, 784.
5. Kirsch 2008, 3.
6. Paris 1961, 4.
7. Roth [1964] 1996; Rummel 2008.
8. Whitechapel 2002.
9. Robertson 1902, 290.
10. Hunt 1994, 79.
11. Rawlings 2006, 1.
12. Quoted in Keen 1969, 708.
13. Peters 1989, 134.
14. Puigblanch 1816, 131.
15. Jenkins 2003.

16. Especially Ellerbe 1995; Kirsch 2008.
17. Contreras and Henningsen 1986; Given 1997; Haliczer 1990; Henningsen 1980; Henningsen and Tedeschi 1986; Kamen 1993; 1997; Levack 1995; Monter 1990; Rawlings 2006.
18. See Henningsen and Tedeschi 1986.
19. Rawlings 2006, 37.
20. Monter 1990.
21. Contreras and Henningsen 1986.
22. Chadwick and Evans 1987, 113.
23. Holinshed [1587] 1965 claims seventy-two thousand were executed by Henry.
24. Dowling [1845] 2002, 16.
25. Kamen 1997, 190; Madden 2003, 30.
26. Rawlings 2006, 33.
27. Peters 1989, 93.
28. Madden 2003, 30.
29. Madden 2003, 29.
30. Daly 1978; Davies 1996, 567; Dworkin 1974; Hughes 1952.
31. Burr 1987, 1.
32. Trethowan 1963, 343.
33. Burckhardt [1885] 1990; Lecky [1865] 1903.
34. Hobbes [1651] 1956, 21.
35. Trevor-Roper [1969] 2001, 112.
36. Briggs 1998.
37. Hyslop 1925, 4
38. Ewen 1929; Levack 1995; Thomas 1971.
39. Briggs 1998; Katz 1994; Levack 1995.
40. Monter 1990.
41. See Stark 2003, 258.
42. Lea 1906–1907, 4:206.
43. Contreras and Henningsen 1986, 103.
44. O'Neil 1981, 11.
45. For a full treatment of these matters see Stark 2003, chap. 3.
46. O'Neil 1987, 90.
47. Kamen 1993, 238.
48. Kamen 1993; 1997.
49. Kamen 1997, 274.
50. Kamen 1997, 274.
51. Robbins 1959, 45.
52. Roth 2002, xi.
53. Decter 2007.
54. Stark 2001, chap. 4.
55. Gerber 1994, 117.

56. For example, "most of the above-mentioned converts were forced" (Netanyahu 2001, xvi). See also Perez 2005.
57. Perez 2005, 10.
58. Roth 2002, 320.
59. Calculated by the author from Contreras and Henningsen 1986 and Monter 1990.
60. Roth [1964] 1996, 132.
61. Netanyahu, 2001, xvi.
62. Chejne 1983.
63. Perez 2005, 45.
64. Bainton [1952] 1985, 131.
65. Peters 1989, 122.
66. Fernandez 1997, 483.
67. Kamen 1997, 268.
68. Kamen 1997, 268.
69. Fernandez 1997, 483.
70. Stark 2003, 258.
71. Goodish 1976.
72. Kamen 1997, 268.
73. Fernandez 1997, 494.
74. Kamen 1997, 134.
75. Monter and Tedeschi 1986.
76. Findlen 1993; Hyde 1964.
77. Ellerbe 1995; Kirsch 2008; MacCulloch 2010.
78. Kirsch 2008.

Chapter 20: Pluralism and American Piety

1. Finke and Stark 1992.
2. Smith 1985.
3. Cobbett 1818, 229.
4. de Tocqueville [1835–1839] 1956, 2: 314.
5. Schaff [1855] 1961, 91.
6. Baird 1844, 188.
7. Gaustad 1987, 15.
8. Whitefield [1756] 1969, 387.
9. Finke and Stark 1992, 27.
10. Finke and Stark 1992; Stark 2008.
11. Grund in Powell 1967, 77, 80.
12. Quoted in Handlin 1949, 261.
13. Bruce 1992, 170.
14. Berger 1969, 133–34.

15. Smith 1998, 106.
16. Neitz 1987, 257–258.
17. Davidman 1991, 204.
18. Berger 1969, 145.
19. Berger 1969, 146.
20. Wilson 1966, 166.
21. Burdick 1993, 8.
22. Finke and Stark 1992.
23. Pew Forum Survey 2007.
24. Quoted in Thumma and Travis 2007, 21.
25. Stark 2008.
26. See Ebaugh 1993.
27. Stark and Finke 2000.
28. Stark 2008.
29. Introvigne 2005.
30. Gill 2005, 5.
31. These statistics come from the Baylor National Surveys of American Religion, 2005 and 2007.
32. See Stark 2008, 55.
33. Hobbes [1651] 1956, 168.
34. Hume 1754, 3:30.
35. Smith [1776] 1981, 793–94.
36. Smith [1776] 1981, 5.1.3.3, entitled "Of the Expense of the Institutions for the Instruction of People of all Ages." So far as I am aware, the only current edition including this chapter is the one published by the Liberty Fund. See the bibliography.

Chapter 21: Secularization

1. Woolston 1735.
2. Quoted in Redman 1949, 26.
3. Wallace 1966, 264–65.
4. Berger 1968, 3.
5. de Tocqueville [1835–1839] 1956, 319.
6. Wilson 1966, 126.
7. Wilson 1982, 152.
8. Martin 1969, 10.
9. Wallis 1986.
10. March 17, 2009.
11. April 13, 2009.
12. Hout and Fischer 2002; Stark 2004, 125; 2008, 141–46.
13. Stark 2008, 125–31.
14. Finke and Stark 1992; Stark 2008.

15. *Christian Century*, October 29, 1997, 972–78.
16. Stark 2007b, 390.
17. Stark 1981, 175.
18. For a wonderful account of this failure see Paul Froese, *The Plot to Kill God* (Berkeley: Univ. of California Press, 2008).
19. Stark and Liu, 2011.
20. Greeley 1995, 63.
21. Greeley 1995; Stark and Finke 2000.
22. Davies 1996; Barrett 1982; Brøndsted 1965; Jones 1968; Sawyer 1982.
23. Stark 1999.
24. Berger, Davie, and Fokas 2008, 16.
25. Schmied 1996.
26. Beckford 1985, 286.
27. Lodberg 1989.
28. Selthoffer 1997.
29. Grim and Finke 2010.
30. *Ude og Hjemme* 24 (2005).
31. Alvarez 2003.
32. Rydenfelt 1985.
33. Quoted in Pettersson 1990, 23.
34. Asberg 1990, 18.
35. Davie 1994.
36. Stark, Hamberg, and Miller 2005.
37. Stark and Iannaccone 1994.
38. Stark, Hamberg, and Miller 2005.
39. Stark 1964.
40. Stark 1965a.
41. Norris and Inglehart 2004.
42. Dennett 2006, 21.
43. Kaufmann 2010.
44. Stark 2001; Wuthnow 2009.
45. Introvigne and Stark 2005.

Chapter 22: Globalization

1. de Flaix and Jackson 1982.
2. Beach 1903.
3. Welliver and Northcutt 2005.
4. Wuthnow 2009.
5. Barrett, Kurian, and Johnson 2001, 843.
6. The very best of these are assembled by David Barrett and his associates.
7. Sun 2005.

8. Jenkins 2002.
9. Robinson 1923.
10. Chesnut 2003b, 61; Gill 1998, 68; Martin 1990, 57–58.
11. Gill 1998, 86.
12. Chesnut 1997; 2003a; 2003b; Gill 1998; Martin 1990; Stoll 1990.
13. *Miami Herald*, October 16, 1992.
14. Klaiber 1970; Montgomery 1979.
15. Gill 1998, 82.
16. Stark and Finke 2000, 153, table 8.
17. Stark 2001.
18. Siewart and Valdez 1997.
19. Welliver and Northcutt 2004, 32.
20. Stoll 1990, 6.
21. Barrett, Kurian, and Johnson 2001.
22. Jenkins 2002, 64.
23. Cox 1995, 168.
24. Drogus 1995, 465.
25. Boff 1986.
26. Burdick 1993.
27. Drogus 1995.
28. Gill 1998.
29. Chesnut 2003b, 55.
30. Chesnut 2003b, 61.
31. Personal communication, Salvatore Martinez, 2009.
32. r = .451, which is significant beyond the .05 level (prob. = .034).
33. Dolan 1975; 1978; Finke and Stark 1992.
34. Sisci 2009.
35. Stark and Liu 2011.
36. Stark 2004, chap. 4.
37. Underhill 1911.
38. Stark 1965b; 2008.
39. Great-grandfather of my colleague and sometime coauthor William Sims Bainbridge.
40. Bainbridge 1882, 270–72.
41. Hutchison 1987, 147.
42. Quoted in Aikman 2003, 5.
43. Stark 2005.

INDEX

Page numbers in *italics* refer to illustrations.